The
Campaigning Handbook

Second Edition

Mark Lattimer

DIRECTORY OF SOCIAL CHANGE

Published by
The Directory of Social Change
24 Stephenson Way
London NW1 2DP
Tel: 020 7209 5151, fax: 020 7209 5049
e-mail: info@dsc.org.uk
from whom further copies and a full publications list are available.

The Directory of Social Change is a Registered Charity no. 800517

ISBN 1 900360 63 2

British Library Cataloguing in Publication Data
A catalogue record for this book is available from the British
Library

Cover designed by Linda Parker
Text designed and typeset by Linda Parker
Printed and bound by Page Bros., Norwich

Other Directory of Social Change departments in London:
Courses and Conferences tel: 020 7209 4949
Charity Centre tel: 020 7209 1015
Research and Marketing tel: 020 7209 4422
Finance tel: 020 7209 0902

Directory of Social Change Northern Office:
Federation House, Hope Street, Liverpool L1 9BW
Courses and Conferences tel: 0151 708 0117
Research tel: 0151 708 0136

To Natasha

Contents

Introduction to the second edition
Campaigning to win   7

Part 1: ORGANISATION

  1 Setting up   14

  2 Charitable status: benefits and constraints   24

  3 Finance for campaigns   35

Part 2: TECHNIQUES

  4 Action research and publications   66

  5 Advertising and publicity   92

  6 Campaigning on the internet   118

  7 Working with the media   131

  8 Using the law   153

  9 Demonstrations and stunts   182

 10 Direct action   199

Part 3: TARGETS

 11 Companies   222

 12 Local authorities   243

 13 Government and Whitehall   263

 14 Parliament   291

 15 The European Union and the international scene   324

Part 4: STRATEGY

 16 Campaign strategy   348

 17 Campaign evaluation   369

Appendices

  A *Charity Commission guidelines on political activities*   375

  B *Useful organisations and addresses*   391

  C *Useful publications*   397

List of Information Boxes   405

List of Influence Maps   407

Index   409

Preface and acknowledgements

Ideally, this book should be read backwards. Starting with a grounding in campaign strategy, the reader would progress to finding out as much as possible about potential target(s) and only then go on to consider which techniques would be most appropriate and the organisation needed to put them into practice. But the book wasn't arranged to be read through, rather to be dipped into, consulted when the need arises, and plundered for ideas.

I would like to thank the dozens of people who generously contributed information or wisdom, including: John Healey, Janet Morrison, Brendan Paddy, John Trampleasure, Nicolas Walter, and the staff of the public information office at the House of Commons. I am particularly grateful to Lindsay Driscoll, Sadakat Kadri and Natasha Walter for reading and commenting on individual chapters. Thank you too to Alison Baxter and the publishing team at the DSC. I would also like to thank the Charity Commission for permission to reprint their new guidelines on political activities and campaigning by charities. Crown Copyright is reproduced with the permission of the Controller of Her Majesty's Stationery Office.

While every attempt has been made to ensure that the information in this book is accurate, it should be treated only as a guide and not as a substitute for professional legal advice.

Introduction to the second edition
Campaigning to win

How can you change society? Is it really possible to challenge the *status quo*, to take on the Establishment, and succeed?

Not only is it possible, but time and again over the last decade campaigners have succeeded in winning fundamental changes in the law, in social policy, and in the day-to-day practices which govern our country. The abolition of the hated poll tax; the introduction of anti-discrimination legislation for disabled people; the eradication of ozone-depleting aerosols and other products that damage the environment; the passing of the UK's first Human Rights Act and the final abolition of the death penalty; the arrest and detention in London of a former foreign head of state for torture; the cancellation of third-world debt – all these milestones and more have been passed, often in the face of determined opposition from the powers that be.

This book attempts to distil from such successes the essential techniques for effective campaigning. Based on the experiences of a wide range of charities and pressure groups over the last decade or so, it explains the techniques that are most likely to work and the strategies that will maximise the chances of success. It is intended as a book not so much about how to protest, as about how to win.

The profession of campaigner is a new one. As long as there has been government, of course, there have been interest groups and lobbyists seeking to influence it, but the public interest campaign has traditionally been the province of the committed amateur. Yet to be effective now, campaigners increasingly need to acquire specialist knowledge and skills. Campaigning has become a professional discipline in its own right.

The best campaigners have many of the skills of the politician, the lawyer, the journalist, the organiser and the marketing manager, but they are not limited to the perspective of any one of those. Ideally, they are able to see and act on the full range of different and sometimes unlikely opportunities for initiating social change. For while other professions will know more about political power, say, or the law, or the media, the campaigner's ultimate focus of expertise is change itself.

The varying imperatives of social change – the need to repeal a bad law, to alter professional practice, to free up a policy blockage in government – call for different techniques. These techniques may themselves have to shift over time, as they become stale or predictable. In the first edition of the *Campaigning Handbook*, I described how the traditional methods of 20th century campaigning, such as the petition, the picket and the mass demonstration, have largely been replaced by a range of low-intensity techniques focused on research, the use of the media and the law, and targeted lobbying.

Five years on, this shift has been confirmed. Collecting hundreds of signatures may have some use as a recruitment tool (an 'engagement mechanism' as the social psychologists put it) but it doesn't impress anyone any more. And while demonstrating public support for your campaign is as important as ever, it is more likely to be done now through opinion polls and e-mail than by getting people out on the streets.

The box covers key features of the new political landscape of Britain in the 21st century. Although many of these have been associated with the New Labour government of Tony Blair, they in fact mark a wider shift in political culture in Britain which has many of its roots in previous administrations.

To negotiate this new landscape, campaigners have pioneered, developed or reconditioned the techniques of pressure and influence. The new trends or innovations in campaigning listed below are all described in detail in this book.

▼ *Virtual organising.* Communicating through direct mail and the internet enables a campaign to attract supporters, raise funds and coordinate lobbies, all without anyone having to go outside their front door. The internet in particular has enabled protests to be organised at little notice right across Europe. *See chapters 3, 6 and 14.*

▼ *Power partnerships.* If you can't beat them, join them. That seems to be the reaction of many charities to the hiving off of large parts of government into quangos and other public agencies. Particularly in the social welfare field, many charities have found that instead of being constantly critical, they can be much more influential by working with the public sector in seeking practical solutions to social problems. *See chapters 4, 12 and 13.*

▼ *Legal actions.* The huge expansion in the use of judicial review currently means that over 10 times a week a governmental decision is overturned by the courts. The passing of the UK's first Human Rights Act further increases the scope for using the law to defend people's rights. *See chapter 8.*

▼ *'Supply-side' campaigning.* Consumer action is one of the oldest techniques in the campaigner's toolkit, but what is new is that

Britain's new political landscape: a guide for campaigners

The appeal to middle England

The majoritarian logic of British politics has always meant that capturing the centre ground is essential for political parties which want to be elected - and for those who want to influence them. In the Thatcher and Major years the talk was of appealing to the C2s, now pundits talk more often of the importance of middle England.

A new populism is certainly evident in political argument. The focus group is perhaps the most celebrated new method for testing out policy ideas on cross-sections of the population and understanding how they are likely to react. Put positively, this new populism places 'ordinary' people at the heart of policy-making, a field which has always been dominated by a small group of experts.

News management

Made notorious by Bernard Ingham's work for Mrs Thatcher (but at least as old as Joe Haines under Harold Wilson), the art of news management and the packaging of policies reached new heights under Tony Blair's press secretary, Alastair Campbell.

News management requires journalistic skills to exploit the media's hunger for new angles or to find the right angle in a story which will turn it your way. But more than anything else, it is about dominating the agenda with the issues that are favourable to you, rather than your opponent. This is a longer-term project, identifying those of your issues or arguments which have the most popular support and ensuring there is a constant stream of new stories highlighting them for the media to use.

The new generation of political advisers

There are now some 70 ministerial special advisers working for the government. These are paid political advisers working within Whitehall, but not part of it. Spin doctors, political fixers, they advise their minister on how policies will go down with the party and with the voters, and help to ensure those policies are presented in the most politically advantageous way. A foil to the impartial and apolitical civil servants, their presence is often criticised as a way of politicising the civil service. They are always interested in things which will put their minister, or party, in a good light.

The Whitehall fringe

From the Social Exclusion Unit, to the new 'Czars' appointed to tackle drug abuse and home-lessness, to a number of new commissions and advisory groups, there are now a plethora of bodies on the Whitehall fringe which have a vital role in putting forward new policies. Unlike the political advisers, these generally represent an attempt to bring technical or executive expertise (and credibility) to the fields to which they are recruited.

The rise of quango culture

With 75% of civil servants now working in executive agencies (or 'Next Steps' agencies) and the continuing rise of other quangos or non-departmental public bodies, the face of Whitehall has changed completely.

In theory this introduces stronger management and a clearer distinction between policy-making (left to ministers and their official advisers) and implementation or practice (left to the agencies),

continued overleaf

but in reality much lower-level policy-making has simply been distanced from parliamentary and public scrutiny.

Limiting the public sector

Governments of every political colour now pride themselves on their ability to keep a tight rein on public finances. Private sector encouragement, rather than stimulating demand through investing in the public sector, is seen as the way to economic growth. Any policies which seek a large increase in the size or responsibilities of the public sector will be difficult to promote.

There is a consequent wariness of creating any new statutory duties. Ensuring that a legal duty was enshrined in legislation was the ultimate goal of many great welfare campaigns, from health to homelessness. But creating new legal duties is now seen as an open-ended, potentially highly expensive, commitment, to be avoided wherever possible. Instead the emphasis is on practical solutions, often involving partnerships between the voluntary, public and private sectors.

Still out of fashion: MPs and the unions

Backbench MPs and the political party democracy have seen their power wane over the last two decades. Thatcher weakened local government and the unions, and although the political language since has been friendlier, they have never really recovered.

Devolution and regional government

The creation of the Scottish Parliament and Welsh and Northern Ireland Assemblies has marked a decentralisation of key areas of policy-making, as well as bolstered powers of scrutiny. Taking the lead from Europe, a new regional tier of government has also come into being with the establishment of the Government Offices of the Regions, as well as mayors for London and other cities.

Europe gets ever stronger

Every decade sees British politicians attack Europe in their rhetoric, but get ever closer to Europe in practice. Heath brought Britain into the European Economic Community; Wilson conducted the great referendum; Thatcher signed the Single European Act; Major signed the Maastricht Treaty; and Blair launched a European rapprochement.

Under the Maastricht Treaty, the European Union has for the first time an embryonic common foreign and defence policy, in addition to free trade and economic and social harmonisation.

The lobby backlash

More and more professional lobbyists have clustered around Whitehall and Westminster, making it harder to get your voice heard over the clamour. Tired of lobbyists for some time, politicians and parliamentarians are now also wary about conflicts of interest and allegations of corruption and sleaze.

Charities and public interest groups may get tarred with the same brush, but they can distinguish themselves from the professional lobbyists by their altruistic credentials and principled message. A time for do-it-yourself rather than hiring consultants.

action against companies has focused on marginal measures that affect corporate competitiveness. Campaigns are targeted on companies' points of weakness in the market place or the production process. *See chapter 11.*

▼ *Direct action.* From the poll tax non-payment campaign that started the decade to the anti-road and GM food actions that ended it, the 1990s saw a stunning revival of peaceful direct action. The new millennium is likely to see the further development of such successful techniques, including the spread of 'hacktivism' or other forms of electronic direct action. *See chapters 6 and 10.*

These techniques and the others described in this book demonstrate that, as successive governments have attempted to dominate or sideline the traditional institutions of democracy, the best campaigners have kept just one step ahead.

Every working day, charities and public interest groups are now involved in consultations and negotiation with government, both national and local. Such a situation would have been unthinkable even a few years ago. This new-found influence is not down to the benevolence of any particular government, but to a growth in the effectiveness of campaign groups that have in many fields replaced MPs, the unions and other traditional representatives as the natural voice of dissent.

People are no longer relying on their elected representatives to make their case; instead, they are choosing to engage directly with government, corporations and the other bastions of power in our society. And the fact that this new face of citizen activism is based not on mass organisations but on simple tools – the press story, the lobby brief, the e-mail, the legal claim, the stunt – means that it is open to practically anyone to have a go. Parliamentary debate, the great constitutional home of democratic opposition, has been relegated to the status of one technique among many.

Whether or not these developments as a whole are positive depends very much on who you are and what you are campaigning for. What they do mean is that the corporate lobbyists and vested interests that have long padded the corridors of power are no longer alone. The environment, minority rights – causes which were never well served by parliamentary representation – now have their advocates at the negotiating table rather than clamouring at the door. And the marginalised and dispossessed in society – homeless people, refugees, those with mental illness – have effective representation perhaps for the first time.

But as I said in the first edition, the *Campaigning Handbook* leaves the ethics to its readers and concentrates on describing what works.

Part 1
Organisation

1 Setting up

This book is about using the freedoms we enjoy in order to change the society in which we live. These include freedom of speech (chapters 4, 5 and 6); of the press (chapter 7); of assembly (chapters 9 and 10); and freedom of petition (chapters 12–15). Perhaps the most basic of our rights and freedoms, however, that which underpins all the others and to which, at the same time, the others are all directed, is the freedom of association. The ability of citizens to join together in pursuit of a common purpose may well be the single most potent instrument for effecting change.

Banning opposition groups and other associations is one of the first steps taken by any repressive regime. Even in many practised democracies the capacity of unofficial or unregistered associations is severely limited. In the UK it is often claimed – with some justification – that many of our liberties suffer restriction and abuse, but spontaneous associations here enjoy wide powers and the right to free association has been almost universally available in mainland Britain in recent decades.

Legal structure

Although there is practically no limit on people's freedom to associate, the more structured or organised forms of association are specifically regulated by law. Most of these were developed primarily for the purposes of business or trade, such as the industrial and provident society, the partnership, or the limited liability company. However, variations of these, or other forms of organisation, are appropriate for pressure groups, charities and other non-profit groups.

Which legal structure, if any, is chosen by a new non-profit group will depend on four main factors:

▼ the relationship between members of the group;

▼ the primary purpose(s) for which the group exists;

▼ legal powers required by the group, such as ability to hold property, enter into contracts and take legal action in its own name;

▼ the level of liability borne by members of the group in the event of contractual default, legal action, etc.

Broadly speaking, the greater the powers and degree of protection offered to a group by a certain legal structure, the higher will be the level of regulation and accountability to which it is required to comply.

The most common forms of legal structure for a pressure group or campaign, with or without charitable status, are the unincorporated association and the company limited by guarantee. These are discussed in turn below, each with their relative advantages and disadvantages, followed by a note on less common forms of legal structure.

If your group intends to seek registration as a charity, this will affect the way in which it is constituted, and you should read this chapter in conjunction with chapter 2. (Unless otherwise stated, it is assumed for the rest of this chapter that the organisations discussed are not seeking charitable status.) Charitable status carries a number of benefits, but it is only open to groups with specified purposes and these *exclude*, among others, seeking a change in the law or in public policy, or garnering support for a political party.

Unincorporated associations

No registration or licence is required to start a campaign or pressure group. Anyone can launch a campaign from their back room simply by inventing a name for it, getting a letterhead printed, raising funds for the campaign and starting to make representations (so long as the purpose of the campaign is not illegal).

As soon as two or more people join together for such a purpose, with agreement over their mutual obligations and how any funds will be held, an unincorporated association effectively comes into being. There are thousands of unincorporated associations in existence up and down the country, including bodies as diverse as community associations, self-help groups, sports clubs, theatre groups and campaigning groups, most of whose members are blissfully unaware of the fact that they belong to something the law has dubbed an unincorporated association.

The term unincorporated means that the association does not have a separate legal identity apart from that of its individual members. Among other things, this means that it cannot borrow money or enter into contracts – such as a tenancy, a hire purchase agreement or a contract of employment – in its own name, but only in the name of one or more of the members acting on behalf of the association.

Although, strictly speaking, nothing is required on paper for an association to exist, in practice it is a good idea to have a written set of rules, which are often known as the constitution. A constitution helps to give the association a stronger sense of identity, to forestall disagree-

The unincorporated association

Advantages

▼ *Informality and speed.* As there is no registration procedure for unincorporated associations, they are quick and easy to set up. Similarly, their rules and methods of working, and even their objects, can be easily altered, so long as the members agree.

▼ *Absence of regulation.* There are no statutory regulations to adhere to, nor any outside body, such as the Registrar of Companies, to answer to. The fact that an unincorporated association is not publicly accountable or subject to outside interference also means that it enjoys substantial privacy. (The Conservative Party's status as an unincorporated association, for example, ensures that its finances remain a closed book to the outside world.)

▼ *Few costs.* No registration or reporting requirements mean that the administrative burden on an unincorporated association will be lighter than on other bodies, and it will have less need for the expensive services of solicitors and accountants.

Disadvantages

▼ *Personal liability.* Officers or members who enter into contracts on behalf of the association are personally liable for any debts incurred. If an association finds, for example, that it can't keep up the rental payments under a tenancy agreement, whoever signed the lease will be responsible for the debt. (Note that some protection is given if the constitution entitles members acting on behalf of the association to an indemnity out of its assets.)

▼ *Difficulty in borrowing money.* Similarly, loans can only be made to officers or members as individuals who will be personally liable for the repayments.

▼ *Difficulty in holding property.* Lack of corporate status means that property always has to be held by individuals on behalf of the association. Either trustees are appointed to hold the property on trust for the members, or the property is vested in two or three members, normally known as custodians, who hold it on a contractual basis for all the members. (The latter avoids some of the complexities of trust law and is preferable for a group whose main purpose is campaigning.) If there are any changes in the trustees or custodians, the property has to be conveyed to the new ones.

▼ *Fewer safeguards.* Even if its constitution is well drafted, the absence of a supervisory body or a statutory framework with which to resolve disputes means that an association can be torn apart in the event of a serious internal dispute.

ments and to protect members from future squabbles (and, if the rules are well drafted, to give them some protection from personal liability). Bearing in mind that an unincorporated association at its simplest is nothing more nor less than a contract between the members, putting the contract in writing makes sense, particularly as the membership of a campaign may grow very quickly. A written constitution will probably also be required for opening a bank account.

The rules or constitution are usually adopted by formal resolution at an early meeting of the association. There is no specified wording or format that a constitution has to follow, but it should set out the name of the association, its objects (i.e. the purposes for which it exists), and the circumstances of membership (e.g. eligibility, admission and resignation of members, etc.). It is also useful to have rules dealing with subscriptions, expulsion, the appointment and powers of committees and officers of the association, the form of general meetings, how the association's finances are managed and how any property is held, as well as powers to alter the rules and to dissolve or wind up the association.

It is useful to look at how similar groups to your own have drafted their rules, but if you intend to use what they have done, make sure it is carefully amended to suit your own requirements.

Campaigns that are structured as unincorporated associations typically include local or community-based groups, like a campaign to stop a road or save a health centre; smaller national campaigns, particularly if they are short-term or employ no paid staff; and networks of other organisations, which share costs between them. The usual procedure is for the day-to-day running of the campaign to be handled by the officers (usually chair, treasurer and secretary) and other members of the management committee, who are elected by the members of the association at a general meeting. Important decisions are also decided by the membership, if necessary on a vote.

The company limited by guarantee

Most companies are set up to make a profit for their members or shareholders and are limited by share capital. This means that the liability of members is limited to the value of the shares they hold in the company.

However, there is another type of company, known as a company limited by guarantee, which is appropriate for non-profit groups. Here members guarantee any debts the company may have on winding up, up to a nominal sum (usually one pound), and their personal liability is limited to that sum.

Incorporating as a company limited by guarantee may well be the answer if the committee members of an unincorporated association feel that they are becoming exposed to too great a degree of liability. This often happens when an organisation starts to employ permanent staff (and with them the considerable obligations laid down in employment law); to trade on a regular basis; or to take on major contracts, such as a long lease or a contract with a funding body to provide services. The process of incorporation will involve formally dissolving the association and transferring its assets to the new company. If you are just thinking of setting up a new pressure group and you intend to undertake any of these activities, it makes sense to seek incorporation from the start.

As a corporate body, the company has a separate legal identity, which means that it can hold property, borrow money and sign contracts in its own name, as well as sue or be sued in the courts.

The constitution of a company consists of a memorandum (stating objects and powers of the company and liability of members) and articles of association (stating the rules and regulations by which the company will be run). The memorandum and articles of association have to be submitted to the Registrar of Companies, as does other information such as an annual return and notice of changes in directors.

Most of the major pressure groups or campaigning groups in the country are constituted as companies limited by guarantee, as are most of the larger service-providing charities. The board of directors of a company is similar to an association's management committee; in fact, many non-profit companies refer to their directors as the management committee. Once again, the directors are usually elected by the members of the company, but the relationship between them, and

---

The company limited by guarantee

Advantages

▼ *Limited personal liability.* A company can employ staff and enter contracts in its own name and will itself be liable for its debts, so the personal liability of members is strictly limited.

▼ *Ability to hold property and borrow money.* As companies can own property, there is no tiresome conveyancing from one set of trustees/custodians to the next. Lenders will make loans more readily to a company, having the security of the company's assets, than to the members of an unincorporated body.

▼ *Statutory framework and safeguards.* The Companies Act 1985 provides a model constitution which organisations can tailor to their own needs. This gives the security of a statutory framework within which problems such as disputes between directors, or directors and members, can be resolved. The duties and rights of directors, and of members, are also set out in law; members always have the right, for example, to remove directors.

Disadvantages

▼ *Outside interference.* Statutory controls, of course, can also prove irksome. The responsibilities of the management committee will be more onerous than with an unincorporated association, and persistent failure to comply with certain requirements in the Companies Act is a criminal offence. Companies regularly have to report to the Registrar of Companies, and details on their activities and on their directors and members are open to public scrutiny.

▼ *Administrative burden.* Company regulation places a considerable workload on the company secretary.

▼ *Cost.* In addition to the cost of the above, companies have to pay a registration fee and annual filing fee to the Registrar of Companies, as well as meeting the rather larger fees of solicitors and auditors.

the rights of each, are defined under the Companies Acts as well as in the company's articles of association. Broadly speaking, the advantages and disadvantages of the company format are the inverse of those of the unincorporated association.

Other types of legal structure

In addition to the unincorporated association and the company limited by guarantee, there are other types of legal structure which it is possible for a non-profit group to adopt. These will almost certainly be inappropriate for a fully-fledged pressure group or campaign, but may be relevant to groups for whom campaigning is only one aspect of their activities.

▼ *The trust.* All trusts share the same basic mechanism: one party (the donor/s) transfers money or property to a second party (the trustees) to hold for the benefit of a third party (the beneficiaries). The beneficiaries under a trust are most often identifiable people. Trusts where the beneficiary class is defined as a purpose (e.g. a proposed trust for the development of a new alphabet, or to preserve the independence of newspapers) are void in law. The major exception to this rule are trusts whose purposes are wholly and exclusively charitable (see chapter 2). Consequently, the only times you'll see campaigns constituted as trusts are when the campaign is for a charitable purpose (e.g. a small charity to educate the public in the needs of disabled people) or for a particular individual or individuals (e.g. a defence fund for an arrested demonstrator). The trust is an unincorporated structure commonly used by grant-making charities and smaller fundraising charities.

▼ *The industrial and provident society (IPS).* This is a corporate structure common among cooperatives, credit unions, housing associations and some social clubs. Incorporating as an IPS involves registering with the Registry of Friendly Societies, and to qualify an organisation has to be a society for carrying on an industry, business or trade *and* either a bona-fide cooperative society *or* intended to be conducted for the benefit of the community. The format carries similar advantages and disadvantages to becoming a limited company (limited liability, less privacy), but the rules and regulations are less onerous.

Objects and powers

Irrespective of how a group is structured, two of the most important elements stated in its constitution are its objects and its powers.

The objects set out the aims or purposes of the organisation and it is important that these are defined broadly enough not to restrict the activities of the organisation unnecessarily, bearing in mind that campaigns develop and circumstances change over time. Today your concern might be securing the passage of a new piece of legislation into law; tomorrow, strengthened by success, you may be concerned with its implementation, or with a public education campaign to persuade people to exercise their rights under the new legislation. The constitutions of many groups state a number of objects; it is also useful to add a phrase at the end of your objects clause such as 'and to do whatever is conducive to the fulfilment of the above objects'. It does not matter if in practice you concentrate your efforts on achieving only part of your objects.

The powers set out the main means, or mechanisms, by which the organisation's objects will be carried out, and their use is discretionary. Once again, it is wise to draft them as widely as possible. They are particularly useful in sanctioning activities which may not appear to follow directly from your objects: the power to make grants to other organisations is a common example. One power that every group should have is the power to alter their constitution.

If the officers or directors of an organisation apply its assets for a purpose which is *ultra vires*, or outside its objects or powers, they can be sued by any of the members. Members of an unincorporated association who act *ultra vires* may also find themselves liable for costs for which they cannot be reimbursed out of the association's funds. Although it is of course possible to alter or add to the powers and, to an extent, the objects of an organisation after it has been set up – providing the constitution allows for this – the process will take time and it may not be easy: as objects set out the purposes for which an organisation exists, it is something on which members will invariably feel strongly.

Democracy and control

Both the unincorporated association and the limited company are in theory very democratic structures. In the classic model, the members elect and can remove the management committee; it is to the members that the management committee answer for their actions; and it is the members who decide on major issues of policy: power comes from below. Among campaigning groups – if not other types of company – it is not uncommon for this model to be followed quite closely.

Such democratic control can leave an organisation vulnerable as it grows in size, however. A number of pressure groups in the eighties encountered problems when a faction of the membership managed to take control of the management committee or to push through resolutions effectively changing the character of the organisation. This could be seen as part of the necessary process of change over time and a natural feature of people power. It is notable, however, that most of the successful pressure groups over the last quarter century have been single-issue groups – those that focused their efforts exclusively on one issue – and attempts to divert or expand the agenda of such a group can substantially reduce its impact.

Conventional safeguards against one clique dominating an organisation include provisions for the regular retirement and re-election of management committee members. An organisation's character and internal dynamics will be affected by how it is constituted in many other ways, however, and in particular by its objects, by who is eligible to be a member, and by the relationship between members, the management committee and any executive staff. It is worth considering these in turn.

Although objects should be drafted to be broad in scope, this is not to say they should be anodyne. Recent debate over a written constitution and bill of rights for the UK has emphasised the effects of having a legally enforceable set of founding principles. Your objects are the charter to which members give their allegiance; they are the rock on which the organisation is built. If you manage to enshrine in your objects the basic principles for which the organisation will strive, those at least should remain secure as times change and people come and go.

While members are few in number, and considerable trust exists between them, problems over control are unlikely. Many organisations restrict membership to workers, long term supporters and others closely associated with the organisation. This does not prevent them from having a wider list of supporters, who contribute to the organisation in different ways but who have no formal control over it. It is also possible to provide in the constitution for two categories of membership, one with voting rights and one without. Activist organisations, however, are based on the active contribution of their members, and it may be impossible to secure the necessary commitment unless members are enfranchised and feel they have a say in how the organisation is run.

Finally, the inter-relationship between members, management committee and hired staff may follow a variety of patterns. Three possible alternatives are given in the box overleaf. (It should be emphasised that these are only models, or abstractions.) The structure of a pressure group could follow any of these models, or a combination of them. It should only be pointed out that in sketching *formal* power structures, they hide the fact that who holds *effective* power in an organisation often depends on personal relationships (the influence of the chief executive, in particular, is underestimated in the diagrams). The balance of power in reality can be held by almost anyone – the chief executive's astrologer, for example.

Local groups

Many national pressure groups have a network of local groups or affiliated organisations. These can undertake a variety of functions: fundraising for the national body, raising local consciousness, run-

Distribution of power within a pressure group

1. 'Charity' model

Model 1 is based on a structure common among charities. The management committee retains responsibility for the policy and actions of the organisation and may be appointed either by an outside body or bodies (e.g. sponsoring organisations), or by the members (if there are members outside the committee), or be self-appointing, with new committee members appointed by the existing committee (or a combination of these methods). The management committee are un-salaried and executive staff therefore cannot sit on the committee.

2. 'Corporate' model

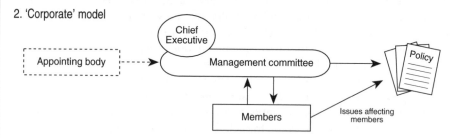

Model 2 has been dubbed 'corporate' because it should be familiar from many for-profit companies. Here the chief executive is an integral part of the management committee, if not its chair. Although the committee is still the driving force behind the organisation's actions, the members have the power to oust committee members (and probably elect them as well) and will be called on to vote on matters which directly affect their interests.

3. 'Grassroots' model

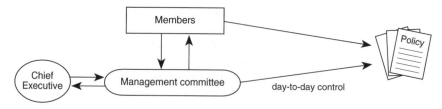

Model 3 is the most democratic structure, but can prove unwieldy. Full control over policy is retained by the members, with day-to-day decisions delegated to the management committee and executive staff.

ning local campaigns or doing the grassroots organising for national mass events or lobbying campaigns.

The relationship between a local group and the national body will generally take one of two forms: the branch or the affiliation. A branch consists of members of the national body and provides simply a convenient local focus for their activities. An affiliated group, on the other hand, is technically a separate association which supports the aims of the national body and abides by its rules. It will tend to be more autonomous. It is also possible to have a bottom-upwards, federated structure where the larger or national body consists entirely of autonomous local groups and is controlled by their delegates: an association of associations, in effect.

The work involved in coordinating local groups, and the problems that arise when a local group unilaterally steps outside the organisation's policy, have led some charities and pressure groups to consider phasing out a local group structure and servicing all their members through direct mail. The disadvantage is that many opportunities for local participation or involvement of members are removed. The decision whether or not to foster a local group structure may ultimately depend on the extent to which a campaign is about locally-based issues.

Help and advice

This chapter should have given you a grounding in what is involved in setting up a new organisation. Although it is worth taking time to get it right, the mechanics really are quite straightforward and shouldn't take too long. You can set up an unincorporated pressure group literally overnight and may well not require the services of a solicitor. Even companies limited by guarantee are now obtainable 'off-the-shelf', ready-formed from a solicitor or legal agency for a fee.

Further help and advice is available from a number of sources (although it should be noted that these are often more experienced in dealing with charities than with non-charitable pressure groups). For a local campaign it might be worth talking to the nearest council for voluntary service or a law centre. Community Matters (a national federation of community organisations) also provide help for community groups. The National Council for Voluntary Organisations represents national non-profit groups and has a legal department which gives advice; there are also separate umbrella councils in Scotland, Wales and Northern Ireland. Finally, the Industrial Common Ownership Movement (ICOM) provides a range of legal and registration services, which gives you the option of paying them to do all the work for you. See appendix B for addresses.

2 Charitable status: benefits and constraints

Some of the most effective pressure groups in the country are charities. Shelter, the national campaign for homeless people, has built up a strong public awareness of the issues surrounding homelessness, challenged existing preconceptions about homeless people and harnessed public pressure for change. The Institute of Economic Affairs, championing the cause of the free market to economists and politicians, could lay claim to having set the foundations for economic policy in late twentieth century Britain. The success of such groups is probably due to a number of different factors, but charitable status is evidently one of them.

Taking the charitable route to creating change will, however, close down some of your options and affect the style of your campaigning. For this reason, it will only be appropriate for a minority of pressure groups.

Specifying exactly who can or cannot be a charity, or what charities can or cannot do, is no easy task because the law in this area is ill-defined. The definitions that do exist come from the centuries-old accumulation of case law, with the judges in each case depending for guidance on the comments of their predecessors and ultimately on an Elizabethan statute of 1601 (the Charitable Uses Act). But as the examples at the start of this chapter demonstrate, common assertions like 'charities cannot campaign' or 'charities cannot undertake political activities' are clearly misleading.

Perhaps the most important distinction to bear in mind is the old one between ends and means. If any of the objects of an organisation are political, it cannot be a charity. If its objects are *exclusively* charitable, on the other hand, it will be a charity, and it will be able to undertake political activity, within limits, which furthers those objects directly. Which purposes are considered charitable, what is meant by the term 'political', and where the limits on political activity are placed, will be considered in turn below.

Charitable purposes

Charity law is a branch of the law of trusts and has its roots in the middle ages when the concept of trusts, or 'uses' as they were then known, first emerged and gifts of property on trust to church bodies were first regulated. The Charitable Uses Act 1601 was an early attempt to limit abuses, and the preamble to the Act describes the principal purposes that were considered charitable at the time. The following extract should give you the tone of the thing, a tone which still dogs charity law today:

> '... Lands, Goods, Chattels and Money have been given by sundry well-disposed Persons for Relief of aged, impotent and poor People, for Maintenance of sick and maimed Soldiers and Mariners, for Maintenance of Schools of Learning, Free Schools and Scholars in Universities, for Repair of Bridges, Ports, Havens, Causeways, Churches, Sea-Banks and Highways, for Education and Preferment of Orphans, for Relief, Stock or Maintenance for Houses of Correction, for Marriages of poor Maids, for Supportation, Aid and Help of young Tradesmen, Handicraftsmen and Persons decayed, for Relief or Redemption of Prisoners or Captives, for Aid or Ease of any poor Inhabitants concerning payment of Fifteens, setting out Soldiers and other Taxes ...'

The 1601 Act has since been repealed, but on the back of this curious list – which was never comprehensive – the courts have slowly built up an understanding of which purposes are legally charitable. Of particular importance was a case in 1891, when Lord Macnaghten went as far as to categorise charities under four main headings, since known as the four heads of charity:

> ' 1. trusts for the relief of poverty;
>
> 2. trusts for the advancement of education;
>
> 3. trusts for the advancement of religion;
>
> 4. and trusts for other purposes beneficial to the community, not falling under any of the preceding heads.'

The objects of a charity can fall under one of the four heads, or under a combination of them, but they must be *wholly and exclusively* charitable. If an organisation's objects are defined to include purposes which are not charitable, it will not be successful in seeking registration with the Charity Commission. More details on the four heads, and on the sorts of charity that can be registered under them, are given in the box overleaf.

Two things should be clear from Lord Macnaghten's words. The first is that all charities, whether they are constituted as limited companies, unincorporated associations or whatever, are subject to trust law. The management committee or directors of a charity will

Charitable purposes

Relief of poverty
What constitutes poverty is not strictly defined. Poverty certainly does not just mean destitution, and the word can be interpreted relatively. However, a trust will not be held charitable under this head if it is clear that others besides those who are poor are eligible to benefit. Note that poverty can be 'relieved' in a multitude of ways, including the provision of advice (citizens advice bureaux and law centres generally include the relief of poverty in their objects).

Advancement of education
As well as the support of pupils and students, and of educational institutions, museums and libraries, and the provision of training, the advancement of education also comprises the promotion of learning and research in a given subject, including the education of the public. Many public education campaigns are registered under this head.

Trusts for the advancement of education which are held to be primarily propagandistic in nature will not be charitable (see main text below), but the line between propaganda and the promotion of learning in a contentious subject can be a fine one. The Centre for Research into Communist Economies, for example, was registered as a charity in 1983.

Advancement of religion
'As between different religions the law stands neutral, but it assumes that any religion is at least likely to be better than none', summed up one judge. The advancement of any religion is charitable, then, but note that a god or gods have to be involved: the advancement of atheism would not qualify, nor would a religion which 'inculcates doctrines adverse to the very foundations of religion', or is 'subversive of all morality'.

Other purposes beneficial to the community
Despite the broad wording, this doesn't mean 'miscellaneous' as much as 'other purposes that the courts have recognised as charitable'. These include:

▾ the relief of sick, disabled or elderly people;
▾ the promotion of the arts;
▾ the provision and maintenance of land and buildings for public use, including recreational facilities;
▾ the preservation of the national heritage (e.g. listed buildings);
▾ the protection of the environment;
▾ animal welfare and the prevention of cruelty to animals;
▾ disaster relief;
▾ the encouragement of good citizenship and moral welfare.

The range of groups registered under this head is very wide. There is a particularly large contingent of medical or health charities, including those promoting alternative therapies, groups for the resettlement of offenders or rehabilitation of drug users, and groups coordinating self-help and campaigning for those suffering from a particular disease. The encouragement of good citizenship and moral welfare includes the promotion of good race relations and a variety of other causes from anthroposophy to humanism. Note that the promotion of peace and good international relations is *not* considered a charitable purpose.

thus also be its trustees, holding the funds of the charity on trust for the purposes defined in its objects.

The second point is that a charity must benefit the community or public, or a sufficiently wide section of it. Note that this does not prevent a charity's objects from limiting the class of beneficiary (e.g. to those under the age of 21, or to those living in the town of Scunthorpe), nor does it preclude those charities which provide a form of benefit extended to the whole community, but by its nature advantageous only to a few (e.g. a charity for those with a particular disability, or a charity to maintain a bridge). The public benefit criterion *does* rule out restricting benefit to members of a family, or to employees of a firm or members of a club. (The only exception to this is certain trusts for the relief of poverty.) Self-help groups, therefore, will not be charitable if their benefits are restricted to members of the group.

Political purposes

It is on account of the public benefit rule that political purposes are held not to be charitable and hence not open to a charity to have as one of its objects. This was first established in a case in 1917, when Lord Parker ruled that a trust for the attainment of a political object was not charitable since 'the court has no way of judging whether a proposed change in the law will or will not be for the public benefit'. To that argument the courts have since added another: that the court must decide a case 'on the principle that the law is right as it stands, since to do otherwise would be to usurp the functions of the legislature'.

Seeking to secure a change in the law, then, is a political purpose, as is opposing a change in the law. There are others. Seeking to reverse government policy, or even a particular government decision, has been ruled a political purpose. This is the case even if such changes appear completely justifiable (indeed, even if the changes are sought in a foreign country and would bring its laws or policy closer in line with our own). Supporting a particular political party or the principles it advocates are also considered political purposes, as you might expect.

These points of law, and the rationale behind them, were usefully summarised in the High Court in 1981 by Mr Justice Slade when he upheld the Charity Commission's decision to refuse charitable status to the Amnesty International Trust. His judgement concluded:

'Indisputably, laws do exist, both in this country and in many foreign countries, which many reasonable persons consider unjust. No less indisputably, laws themselves will from time to time be administered by governmental authorities in a manner which many reasonable persons consider unjust, inhuman or degrading. Amnesty International, in striving to remedy what it considers to be such injustices, is performing a function which many will regard as

---

Political purposes

The following purposes are considered by the courts to be political in nature:

▼ advocating a change in the law, or opposing a change in the law, whether in the UK or in a foreign country;

▼ seeking the reversal of government policy, or of a particular government decision, whether in the UK or in a foreign country;

▼ furthering the interests of a particular political party or the principles propounded by a particular party.

An organisation which has any of these purposes as its object cannot be a charity. Furthermore, if an organisation with educational objects has as its real aim any of the above purposes, i.e. it is primarily propagandist in nature, it cannot be a charity.

---

being of great value to humanity. Fortunately, the laws of this country place very few restrictions on the rights of philanthropic organisations such as this, or of individuals, to strive for the remedy of what they regard as instances of injustice, whether occurring here or abroad. However ... the elimination of injustice has not as such ever been held to be a trust purpose which qualifies for the privileges afforded to charities by English law. I cannot hold it to be a charitable purpose now.'

Finally, the courts have also refused charitable status to trusts which have ostensibly educational objects but whose main purpose is the promotion of a particular set of political principles. 'Political propaganda masquerading ... as education is not education,' as one judge pointed out. Thus in 1975 a trust for furthering knowledge of socialised medicine and demonstrating that its full advantage could only be enjoyed in a socialist state was held not to be charitable.

Registration

Charities in England and Wales are required to register with the Charity Commission, unless their annual income is less than £1,000 and they have no permanent endowment and do not use or occupy land. A few classes of charity, listed at the back of the Charities Act 1993, are exempt from registration, but they are primarily those for whom a regulatory mechanism already exists (e.g. some universities, or charitable societies registered under the Industrial and Provident Societies Act). The registration process usually takes about three months but may take much longer if the objects or activities of the proposed charity are unusual. The Charity Commission's remit does not extend to Scotland or Northern Ireland: Scottish charities should register with the Inland Revenue in Edinburgh; in Northern Ireland there is no system of registration but the Inland Revenue (in Merseyside) will advise on charitable status for tax purposes.

On initial application, the Charity Commission sends out a registration pack. Following a new, streamlined registration process introduced in 1996, a new organisation can only apply for registration as a charity once it has formally approved its constitution or governing document.

The Commission will look at the objects to confirm they are charitable, at the powers and the rest of the constitution to make sure they are consistent with charitable status, and at the proposed activities of the charity to check they are consistent with its objects and powers. If the charity does not fall within established precedents the Commission will also consult with the Inland Revenue. If you have trouble at any stage you may need to employ a solicitor experienced in this sort of work to help you in dealing with the Commission.

In addition to the Charity Commission itself, the organisations listed at the end of chapter 1 will give advice on registering as a charity. Both the Commission and the National Council for Voluntary Organisations have model constitutions for a charitable trust, a charitable company and a charitable unincorporated association, and Community Matters have a model constitution for a charitable community association. The advantage of using a tried and tested model is that the registration process will be easier, but note that the model constitutions will not be appropriate as they stand for every variety of group and may well need tailoring to individual requirements.

Benefits and constraints

Charitable status is a two-edged sword: it provides a group with valuable benefits but it will constrain its freedoms and may even provide opponents with an opportunity to attack it. But let us consider the benefits first.

▼ *Tax reliefs.* Charities do not pay income or corporation tax on income which is applied to charitable purposes. They do not pay any capital gains tax and receive 80% mandatory rate relief. Gifts to a charity are also exempt from capital gains tax and inheritance tax. In addition, charities can reclaim basic rate tax paid by the donor on donations made under the Gift Aid scheme, provided that the donor has made a Gift Aid declaration. Higher rate taxpayers are also entitled to higher rate relief. Further information on tax reliefs is available from the Charities Division of the Inland Revenue Claims Branch in Merseyside.

In practice the value of tax reliefs to an organisation will depend on its sources of income. In rare cases, they could be worth over 40% of income. However, a charity with few investments whose main source of income was membership subscriptions and small donations from the general public might find the value of tax reliefs negligible.

▼ *Eligibility for grants.* Some funding agencies, in particular many charitable trusts and foundations, will only make grants to registered charities.

▼ *Fundraising appeal.* Being able to say that you are a charity can make it much easier to raise money from the general public, who are impressed or reassured by such things.

▼ *Badge of independence.* Charitable status is a badge of respectability that can carry benefits far beyond fundraising. As a charity cannot have political objects, charitable status is effectively a guarantee of independence. In contrast to politicians and to other interest groups, charities are generally regarded as having no personal axe to grind, and to be speaking on behalf of their beneficiaries, as often as not the poor, the powerless and the dispossessed. This advocacy role – whether justified or not – can give their arguments an unusual weight and integrity. Charitable status, in fact, can teach any campaigner a vital discipline: the importance of establishing and guarding the independent credentials of a group and of ensuring that in any contentious debate its own point of view is positioned at the *centre*, or (particularly if the issue is highly politicised) outside and above the debate.

In return for the above benefits, a charity will be subject to the following constraints:

▼ *Ban on distributing profits.* A charity cannot have as one of its objects the making or distributing of profits. Those involved in the running of the charity cannot profit from its activities, and if the charity does declare a surplus or profit at the end of the year this cannot be distributed amongst the members or workers. Note that this does not prevent a charity from employing paid staff, charging for its (charitable) services, or even making a small surplus, provided it is ploughed back into its charitable activities.

▼ *Limits on trading activities.* Consequently, any trading undertaken by a charity must be ancillary to its objects. The trade must either further directly the primary purposes of the charity (e.g. the sale of this book by the Directory of Social Change, or the sale of goods from a sheltered workshop) or, if undertaken simply to make money for the charity, it must be limited in scale. (For more information on trading, including its tax treatment, see chapter 3.)

▼ *Safeguards imposed by charity law.* The management committee or directors of a charity cannot normally be paid a salary or otherwise remunerated, except for out-of-pocket expenses. As trustees of the charity's funds, it is their duty to ensure that those funds are applied solely to further the charity's objects – applying funds for any other purpose would constitute breach of trust. They are not able to alter or amend the objects and if a group's constitution includes the power to alter its objects it will not be accepted for registration by the Charity Commission. Charities will normally be required to submit to the Commission an annual report and accounts and an annual return.

▼ *Limits on political activities.* See below.

Political activities by charities

This is one of the most difficult areas of charity law, partly because the concepts involved are not clearly defined but also because there is some disparity between the law and what happens in practice. For this reason it will be useful to consider first the case law, then the position taken by the regulatory authorities (the Charity Commission and the Inland Revenue), and finally the possible sanctions that could be applied to an errant charity.

Nearly all the cases dealing with political activities and charity are concerned with whether or not the proposed objects of a charity are political (see above) rather than with what a group is able to do once the charitable nature of its objects is not in doubt. Mr Justice Slade, in the Amnesty case cited above, was at pains to make the distinction clear: 'I would further emphasise that [my comments] are directed to trusts of which the purposes are political ... the mere fact that trustees may be at liberty to employ political means in furthering the non-political purposes of a trust does not necessarily render it non-charitable.'

The distinction is between ends and means. Charities are able to carry out a wide range of activities which in themselves are not charitable (e.g. raising and investing money) provided that they are undertaken to further directly their objects. Slade J again: 'The distinction is thus one between a) those non-charitable activities authorised by the trust instrument which are merely subsidiary or incidental to a charitable purpose' – which are OK – 'and b) those non-charitable activities so authorised which in themselves form part of the trust purpose' – which are not OK. Thus, to quote an actual case, a charity for the advancement of Christian principles may, as a subsidiary activity, campaign 'to minimise and extinguish the drink traffic' (combating the drink traffic being an application of Christian principles).

Unfortunately this distinction often blurs in practice, and establishing whether a given purpose is a) 'subsidiary', 'incidental' or 'ancillary', or b) a main or primary purpose is, as one law lord put it, a question of degree. To be considered a main purpose by the courts, an activity will not necessarily have to be written into the charity's objects. Thus in 1991 a students' union, an educational charity, was prevented from spending money on a campaign against the Gulf War, on the grounds that 'far from being an educational purpose, any educational effect [the campaign] might have was incidental to the main purpose of attempting to influence public opinion.'

On this legal skeleton the Charity Commissioners have attempted to construct detailed advice for charities. (Their published guidelines on political activities by charities were last revised in 1997, and are reprinted in appendix A.) On the plus side, the Commissioners have confirmed on numerous occasions that charities may be able to undertake certain activities of a political nature provided that they are in direct furtherance of their objects and within the powers conferred by their constitution. However, their guidance also places considerable stress on the style and tone of a campaign, emphasising that it should be 'reasoned' and 'responsible':

'A charity may advocate a change in the law or public policy which can reasonably be expected to help it to achieve its charitable purposes and may oppose a change in the law or public policy which can reasonably be expected to hinder its ability to do so. In either case the charity can present government with a reasoned memorandum or written argument in support of its position. It may well publish its views and may seek to influence public opinion in favour of its position by well-founded reasoned argument.'

In particular, the Commissioners stipulate that a charity must not seek to influence government or public opinion 'on the basis of material which is merely emotive', and must not invite its supporters or the public to write to their MPs or the government 'without providing them with sufficient information to enable them to advance a reasoned argument in favour of the charity's position'.

In a rare inquiry into a charity's political activities, the Commissioners ruled in 1991 that Oxfam had on occasion gone beyond what was allowable. Most of the points made were substantive: Oxfam's advocacy of sanctions against South Africa was criticised, for example, on the grounds that there was no reasonable proof that such action would be of direct benefit to Oxfam's beneficiaries. The tone of some of the charity's work was also criticised, however. On Oxfam's Cambodia campaign the inquiry commented, ridiculously: 'The peculiar horror of the Pol Pot regime adds strength to any campaign, but a balance should be maintained. This campaign had been prosecuted with too much vigour.'

More frequently, the Charity Commission has questioned the activities of a proposed charity at the registration stage. There is some unevenness in how different applications are treated, and on occasion the Commission has appeared to regard any political activity as prejudicial to a group's achieving charitable status. It is also possible that the Inland Revenue can take a dim view of *any* non-charitable activity and withhold tax relief, on the grounds that the taxes acts only extend tax relief to income which is *applied* for charitable purposes.

In addition to losing tax relief on the funds spent on any political activity found unacceptable, the trustees of a charity risk being in breach of trust. This means that they can be held personally liable to repay to the charity the funds spent on such activity. (Note that the penalty is not being stripped of charitable status, as is often assumed.) In practice this sanction is very rarely applied. In the case of Oxfam, the Commissioners took the view that the trustees acted in good faith and consequently did not seek reimbursement.

In fact, the Charity Commission hardly ever looks into the political activities of established charities, relying instead on the media and on complaints from members of the public to spur it into action. Don't derive from this a false sense of security: any campaigning group worth its salt will acquire enemies in whose interest it is to complain to the Commission or to try and place stories in the media. Oxfam, for example, was the target of a concerted campaign by the International Freedom Foundation, a far-right pressure group.

But hundreds of charities up and down the land campaign, often quite vigorously, on issues that affect their beneficiaries, and do so without interference. The box below gives a few pointers to help ensure that a charity's political activities remain within what is allowable. If the Charity Commission guidelines do seem to you unduly restrictive, try looking at them as a lesson in campaigning technique: in suggesting that charities may present their argument in the form of a reasoned memorandum, the Commission is in effect pushing them towards the style of campaigning employed – often with great success – by most parts of the establishment.

Charities undertaking political activities: how to stay out of trouble

1. Ensure that you only undertake political activity which directly furthers your objects. If your charity has a distinct class of beneficiary, you should be able to demonstrate with reasonable certainty that any measure you campaign for will be of direct benefit to your beneficiaries. (A disability charity, for example, may be able to campaign on a new disability bill which would affect its beneficiaries, but it would not be able to support the election of a parliamentary candidate whom it thought sympathetic to its cause.)

2. Ensure that any political activity you undertake is within the powers conferred by your constitution. In particular, if you intend to mount a public campaign, make sure that your constitution includes the power to inform and educate the public (and if it does not, get it amended).

3. If you are planning a campaign which is high-profile, long-term or involves substantial resources, get legal advice from someone with experience in this field, or seek clearance from the Charity Commission (but note that the Commission may find it easier to refuse permission than to approve something which may set a precedent for other groups to follow).

4. If you have staff or volunteers who will be representing your charity, particularly in any campaigning activities, make sure they have a clear policy line to follow. Consider compiling a list of dos and don'ts that staff can use as a guide.

Another option if a charity envisages carrying out significant high profile political activities is to hive off those activities into a separate campaigning arm with a related name, making two different organisations. The charity War on Want thus set up WoW Campaigns Ltd. A non-charitable group can similarly establish a charity to handle its charitable activities; Liberty (the National Council for Civil Liberties) did this with the Civil Liberties Trust. The Charity Commission can be somewhat wary of registering this kind of associated charity, however, because of the difficulties involved in keeping the activities of the two groups separate. The management committees of the two groups, charitable and non-charitable, can include the same people (indeed at least some overlap is useful to ensure coordination), but problems do occur with having to set up separate accounting structures, particularly when it comes to apportioning costs or sharing resources. Most members of the public, of course, won't know the difference.

Changing the regime

It is probable that the regime restricting charities' political activity will change in the future, but in which direction it is hard to say. Looking back, it is clear that the restrictions are largely a creation of the twentieth century: in the last century charities were accepted with objects such as 'the abolition of all forms of forced labour', 'the suppression of vivisection' and 'the furtherance of Conservative principles'.

Many charities currently resist a legal clarification of what is permissible, fearing a tightening of the regime. However, there are strong arguments for loosening or removing the restrictions on charities' behaviour. Many people have argued that charities are unique among organisations in our society in having their freedom of speech checked in this way, and that commercial companies or individuals (who may well be the recipients of tax reliefs or benefits) are free to campaign as much as they like.

But perhaps the most compelling argument for removing the restrictions altogether derives from a technicality. Although in practice a new organisation might choose not to register as a charity, strictly speaking charitable status is not optional. If a new fund is set up, or a legacy or a gift is made, on trust for purposes which happen to be exclusively charitable, then a charity will have been created. The effect of the current restrictions, then, is to deny proper advocacy to all those causes, and exclusively to those causes, that our society has come over the last 800 years to recognise as most laudable and beneficial.

3 Finance for campaigns

Sans argent, l'honneur n'est qu'une maladie – Racine

There is now a considerable literature on raising money for non-profit organisations, covering both techniques – from direct mail to 'relationship' fundraising – and funding sources, from the government to companies to the public. Most of this material, however, is aimed at charities. Although this chapter will be relevant to any organisation raising funds to run a campaign, it will concentrate on finance for pressure groups or other non-profits without charitable status. In particular, it will discuss those areas that provide most support for campaigns, outline which charitable sources are still open to non-charities and highlight possible new areas for developing support.

The income account for a pressure group typically looks like a cross between that of a charity and a political party. Sources of finance will in practice depend on the type of campaign (e.g. whether it is membership-based), on its natural allies (and whether they have money) and on the degree to which its activities are charitable.

Political fundraising in the UK is becoming more and more sophisticated, partly on account of innovations imported from the United States. These often are designed to exploit the high level of commitment which potentially exists among members or supporters of political organisations. Telephone solicitation, for example, which usually involves calling members or existing donors to get them to commit further donations, has been successfully pioneered in this country by a couple of American firms whose clients range from political parties to pressure groups to charities.

There are four main sources of finance for pressure groups or campaigns:

▼ the membership;
▼ the wider public;
▼ independent bodies, including unions, companies and foundations;
▼ government (sometimes).

The best funding sources of all are allied interest groups. They effectively form a sub-set of each of the four categories listed above. Those, whether individuals or institutions, who hold an interest (financial or otherwise) in the successful outcome of your campaign will usually prove the most profitable targets for fundraising, and should always be considered first. The obvious example of this historically is the political parties: the Conservatives receive the bulk of their funds from corporations, wealthy individuals and businesspeople; Labour from the trades unions; while the Liberal Democrats, a newly restructured party without a clear economic constituency, have to rely on members for most of their income.

Always ask yourself the two questions: Who stands to gain from the success of the campaign? Do they have any money?

The membership

The membership remains the bedrock of campaign finance for many public interest pressure groups and smaller political parties. It certainly has one great advantage over most of the other sources of money discussed in this chapter: if well managed, a membership can provide a *stable, recurrent source of core income* that can give a campaign great freedom of movement.

Establishing a membership for fundraising or campaigning purposes need not have repercussions for the formal control of your organisation. 'Membership' of a pressure group or charity does not confer any rights (e.g. voting at AGMs, etc.) unless this is stated in the group's constitution (see chapter 1) and it can simply be a mechanism for expressing continuing support. The membership of most groups is in fact structured in this way. You can launch a membership scheme simply as a means of securing a core of committed supporters and of demonstrating the breadth of your support to the world at large.

Building membership

Establishing a membership for a new group usually involves a public launch – based on a stirring campaign message with, hopefully, good media coverage – and a coordinated programme of adverts, inserts or mailshots to bring home the subscriptions once people are aware of your existence. More information on these different types of advertising are given in chapter 5, but the key to the success of any membership drive is targeting: making sure advertisements or letters get to the people most likely to want to be members.

The better-defined your constituency is, the more straightforward this will be. A campaign to remove a local traffic blackspot might: arrange coverage in a local newspaper; write to, or leaflet, households in adjoining roads; place notices in local community or neighbourhood centres; arrange piggy-back mailings with the local branches of automobile clubs or amenity societies; put a notice in the council newsletter; and so on.

National or even international campaigns may also have natural constituencies that can be easily targeted. The branches of International Physicians for the Prevention of Nuclear War the world over organise appropriate publicity in hospitals, clinics, health centres and doctors' or nurses' homes; target professional associations in the health field, members of the health unions, and medical students; and mail to others active in the wider peace movement.

For other national campaigns, targeting potential members may not be so easy. There are now a large number of single-issue campaigns active, many of them with a youngish, high-turnover membership. Attracting members to any new liberal cause will therefore involve targeting people who are likely already to be members of other groups. This is not so bad as it sounds: it does at least give you somewhere to start. Ideally you could buy a mailing list from another group, similar to your own, but most organisations are loathe to part with such information, even for a sizeable fee. They may, however, agree to let you piggy-back one of their own mailings. A programme of inserts in other campaign newsletters or appropriate publications is a favourite option. Donor profile information (details on the demography and lifestyle of potential or existing donors that enable you to target mailings) could be obtained from other related campaigns, from your own research (see chapter 4), or even from relevant opinion polls or social attitude surveys. More on this under 'Direct Mail' below.

One of the cheapest and most effective ways of expanding your membership once established is to launch a member-get-member scheme. This is Americanese for persuading existing members to find new ones among their friends, relatives, colleagues, etc. It is useful to be able to offer an incentive to the member doing the recruiting – a free publication, T-shirt, or a one-off reduction in their own membership fee, for example.

Subscriptions and donations

The membership subscription for a campaign or interest group can vary from a couple of pounds for a local campaign to over £200 to join a professional association which provides benefits to members, like the British Medical Association. The level at which a campaign sets its membership subscription generally depends on three factors:

▼ the level of services offered to members;

▼ what members can afford (or how price-elastic take-up is);

▼ how the membership is used by the campaign.

One rule is that subscription income should, at the very least, cover the cost of servicing the membership. Where the subscription charged is so low that the organisation is in effect subsidising its membership this can lead to serious problems. (This is particularly so as it is difficult to raise the price substantially once it has been set.) If you provide services to members in addition to the standard publicity mailings and newsletter, such as technical briefings or individual advice or advocacy, it is better to spell out the higher costs involved and reflect them in the price of membership.

Many campaigns are constrained by what they think their members will be able to afford. This can often lead them to under-price membership subscriptions, especially if they do not have an accurate idea of the relative wealth of their members. It is still common for national campaigns to set their individual rate at £10 or under, which is really very low.

Some groups deliberately keep membership subscriptions cheap on the basis that once members have signed on the dotted line, they can be more successfully approached for donations in the future. However, there is rarely anything to indicate that this tactic will in fact attract more members – or that once attracted, they will be willing to donate more subsequently. On the contrary, it is probably worth trying to gauge how price-elastic the membership response really is: in this case, how high you could put up the price before a significant proportion of people are put off buying membership. (Pricing theory suggests that this margin can be quite wide.) Once again, this sort of information is best gleaned from donor profile research.

You can also boost subscription income and avoid discouraging members at the same time by using discretionary pricing. This has two aspects. The first, varying rates by members' income, is more common: having a concessionary rate for low income or unwaged people, a standard rate, and possibly a premium rate for higher-rate taxpayers or those with large incomes. The important thing here is that it enables you to set the standard rate quite high. The other method is to introduce different categories of membership at different prices. This is often used by the big arts or heritage charities, who have two or three categories (e.g. 'member' and 'associate'; or 'standard', 'silver', 'gold') which may or may not

---

Checklist: options for boosting membership income

▼ Raise membership fees

▼ Set subscription rates on a scale

▼ Introduce new categories of member

▼ Mail members more frequently

▼ Segment mailing list to target stronger supporters more often

▼ Suggest higher levels of donation

▼ Link donations to campaign actions

▼ Encourage payment by standing order or direct debit

▼ Encourage donations by Gift Aid (for charities only)

Attract new members through:

▼ Launching member-get-member scheme

▼ Programme of inserts or piggy-back mailings

▼ Advertising

▼ Compiling, swapping, or hiring other mailing lists

carry additional perks for members. This can seem a bit elitist: a good way round it is just to invent a nominal category of 'supporting member' at, say, double the standard rate. When their membership comes up for renewal, supporting members can be simply prompted to continue paying at the higher rate. Introducing a category of life member can also be a way of securing a large donation straight off.

Some people will wish to support your campaign but will be reluctant to become members because they see this as committing themselves in some way. On any membership invitation or leaflet you produce it is therefore important to give people the option of donating instead of (or in addition to!) becoming members. Such invitations should always include a tear-off form, making it easy for the recipient to act immediately. Ideally the form should prompt the potential member at every stage, leaving them to make as few decisions as possible (see example below).

Specimen membership form

ACT NOW!

Name Mr/Ms/Mrs/Miss _____

Address _____

_____ Postcode _____

I would like to become a member (please tick)

☐ Single £19   ☐ Family £28   ☐ Unwaged £9   ☐ Supporting member (with free T-shirt) £38

Additional donation of £_____

If you can afford to give more, we will use your money to carry out more actions.

I enclose a cheque/PO. for £_____ made payable to **Action For Its Own Sake Ltd.**

Better still, please complete this Banker's Order:

BANKER'S ORDER

To: The Manager of_____Bank

Address _____

Postcode _____ Sort code _ _/_ _/_ _

Please pay Action For Its Own Sake Ltd. the sum of £_____every month/year, starting on _____(date), and debit my account no. _____

Signed _____

Pay to Action For Its Own Sake Ltd., A/c 98437609, CredoBank, 279 Baker Street, London NW1 (Sort code 40-43-05)

Please send this form to Action For Its Own Sake, *not* to your bank

It was mentioned above that one of the great advantages of membership income is that it is relatively reliable. However, this is only the case if an efficient system for renewing subscriptions, soliciting donations and attracting new members is implemented. It was – and still is – possible to do this through a card index system, but for all except the smallest organisations a computer database package is now essential. As this section and the following one on direct mail emphasise, many fundraising techniques depend on segmenting lists of supporters in various ways, so it is worthwhile investing in a software package that is sophisticated enough to sort on different data fields (e.g. name, postcode, amount of donation); to merge information in different fields (e.g. donation and subscription information); and, ideally, to sort using comparison operators (e.g. 'greater than' and 'less than' commands, as in 'those donating more than £100').

New members will join at any point throughout the year, so it is important to establish a system for sending out subscription renewal notices at regular intervals. It is often easiest to do this on a quarterly or bi-monthly basis, sending notices in one block to all those members whose subscriptions expired over the preceding 2–3 months and then a reminder a few weeks later to those who don't reply. One good way of letting inertia work in your favour, and making your income more reliable at the same time, is to persuade people to pay their subscriptions by standing order or direct debit.

Direct mail

The mail is the principal method for soliciting donations from members and other individual donors. So long as mailings are confined to such existing supporters, it can be a very effective way of raising money.

To communicate with people well, you need to know who they are. This means knowing something about their lifestyle, values, disposable income, etc. A few years ago Shelter, the National Campaign for the Homeless, commissioned a donor profiling exercise in order to find out more about its 41,000 active supporters. Some of the findings are given in the box opposite, and are not necessarily what one might expect: the two largest categories of donor are predominantly traditional, small-c conservative, older people. Knowing in which demographic or lifestyle categories its supporters are concentrated, and how they differ from the norm, will affect the way in which Shelter uses direct mail and other publicity. It will enable it, for example, to target cold mailings by using lists which match these characteristics.

It will also affect the tone of any publicity. Direct mail letters are often written to a 'typical' donor. Shelter's research produced the following profile for a typical Shelter donor: 65 plus in age; married;

Donor profiling for Shelter

Shelter donors were classified under a number of headings based on demographic and lifestyle characteristics, and the results compared with the national average. The headings or 'personas' are those used in market research into consumer behaviour. Most should be self-explanatory, but the two containing the highest proportion of Shelter donors are described here.

Tradition and Charity:- 'Long established in their work and where they live, this well educated and financially secure group are approaching retirement or already retired. Equally their eating habits are established, they buy wholesome, good quality and traditional items; no convenience or fast food for them. As pillars of the community they are likely supporters of good causes, charities and the National Trust. They take an interest in the world about them, continuing to increase their knowledge which is helped by foreign travel to far away places, especially North America.'

Wildlife and Trustees:- 'Now that the children have left home and their mortgage is probably paid off this group, as they approach or enter retirement, can spend more time enjoying the countryside, its landscape and its natural wonder. Just as they enjoy British historical traditions in architecture and historic homes so they savour traditional foods, none of which are health or vegetarian foods but wholesome nutritious fare.'

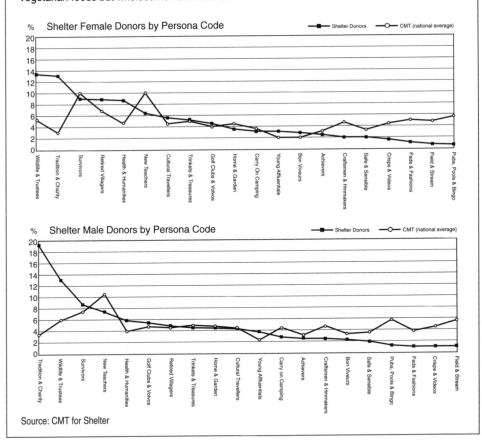

Source: CMT for Shelter

income over £35,000; retired or professional/senior management; home owner; no children at home; high use of credit cards; drives personal car; lives in London; reads quality newspapers; gives to many charities by post or covenant; likes: religion, charities, arts, books and current affairs; dislikes: videos, pools, pubs and TV. On the practical side, the appeal should therefore give the donor an oppor- tunity to pay by credit card and sign a covenant, and prompt a level of giving that is quite high; on the emotional side, it may appeal to a sense of community, to the idea of others being less secure than ourselves and to anxiety for young people having to make their own way in the world.

Perhaps the most important lesson from all this is not to make too many assumptions about who the bulk of your donors are, at least until you have done some research.

The limit on what you can include in a direct mailshot will be set by the postage rate. The best way to get ideas for your own mailings and a feel for copywriting is to look at mailings from other groups. One thing to look out for especially are methods for personalising letters: handwriting the salutation and signature, adding a handwritten PS (even if it is then printed), using typed or handwritten addresses on envelopes rather than labels, etc. If people feel they've been written to by a Xerox machine, you'll end up communicating with nothing except the trash can.

Used most effectively, direct mail involves dividing up your mailing list so that you can vary the message, and the frequency of mailing, to each sub-list as appropriate. Recent or major donors, for example, should be approached more often. The exception to this is those who pay by standing order or covenant, who could well be put-off by numerous additional appeals. A sample annual mailing plan is given overleaf.

It is now customary to mail supporters much more frequently than was once the case. In the US, it is not uncommon for non-profit groups to appeal to supporters eight, ten or even more times in a year. This may still be a bit much for British sensibilities, but a programme of six mailings a year is a good target. Generally speaking, mailing more often might reduce your *average* take, but boost the *total* income considerably. It is particularly important in this respect to segment your list, so that you can mail selectively, which will also keep mailing costs down (see sample plan).

If you are sending appeals as often as six times a year, it is a challenge to make each one fresh and compelling. It is useful to be able to construct mailings around a particular event: calamities are ideal, but other examples include Christmas or other seasons of goodwill, an election, a change in government policy, or a special anniversary (Hiroshima Day is often used by peace groups). Greenpeace pulled in a lot of new support with its publicity after the Shetlands oil disaster.

A sample annual mailing plan

Donor Group	Feb	April	June	Aug	Oct	Dec
Standing orders			R			A
Covenants			R			A
Recent major donors	A	A	R	A	A	A
Recent donors	A	A	A	A	A	A
Old donors			A			A
Enquirers			A			A

A = appeal sent out   R = annual report sent out

An example of how a small charity might structure its mailing programme, taking into account the need to appeal more often to good but uncommitted donors, to report back to major donors with an annual report, and to appeal less frequently to enquirers or lapsed donors. Each of the segments in the plan will demand a different package even if appeals are going out at the same time. *Source: Complete Fundraising Handbook, see appendix C.*

So far we have talked about direct mail as a method of raising money from existing supporters. It is also possible to mail *cold*, to people whom you have not contacted before. The response rate will depend on the quality of the mailing list you use, but is unlikely to be high: the average for cold mailings is about 1–2 per cent. For this reason, cold mailings are seen principally as an investment, a way of gaining new supporters – who can be mailed repeatedly in the future – rather than a means of raising money directly. As direct mail is most cost-effective when it is used to communicate with very large groups of people – 10,000 is a frequently quoted benchmark – the investment required to build up such a long list of supporters is considerable.

Mailing lists can be obtained from other groups (rent or exchange), compiled from directories or membership lists, or rented from a list broker. A short directory of about 80 accredited list brokers can be obtained from the Direct Marketing Association (see appendix B).

The quality of lists can vary greatly, both in terms of how up-to-date they are and how receptive to your services and cause the people listed will be. The broad aim is to get to the sort of people you have identified in your donor profile research. It is often a good idea to test mail a part of a list first, to gauge what the response rate will be like.

More generally, it is important to develop a way of keeping track of all the different approaches you use, so that you know exactly which ones are more successful and need developing further. At its simplest, this means ensuring that the return forms from each mailing, insert or advertisement, are separately identifiable and that every donation or response received is recorded.

Telephone fundraising

One step further than sending individualised mailshots to people is to ask them directly for money over the phone. At the moment this is only practised to any significant extent with existing supporters, in order to persuade them to upgrade their giving. A common structure for the call is to begin by thanking the person for their past support, to take the opportunity to fill them in about what you have been able to do with their money, and then to ask them whether they have considered giving by standing order, becoming a supporting member, etc. You need a script so that you speak fluently and know what to say in response to different questions and reactions.

The response rate is generally considerably higher than with direct mail, but there is a danger of alienating some supporters unless considerable tact is employed. Raising money through the telephone is certainly demanding, and not just on your telephone manner. Most supporter lists or databases do not include telephone numbers, which will have to be researched first. Once calls are made, all those that pledge money need to be contacted as quickly as possible in writing to clinch the donations. Even so, about a third of the pledges may not be translated into cash.

There are some professional agencies who specialise in telephone fundraising. These can handle all the above work, have the advantage of employing telephone operators trained to be both tactful and thick-skinned, but are not cheap. Charges are generally made per person contacted, with follow-up. Note that hiring a telemarketing agency to make telephone appeals would require a written agreement under the terms of the Charities Act 1992 (see below under 'Professional fundraisers').

Telephone solicitation is a very expensive fundraising medium: an average call may last over 10 minutes. Even if you do it yourself, it is clearly not cost-effective if you are only getting people to pledge small amounts, £5 or £10, particularly as you will not see all the money at the end of the day. Conversely, if you aim high enough, and there exists a depth of commitment among your supporters, the rewards can be considerable: the Labour Party used telemarketing to boost standing orders pledged to the party up to £1 million a year, an increase of four times in as many years.

Public collections

Public charitable collections are regulated under Part III of the Charities Act 1992, although as of January 2000 still not brought into force. Any group undertaking a street or house to house collection must obtain a permit from the relevant local authority (i.e. a district council or London borough). This applies not only to registered charities, but to any appeal for 'charitable, benevolent or philanthropic purposes' (a definition that is yet to be tested in the courts but is likely to encompass most pressure group activity). Permits normally have to be applied for at least one month in advance of the proposed collection and the local authority may specify conditions regarding dates, times, frequency, etc. Charities only can apply to the Charity Commission for a national exemption order if the proposed collection(s) are to be promoted throughout a substantial part of England and Wales. Promoting a public collection without the relevant permit or exemption order is a criminal offence.

So long as a collection is not made in a public place or by means of house to house visits, a permit is not required. No permit is needed for collections made:

▾ in the course of public meetings;

▾ in a place to which public access is controlled by ticket or entry fee;

▾ in shops, theatres, hospitals, etc. (though the consent of the owner or managing authority should be obtained);

▾ by means of unattended collection boxes.

Permits *are* required, however, for collections made in shopping precincts, on the forecourts of railway stations, etc.

Most public charitable collections consist of volunteers rattling collection tins in busy thoroughfares where passers-by are forced to look them in the eye. Often run by household-name charities, they rely to a large extent on an 'It's for charity' reflex. Pressure groups may find it hard to tap into this reflex unless they can get a message across convincingly in less than a couple of seconds.

Two successful alternatives both involve drawing the passer-by into conversation. Exiled Iranians from the refugee charity IranAid used to use a dossier documenting, and illustrating, ill-treatment to their compatriots to engage the attention and sympathy of the passer-by. A sponsorship sheet already recording large donations is used to prompt a similar level of gift. Workers Against Racism, on the other hand, approach people on the street to sign an anti-racist petition and then prompt signatories to make a donation. Getting someone to express their commitment before asking them for money is one way of turning the age-old tradition of signing petitions to substantive use.

Trading

As concern grows about 'giving fatigue' among the donating public and the number of non-profit groups proliferate, more and more of them are turning to semi-commercial activities to raise money. Things sold typically include: pamphlets and other campaign materials; Christmas cards, T-shirts and other small gifts; goods produced in sheltered workshops and in less-developed countries; and donated goods like second-hand clothes and books. The bulk of this stuff, donated goods excepted, is sold through mail order catalogue.

Aside from the ubiquitous local jumble sale, it is difficult to make money out of selling donated goods unless you have a developed system for acquiring goods that other people would want to buy and a retail outlet with low overheads. Even Oxfam, which leads the field in raising money this way and which relies heavily on volunteer input and its network of high-street outlets, now sells a large range of new goods in its thrift shops.

More generally, probably too much trading now goes on. This is not just because the world already has a more than adequate supply of souvenir mugs and tea towels, but also because selling them is rarely very profitable. Organisations often find themselves committing more and more staff time to their trading activities when the return on them is very small or negligible. In addition, supporters will often regard buying from a campaign catalogue as a form of soft donation, so there is a risk of diverting donations (on which the 'return' is near 100%) into sales (where the return rarely exceeds 50%).

Before undertaking any trading, it is important to calculate the profit margin and break-even point for any project (see box for an example). The relative difficulty involved in breaking even represents the level of risk in a venture. Up to break-even, you will effectively be running at a loss. Risk can be minimised to the extent that you can get goods on a sale-or-return basis and keep overheads low by attracting volunteer input or gifts-in-kind (e.g. free publicity or retail space).

It is particularly important to cost out overheads fully because any profit made on trading activities may be liable to tax. Non-charitable companies are liable for corporation tax on their trading profits, as are unincorporated associations without charitable status (which come within the definition of 'company' for the purposes of the relevant taxes acts). The small companies rate will generally apply. It is worth noting that for the purposes of tax assessment a trading loss made during the year can be offset against other profits made (e.g. from investments).

Charities are exempted under statute from paying tax on trading profits 'if the profits are applied solely to the purposes of the charity and either: i) the trade is exercised in the course of the actual carrying out of a primary purpose of the charity; or ii) the work in connection with the trade is mainly carried out by beneficiaries of the charity' (*Income and Corporation Taxes Act 1988*). The first category covers such things as charging for the charity's services or selling its publications and the second mainly refers to sheltered workplaces and the sale of goods made by disadvantaged people. Charities also benefit from an Inland Revenue concession exempting from tax the profits from small-scale, irregular trading such as charity fêtes, premières and dinners. However, any trading not covered by the above will be liable to tax and substantial trading activities may compromise an organisation's charitable status. A common method of getting round both these problems is for the charity to set up a subsidiary company to carry out the trading and covenant profits back to the charity.

One of the most fruitful areas for developing trading activities is selling items directly connected with the campaign, including pamphlets, books and posters.

A few organisations in the eighties made trading one of the most successful elements of their campaign. The anti-fur group Lynx countered one element in the clothes trade by pushing another: selling Lynx designer T-shirts which turned people into walking adverts for the campaign. In similar vein, the Nicaragua Solidarity Campaign's sale of shirts and other fashion accessories helped make solidarity with the Sandinistas an integral part of eighties youth culture.

Looked at another way, few organisations take full advantage of the commercial opportunities that exist within their campaigning activities. Applying a realistic pricing policy to campaign materials or publications can enable parts of a campaign to become self-financing and may even make dissemination more effective (people are more likely to read things they have had to buy).

Benefits and events

Concerts, dinners, premières and other social events are a natural way of raising money for campaigns seeking publicity. The last few years have seen a number of spectacular events run by cause groups, many of them raising thousands and even millions of pounds and boosting the profile of the cause substantially at the same time. The huge 1988 Mandela '70th birthday tribute' at Wembley brought in £1.2 million for the Anti-Apartheid Movement and various development NGOs and upped the pressure for Nelson Mandela's release from prison. Amnesty International benefited handsomely from selling the TV rights for the Secret Policeman's Ball. On a much smaller level, the traditional gamut of fundraising activities from fêtes to sponsored events to car-boot sales can all be run by volunteers to bring in money.

Calculating break-even point

Proposal: to sell campaign T-shirts by mail order

Deduct direct costs from selling price to give gross profit:

Selling price	£10
Wholesale cost (per T-shirt)	4
Gross profit	6

$$\text{Gross profit margin} = \frac{\text{Gross profit}}{\text{selling price}} \times 100 = \frac{6}{10} \times 100 = 60\%$$

Calculate overheads:

Staff costs	350
Publicity	150
Office overheads	100
Total overheads	600

Divide overheads by gross profit per unit to give required volume of sales to break even:

$600 \div 6 = 100$

Break-even point will be reached when 100 T-shirts have been sold, giving a gross profit of £600 on a total income of £1,000.

Estimated profit/loss for different levels of sales:

Number sold	50	100	200	400
Income	500	1000	2000	4000
Cost of sales	200	400	800	1600
Gross profit	300	600	1200	2400
Overheads	600	600	600	600
Profit/loss	(300)	–	600	1800

However, money can be lost as well as made on events. The level of risk is generally higher with events than with most trading activities because their one-off nature makes them vulnerable to anything from bad weather to last-minute cancellations to poor attendance. It is therefore particularly important to draw up a thorough financial plan, including a budget for contingencies, and to ensure that the profit margin is wide enough to justify the risk (and possibly to absorb the cost of some things going wrong).

A number of things can be done to lower the costs of an event and minimise the risks:

▼ *Free appearances.* Whether it is a rock group or an after-dinner speaker, it should be possible to get your star attraction to give their services free of charge. For speakers, call in favours from your more illustrious patrons or supporters. Pop stars are obviously in great demand but, if the cause is right, performing for free can be a relatively cheap way for them of showing their support (and picking up healthy publicity at the same time). Both George Michael and Elton John, for example, have done shows for AIDS causes. Film premières follow a similar logic. Film producers/distributors are often keen on charity premières and not necessarily just those that involve royalty and big name charities. The marketing of cause-related films can benefit from an association with a pressure group. The El Salvador Committee for Human Rights pulled in £10,000 from the London première of *Romero*, a biopic of Archbishop Romero of San Salvador, and the first showing here of *Thunderheart*, a film about Native American reservations, was given to Shelter.

▼ *Sponsorship.* Try and get sponsorship or gifts-in-kind to cover as much of what you need as possible – from the venue to the catering to the ticket printing.

▼ *Volunteer input.* Events are labour-intensive and are an ideal opportunity to draw on the enthusiasm of volunteers. Ideally, each should be assigned a specific role, but a plethora of hands on the day can seal over many a crack in the event planning.

▼ *Advance sales.* Tickets for any event should be sold as far as possible in advance, rather than on the door. Apart from easing administration at the event itself, advance sales will tell you how successful the event will be. If not enough tickets are sold, you can arrange more publicity, cut costs and scale down the event, or cancel it (as the event date approaches, these options narrow quickly).

▼ *Insurance.* It is possible to insure against most contingencies, including cancellation. A list of specialist firms offering event insurance is contained in *Corporate Events Services*, which is published annually by Showcase Publications (see appendix C). The guide also lists professional event organisers and suppliers of everything from grandstands to dry ice, pavilions to pyrotechnics.

Much of the real benefit from organising events often comes not from the main attraction but from associated trading and fundraising. You can often get better profit margins on the sale of programmes, food and drink, etc. than on the event tickets themselves (if you intend to sell alcohol contact the local magistrates court about obtaining a licence or occasional permission). Take the opportunity to run a stall selling campaign materials and ensure that structured fundraising and member-gathering activities are built into the event.

Professional fundraisers

There are a growing number of consultants specialising in fundraising, most of whom originally cut their teeth in one of the big fundraising charities. Most charge on an hourly or daily rate (generally from £150 to £600 a day), after an initial free consultation. The Institute of Charity Fundraising Managers (see appendix B) holds a list of accredited members who offer consultancy services.

Fundraising consultants are often hired to run or advise on big capital appeals. Their fee structure makes them very expensive to retain over long periods of time so if you have indefinite fundraising needs it is probably more cost-effective to employ someone to raise money as a member of staff, even if that involves an element of training in post. For pressure groups, check that any consultant hired has experience in raising money for similar kinds of organisation.

The hire of fundraising consultants is regulated under the Charities Act 1992 and the Charitable Institutions (Fundraising) Regulations 1994. As with the provisions on public collections, this does not just apply to charities, but to any 'charitable institution', defined as an institution established 'for charitable, benevolent or philanthropic purposes'. (It would probably be wise to construe this as including any non-profit campaigning group.) The provisions require a written agreement in specified form between the institution and any 'professional fundraiser', defined as 'any person who carries on a fundraising business, or ... who for reward solicits money or other property for the benefit of a charitable institution' (the institution's own staff and volunteers are excluded). In addition, professional fundraisers have to come clean with the public about which institution(s) are to benefit, in which proportions, and how they themselves are remunerated. The Act also places similar requirements on 'commercial participators', or those who encourage the purchase of goods or services on the grounds that some of the proceeds will go to a charitable institution. Professional fundraisers and commercial participators should be aware of the specified form of agreement required, as without it their clients would be able to refuse to pay them.

Wealthy individuals

Some people are wealthy enough to be worth targeting individually. These will mostly be successful businesspeople or those that have inherited wealth, although some entertainers can also get pretty rich.

There are a growing number of sources of information on rich people. *The Millionaire Givers*, a book published by the Directory of Social Change in 1994 but now out of print, gives details on the charitable giving of over 270 of Britain's wealthiest individuals and families. The *Sunday Times* publishes a list of Britain's richest people every Spring and *Forbes* magazine in the US publishes regular information on the rich. Look for any evidence of interest in your cause, or related ones. It is worth cross-referencing these entries with *Who's Who* and *Who's Who in the City*, as well as keeping an eye on the business pages in the newspapers. Check your management committee, patrons and prominent supporters to see if any of them have contacts among the moneyed.

It is next to useless to send written appeals to such people. They need to be approached in person, preferably by someone they know well. If you can't come up with any direct contacts, consider an approach via one of their other charitable, political or business interests. The exception to this is those that give regularly to non-profit groups through the mechanism of a charitable trust or through their companies (see below) – here a written approach may bring some response. Timing is very important: news coverage or other media interest can leave people predisposed to help out. News despatches from the Bosnian conflict prompted US financier George Soros to write out a cheque for $50 million to various UK and international aid agencies.

There is an informal association of rich people who support progressive causes, called the Network for Social Change, which has been meeting since the mid-eighties. A list of members is unfortunately not available. More on this under 'Non-charitable trusts' below.

Approaching wealthy individuals for support is something of a long shot, but some pressure groups have received a large part of their income from just one individual. Property developer Godfrey Bradman supported a number of campaigning groups for many years, including Friends of the Earth and CLEAR, the Campaign for Lead-Free Air.

Charitable trusts and foundations

Grant-making trusts or foundations are independent bodies that give financial support to non-profit organisations. They are often referred to somewhat loosely as 'trusts', but they are in fact only a particular type of trust (as defined in chapter 1). Their money generally comes from the investment income on an endowment (e.g. Leverhulme Trust, Nuffield Foundation, Gatsby Charitable Foundation), from public appeals (e.g. Comic Relief, BBC Children in Need), or from covenanted gifts from a regular donor.

It is important that any projects you approach a foundation to support come within the foundation's own objects and priorities. There are thousands of foundations in the UK and although many of them give to a wide range of causes, many others will only make grants in specific fields (e.g. third world development or medical research) and have fairly exacting criteria.

However, there is a widespread misconception that foundations generally cannot give money to pressure groups or campaigning organisations. In actual fact, most foundations are charities and as such are constrained to making grants for *charitable purposes*, but not necessarily just to *charities*. What follows from this is that a foundation can usually make a grant to anyone, even a pressure group, so long as the money is actually spent for a purpose which is charitable by law (and which falls within the foundation's own objects).

A very small number of foundations are not charities and can therefore also give for non-charitable purposes. These are considered in a separate section below. Conversely, some foundations are only empowered to give to registered charities. This would indeed seem to

---

Sources of information on grant-making trusts and foundations

Directory of Grant Making Trusts

Published biennially by the Charities Aid Foundation (2000 price for three volumes: £89.95). Includes a register of 3,500 trusts, including hundreds of newly registered trusts. Also available on CD-ROM. Available from the Directory of Social Change (DSC – see appendix B for address).

A Guide to the Major Trusts

Published biennially by the Directory of Social Change in three volumes (2000 price: £19.95 each for volumes 1 and 2, £17.95 for volume 3). Covers in more detail the top 300 trusts (Vol. 1), the next 700 (Vol. 2), more UK-wide trusts as well as major trusts giving in Northern Ireland, Scotland and Wales (Vol. 3). Also available on CD-ROM. Available from DSC.

Trust Monitor

The thrice-yearly journal on foundations, it covers news on what they are doing, changes in policy, and details of new trusts that are set up, as well as general analysis and debate (2000 subscription price £30 a year). Available from DSC.

Charity Commission

Charitable trusts are required by law to file their accounts with the Charity Commission, where they are available for public reference. The Commission has offices in London, Liverpool and Taunton (see appendix B for addresses). The telephone line for general enquiries is 0870 333 0123. The central register of charities is now maintained on a database; this is partly accessible from the Commission's website at *www.charity-commission.gov.uk*

Checklist: fundraising from foundations

1. If you are not a charity, identify those projects or parts of your work that are charitable.

2. Find the foundations whose policy covers this work (there may not be very many).

3. Match carefully your projects and specific project costs with the requirements of individual foundations.

4. Check that the foundations you have identified are not limited to supporting registered charities. If they are, find a charity in your local area or field of work that would be willing to accept the grant on your behalf.

5. If possible, sound out a potential application with the administrator.

6. Write a concise letter of application, giving information on your organisation, the project that requires funding and how much you need. Attach a breakdown of project costs and a copy of your most recent accounts.

7. Point out that the work for which you are applying for funding is charitable.

8. If you receive a grant from a foundation, acknowledge it, send reports, and generally keep in touch – you may be able to turn it into a regular supporter.

debar grants to pressure groups altogether, unless the grant could be paid through an intermediary organisation that was a registered charity. 'Laundering' money in this way is quite common (and perfectly legal) in the case of donations to small community groups, arts groups, etc., where the charitable purpose is obvious and where the money can be paid through a local Council for Voluntary Service or arts association. It is rarer in the case of pressure groups, if only because charitable purpose is less clear, but some trusts do use the mechanism effectively. A grant could be paid via a large charity that was sympathetic to your aims or even a college or university department.

Most foundations, however, would be able directly to support charitable work undertaken by a campaigning organisation, such as educational or service-providing activities, provided that it came within their field of operation. See chapter 2 for more information on which sorts of activities are charitable. It is worth pointing out that foundations themselves are not always aware of where the boundaries lie.

The trick is to identify as much of your work as possible which will fall under the charitable net. A number of campaigns have done this and received a substantial part of their funds from foundations. An example is the Healthcare Foundation's support of Parents Against Tobacco, a group prominent in lobbying for a very successful private member's bill a few years ago.

As you can only approach a foundation to fund your project if it comes within the foundation's own objects and priorities, basic research is essential. This might involve using reference books on foundations (see box), speaking to other organisations working in your field, getting annual reports and funding criteria from the foundations themselves, or even looking up foundation files at the Charity Commission. The single most common error made by people starting to fundraise from foundations is to send out a large number of application letters fairly indiscriminately. If appropriate foundations are researched thoroughly first, the chances of success will improve considerably.

It is difficult to generalise about such a large and diverse group of organisations, but foundations are often more willing to fund project-specific costs, preferably one-off, rather than supporting general running costs. Potential applications should be matched as closely as possible with an appropriate foundation, regarding:

▼ the foundation's policy and field of operation;

▼ its beneficial (geographical) area;

▼ the type of costs supported;

▼ the amount required.

The initial skill in foundation fundraising consists of targeting appropriate foundations and pitching the application at the right level. Many have a preferred method of support – making grants for capital, for example – and even an habitual level of grant. If you are a local organisation, try local foundations first.

Few foundations have forms to fill in and most will just require a letter of application. These should always be personalised and should include budget details. Make it clear why you are applying to that particular foundation. Wherever possible, sound out a potential application on the telephone with the foundation administrator first – this saves a lot of wasted applications and you can pick up some useful guidance. Foundations can take some time to come to a decision, often a few months.

Apply to foundations to fund your charitable activities and use other sources of income to finance your political work. This is in fact only a particular application of the more general rule that you should always try and raise money for those things for which it is easiest to raise money. If you are lucky enough to be on the receiving end of a core grant, substantial membership income, or other funds that are not earmarked for a specific purpose, that leaves you at liberty to choose from among your budgeted activities those most attractive for fundraising purposes and then apply for a grant for them. A foundation grant, received for – and spent on – charitable work, can effectively enable an organisation to undertake political activities that it would not have been able to otherwise, simply by freeing other funds for this purpose.

Non-charitable foundations

A handful of foundations have forgone charitable status – and its considerable financial advantages – in order to remain free to fund political or campaigning activity. Most of their support goes to pressure groups.

The Joseph Rowntree Reform Trust

The Joseph Rowntree Reform Trust spends about £750,000 a year on either specific project funding or kick-start grants to enable campaigns to get off the ground. It is not to be confused with two other foundations set up by Joseph Rowntree, both of which are charities.

Many leading campaigns and public interest groups received start-up grants from the Trust, including Amnesty International, the Child Poverty Action Group and Friends of the Earth. The Trust's remit is very general, but most of its grants focus on social justice or on reform of the political system. The latter aim is pursued partly through grants to political groups such as the Association of Liberal Democrat Councillors, the Electoral Reform Society, the Tory Reform Group and the Labour Coordinating Committee.

The Trust explains that its principal concern is 'the continuity of reform within the democratic system ... the trust looks for ideas whose time has come, or is about to come ... the trust aims to correct imbalances of power; strengthening the hand of individuals, groups and organisations who are striving for reform'. Recipients of grants include Charter 88, the Plain English Campaign, the Campaign for Press and Broadcasting Freedom, WaterWatch, the Genetics Forum and Inquest.

The Trust will not fund research or any other charitable activity, reserving its support for projects which are ineligible for charitable funding. It rarely funds projects outside the UK.

Applications outlining the nature of the project and what it hopes to achieve, with a budget and supporting documentation, should be sent to the trust secretary (see appendix B).

The Barrow Cadbury Fund Ltd

There are a large number of different foundations set up by members of the Cadbury families. The Barrow Cadbury Fund is the non-charitable arm of the Barrow Cadbury Trust. The two organisations share the same board and secretariat, and the same interests, with the Barrow Cadbury Fund going where the Trust (because of its charitable status) cannot tread. The Fund now distributes about £250,000 a year, and its big sister some ten times as much.

The Fund seeks to support 'projects of an innovatory nature and national significance which aim to realise a more just and democratic society'. The main areas of interest are:

▼ community democracy, and justice and peace: education and training programmes in community organising; and the promotion of a just and peaceful civil society, particularly in Northern Ireland;

▼ gender: women-led initiatives enabling women to take a full part in creating a just, equal and democratic society, including support for projects local to the West Midlands or to Northern Ireland;

▼ racial justice: support for black and multi-racial projects fostering self advocacy and inter-ethnic and religious understanding;

▼ disability: national projects promoting inclusive education and an inclusive society for those with learning difficulties;

▼ civil rights: support for the settlement needs of refugees and the rights of asylum seekers and immigrants;

▼ penal affairs: promotion of a humane and just prison and remand service and an equitable system of justice.

Further information from the Director or Deputy Director (see appendix B for address).

The Network for Social Change

The Network for Social Change, mentioned under 'Wealthy individuals' above, channels some of its support through a charitable body, the Network Foundation, as well as through a non-charitable arm, the Network for Social Change Ltd. A list of the members of the network is not available, although the trustees of the foundation (whose grant expenditure in 1996 exceeded £500,000) were listed as Patrick Boase, John and Ingrid Broad, Samuel Clark, Oliver Gillie, Hugh MacPherson, Sara Robin, Fred Mulder, P Hadwick and C Carolan.

The Network has been described as 'a community of wealthy individuals seeking to realise their visions in ways that enable others'. As recently as 1996, applications were assessed under four headings: Human Rights and Solidarity; Health and Wholeness; Peace and Preservation of the Earth; and Arts and Media. The majority of grants made appear to be in the range £5,000 to £15,000.

The Network does not consider unsolicited applications, only those which are 'sponsored' by a member of the Network – you'll have to find and try to interest the individuals concerned. (See appendix B for address.)

The National Lottery Charities Board

The National Lottery Charities Board is the single largest new source of funding for charities and public interest groups in the UK, distributing some £250 million every year. Although it is in fact a public authority, established by statute, the Board operates in many ways like an independent foundation and has maintained a healthy distance from government. It is only one of a number of organisations distributing money from the National Lottery: others distribute money specifically for sports, arts and heritage schemes.

Despite its name, the Board makes grants not just to charities but also to community groups or campaign groups, so long as they are 'philanthropic or benevolent', This means that they must be humanitarian or altruistic, strictly non-profit, and not dominated by purposes which are political or doctrinaire.

The Board makes grants under a series of programmes. The relevant ones are briefly described below.

▼ *Poverty and disadvantage*. With the broad aim of improving the quality of life of people and communities who are disadvantaged by poverty or who are at risk of poverty, this programme focuses on people on low incomes; people living in deprived areas; and preventing or minimising future poverty. Groups targeted include older people, minority ethnic groups, women and children (especially lone parents) and disabled people.

▼ *Community involvement*. This programme supports projects which enable people to become involved in activities which improve the quality of life for the whole community, with a particular focus on those who are excluded from the community. This includes community buildings and activities, volunteering and community action, and development and support services for community groups.

▼ *International grants*. The Board supports UK-based agencies working abroad on development projects which make a significant impact addressing the causes of poverty and inequality. A wide range of projects are supported, covering sustainable livelihoods, environmental management, access to basic services, advocacy promotion, protection of human rights, development education, and the development of non-governmental organisations in Eastern and Central Europe.

▼ *Small grants*. Under the 'Awards for All' scheme run in conjunction with the other National Lottery distributing bodies, small grants of between £500 and £5,000 are made to any kind of charitable or community group through a simplified application procedure. Local groups with an income of less than £15,000 a year get priority.

The National Lottery Charities Board has made many thousands of grants since it was first established in 1994, but examples of larger recent grants include: £1 million to Oxfam's UK poverty programme, including work on gender bias, user-led research and lobbying; £590,000 for the Groundswell network of groups of homeless or ex-homeless people coordinated by the National Homeless Alliance;

£200,000 for the London Lesbian and Gay Switchboard; £140,000 for the Environmental Law Foundation for their advice service covering environmental rights; and £890,000 to Going For Green for a sustainable communities project aimed at involving people in community-based environmental action. International grants have included those to War on Want, the Westminster Foundation for Democracy, Interights, Amnesty International and the Minority Rights Group.

One particular achievement of the Board has been its sustained support for black and minority ethnic groups, including those working with refugees and asylum seekers; for example, the Tamil Refugee Centre, the Greater Manchester Immigration Aid Unit, the Migrant and Refugee Communities Forum, the Electronic Immigration Network, London Black Women's Health Action Project and the Sudanese Coptic Association all received grants ranging from £30,000 to £180,000.

To apply for a grant you need to fill out one of the Board's detailed application forms. Further information from the address in appendix B.

Companies

Non-profit groups can also get support from commerce and industry, although, as a general rule, less money is available than from foundations, and more of it goes to the well-established charities. Companies, naturally, have a history of supporting institutes and cause groups which further their own interests, from the Industry and Parliament Trust to Aims of Industry. The Adam Smith Institute, for example, has received about half its income from companies since the early eighties. There are no hard and fast rules, however: Demos, the non-aligned think-tank set up by a former editor of *Marxism Today*, has been surprisingly successful in pulling in corporate donations.

Companies can offer support in a variety of ways, of which donations and sponsorship are the most important:

▼ Donations are generally handled by the community affairs department, donations committee or simply the company chairperson's office. They are paid out of a company's after-tax profits and, if made for a charitable purpose, are eligible for charitable tax reliefs. The company does not receive any appreciable benefit in return for the donation.

▼ Sponsorship is a term often used to cover any type of company support but, strictly understood, it refers to a business arrangement in which the non-profit group is typically paid a fee and the company gets a ringing endorsement, use of a logo, or other elements of a PR package. The fee will be paid out of the company's marketing budget and is treated for tax purposes as a normal business expense.

Information on companies that have a history of making donations is available in a big book called *The Guide to UK Company Giving*, published by the Directory of Social Change. It profiles over 500 top companies with details of their donations and community support, contact addresses and advice for applicants. The information is also available on CD-ROM (see appendix C).

The big sums in company support tend to come through sponsorship deals, but these are unlikely to be forthcoming unless you already have an established image that could appeal to the corporate marketing imagination. In a publicity leaflet aimed at corporate sponsors, Amnesty International invited companies to 'raise their profile *and* raise awareness', and explained: 'Those who have associated themselves with us already are companies making a difference in their own right: The Body Shop, Virgin, The Independent, The Guardian, Time Out, Waterstones, HMV. Others such as Reebok, Red Stripe Lager, Becks Beer, and Our Price want to project a young, active image, consistent with Amnesty's profile.'

As with any business transaction, each side of the bargain should be carefully controlled. Save the Sealife Campaign may walk away from its new sponsorship deal thinking it has got money for nothing, but unless it has taken care it might find itself associated with Viscous Oil plc for the rest of its (short) life.

Finally, it is possible to get help from companies in the form of gifts-in-kind: spare office or warehouse space, the loan of equipment, outmoded or end-of-line products, etc. This is a relatively cheap way for a company to offer support: even if it involves new products, the cost to the company itself will only be a fraction of the retail price.

Unions and professional associations

The trades unions have been a traditional source of support for many pressure groups, although this has usually taken the form of small solidarity donations or a modest annual 'affiliation' fee. Figures for donations made centrally by some of the largest unions are given below. These figures do not reflect support from local branches or chapters, which added together probably amounts to as much or more than is available from the head offices.

In addition to supporting outside organisations from its general fund, a union is able to spend money on 'political' objects, generally the support of political parties and associated groups, as regulated by Chapter VI of the Trade Unions and Labour Relations (Consolidation) Act 1992. With most unions, the largest beneficiary of such expenditure is the Labour Party. Similarly, the bulk of donations and affiliation payments made by unions from general funds go to non-political organisations within the labour movement.

However, small grants are often made to other non-profit groups out of general funds and occasionally out of political funds. One year USDAW, for example, supported the Low Pay Unit (£900), One World (£250), the Low Pay Forum (£3,000), Liberty (£110), the Campaign for Press and Broadcasting Freedom (£375) and Anti-Slavery International (£250), among others. Grants were made out of political funds to the United Nations Association (£100), the Fabian Society (£330) and Maternity Alliance (£120).

There is no standard procedure for applying to unions for support and, generally, no application forms. Decisions on grants are often left to the finance committee.

Annual accounts for trades unions, which give some information on the value of past donations, can be inspected at the Certification Office for Trades Unions and Employers Associations (see appendix B). The office can also send out photocopies, for a fee.

Government

Government is the single most frequent target of pressure groups and campaigns. This might make it seem an unlikely source of finance. Some campaigning organisations, for example Amnesty International, go as far as to refuse to accept government money on principle.

Some government bodies have supported campaigns, however. This is probably more common at either local level or international level than it is with national government, which presumably feels that financing campaigns is a bit like sharpening the stick with which it is going to be beaten. The government does of course core fund a number of charities, even some that function largely as interest groups, like the National Council for Voluntary Organisations. Money can also be got from government departments if campaigns aimed at the general public reflect current government policy. For example, ASH (Action on Smoking and Health) and Action for Victims of Medical Accidents receive support from the Department of Health, and Peace through NATO, the non-charitable arm of the British Atlantic Committee, has received support from the Foreign and Commonwealth Office. Quangos may also, on occasion, back campaigns: the National Childcare Campaign and other groups have been supported by the Equal Opportunities Commission, for example.

Detailed information on finance available from government departments is given in the *Guide to Funding from Government Departments and Agencies,* published by the Directory of Social Change (see appendix C). Applications are generally made under a specific programme or budget head and can take a long time.

Local government

Local government is the single largest funder of non-profit groups working at the local level. However, local authority support for local campaigning organisations frequently depends on the political composition of the council. Labour councils have traditionally been freer in spending money on campaigns although not necessarily on non-profit groups generally. When Ken Livingstone was leader of the Greater London Council he noted that there was a tide of opinion in the Labour Party which felt that it was much easier to achieve a political aim by finding a local group which sought to provide a service or draw attention to a need than to do it through the council bureaucracy.

Times change. The Local Government Act 1986 brought in some restrictions on what local authorities were able to fund, partly intended to halt just the sort of activity that Ken Livingstone was talking about. In addition, the capping of locally-raised taxes, adverse publicity and a general turn in the political climate all dented the willingness, or the ability, of councils to support campaigning groups. Politically-aligned or politically-identified groups have always suffered when control of a council changed hands, but now such groups generally are getting a tougher ride.

Local authorities can only spend money or provide financial support if they are legally empowered to do so. Their powers to support specific activities are given in a number of different pieces of legislation; e.g. under Section 73 of the Housing Act 1985 district councils and London boroughs can support organisations working on homelessness; under Section 65 of the Health Services and Public Health Act 1968 authorities can support groups to provide or promote a range of welfare and care services.

More generally, local authorities have very wide powers under the Local Government Act 1972 to support unspecified activities which will help them to discharge their functions or which will be of benefit to their area and its inhabitants. However, the Local Government Act 1986 constrained these powers particularly with regard to publicity campaigns.

It is not strictly necessary to know the legal position when applying to a local authority for a grant – the authority should be aware of the powers under which it can fund your work – but it can help, particularly in the case of campaigning groups where some authorities will be unsure. Being able to suggest a relevant power might alert them to an opportunity they were unaware of or at least swiftly rebut a claim that they have not got the power to fund you.

The first thing to note is that if your organisation is also involved in providing services locally, you probably stand more chance of winning a local authority grant for such work than for campaigning activities. Unless the council has a central grants committee, you will need to contact the relevant council department for advice on how to apply, forms, closing dates, etc. (If you do not know which department to approach the Chief Executive's department will advise.)

If you *are* applying for funding for a publicity campaign, there may be a specific power which covers your field of work: a well-known example is Section 65 of the Health Services and Public Health Act 1969, mentioned above. If there is no such specific power, you may have to fall back on one of the more general powers contained in the Local Government Act 1972 or elsewhere. A summary of the main ones, as amended by the recent legislation, is given below.

General local authority powers to fund publicity and campaigns

Local Government Act 1972

Section 111: enables local authorities to do anything which is intended to facilitate the discharge of any of their functions or is conducive or incidental to this. This can only be used in conjunction with other powers but can be very useful in widening existing powers to include the support of outside organisations.

Section 137: enables local authorities to spend money on anything which is in the interests of the area or a part of it or of its inhabitants. *Can only be used within a strict financial limit and when no other power is available.* Under sub-section (2C) such spending can only be to assist non-profit bodies on publicity where the publicity is incidental to the main purpose for which the assistance is given. Under sub-section (3) contributions can be made to any charitable body or to any body which provides a public service other than for gain (probably not limited by the condition in (2C)).

Section 142: enables local authorities to support the provision of information about available services provided by public or non-profit bodies or about individuals' rights or obligations. If the information does not relate to the functions of the authority, then it can only be supported if it is to be made available on request rather than distributed unsolicited. Case law has established that publicity material funded under Section 142 must be informative rather than 'persuasive'. This section also enables local authorities to support representation or communications made on behalf of individuals in asserting their rights.

Local Government Act 1985

Section 88: enables metropolitan district councils and London boroughs to support research and the collection of information relating to or concerning part or all of their metropolitan area and its dissemination to the public or to government. A similar power is available to county councils under Section 141 of the Local Government Act 1972. Material must be informative rather than persuasive.

Incorporates amendments contained in the Local Government Act 1986 and the Local Government and Housing Act 1989.

This list is not exhaustive.

The Local Government Acts of 1986 and 1988 also introduced a blanket ban on the support of anything which could be construed as party political. The exact restrictions are given below. When the bills were debated in the Houses of Parliament, the government did emphasise that in introducing these measures it was not their intention to place new restrictions on non-profit groups and their campaigning. As the ban centres on influencing support for political parties, most campaigning groups should indeed remain unaffected. However, many anti-racist groups are undoubtedly affected, in that some of the far-right groups they seek to discredit are in fact political parties (e.g. the National Front). The 1988 Act also included the notorious Section 28, prohibiting local authorities from intentionally promoting homosexuality (which includes supporting other organisations that do so), although the present government has said it will repeal this provision.

If you manage to get a local authority interested in your work and it is keen to support you then it will usually find an appropriate power to enable it to do so (unless the activity comes within one of the blanket bans noted above). Conversely, authorities which, for one reason or another, don't appreciate your efforts, may cite legal or financial reasons for refusing a grant. Some tactful lobbying could help your chances considerably: testing out the waters in advance, getting some advice from a friendly officer, ensuring that an application is favourably worded, clarifying the power(s) under which it could be funded and enlisting the support of some of the councillors (and preferably the chair) of the relevant committee. Influence map 4 (chapter 12) outlines the main steps in lobbying for a local authority grant.

If you have no luck with one branch of local government you may be able to try another. In the shires many functions or areas of responsibility are shared by district and county councils, so there is often scope to try the county council if you have had no luck at district level (and *vice versa*) particularly if they are under different political control. In London and the metropolitan

---

Restrictions on local authority support of political publicity

(1) A local authority shall not publish any material which, in whole or in part, appears to be designed to affect public support for a political party.

(2) In determining whether material falls within the prohibition regard shall be had to the content and style of the material, the time and other circumstances of publication and the likely effect on those to whom it is directed and, in particular, to the following matters –

(a) whether the material refers to a political party or to persons identified with a political party or promotes or opposes a point of view on a question of political controversy which is identifiable as the view of one political party and not of another;

(b) where the material is part of a campaign, the effect which the campaign appears to be designed to achieve.

(3) A local authority shall not give financial or other assistance to a person for the publication of material which the authority are prohibited by this section from publishing themselves.

Section 2 of the Local Government Act 1986 as amended by section 27 of the Local Government Act 1988

districts there are also schemes for funding non-profit groups operating in more than one district or London borough, e.g. the London Boroughs Grants Scheme.

One other valuable form of support available from local authorities is rate relief on offices and other non-residential premises.

Finally, some health authorities are using non-profits increasingly to help accomplish their aims, and are a natural source of finance for public health campaigns.

European and International sources

Other countries in Europe do not have the same concept of charitable status as the UK and the paranoia regarding political activity that goes with it. On the other hand, the non-profit sector is considerably less developed in some parts of Europe. Many countries in the European Union grant tax reliefs on donations to pressure groups unless they are engaged in party political activities, and some countries even then. The Netherlands, for example, extends tax reliefs to political parties provided they do not advocate violence.

Although grants from the European Commission are consequently not limited to charities, much EU money for UK non-profit bodies is for vocational training initiatives, most of it from the European Social Fund, which depends on securing matching grants from public bodies in the UK. However, there are numerous other EU budget lines of potential interest to a campaign, particularly if it has a Europe-wide remit or is active in a field covered by EU policy. There are, for example, a number of different appropriations or budget lines for supporting public information campaigns in the health and environmental fields. These are all listed in the EU's voluminous annual budget, but it is worth noting that although many budget lines might be open to voluntary groups, hardly any are designated specially for them. In addition, smaller pots of money exist in some Commission departments or Directorates-General (DGs): once you have identified the relevant DG (see chapter 15) it may be possible to get an occasional grant for an event like a conference or even for a trip to Brussels to talk to Commission officials.

The EU budget is generally agreed each December for the following calendar year. January and February are supposed to be peak spending time at the Commission. However, many funding programmes operate over a number of years and the money can be allocated early in the cycle.

Grants from foundations or independent institutes in Europe are very thin on the ground, but it may be possible to get some funding for international relations or human rights work. See the box on page 64 for listings of potential funding sources.

Casting the net wider still, another long-shot for finance could be the United States. A number of US foundations have supported campaigning groups based in the UK, once again particularly those active in the fields of peace, international relations or human rights. Support seems to be divided fairly evenly between liberal and right-leaning groups. On the progressive side, the MacArthur Foundation has funded peace research at British universities and supported GreenNet; and the Ford Foundation has supported the publication of Index on Censorship and the International Centre for the Legal Protection of Human Rights (INTERIGHTS) in London. The W Alton Jones Foundation has supported environmental protection and world security, with the latter ranging from arms control initiatives to the development of grassroots citizen action.

Sources of information on international grants

A Guide to European Union Funding

Details of over 150 programmes relevant to non-profit groups, including examples of work that has been supported and practical tips on making an approach. Published in 1999 at £18.95. Available from DSC (see appendix B for address).

Grants from Europe

Published periodically by NCVO Publications. Covers the main sources of EU grants for non-profits by subject area. 1997 edition – £12.50. Available from Hamilton House Mailings Ltd (see appendix B for address).

The Foundation Directory

Published by the Foundation Center, New York. Contains details on over 6,000 US Foundations. 1999 edition - $185. Available from the Foundation Center (see appendix B for address).

Fundraising from America – The complete guide for charitable organisations outside the USA

Published by Chapel & York. Practical advice on getting money from US donors, companies and foundations. Available at £36.50 from DSC.

Directory of American Grantmakers

Published by Chapel & York. Profiles 300 American foundations that fund charitable organisations and individuals outside the USA Available at £45.00 from DSC.

International Foundation Directory

1998 edition – £105. Details on over 1,200 foundations in more than 70 countries. Will always be a long shot. Available from Europa Publications (see appendix B for address).

Part 2
Techniques

4 Action research and publications

Comment is free, but facts are sacred – C P Scott

The opinion of the ordinary citizen doesn't count for much. The opinions expressed by pressure groups gain credibility in two major ways: firstly, through the number of supporters they can claim, and secondly, through the hard facts they can deploy to back up their cause. The publication of research generates far more stories in the press for pressure groups than any other activity; indeed, probably more than all their other activities put together.

Primarily, research is needed to bring to the attention of policy-makers or the public the problem which a campaign was set up to address. Research supplies factual weight to arguments; it enables a campaign to monitor what is going on and provides intelligence on the opposition; and it builds confidence: establishing not just *whether* the campaign is right, but *why* it is right. Research is a campaign's ticket to the middle ground; with it, it can speak with the voice of reason. Without it, a campaign can always be marginalised. Good research enables campaigners to acquire the status of expert, to whom the media naturally turn for comment; it transforms them from people with a chip on their shoulder to people in the know.

In an open society, the power of information can hardly be over-estimated. Many famous campaigns were launched on the back of a piece of research; few do without the handful of punchy statistics that are used to shock a complacent audience into recognising that a problem exists. The publication of Ralph Nader's *Unsafe at any Speed*, an indictment of General Motors, launched not only a major campaign but a whole new culture of citizen action in the US. In 1963 the Spies for Peace demonstrated that the release of information can itself be a subversive act, when they published details of the emergency state that was planned to take over in the event of nuclear catastrophe.

Action research is distinguished from the great mass of information and research that clutters everyday life by two overriding properties: it must be current, and it must have a clear objective. It is not published just to increase the general level of understanding on a subject; it is there to back new legislation, expose a scandal, win a grant, shut down a factory (or keep it open), or force a change in policy.

Using existing research

There are essentially two kinds of research: your own, and other people's. The latter has three distinct advantages:

▼ it is generally cheaper and quicker to obtain and use;

▼ because you are dealing with the finished product, rather than just a research brief or plan, it is much easier to decide whether it will provide you with the results you want;

▼ it is backed by the authority of the researcher(s) and/or publisher. This means that existing research comes with a credibility rating attached, dependent on who produced it. Being able to quote independent, authoritative research is particularly important if your own group is seen to be an interested party.

Existing research does have the disadvantage that it will often have already been published, which will limit its news appeal. However, there is much research produced by government or by academics which has never been exploited. National campaigns spend a lot of time extracting figures or documents from government and then publishing them or leaking them to the press.

The vast bulk of published information is in fact the work of many parties and most existing research that is potentially of use to you will need adapting, expanding or reworking. If you are in the rare position that you just wish to reproduce something, you will have to consider copyright restrictions (see chapter 5).

A trawl through existing publications, information, press cuttings and other research is a prerequisite for any new campaign. If you are hoping to go on and do your own original research, a literature survey will prevent duplication, develop expertise and help immeasurably in designing the research.

Research credibility

All facts are true, but some are more true than others. Both policy-makers and the press, who spend a lot of time generating facts themselves, appreciate this, and before deciding whether to use your research they will make an assessment of its credibility. As they may not be well versed in the subject matter, they tend to rely on a number of more general factors:

▼ *The producer organisation.* 'Who says?' is the first question prompted by any new statement of fact. The first guarantee of credible research is the credibility of the organisation that produced it: its size, reputation, independence, government links, research history, etc.

▼ *Presentation and tone.* The media, in particular, are influenced by the way in which research is presented and published. This is not so much a question of using glossy paper (although professionalism in print design and production certainly helps) as ensuring that the format and tone is appropriate to a piece of thorough and impartial research. Any figures quoted should be accompanied by their source or method of calculation, the methods employed in carrying out any original research should be explained and justified, and conclusions and argument must appear to stem directly from the research findings.

▼ *Quality of research as regards design and implementation.* The actual quality of the research itself will depend on many factors. If it draws on existing work, is it comprehensive or has something important been omitted? If original research, does the sample accurately reflect the population? Are the survey methods impartial, or do they introduce a weighting or bias into the results? (See 'The rules of the game' below.)

More store is often set on where research comes from and its presentation than on its actual quality. If you don't have an established reputation on which to build, you will have to concentrate on ensuring that any work you produce is of high quality and professionally presented.

Government research has the highest credibility rating of all, despite the continual scandals over the massaging of statistics in areas such as unemployment and the NHS. For one thing, government puts enormous resources into undertaking or commissioning research into just about every field of activity; for another, it has unique powers to access information. Most importantly, perhaps, government will never question its own figures, while treating everyone else's with a powerful scepticism. Always try and get official figures to support your own, particularly if government is one of the targets of your campaign.

New information does not appear in a void but on a stage on which the positioning of interest groups is already in play; and any pronouncement will be judged according to which of the actors it comes from. This makes it doubly important that your own research should project a voice of impartiality. It also means that if you can get hold of research produced by the target of your campaign and use it against them, that will be more effective than anything you produce yourself.

Sources of information

The main sources of written information are described below. The internet is covered in chapter 6. More detail on the major institutions in our society, such as corporations, local authorities or central government, and how to find out about them, is given in part 3 of this book on targets.

Few campaigns, however, could operate effectively without in addition developing personal contacts and becoming part of the formal or informal networks in their chosen field. Ring round, find out what people know, get your name on press lists or mailing lists and build your own network of contacts who can feed you information and alert you early to new developments.

The press

The press is both a good source of current information and a ready index of the level of interest in an issue. Most newspapers' websites enable access to archive material and many good libraries keep recent back issues of the major newspapers. The *Times, Financial Times, Guardian* and *Independent* are also available on microfilm, enabling libraries to store many years' worth.

Tracing press articles or recent coverage on a given subject is quite straightforward, thanks to a number of cuttings indices and online information systems that have been developed.

▼ Most of the broadsheet or quality newspapers now publish a regular index of their content, but how far back in time they stretch varies. The oldest is the *Times* index which has monthly updates. The *Clover Newspaper Index* is particularly useful because it covers all the national broadsheet papers, including the Sundays, plus one or two of the more important weeklies, and is published every week. You can search by name, or by subject. All good reference libraries should have copies.

▼ There are also computer databases of press content which are considerably more sophisticated, but expensive to access. They include databases produced by Reuters, the Dialog Corporation and the *Financial Times* (but covering all the main papers). These have the advantage of being able to search on any word, including, for example, the name of the journalist, and make life a lot easier if you are looking for a particular article but have little idea when it appeared.

▼ Short of subscribing to a database yourself, there are a number of commercial research services which will get you access to the information. As cheap as any is the British Library's charged research service, on 020 7412 7457, which has both Reuters and the *Financial Times* databases, as well as many specialist databases. If you are just starting up a campaign or moving into a new field, it may be worth investing the £50–£100 to get them to do a search through the press for the last six months or so. Alternatively, the newspaper library at Colindale (see below) has a rather more basic press cuttings index on CD–ROM, starting from 1991.

▼ The national newspapers themselves have cuttings libraries which use computerised databases. Although these are generally not accessible to the public, some provide a reader's service at little or no cost which will help with simple queries about articles that have appeared in the paper.

▼ For back issues of local newspapers you will have to rely on local libraries or on the office of the newspaper itself. Some libraries will keep press cuttings files on subjects of municipal interest.

Details on the local and specialist press are contained in *Willing's Press Guide* and *Benn's Media* , both of which list thousands of newspapers and periodicals with contact and publication details.

Difficulty in finding back issues of any newspaper or periodical can nearly always be resolved by contacting the British Library's newspaper library at Colindale in London, which holds by far the best collection in the country. You can order photocopies of particular articles by post or through a local library service, as well as visiting in person. The address is in appendix B.

For keeping a watching brief on news and articles as they appear, there are a number of press cuttings agencies which monitor the national press. They operate by company name or key-word searches, and forward photocopies of any articles that appear containing the required words. Most charge a subscription plus a per cutting fee; expect to pay £300 a year upwards. Regional agencies should be cheaper. Details in the Yellow Pages.

Libraries and registers

Public libraries vary considerably in quality, but few places in the UK are very far from a good reference library. Many will answer queries on the telephone.

Reference libraries may hold invaluable local information like the minutes of council meetings, council consultation papers and other documents, copies of planning applications, the electoral register and possibly the rates register. Main libraries will hold a copy of the Data Protection Register, in which data users who store personal details on individuals are required to register. Most of the expensive publications referred to in this book, from *Who's Who* to the *Civil Service Yearbook* to Acts of Parliament, you should find in any reference library.

In addition to their collections, libraries also contain librarians, a highly-skilled and generally undervalued bunch. The first problem that a researcher confronts is often the hardest: How do you begin? Where do you start looking? *Current British Directories*, for example, lists some 3,000 directories in print. Librarians are professionals at finding and accessing information sources, and a good one will nearly always be able to set you on the right track.

If a main reference library doesn't stock what you want, you may need to go further afield. A Macmillan book called *British Archives* gives details of over 700 libraries, archives and record offices which hold public records. The *Aslib Directory of Information Sources* is particularly good on specialist libraries kept by other organisations, whether they are public bodies, private companies, professional associations or other voluntary bodies.

Information on companies and independent organisations

Companies House
21 Bloomsbury Street, London WC1B 3XD, Tel: 029 2038 0801
Crown Way, Cardiff CF14 3UZ, Tel: 029 2038 8588
37 Castle Terrace, Edinburgh EH1 2EB, Tel: 0131 535 5800
IDB House, Chichester Street, Belfast BT1 4JX
www.companies-house.gov.uk

Every company, whether public, private or non-profit, must submit an annual return to Companies House. The files reveal a wealth of information, including accounts, auditors' reports, details of shareholders, the registered address and names of directors and company secretary. You can get a copy of a particular company's file in the form of a microfiche; the fees are £5 per company for personal callers and £8 for the information by post. The only information supplied free of charge on the telephone is the registration number, date of incorporation and date of last annual return.

Charity Commission
The Charity Commission holds a register of some 180,000 charities in England and Wales. The public files should contain a copy of each charity's constitution and annual accounts and reports, but are not always complete. There are offices in London, Liverpool and Taunton (see appendix B for addresses). Files have to be ordered in advance, but for a small fee the Commission will supply photocopies of documents on file and the Commission's website at *www.charity-commission.gov.uk* provides basic information from the register. In Scotland, the Inland Revenue now maintains a public index of Scottish charities.

Certification Office for Trade Unions and Employers Associations
Brandon House, 180 Borough High Street, London SE1 1LW, Tel: 020 7210 3734

Registry of Friendly Societies
Victory House, 30–34 Kingsway, London WC2B 6ES, Tel: 020 7663 5025
Both the Certification Office for Trade Unions and the Registry of Friendly Societies also hold files for public inspection, but are less frequented than either Companies House or the Charity Commission so you should ring and make an appointment first. The Registry of Friendly Societies covers organisations as diverse as credit unions, building societies, industrial and provident societies and housing associations, and inspection charges are £8 a file.

The British Library is a copyright library which in theory receives copies of every book published in the UK. Its main staffed reference service is called the Business Research Service and takes enquiries on 020 7412 7454. Simple enquiries (up to 10 minutes of staff time) are answered free of charge. For more in-depth research, you will either have to pay, or do it yourself at the British Library (see appendix B for address).

Most types of commercial or non-profit organisation in the UK are required under statute to register with a government office or registrar, and generally the files are open to public inspection. The most important registers are detailed in the box opposite.

Government

The state publishes an enormous quantity of information both about itself and about the people and land it governs. It is in many ways the archetypal producer of information (the 'state' is the etymological root for 'statistic'). Bearing in mind the high credibility that government research commands, it is worthwhile for any action researcher to get acquainted with this output.

The Stationery Office is the UK government's publisher, producing some 10,000 new items each year. Its primary task is to publish the mass of papers that enable Parliament and the legislative process to function, including Hansard (the verbatim report of Parliamentary debates), White Papers (plans for new legislation), bills and statutes, the reports of Select Committees and Royal Commissions, etc. More on this in chapters 13 and 14.

In addition to Parliamentary papers, the Stationery Office publishes material for government departments, agencies and other national bodies (note that not all Stationery Office publications are produced by government). It also acts as the UK sales agent for a number of major international institutions including the EU, the Council of Europe and the United Nations and its agencies.

Stationery Office publications are available from Stationery Office bookshops in London, Edinburgh, Belfast, Manchester, Birmingham and Bristol, as well as other bookshops. You can also order by post to the Stationery Office Publications Centre (see appendix B), or by telephone – expect to be kept waiting. Stationery Office publications are not cheap; luckily, reference libraries often have a good stock.

Among the most useful of its publications are those the Stationery Office produces for the Office for National Statistics (ONS). Alongside the *Blue Book* and the *Pink Book* (UK national accounts and balance of payments) and the *Annual Abstract of Statistics*, the Office for National Statistics produces annually *Social Trends* and *Regional Trends*, perhaps the most widely quoted authoritative sets of current figures on everything from employment to education, health and social services to income and wealth, the environment to law enforcement ('... grippingly revealing ... the zenith of the British number-lover's year', according to the *Times*). *Social Trends* has, however, on occasions been as notable for the embarrassing figures it doesn't contain as those it includes. Note also the *Guide to Official Statistics*, a guide to tracing primary sources of statistics on a very wide range of subjects.

The ONS analyses the decennial census of the population in England and Wales, with the General Register Office in Edinburgh and the Census Office in Belfast performing the same function in Scotland and Northern Ireland respectively. A full census has been taken every ten years since 1801 (except in 1941), and there is one in 2001. Having collected the data on population, housing, employment and other topics, the statisticians then spend the best part of the next five years analysing and publishing it. See the box overleaf for details of what is available.

The census is unique in that participation is compulsory and it involves the *entire* population, not just a sample from which inferences are made as in other surveys. The comprehensive and detailed nature of the data make it suitable for a vast number of different applications: it is relatively straightforward, for example, to compare the prevalence of unemployment, or owner-occupation, in one area or one social group with another or with the national average. The census data is collected in enumeration districts of 150-200 households and these districts are then used as building blocks to compute figures for wards, parishes, health districts, parliamentary constituencies, counties, etc. You can obtain the data for any of these areas, or for the enumeration districts themselves, in the form of Local and Small Area Statistics, which are available for purchase from Census Customer Services.

In addition to Stationery Office publications, many reports, consultation papers and other documents are available direct from government departments and agencies. (As a general rule, if a publication is issued free of charge, it will *not* be obtainable from the Stationery Office.)

The extent to which other information is available, including unpublished figures and executive instructions to statutory bodies, depends partly on how politically sensitive it is, but probably more on the attitude of the individual civil servant(s) holding the information. Under the Code of Practice on Access to Government Information, first introduced in 1994, officials should make information available to the public unless there is a good reason for withholding it, but there is no right of access to the original documentation. A leaflet explaining the code and how to complain is available from the Parliamentary Commissioner for Administration (see 'The Ombudsman', chapter 8).

The proposed Freedom of Information Bill, which at the time of writing was due to go through Parliament in 2000, will include a

Census data from the Office for National Statistics

*Or the General Register Office in Scotland and the Census Office in Northern Ireland

County Monitors
Summary statistics for each county in England and Wales and each Region and Islands Area in Scotland. The 12 tables cover many of the topics in the *County Reports*, but in brief.

County Reports
Each report is published in two parts. Part One includes results based on processing all census returns, with main tables presented for the county as a whole and for each local authority district. Part Two includes results based on subsequent processing of a one in ten sample of the returns.

Main topics in Part One:

▼ age and marital status
▼ communal establishments
▼ country of birth
▼ ethnic group
▼ long-term illness
▼ economic position
▼ migration
▼ tenure
▼ rooms and household size

▼ household amenities
▼ availability of cars and vans
▼ household composition
▼ shared accommodation
▼ household spaces and dwellings
▼ students
▼ pensioners
▼ Welsh/Gaelic language

Topics in Part Two:

▼ economic and
   employment status
▼ occupation
▼ industry
▼ hours worked
▼ travel to work
▼ qualified manpower
▼ family type

Topic Reports
A series of topic and national summaries, e.g. Age, Sex and Marital Status; Ethnic Group; etc.

The above publications are all available from the Stationery Office

Local and Small Area Statistics
The Local Base Statistics (LBS) and Small Area Statistics (SAS) are the standard census outputs which are available for a variety of areas throughout Great Britain, including counties, Scottish regions and islands, local authority districts and wards, health authorities, parliamentary constituencies, parishes, standard English regions, and at national level. They are sometimes referred to as the 'unpublished data', but are obtainable in either printed or magnetic media form (at a price) from the relevant census customer services. Similar data covering the smaller areas in Northern Ireland (ward level and below) are available from the Census Office in Belfast.

ONS	GRO (S)	Census Office
Segensworth Road	Ladywell House	McAuley House
Titchfield	Ladywell Road	2–14 Castle Streety
Hampshire PO15 5RR	Edinburgh EH12 7TF	Belfast BT1 1SA
Tel: 01329 813800	Tel: 0131 314 4254	Tel: 028 9052 0500

The Census Information Gateway is at *www.census.ac.uk*

statutory right of access to information held by public bodies, regulated by a new information commissioner. Bodies such as health authorities and the police, which are not covered by the open government Code of Practice, will have to disclose information for the first time.

However, the draft bill contains so many exemptions to disclosure, including information about accident or malpractice investigations which could lead to criminal charges, and all information relating to 'the formulation and development of government policy', that it is unclear whether it will result in any significant increase in information rights. Information may still be withheld if disclosure would 'prejudice' the interests of government bodies or relevant parties. The Campaign for Freedom of Information points out that under the bill's proposals, the public would have no right to see scientific advice about health hazards such as BSE or to see official assessments of the safety implications of privatising the Underground or the air traffic control system.

The time-honoured method of extracting further information from government departments is through written parliamentary questions. PQs have to be tabled in Parliament by an MP and addressed to the senior minister in the relevant government department. They are generally answered within a week to ten days, the answers appear at the back of daily *Hansard*, and they often contain information that would not normally have been published. There is no limit to how many written PQs an MP can table, and it shouldn't be difficult to get your local MP or one interested in your cause to table one or two for you. More on PQs in chapter 14.

If a minister refuses to give an answer to a PQ, the reason usually given is that either the information is not available or that rooting it out would result in 'disproportionate cost' to the civil service (generally calculated as anything over £500). If you get either reply, but particularly the former, it is often worth varying the terms of the question. In the *Freedom of Information Handbook* (see appendix C), David Northmore notes that as Prime Minister, Margaret Thatcher refused to say how many questions she had declined to answer since coming to power, saying that answering that question would itself involve disproportionate cost. 'But ministers are free to spend any amount they wish on an answer. In June 1989, the Prime Minister was asked to list the government's achievements since 1979. The reply covered 34 columns of *Hansard*, and the cost was later disclosed to have been £4,600.'

If you are seeking information from a relatively junior civil servant, the threat of a PQ – tactfully enunciated, of course – can often work wonders. Drafting PQs is a lot of work for officials; so much simpler for them just to photocopy the two pages you want and pop them in the post.

Unless you have some idea of what is going on inside government, or know what kind of information they are producing, you will be unable to use it to embarrass them or strengthen your own position. To leak a document to the press, you have to get hold of it; in order to get hold of it, you have to know it exists. This is an argument for developing as many contacts as possible, at any level, in Whitehall or on the Whitehall periphery, i.e. consultants, advisers, journalists, and people in other statutory bodies like local authorities or health authorities who are in regular contact with the civil servants. The weak point, for the purposes of information security, is the circulation list. An executive letter from the Department of Health may only go to one person in each health authority, but that's over 200 letters (which will then be copied to each auditor, chief executive's office, etc.) and you only have to get a copy of one of them.

The only unpublished government documents to which it should always be straightforward to gain access are those yellowed with age. The Public Records Office (see appendix B for address) holds a unique collection of central government files which have been released under the thirty-year rule; the really sensitive (i.e. interesting) stuff is kept under wraps for much longer, so if you still entertain any suspicions about Britain's scorched-earth policy in the former Malaya in the 1940s or even the jailing of Emmeline Pankhurst in 1913, the satisfaction of confirming (or denying) them may be left to your children. The staff can help with initial queries but you will have to do the digging around yourself.

Charities, think-tanks and academia

Other pressure groups, charities, think-tanks and institutes can provide fertile ground for the action researcher. Most will have produced information or published research which supports their own point of view and will be anxious to disseminate it as widely as possible.

However, this kind of research tends to have a short shelf-life: once it has been published and press-released it will fall quickly into oblivion, and usually no attempt will be made to keep it in print.

One of the richest research resources that service-providing organisations possess is their client files. If your own organisation provides advice services, or takes on any other form of case-work, it is important to realise the unique opportunity this presents, and to keep figures and other information on your case-work in a usable and up-to-date form. One of the main reasons government listens to non-profit groups is because of the link they provide with welfare consumers and other users of services: if you know what percentage of your clients are on income support, how many of them are affected by the new Social Security Act *and in which ways*, that can prove invaluable information. The wealth of case-study material that clients present is also a strong asset for attracting media interest, with its need for a human angle.

The need for confidentiality will make most charities and other service providers reluctant to give outsiders access to their case-files, but if they are persuaded that it is in their interest, they may agree to make available an abstract of the information, or to cooperate with a piece of research.

The think-tanks are the guerilla fighters in the field of policy formulation: small, flexible research institutes, they operate by publishing research monographs and pamphlets, running seminars and promoting themselves as advisers to the powerful. Their key skill is not researching, or even thinking, but being at the right place at the right time with a serviceable idea. Historically, the most influential think-tanks have been the Fabian Society, which helped to think the foundations of British socialism in the early years of the century, and the Institute of Economic Affairs, which had promoted free-market liberalism for some twenty years when, in the mid-1970s, the message got through to the top of the Tory Party and provided the dominant theme for the next twenty.

A rash of new think-tanks or institutes has been set up in recent years to try and influence a political world that is less polarised. It is certainly noticeable that the institutes, new and old, whose commentary is now most sought after are those which are politically non-aligned and whose expertise appears technical rather than ideological. The Royal Institute of International Affairs (Chatham House) and the Institute of Fiscal Studies spring to mind.

The box opposite details most of the better known think-tanks. Their work can provide some good figures and an up-to-the-moment picture of issues and debate in a given field, but as much can be learnt from the style as from the substance. At its best think-tank research is current, concise and positive: making improvements seem possible in a world which continually stresses the negative and the impossible.

By contrast, the research produced in universities and by academia generally can often seem, well, academic. Because it is undertaken with relative freedom from policy constraints, however, it can be both less partial and more thorough. Academics certainly share with pressure groups and think-tanks the desire to have their work publicised, albeit for slightly different reasons. The problem is locating and turning to good use studies which have often been designed and carried out largely as ends in themselves.

Current research is hard to trace systematically, but luckily academics are better at networking than repute suggests: ivory towers maybe, but competition in academia means that these days they have radar installed. Any good academic should be able to brief you on the leading work being done in their field. In some specialisms there is a college or department which has managed to carve itself a special reputation; the School of Peace Studies at Bradford University, for example, is unusual in its concentrated work on peace theory, arms reduction, alternative security and conflict resolution.

The think-tanks at a glance

Adam Smith Institute
23 Great Smith Street, London SW1P 3DJ   Tel: 020 7222 4995 *www.adamsmith.org.uk*
Profile: Independent, but claimed credit for many Tory policies in the 1980s, including the poll tax.

Centre for Policy Studies
57 Tufton Street, London SW1P 3QL   Tel: 020 7222 4488 *www.cps.org.uk*
Profile: Conservative Party think-tank, set up by Thatcher and Keith Joseph in the 1970s.

Demos
Panton House, 25 Haymarket, London SW1Y 4EN Tel: 020 7321 2200 *www.demos.co.uk*
Profile: New Labour connections, long-termist orientation, but still best at labels and capturing the *zeitgeist.*

Employment Policy Institute
South Bank House, Black Prince Road, London SE1 7SJ, Tel: 020 7735 0777
Profile: Serious economists aiming at full employment

Fabian Society
11 Dartmouth Street, London SW1H 9BN   Tel: 020 7222 8877 *www.fabian-society.org.uk*
Profile: Close to the Labour Party, no longer very Fabian.

Foreign Policy Centre
Panton House, 25 Haymarket, London SW1Y 4EN, Tel: 020 7925 1800
Profile: Rethinking Britain's relations with the world, with New Labour's blessing.

Institute for Public Policy Research
30–32 Southampton Street, London WC2E 7RA   Tel: 020 7470 6100 *www.ippr.org.uk*
Profile: Associated with Labour modernisers, but never seemed to carve out the influence that was its due.

Institute of Economic Affairs
2 Lord North Street, London SW1P 3LB   Tel: 020 7799 8900 *www.iea.org.uk*
Profile: The classic *laissez-faire* think-tank. Helped set up the Social Affairs Unit, which spends its time baiting the public sector.

Institute of Fiscal Studies
7 Ridgemount Street, London WC1E 7AE   Tel: 020 7291 4800
Profile: Authoritative, non-aligned, expertise ranges from benefits to budget deficits.

Policy Studies Institute
100 Park Village East, London NW1 3SR   Tel: 020 7468 2201
Profile: Large, wide-ranging, academic: more of a research agency than a think-tank.

Royal Institute of International Affairs (Chatham House)
10 St James's Square, London SW1Y 4LE   Tel: 020 7957 5700 *www.riia.org*
Profile: Large, foreign affairs think-tank. Quite establishment, but has no political axes to grind.

Social Market Foundation
11 Tufton Street, London SW1P 3QB, Tel: 020 7222 7060 *www.smf.co.uk*
Profile: Originally associated with the SDP; out to prove that the social market is more than just a label.

Market research

Finally, market research presents a huge body of data that could be exploited by campaigning groups, particularly unions, professional associations, or those working in the areas of employment, corporate ethics or the environment. It will provide answers to questions such as: How labour-intensive is a particular business, and how have labour costs moved over time? What are the main trends in the sale of 'green' detergents as compared with conventional detergents? Which are the companies that manufacture a certain product?

Much market research is commissioned by individual companies for their exclusive use, but there is also a growing range of companies that publish, for general sale, market surveys or other information on particular industries, industry sectors or products. Among the best known are Mintel, Euromonitor and Key Note Publications. Market research is expensive and copyright is protected fiercely. Mintel produces a cumulative monthly index of its research surveys, covering everything from air treatment to health insurance to waste management.

Original research

If existing research does not provide sufficient figures or information for you to make a good case, or the information that is available is out of date, you will have to consider undertaking or commissioning some original research. This will have the advantages of currency and of being tailor-made to your campaign needs.

The design of new research should always be driven by clear campaign objectives. Take the example of a welfare benefits campaign. The research requirements for amending a new social security bill in Parliament, with the emphasis on identifying specific loopholes and producing individual examples, will be very different from a campaign to raise levels of benefit, where the stress might lie on identifying measures of general disadvantage and providing evidence for their existence in a large proportion of the claimant population.

The Urban Trust, an organisation set up in 1987 to channel grant money into black communities, was convinced that relatively little money from traditional funding bodies was finding its way to black and ethnic minority groups, although few of the funding institutions appeared to accept this. The Urban Trust, then, needed some strong evidence. The Trust analysed the accounts of a random sample of 50 of the larger foundations held on file at the Charity Commission and complemented this with an attitudinal survey of 100 further foundations and corporate funders. It discovered that as little as one per cent of the funders' money was going to black groups, but that over 80% of funders were rigidly adhering to a policy of 'colour-blindness' (i.e.

disregarding ethnic or cultural differences) when assessing applications, in the belief that this was a fair and equitable approach. The Trust now had the evidence it needed, and because it had been gleaned from audited accounts and from the funders themselves it was difficult for anyone to question the results.

One thing it is important not to overlook in any research programme is the value of making positive proposals or at least providing instances of good practice. These can lead more directly to the achievement of an organisation's objectives than unremitting criticism or condemnation. (The Urban Trust, as a financial intermediary between funders and black communities, could tactfully put itself forward as a ready-made solution to the problems it highlighted in research.) Taking a wholly negative approach will often lead to an easy dismissal by policy-makers – who often feel they are being criticised on all sides – and resignation and ultimately apathy amongst supporters.

Comparing good and bad practice is a particularly effective motor for change. If you criticise the practices of some local authorities, or some companies, do provide examples of others that are getting it right; this should both give a clear direction for improvement and embarrass the offenders into taking it. The work of the environmental movement in damning the polluting behaviour of some companies while encouraging green corporate practices is a very successful example of this technique.

One thing for which policy-makers are universally desperate are practical, tested solutions to problems, particularly if they do not require legislation or substantial resources. Why not give them a few ideas?

The rules of the game

Pressure groups only publicise research if it supports their argument. This is the basic credibility problem with which any group has to contend. It immediately places the work they do under the spotlight, and a scientific approach is needed to survive scrutiny.

A scientific approach to research is based on the principle of scepticism. (Statistical inquiry, for example, commonly progresses by testing hypotheses that results are due to a quirk of chance.) Results, ideally, are not cultivated or nurtured; they should spring up and hit you in the face despite your gallant attempts to knock them down.

The biased presentation of data is both familiar and galling: the statement, for example, that '50% more people in the local community support rather than oppose the proposal for a new road', based on a survey where 18% were in favour of the new road, 12% were against, 12% undecided and 58% had never heard of the proposal. However, bias or imbalance can enter a piece of research at almost any point. It can be introduced in the selection of information sources, in the methods used to extract data from them, and in the collation and processing of that data. When publishing research you will need to explain the methods employed to obtain the information and if there is any obvious element of bias present which you have not controlled for, or at least explained, this will put your results in question. Some common sources of bias in the design of questionnaires and interviews are described in the relevant section below.

If data is obtained from a sample rather than from the full population (i.e. from just a selection of the people or things that you want to make conclusions about rather than from all of them) particular care should be taken. Will the sample be weighted towards one geographical area or one interest group? Will the method of selection prejudice the sample and make it unrepresentative of the population? If your research is based on using sample data to infer conclusions about a general state of affairs the onus will be on you to demonstrate that the sample is representative.

Most research is about establishing relationships: the relationship between where people live and incidence of cancer, for example, or between social class and educational qualifications. It is important to be aware of what sort of relationship is suggested by the evidence from the research, and to be wary of claims which the data does not justify.

This last point is particularly pertinent when it comes to causal relationships. Sets of figures can establish the existence of a *correlation* between two or more factors (or variables, as they are known), but never a *cause*. Take the example of crime and marital break-up on a number of different housing estates. A researcher carries out a survey and notices that the greater the prevalence of crime on one estate compared to the next, the higher the incidence of separation and divorce; i.e. there is a positive correlation between crime and marital break-up. Does this mean that crime causes people's marriages to fail? Not necessarily. It may mean that marriages breaking up leads to more crime. Or both. Or maybe the increase in crime and broken marriages are both caused by a third variable: poverty, for example. Or perhaps there are yet more links in the chain: it may be that broken marriages are more common among younger people, who also happen to have lower disposable incomes, which makes them more likely to be pushed to commit crime … The point is that statistics can give the correlation, but you will have to turn to philosophy to give you the causes.

In fact, establishing that a correlation exists may be all you need to do. Simply showing that crime and family breakdown had reached unprecedented levels on a housing estate might be enough to push the local authority into taking decisive action to improve conditions on the estate. Some of the most effective action research is of this kind: bald, unencumbered by rhetoric or ideology, it lets the figures speak for themselves.

Most of the original research we have considered so far is *quantitative*: it relies on data collected in numerical form which is then analysed to give information about a sample or population.

If you need to show that a causal relationship exists, however, you will have to rely on making a logical or reasoned case for this. Even though figures cannot prove your case, they may lend support to it. You can also strengthen your case by using *qualitative* techniques, like collecting anecdotal evidence or conducting in-depth interviews.

Quantitative research has a number of disadvantages: the questions it is able to ask have to be kept simple in order that the data collected is directly comparable; and it becomes very unwieldy when dealing with a number of different variables. Qualitative research, on the other hand, enables you to unlock quite complex issues or deal with several issues at one time, particularly if they involve people's impressions, attitudes or motivations. It can also alert you to new

---

Ensuring data are comparable: how to adjust prices for inflation

The Retail Prices Index (RPI) is calculated every month. There are indices for everything from 'alcoholic drinks' to 'housing' and an 'all items' index. The RPI measures price changes, not price levels. The 'rate of inflation' is simply the percentage change over twelve months in the all items index.

Retail price indices are published by the Stationery Office (most recent indices appear in the *Monthly Digest of Statistics*).

The table below is an extract from the all items RPI:

Indices: January 1987 = 100

	Jan	Feb	Mar	Apr	May	Jun	Jul	Aug	Sep	Oct	Nov	Dec
1987	100.0	100.4	100.6	101.8	101.9	101.9	101.8	102.1	102.4	102.9	103.4	103.3
1988	103.3	103.7	104.1	105.8	106.2	106.6	106.7	107.9	108.4	109.5	110.0	110.3
1989	111.0	111.8	112.3	114.3	115.0	115.4	115.5	115.8	116.6	117.5	118.5	118.8
1990	119.5	120.2	121.4	125.1	126.2	126.7	126.8	128.1	129.3	130.3	130.0	129.9

Q. How much money was required in May 1987 to have the same purchasing power as £32 in November 1990?

A. £32 x $\dfrac{\text{earlier date RPI}}{\text{later date RPI}}$ = £32 x $\dfrac{101.9}{130.0}$ = **£25.08**

Q. How much would be needed in January 1990 to be able to buy as much as one pound in January 1988?

A. £1 x $\dfrac{\text{later date RPI}}{\text{earlier date RPI}}$ = £1 x $\dfrac{119.5}{103.3}$ = **£1.16**

factors or those unanticipated in the research design. The disadvantage is that it does not provide a safe base for making generalisations about such impressions, attitudes, etc. in a wider group.

In the Urban Trust research into the funding of black groups described above, the quantitative surveys were complemented with some in-depth interviews with officers from funding agencies. The open-response format allowed funders to raise their own concerns and uncovered more complex attitudes towards the funding of black groups than was possible through the written (closed response) surveys, helping to shed light on the decision-making processes involved.

Finally, it is worth noting that if the issues on which you are working are very contentious and your results likely to be disputed, or the information sources available are all imperfect in some way, you could employ a variety of different methods, all focusing on the same issue. This can add credibility to your research and make it more difficult for other people to question your conclusions.

Using statistics: samples and significance

It is useful to make a distinction between descriptive and inferential statistics. *Descriptive* statistics are used to summarise a set of data. Through tables, graphs and figures they help to bring out trends or characteristics. Of particular interest are figures which measure the central tendency in a set of data (e.g. the mean, median or mode) and those which give a measure of dispersion (e.g. the standard deviation, or the range). A hostel for homeless people, for example, might work out from its records that the average (mean) age of its residents last year was only 24, while the year before it was 36.2, and use the information to help it provide more appropriate services, or to campaign for a better deal for its clients. A few hints on presenting statistics in graphic form are given overleaf.

Inferential statistics use data from a small group, or sample, to make estimates or predictions about the wider group, or population, from which the sample is drawn. Pre-election opinion polls are a common example. In particular, inferential techniques are used to evaluate to what extent the estimates made about a population will be due to chance in the choice of sample. The make-up of the sample of voters polled, for instance, will differ somewhat through chance from the make-up of the entire constituency, so in addition to saying 'liberal democrats: 18%' (the sample result), we can use mathematical probability to calculate that there is a 95% chance (or we can be 95% confident) that liberal democrat support in the constituency is between 16-20%. This is known as a confidence interval.

Other inferential techniques, known as tests of significance, are used by statisticians to evaluate whether differing results from two or more samples are due to chance or to the fact that they come from

Presenting statistics

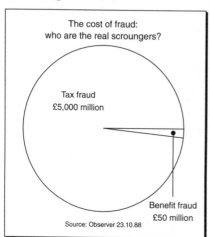

The cost of fraud:
who are the real scroungers?

Tax fraud
£5,000 million

Benefit fraud
£50 million

Source: Observer 23.10.88

◀ Pie-charts are useful for comparing the size of each category with the whole.

▼ Bar-charts are good for comparing the size of each category with the size of the others.

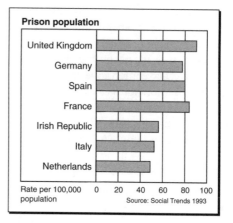

Prison population

United Kingdom

Germany

Spain

France

Irish Republic

Italy

Netherlands

Rate per 100,000   0   20   40   60   80   100
population   Source: Social Trends 1993

▼ Pictograms are a fun way of doing this if there aren't too many categories

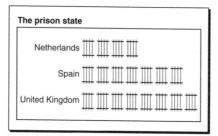

The prison state

Netherlands

Spain

United Kingdom

▼ Cropping the scale on a chart or graph can emphasise differences

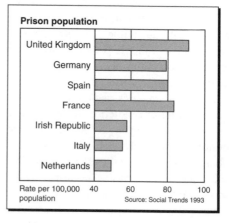

Prison population

United Kingdom

Germany

Spain

France

Irish Republic

Italy

Netherlands

Rate per 100,000   40   60   80   100
population   Source: Social Trends 1993

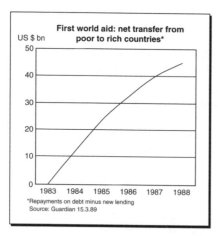

First world aid: net transfer from
US $ bn   **poor to rich countries***
50

40

30

20

10

0
    1983   1984   1985   1986   1987   1988
*Repayments on debt minus new lending
Source: Guardian 15.3.89

◀ Linear graphs show continuous change, e.g. change over time (but bar-charts may be more appropriate if the data is grouped by year, week, etc.)

different populations (or from a population that has changed from the time one sample was taken to the next). If a further opinion poll was taken a week after the first, and the liberal democrats only polled 16%, a significance test could be used to check whether the 2 per cent drop in their polled vote was a safe indication of an actual slide in liberal democrat support in the constituency. A significant result would be one where we could be reasonably confident that the difference in the two results had not occurred just by chance. 'Significant' in this context does not mean 'large' or 'important'; it just means 'reliable'.

Take another example. The hostel for homeless people mentioned at the start of this section might use its information on the drop in the mean age of its residents to claim that the mean age of homeless people had dropped from 36 to 24 (approximately). But would it be justified in making such a claim? No. We have already noted that the selection of a sample may be subject to bias. There are any number of reasons why the hostel residents may not be a representative sample of the population of homeless people (the new receptionist's habit of playing loud music may have put off older people, for example). Performing a significance test for this inference would therefore be nonsensical: there are other factors involved in the selection of the sample than just pure chance. This is not to say, however that the observed drop in age is not powerful anecdotal evidence, particularly if it is reflected in other hostels.

The only samples from which inferences can be made with safety are those selected through a random procedure. (Note that a random sample is not one that has been casually chosen, but one for which every element in the population has had an equal chance of being selected.) One method is to number the elements in the population and then to read off the numbers in a random numbers table, selecting those elements which correspond. Any scientific pocket calculator will also be able to generate random numbers.

The problem with this method of selecting a random sample is that it requires a list of all the elements in the population. For most social research, such a list will not be available, so the only alternative is to try and approximate a random procedure: the pollsters' method of accosting every fifth person in the street is one such method. As was noted above, selecting a sample that is representative of the population will depend on a mixture of experience and common sense in removing potential sources of bias.

Opinion in the statistical world differs on the value of inferences made from such approximated 'random' samples, and in particular on the usefulness of carrying out tests of significance on them, as it is clear that they will be affected by factors other than just chance. Perhaps the most important point to bear in mind is that the quality, and hence the credibility, of any research you do will depend on a consistent, objective approach, and that poor or unreliable source data cannot be improved by any amount of fancy statistics.

Questionnaires and interviews

The examples used in the last section were based on a survey of records or a straightforward poll. In many cases adequate records will not exist and research will require obtaining more detailed information direct from people themselves.

Questionnaires and interviews range from a few tick-boxes typed on a sheet of paper to face-to-face recorded interviews. Generally speaking, the more structured the method, the easier it will be to compare groups of results, or one person's responses with those of another. In particular, closed (or selected) response formats, in which the respondent has to select their answer(s) from among those given, provide a better basis for comparing results and compiling statistics than open (or constructed) response formats, where the respondent is at liberty to construct their own answer.

The advantage usually claimed for open response is that it produces more information, even if that information is harder to handle. It will also avoid the respondent feeling frustrated at being pushed into making over-simple or stereotyped responses, which often happens with closed response formats. In word-of-mouth surveys, the less structured the survey, the more knowledge and experience is required of the interviewer, clarifying questions asked or probing for fuller responses.

Conversely, if a researcher intends to categorise or tabulate the results anyway, it makes sense to let the respondent do it. For a written questionnaire, most people also find closed response questions quicker or easier to complete, which may improve your

---

Using closed response formats: attitudes towards funding ethnic minority groups

8. For each of the following statements, please tick on the scale to what extent you agree with what is written (e.g. 1=strongly agree, 5=strongly disagree).

	Strongly agree (1)	Agree (2)	Undecided (3)	Disagree (4)	Strongly disagree (5)
Ethnic minority voluntary groups in general receive a lower level of funding than other voluntary groups.	O	O	O	O	O
Each application for funding should be considered solely on its individual merits, regardless of the ethnic background of the organisation making the application.	O	O	O	O	O
Grant-makers in general should do more to encourage applications from ethnic minority organisations.	O	O	O	O	O
Grant-makers should, if necessary, employ positive discrimination to ensure that the grants they make reflect the ethnic balance of their beneficial area.	O	O	O	O	O
Applications from ethnic minority groups are generally of a poorer standard than those from other groups.	O	O	O	O	O
The needs of ethnic minorities are already well catered for by existing (multicultural) service-providing agencies.	O	O	O	O	O

response rate, particularly if the questionnaire is laid out attractively. Finally, if the questions are well-designed it is possible to glean quite complex information from closed response, even on people's attitudes. The box below left shows part of a written questionnaire used in the Urban Trust research to untangle a mesh of complex attitudes held by funding officers towards ethnic minority groups: although closed response, the format allowed respondents scope to express quite sophisticated shades of opinion.

Note that each of the statements used in the example contain just one idea and that as a whole the statements are broadly balanced. If a question used in a survey contains more than one idea this will create problems in interpreting the results and can lead to accusations of bias. 'Do you think this new piece of legislation should be scrapped and replaced by a charter for consumers?', for example, will fail to pick up or distinguish those people who oppose the legislation but think a consumers' charter is a bad idea, those who think there should be a charter in addition to the legislation, or those who feel strongly about either the legislation or the charter but are undecided on the other.

Common sources of bias in questionnaires are described in the box below.

Common sources of bias in questionnaires and interviews

Self-reporting. If people are questioned about their own actions or behaviour, they may have a reason for not answering honestly. If a GP asks her patients how many cigarettes they smoke, there may be a tendency to underestimation; if people are asked how much they give to charity, a degree of exaggeration might be expected. To an extent this bias can be minimised by conducting surveys anonymously, but self-report procedures are best avoided on issues where respondents are unlikely – or unable – to provide accurate information.

Loaded questions. The way in which questions are put by a questionnaire or an interviewer can also weight the responses. Examples of loaded questions include:

▼ Do you support this vicious new piece of legislation?

▼ How do you think people will suffer from this legislation?

▼ Do you think the new legislation is a) acceptable; b) damaging; c) an outrage?

Any question which taints or pre-empts some of the possible responses, or which provides more opportunity to answer one way rather than another, should be avoided. A more subtle type of weighting occurs in interviews where responses can be affected by the interviewer's tone.

Self-selection. If the respondents in a survey are those that have themselves elected to take part, the sample will be flawed. It could, for example, be weighted towards those with an existing interest in, or sympathy with, the subject matter. This is a problem with interviews, where only one out of three people approached may agree to take part, and with nearly all postal questionnaires.

The manner in which people respond to a survey can be wholly unpredictable, particularly if they are unacquainted with the issues you are researching, *or the language you use.* Once the questionnaire/ interview has been designed, try it out on a small sample first: this will help you sharpen the design and hopefully alert you to any serious misunderstandings which could make your results unusable.

One of the knottiest problems with any survey is achieving a good response rate, bearing in mind that a low response will not only leave you with less information but will also affect the credibility of the results. Response rate will depend on a number of factors including the subject matter, the survey method employed, the status of the researcher and the extent to which the respondents are a captive audience (e.g. pupils in a class, employees in a firm) or are committed to the research. For most postal questionnaires you will have to work particularly hard at getting a good response. A few tips:

▼ enclose a reply-paid envelope;

▼ make the questionnaire as short and simple as possible (it is worth aiming for something that people will complete immediately on opening your letter, rather than putting to one side for later consideration);

▼ be wary of asking for information which respondents will not have easily to hand;

▼ consider offering an incentive, e.g. a prize for the first 20 completed questionnaires (but be careful not to introduce bias this way);

▼ give a deadline for return of questionnaires (10 days is fine);

▼ send any reminder letters quickly, with another copy of the questionnaire. A stamped reminder message may help. The one shown here has worked for me in the past.

Stamped message for a reminder mailing

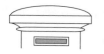

Your opinion counts...
If you don't send it
we can't count it

Omnibus surveys and commissioned research

The Market Research Society (see appendix B for address) produces a guide to organisations and individuals providing market research services, including famous names like MORI and Gallup. Many of these specialise in social research. Apart from the advantage of getting someone else to do the work, commissioning research from a respected independent agency can be a way of making your information appear more impartial.

The Society gives a few guidelines on commissioning survey research. It suggests that the brief you give should include a statement of the research problems, setting them in their general background and context; an indication of the sorts of decisions that are likely to be influenced by the research results and the uses to which the results are to be put (e.g. whether publication is envisaged); and a broad indication of the budget available.

Survey research doesn't come cheap. One method which might meet your aims and not come too expensive is the omnibus survey. A number of market research agencies run these surveys which give you the chance to put two or three questions on an opinion poll administered to a sample of the general public. This can be a good way of gauging public opinion on an issue central to your campaign. If the results are positive you can then publicise them widely, with the credibility of the research agency to back you up. Three questions administered to a representative sample of the public costs about £400.

Publishing research

Action research is above all action*able* research: research that can be acted upon or persuade others to act. The format, tone and presentation of a piece of research can make all the difference between it gathering dust on a shelf or being read, talked about, covered in the media and influencing decisions.

A few years ago the Joseph Rowntree Foundation, a leading charity which supports social research, realised that most of the material it produced, although of high quality, was not getting out of the academic social policy ghetto. It decided to devote more effort to dissemination: to producing attractive, bite-sized chunks of research, whether in booklet or magazine format, and making sure that they got onto the desks of the right people and were reported in the newspapers those people read. Some of the policies its research has supported – even large-scale, difficult ones like the phasing out of mortgage interest tax relief – are now being discussed seriously by politicians for the first time. The Foundation calls it 'insemination ... the active introduction of ideas, knowledge and practice into existing systems'.

Journalistic qualities

Perhaps the key to understanding what makes persuasive research is an appreciation of its journalistic qualities. Action research, like good journalism, should be:

▼ *Targeted at a particular readership.* Who will be reading this research? Whom is it intended to influence? How much do they already know? Once these questions have been answered you can work at arousing their interest, addressing their negative perceptions and talking throughout on their level.

▼ *Current and up-to-date.* Research should demonstrate an awareness of current issues in its field and discuss latest developments.

It also helps to be topical: to tie in with more general subjects or issues that are in the news (this is particularly important if you want national media coverage).

▼ *Exciting and accessible.* Hard to define but easy to spot – just look at a feature article in a Sunday newspaper and open up any research report, and note the difference.

The above qualities are in fact so rare in published research that if you manage to acquire them you will be almost guaranteed an impact.

The print or broadcast media will only cover one story, or angle, at a time. It can be galling to produce a learned tome and then to discover later that a 12-page briefing can generate as much media coverage (or more, if the journalists find it hard to extract a clear story from your tome). There is clearly a balance to be struck here because your work must appear authoritative, and not lightweight, but it may be worth publishing research in manageable portions, almost one story at a time, to maximise the impact. If you produce reports of any length or complexity include a one- or two-page summary of the main conclusions, in bullet-point form, right at the front.

Policy-makers have a predisposition for practical points, and the media for human interest stories. Both can be satisfied through case-studies: short examples of how the problems or advantages of a particular policy work out in practice, and the effect they have on individuals. More on this in chapter 7.

Dissemination and marketing

Producing simple publications is now much easier than it used to be. Print production has been revolutionised in recent years with the introduction of desktop publishing (DTP) and this has made the physical side of publishing much simpler and quicker. Companies will often handle both the design/typesetting and the printing for simple publications like research reports. The typesetting and print-ing costs for 500 copies of a 64-page A4 research report, saddle-stitched with an artboard cover (one-colour) would probably start from about £1,700 and you could get a limited number produced on compact disc for a few pounds each.

The product is only a quarter of the story as far as marketing is concerned. Also to be considered are the other three 'p's: price, place, and promotion.

▼ *Price.* It may seem strange to charge for information when the principal aim is to get it through to as many people as possible. However, an appropriate pricing policy can actually help in this regard. Publications that can be obtained free of charge (particu-larly in bulk) end up on the shelf: where some effort and expense is required to get hold of them, they stand more chance of getting read. Charging for a piece of research will also make it more likely to get reviewed and may even mean that people will take the results more seriously.

Setting a price will of course not prevent you from sending free copies to policy-makers or others whom you wish to influence. (Note that even here there is still a difference between someone getting a free publication and getting a publication *for free*.) Try and make sure that it arrives not just at the right organisation, but at the right desk. Rather than sending a copy to the minister – who won't read it – send it to the Grade 7 civil servant who is actually working on the policy.

▼ *Place.* There are a number of potential channels through which a book can get from the publisher to the reader. The bulk of pressure group material is distributed by mail order, either to existing supporters or to others who are responding to an advertisement, a review or listing, or a recommendation.

Most general bookshops won't be interested in taking research reports. There are, however, some specialist bookshops and book distributors, making up what is sometimes known as the alternative book trade, dealing with publications on subjects such as peace and the environment, alternative living, community politics, trade unions, etc. Other groups in your field may also be happy to sell your publications, if they think them relevant, and you might consider doing the same for them. Any bookshop or retail distributor will expect to take publications from you at a 35% discount.

Take advantage of occasional opportunities to sell your publication(s) and to help your publications sell your organisation: book stalls at exhibitions and fairs (or at the front of your office), seminars and conferences (try including the price of the publication in the seminar fee), public meetings, etc.

▼ *Promotion.* Promotional activities, from advertisements to news releases, are covered in some detail in the next two chapters. With the publication of a research report you will probably be aiming for some news coverage but don't miss the opportunity to get review coverage as well: book reviews, listings, catalogues and bibliographies will all help to shift copies and disseminate the findings. Include a copy of the conclusions of the research in summary (i.e. one sheet) with news releases. The simplest promotional material is a flyer, a one-sheet advertisement with the front cover of the publication reproduced on one side and a short description and order form on the reverse. This can be handed out at events, mailed, or inserted in other publications and magazines.

5 Advertising and publicity

Advertising is a set of techniques developed to sell commodities. These techniques include press, radio and TV advertisements, posters, hand bills, direct mail, catalogues, exhibitions, and everything from sales displays to prize draws and free gifts. But whether it is direct or subtle, advertising by commercial companies always has the same end in view: a sale. And when campaigners advertise they are using the techniques of selling, even though they may not literally be selling anything.

Advertising is so influential partly because it works cumulatively and partly because its battery of techniques is focused on prompting one very simple act: a purchase. The more complex or considered a response that an advertisement requires, the harder it will be to gauge its success. A single leaflet or advertisement, or even an entire publicity campaign, is unlikely to persuade someone to change their lifestyle. This is the problem faced by most public education advertisements, which have questionable efficacy even when their aim is to prompt concrete actions like stopping smoking or wearing a condom.

Where does this leave the non-profit group whose aim is to raise consciousness, to change people's behaviour or to influence policy-making? Advertising may be a very imperfect method of achieving any of these long-term aims, but, *if linked to specific action by the target audience*, it can provide the hook which will draw in new supporters or advocates. The audience must be given the opportunity to respond, and once that response is made they can be presented with further opportunities to act for the campaign.

A group could use advertising to solicit donations, to attract new members, to sell a publication, to get people to a meeting, to persuade them to vote a certain way, to write to their MP, or just to request further information. In each case the call to action is clear. Just as the sales advertisement will prompt the initial enquiry that can lead to securing a loyal customer, so advertising by non-profits should be seen as one link in a chain of actions, each one reinforcing the others and deepening support for the cause.

Positioning

The fact that campaigning groups are not in the business of selling for profit can also be a great advantage in advertising terms. It will be a major element in how they position themselves in relation to other advertisers.

There are three main elements in positioning, or the process by which organisations situate themselves and their products or offers in the marketplace.

Advertising should directly address the **target** audience. This will often be those people who are most likely to respond, but sometimes the target audience will be predetermined (e.g. public education campaigns aimed at a specific at-risk group). How the target audience will **benefit** from the offer, emotionally as well as materially, should be clear. The offer should also be distinguished from the **competition**, or other conflicting calls on the audience's time and resources.

In contrast to the one-dimensional political positioning which has opinions or groups located on a continuum from left to right, market positioning, being three-dimensional, is considerably more specific. How this is conveyed in an advertisement can be merely implicit, or suggested by the tone or the image used rather than the words, but it is what establishes the line of communication from advertiser to consumer. It is the bedrock of advertising on which the flashy, creative stuff is based, and if you are using an advertising agency it will form the basis of the brief that you need to give them.

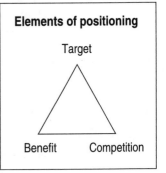

It is a useful discipline to compose just one sentence which welds together the three elements that position your own offer, even if you are unlikely to use it *verbatim* in an actual advertisement: 'Joining Action for its Own Sake is now the only [*competition*] way in which disgruntled citizens [*target*] can know they are making a difference [*benefit*]', for example. Rewrite it a few times. Spend some time looking critically at other press and poster ads, both commercial and non-profit, and evaluate their positioning.

Notes on using audience research or donor profiles for the purposes of targeting are given in chapter 3 under 'Direct mail'. Generally, targeting should be as focused as possible, without being unnecessarily exclusive. If you are advertising to increase your support, it is worth reiterating that it is sensible not to make too many assumptions about potential supporters, in terms of their lifestyle, age, etc. unless you have first done some research on your existing supporters.

The challenge faced by any advertisement is to ring out loud and clear from the cacophony of advertisers' messages that surrounds us every day. This is the wider competition. Non-profit advertisers generically have a number of competitive advantages over the rest of the field:

▼ they are not selling anything;

▼ they are not in it for themselves;

▼ they are often dealing with major social issues.

Compared to the banality of washing powder and breakfast cereals, the subject matter of pressure group advertising will also seem weighty, compelling or even shocking and, particularly in the press, it can often be made to straddle the boundary between advertising and editorial coverage. Responding to a call from a social welfare, human rights or environmental campaign can provide an immediate outlet for the anger or frustration occasioned by the doom, gloom and affairs of state that make up the news.

In creating such an outlet, the campaign is providing an emotional benefit. Such emotional or psychological benefits are very important to a campaign's positioning, particularly as it may be able to supply a depth of benefit which commercial advertisers cannot reach. Other examples are given in the box below. They are the non-profit equivalent to the feel-good factor which commercial advertisers always attempt to capture. Successful advertising, whether commercial or non-profit, must always appeal to self-interest to the extent that it enables people to feel good about themselves.

The extent to which commercial advertisers appreciate the innate advantages that pressure groups possess is evidenced by the growing number of joint commercial/charity promotions, by the avidity with

---

Psychological benefits for campaign positioning

A campaign can:

▼ provide a constructive outlet for the anger or frustration provoked by events;

▼ offer people the chance to register their dissent;

▼ absolve them from the implication that they are condoning policies or practices through their silence or inaction;

▼ provide them with a role in the big issues;

▼ enable them to feel that they are contributing or 'doing their bit';

▼ relieve anxieties about their responsibility for others or the world around them;

▼ enable them to feel that they are planning for the future, particularly as it may affect themselves or their loved ones;

▼ help people to position *themselves* as radicals, as innovators, or simply as people of action rather than passive subjects.

which sales messages now stress the environmental or ethical benefits of their products, and, ultimately, by the shock tactics employed in commercial advertisements like the infamous Bennetton series, which projected images of Mafia victims, people dying from AIDS, and tragedy and war in the third world.

So far we have concentrated on the positioning of non-profit advertising generally, or as distinguished from commercial offers. But positioning is all about making your own offer distinctive, or unique, and that means taking into account the immediate competition as well: other pressure groups, charities and campaigns. This will be of particular importance in those areas, such as animal welfare or the environment, where there are already a considerable number of such groups. To what extent is your target audience different from theirs? What are the distinct benefits you can offer your supporters?

Perhaps the best way to explain how positioning can help in this situation is to use an example. Friends of the Earth and Greenpeace were both very successful during the eighties in attracting support. Yet at first glance their agendas are disarmingly similar: protection of the environment, opposition to air and water pollution. They do of course have a different balance of priorities, and run different campaigns at different times, but, crucially, their appeal to their supporters is structured around a more basic emotional distinction. With its network of local groups and attention to countryside issues, Friends of the Earth engages parochial sympathies and champions the importance of recycling and other constructive alternatives to environmentally damaging practices: its appeal centres on conservation and quality of life. Greenpeace, by contrast, is deliberately confrontational. Best-known for its direct actions, it offers its supporters the feeling of making an uncompromising stand, of sharing in the heroic, encapsulated in advertising slogans such as 'Against all odds'.

The distinctive positioning of the two groups means they appeal to differing audiences. At the same time, each can benefit from the success of the other in raising environmental awareness, and those who have become members of both groups clearly feel they each have something distinct to offer. By the early nineties, Friends of the Earth could boast 240,000 members and Greenpeace a massive 400,000: more than any of the political parties.

Copywriting and design

This section, which covers the process of turning a positioning statement or brief into an actual advertisement, was written with a press advertisement in mind, but is relevant to most printed publicity material from posters to leaflets, flyers and inserts. Choice of media is discussed later, but bear in mind that this will influence both layout and copy.

General principles

For every rule there will always be people ready to break it, in order to make their advertisement(s) stand out from the rest. There are, however, three general principles that apply almost universally.

▼ *Simplicity*. The limited time and space that the advertiser has in which to get her message across makes simplicity a necessity. This will often mean concentrating on just one message or one image. The more elements, whether textual or graphic, that are emphasised, the more they compete with each other, the less the advertisement as a whole will stand out.

▼ *Repetition*. Numerous studies have shown that the public's recall of advertisements improves considerably with the use of repetition. This applies both to repetition *within* an advertisement, whether it is the reiteration of a slogan or the name of the product or campaign, and to repetition *of* the advertisement, or a similar one, as part of a coordinated publicity drive.

▼ *Corporate identity*. This is the name given to the visual characteristics that distinguish an organisation, such as the logo, typography and colour scheme. They should naturally be as attractive and distinctive as possible, but above all they should be consistent across the range of organisational products, from letters to publications to publicity materials to T-shirts. Employing similar typography, colour scheme or other design elements in printed materials will help them to reinforce each other and maximise recognition.

The copy

Once you have worked out your positioning, the next step is to devise a **copy platform** that will make it come alive. The copy platform is the theme or story on which the advertisement is based: it may be that a small donation could save a life – in the *first* world; that joining a campaign gives someone the chance to say what they've always wanted to say to the prime minister; or that buying a fur coat will make one instantly repellent to members of the opposite sex. As the above examples show, subverting expectations, particularly with humour, is the stock-in-trade of much advertising.

In fact, copy platforms in charity and pressure group advertisements frequently work through comparing the good luck of the person addressed with the ill fortune of others (a variation of the feel-good factor). 'Fresh food is now flying in to Biafra', pointed out one famous Christian Aid advertisement, next to a huge picture of an edible fly; 'Your holiday photos are enclosed' reads the outside of a direct mail letter from Amnesty International containing a photograph of a torture victim with the message 'This torture and ill-treatment happens so often in the very sunspots where you and I might go for our holidays'. It is worth noting that, in contrast to these very negative comparisons, most commercial advertising accentuates the positive, relying on the implication that if you buy the product on offer you will be that much more attractive/satisfied/happy.

Why bother with all these positions and platforms? Why not just get on with thinking up good lines? There are two main reasons: firstly, good lines will be easier to create if they have a good story behind them, and secondly, clever, funny or even original advertisements are not necessarily

> **Copywriting: the AIDA formula**
>
> **A** attract the *attention* of the target
>
> **I** raise *interest* in the message or offer
>
> **D** encourage a feeling of *desire*
>
> **A** prompt *action*, whether it is joining the campaign, writing to a councillor, making a donation, sending for more information, voting, buying a book, attending a demonstration, lobbying an MP, recycling the advert....

the most effective (the reason all those washing powder advertisements are so tediously similar is because they work). To achieve a high response, an advertisement should present a sympathetic story or theme that will appeal directly to its target audience, and the role of the actual copy should always remain subordinate to that.

Charity advertisers have discovered over time that the best response to fundraising advertisements often comes from presenting cries for help from people in obvious need. Consequently they have publicised the needs of beneficiaries in increasingly desperate and, arguably, humiliating ways, whether it is starving children in less-developed countries or physically disabled people at home. Quite apart from the fact that such an approach may be counter-productive to an organisation's wider educational or campaigning goals, it may not be very effective in any case if the aim is to raise more than just donations. To attract commitment a campaign needs to evoke a sense of solidarity and the possibility of lasting change, not just pity.

Perhaps the best advice on how to write good copy is to keep reading other people's. The textbooks emphasise the AIDA formula (see box, above) which helps you keep the main aims in mind, but, as with all formulas, can encourage a rather laborious approach. A few other points to note:

▼ The conventional rules of grammar and punctuation are often broken in advertisements for rhetorical effect. Sentences may be without a main verb, or consist of just one word. The following copy is from a Health Education Authority advertisement:

'Perfect eyesight. Clear skin. Normal weight. Healthy appetite. Some of the signs of HIV to look out for in your next sexual partner.

AIDS.

You're as safe as you want to be.'

▼ Short action words, like Send, Save, Go, Fight, Get, Do, Write, etc., are used to heighten pace and stimulate reaction. Conversely, difficult words, long sentences or any grammatical impediment to instant comprehension should be removed from the copy.

▼ Conciseness is all. When it comes to advertising, the complete version is the one that is completely ignored. An anti-war poster that graced the walls of student rooms for the best part of a decade carried the photo of a shot soldier with just the single word 'Why?'

Layout and typography

The optical centre of a page is about a third of the way down vertically and half way along horizontally; i.e. straight between the eyes on a portrait (see below). This is the point on which the eye of the reader naturally falls first. All things being equal, it would then move downwards, but where it travels in practice will depend on how the page is laid out. Good design is about making the eye's journey as pleasing and exciting as possible. The basic principles of good design are balance, contrast, unity, proportion and rhythm.

Most advertisements will have at least one axis which divides the different elements in the layout, whether textual or graphic. If the layout is arranged around an axis half way down or across (i.e. at the mathematical centre) then it will be symmetrically balanced. Symmetry is attractive, but because it divides a space so neatly it can make an advertisement appear smaller than it is, or even disjointed. Dynamic balance, which operates around the optical centre, is more dramatic and encourages greater eye movement. Two examples of simple dynamic balance are given below.

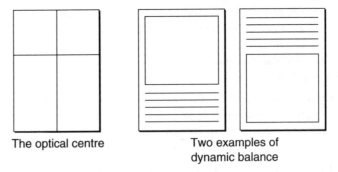

The optical centre   Two examples of
                                   dynamic balance

Not only should the different elements in a layout balance each other, they should also contrast with each other, either in shade, size, or shape. Contrast is what gives individual elements emphasis. It prevents them from either shouting each other down or merging into a background murmur.

One element in a layout which should not be overlooked, and which is very useful for the purpose of providing contrast, is blank or white space. White space is particularly effective in a press advertisement because it is in short supply anywhere else in a newspaper where text and photos cover all the available space. Anything that is surrounded by white space will immediately stand out. However, if you squander your white space by distributing it evenly through the layout, with each headline, graphic or block of text sitting in its own pool of space, you will lose emphasis and end up with a very disjointed result.

Unity will also be hard to achieve if too many typefaces or typestyles are used within an advertisement. It is safe to stick to just two, one for the headline(s) and one for the main or body text, making sure that they are sufficiently contrasted. Blocks of body text should normally be of the same proportions to each other.

Although the different elements in a layout should be of compatible proportions and hold together well enough to give unity to the whole, you don't want to make them too regular or regimented as to make the result boring. The repetition of similar elements, whether graphics, drop capitals, headings or text blocks, strategically placed in a layout will cause the eye to follow them. This is known as rhythm and is another good way of imparting dynamism to your design.

Just as people recognise quotes or photographs, so they recognise typefaces or designs and associate them with particular periods, activities or qualities. Designers use this for effect. A few years ago many charity advertisements used a typewriter-style typeface in order to give a thrifty, low-budget impression. Publicity materials produced by the Socialist Workers' Party make heavy use of monumental block capitals reminiscent of Bolshevik agitation. An interesting variant of this is to design advertisements to suggest other campaigning media. Designing an advertisement in the style of newsprint, for example, can help to stress the importance and currency of the subject. Charter 88 successfully ran petition

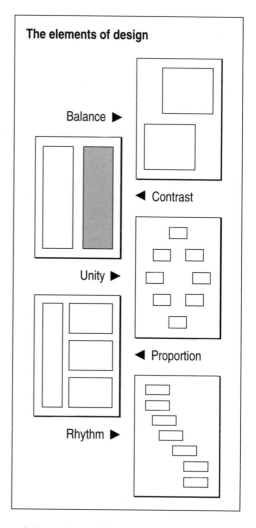

The elements of design

Balance ▶

◀ Contrast

Unity ▶

◀ Proportion

Rhythm ▶

advertisements, calling for signatories off the page, which fitted well with one of their aims which was to revive traditional forms of political activity.

Using agencies

Advertising media are now often divided into above-the-line and below-the-line. Above-the-line media are those which pay commission to recognised advertising agencies and broadly consist of broadcast, press, cinema and outdoor (poster) advertising. The agency's main source of remuneration is technically not the client or advertiser but commission from the media owner with whom the advertisements are placed. Media which do not carry the possibility of commission, like direct mail, hand bills and sales displays or literature, are known as below-the-line. If an agency or consultant is employed on below-the-line work they will normally be paid on a fee basis.

Pressure group work can certainly be attractive to a creative agency – it is easier to be original and hard-hitting if the advertising is for a cause and many of the awards won by agencies are for non-profit advertisements.

The conventional wisdom is that above-the-line advertising is so expensive (even a single quarter-page press advertisement in one of the nationals costs several thousand pounds) that it is important to hire a professional agency to plan and design a campaign in order to get it right. As the cost of the agency is usually bound up with the cost of the media space, attempting a do-it-yourself approach may also save less money than you think.

There now exists, however, a wide variety of agencies who offer different services and are remunerated in different ways, often through a combination of fees and commission. It should be possible to find a package that suits your needs. The big, full-service agencies concentrate on above-the-line mass media advertising and are still paid largely through the commission system. Each client will have one main point of contact in the agency, known as an account executive, but different teams of people are generally used to plan the campaign, design the actual materials and book the media space, as well as providing other marketing or market research services. The smaller creative or *à la carte* agencies, which stick to planning and creating advertising, do not buy media and therefore charge full fees. There are also media buyers or media independents who just plan and book media space; some of these work under contract for, or are even owned by, the bigger agencies. The other main type of agency that may be of interest to pressure groups are direct marketing consultancies; these plan and design direct mail and insert campaigns and are often used by bigger fundraising charities.

Constrained by tight budgets, much pressure group advertising will be small-scale (often below-the-line) and put together without the help of an agency. It is considered first below. On above-the-line work, dealing directly with media owners or with smaller creative agencies can have its advantages: you are more likely to get discounted advertising space, particularly if you are a charity.

The recommendations of other non-profits are useful if you are choosing an agency. The main advertising trade journal, *Campaign*, may also give some leads. Depending on the size of your budget, you may want to ask two or three agencies to pitch for the work in competition with each other. Some groups have used the Advertising Agency Register (AAR – see appendix B for address), an independent organisation which supplies a list of relevant agencies to a client's brief and arranges for it to screen the current work and experience of a chosen short-list.

Below-the-line media

Direct mail

Direct mail is principally used by pressure groups as a means of raising funds and is covered in chapter 3. It is worth reiterating that what sets direct mail apart from most other forms of advertising is that it is a personal form of communication, arriving on the doormat of each recipient, and is therefore guaranteed at least cursory attention. To take advantage of this, the success of direct mail depends heavily on personalisation and emotional appeal.

Leaflets and hand bills

The simple membership leaflet or double-sided hand bill is probably the first piece of advertising that most groups undertake, and one of the most effective. An attractive result can be created using a good word-processor and a high-street 'instant' printer, for little more than the direct costs of photocopying.

The most popular format for membership leaflets is one sheet of A4 size folded into three vertical panels. As these will be used again and again to send to potential members, donors and colleagues, or just to reply to routine inquiries, it is worth investing enough to get them properly designed and printed on a quality paper or artboard. The content should include three things: what the problem is, what the group is doing about it, and what the reader can do. An example of a reply form or coupon for a membership leaflet is given in Chapter 3.

One great advantage of hand bills or leaflets is their versatility: they can be used to advertise everything from publications to events to campaign actions. They can be included in direct mail packages, displayed prominently in offices, meeting rooms, shops or stalls, or handed out at events or demonstrations. *Make sure that everything you put out has a reply coupon*, or at least a contact address, and is branded with the identity of the campaign.

Display posters and fly posting

There are many opportunities for displaying posters other than buying commercial advertising space on hoardings (which is covered in the next section). Silk screen printing methods enable colour posters to be produced quite inexpensively. Opportunities include advertisements in shop windows, on empty walls or fences, and in cafés, halls and offices. Posters and other printed materials are required by law to carry the name and address of the printer or publisher, known as the imprint.

The display of advertisements is controlled by local authorities through regulations made under the Town and Country Planning Act 1990, although they are inconsistently applied. Anything vaguely resembling a notice, placard or advertisement is covered by the regulations, which divide advertisements into three main categories: those excepted from control, like traffic signs or advertisements in the interiors of buildings; those requiring express consent from the local authority, for which a fee is normally payable; and those for which the regulations provide a 'deemed consent'.

Any advertisement has to conform to a number of standard conditions, which mostly have to do with safety and tidiness, but which also stipulate that *no advertisement can be displayed without the permission of the owner of the site used*. Advertisements displayed inside buildings, including those open to the public such as cafés or meeting halls, are excepted from any further control so long as they are not within one metre of any external door, window, or other opening through which they are visible from outside.

A wide variety of other advertisements are granted deemed consent and therefore do not require consent from the local authority. These include most advertisements relating to a group based at the premises where the advertisement is displayed, and any temporary advertisement announcing a local event of a religious, educational, political, social or recreational character, which is not carried on for commercial purposes. In the latter case the advertisement must not be bigger than 0.6 square metre (just under quad crown size), cannot be put up earlier than 28 days before the first day of the event and should be removed within 14 days after the event.

The majority of pressure group posters should fall into one of the above categories, but in other cases express consent may be needed from the local authority. The Act provides that any person who displays an advertisement without the required consent shall be guilty of an offence and liable to a fine on summary conviction, but the local authority would normally request the person to apply for consent or remove the advertisement before prosecuting.

Putting up posters without the consent of the site owner or occupier is known as fly-posting, and is illegal. It is of course very common, particularly on empty shop fronts and fencing enclosing building sites, and the main perpetrators are people advertising local concerts or gigs. Local authorities find it hard to clamp down on, partly because of the time commitment and because most posters will only be on display for a very short time (in fact, the main disincentive appears to be not law enforcement but other fly-posters, who will guard their own patch aggressively). The Act also provides that the person whose activities are advertised, or who benefits from the advertisement, shall not be guilty of an offence if that person can prove that the fly-posing was done without their knowledge or consent. Guidance from the Department of the Environment to enforcement officers is quoted in the box below, and demonstrates the lengths to which they have to go to secure prosecutions.

A variation on fly-posting is the use of small stickers, stuck on everything from lampposts to the inside of tube trains, which some groups have used almost as a simpler and smarter alternative to

---

Control of fly-posting

'LPAs [local planning authorities] may find the following procedures useful as means of bringing successful prosecution of fly-posting under section 224(3) of the 1990 Act:

(1) enforcement officers' duties would include keeping regular watch for any new fly-posting;

(2) enforcement officers should note all new fly-posting sites, photograph them (and date the photographs) and, where possible, remove a copy of the illegal poster for exhibition in Court;

(3) the LPA should take positive steps to find the person who benefits from the advertisement, either by a personal call from an enforcement officer at an address shown, or on the company who printed the posters, or by enquiring at the venue of the function (perhaps necessitating a visit to the function out of normal working hours);

(4) the LPA should advise the person responsible, usually the organiser of an advertised event, that the posters contravene the Control of Advertisements Regulations and give that person a detailed description of the places where they are displayed. (This should be confirmed by recorded delivery letter and the person responsible asked to remove the advertisements);

(5) if the posters are not removed within a reasonable time, the LPA should issue summonses; and

(6) with guidance from the authority's legal adviser, the enforcement officer should prepare a brief statement, supported by photographs and/or a copy of the poster and a copy of the recorded delivery letter which warned the person responsible that the event had been illegally fly-posted.

LPAs using these procedures have been able to satisfy Magistrates' Courts that adequate warning was given, so that the organiser or promoter could no longer claim to be unaware of the illegal advertising. Quite frequently the preliminary warning letter (sub-paragraph (4) above) has been enough by itself to ensure that posters are removed.'

DoE circular 5/92 para 52

graffiti. They also provide a means of twisting the message of existing commercial advertising. Done systematically, either graffiti or stickers have the potential for reversing the effect of an entire corporate advertising campaign. In 1990 a number of big companies backed a campaign for the new employment training scheme, lining up to claim, on huge 48-sheet posters, that they were 'training the workers without jobs to do the jobs without workers'. The slogan had been cleverly chosen partly to counter criticisms that trainees would in effect be removing jobs from paid workers. However, the last word of the slogan was defaced on hundreds of the posters, often overlapped in matching lettering, so that the posters read 'training the workers without jobs to do the jobs without *wages*'.

Other media

Almost any point of contact between your organisation and the outside world presents an opportunity for advertising. Cumulatively, such occasions can make a big difference to the visibility of your campaign. Advertising media include:

▼ *Banners and placards*. Consider getting these printed up, preferably with bold use of colour. If you don't want to lose the element of spontaneity, particularly at demonstrations, produce blank sheets branded with the campaign logo or colours on which slogans can then be handwritten, stamped or stencilled.

▼ *Inserts*. An alternative to buying advertising space in the press is to arrange for leaflets or flyers to be inserted between the pages of a journal or periodical. The advantage is that you can include a lot more information in an insert than in a display advertisement. Inserts will not necessarily be cheaper than buying advertising space, but it is not uncommon in the non-profit press for people to agree to include them without charge.

▼ *Sales displays at stalls or shops*. Table coverings, baskets, backdrops and just about anything else can carry advertising messages. There are now a growing number of fairs and exhibitions organised by and for different parts of the non-profit sector, which can be useful for raising your profile among potential supporters and allies.

▼ *Carrier bags*. Highly visible and providing concrete evidence of demand, distinctive carrier bags can do a lot for high-street shops but are unlikely to work for a pressure group unless it is already well-known.

▼ *Badges and T-shirts*. These are walking advertisements that you can sell.

▼ *Videos*. Good for showing at exhibitions or proselytising in schools or clubs, videos provide both the time and the visual impact to get a message across persuasively. You do need to be able to get captive or semi-captive audiences, even if just for a few minutes. CND's brilliant film *The War Game* (not a video originally of course) formed the bulwark of local groups' consciousness-raising for many years. CSV Media (see appendix B for address), the social action broadcasting arm of Community Service Volunteers, provides media training and support services, including video production. Similar services are provided by the Media Trust (see appendix B for address), which exists to promote the use of the media for social and community purposes.

Perhaps the most important publicity channel of all for campaigns has not yet been mentioned, however. That is word-of-mouth. Unlike commodities, causes do not often take to the fleeting or even subliminal messages that are the currency of modern advertising techniques. A committed supporter, on the other hand, can have a considerable influence on her peer-group, whether through active argument or just the recommendation implicit in her membership of a group. Member-get-member schemes (see chapter 3) are an attempt to formalise the effect of word-of-mouth recommendation.

Above-the-line media

This section deals with the high profile media commonly referred to as above-the-line, although their use will not necessarily involve working with commission-earning agencies. Broadcast advertising by charities, for example, more often takes the form of free appeal slots rather than the more conventional bought advertising space.

The press

Press is by far the most widely used by pressure groups of the above-the-line media, for several reasons. The sheer number and variety of newspapers, magazines and journals in circulation make it very effective for targeting a particular audience. It makes possible a quick response to events or to changing circumstances as space can usually be booked without much notice and the production of advertisements is straightforward. This latter point is also one reason why it is relatively inexpensive compared with TV or billboard advertising, say, which involve costly production processes.

The advertising rates and certified circulation figures for over 12,000 newspapers and periodicals are given in a publication called *British Rate and Data* (BRAD), which is updated monthly. What distinguishes one periodical from another, for advertising purposes, is the size and nature of the readership. Periodicals are commonly classified by circulation coverage (e.g. national, local or regional); frequency (daily, weekly, monthly); principal method of circulation (newsstand, subscription, in-house); and specialist or professional interest.

There is a tendency to be drawn to the larger circulation press, but this may often prove very expensive for the rate of response that it delivers. The ideal advertising medium is a journal whose readership closely matches your own target audience. Note that many local papers are desperate for news stories, so a local pressure group seeking a high profile is probably better off trying to get frequent editorial coverage, rather than buying the advertising space.

The national daily and Sunday newspapers are often divided into the tabloid or popular press and the broadsheet or quality press. More specific readership categorisation follows age, sex and socio-economic groupings. An example of standard rates and circulation figures for the main daily newspapers is given in the box below.

The cost of space will depend not only on the choice of newspaper and the size of the advertisement, but also on factors such as its position within the paper, whether it is located next to editorial material rather than buried among other advertisements, and whether it is the only advertisement on a page (known as a solus position). The unit of measurement used is the single column centimetre or scc (the width of one newspaper column across by one centimetre down). The most popular size amongst non-profits is the 20 centimetre by two-column advertisement, which has the advantage of fitting the front-page and leader page solus positions.

Opting for popular positions will reduce your chances of getting discounts, however. Some newspapers will give discounts to chari-

Advertising rates for national dailies

	scc rate	page rate	20 x 2 col. front solus	readership profile						circulation
				A	B	C1	C2	D	E	
The Express	£97	£23,765	-	93	111	130	97	82	44	1,115,000
Daily Mail	£138	£31,500	-	157	135	126	88	67	42	2,350,000
The Mirror	£133	£31,600	-	26	41	83	136	149	109	2,323,000
Daily Telegraph	£94	£44,500	£6,600	392	222	116	45	23	19	1,050,000
Financial Times	£82	£46,200	-	434	297	77	24	32	6	373,000
The Guardian	£38	£16,300	£6,000	222	274	108	29	22	25	393,000
The Independent	£35	£15,000	£2,400	324	234	112	48	28	13	221,000
The Sun	£146	£34,700	-	28	37	82	142	141	120	3,682,000
The Times	£62	£25,300	-	449	252	93	31	31	26	751,000

Page rates are not directly comparable. Note that broadsheet page is considerably larger than tabloid
Readership profile figures compare to an average of 100 for each group

All figures vary over time and should be taken as approximate   *Source: BRAD, August 1999*

ties and possibly other non-profit groups, but the big reductions come on distress space, i.e. last-minute unfilled space which may be offered at much less than the published rate. To take advantage of this sort of opportunity, you need to be able to move fast. It also helps to know the market – few sales people will admit that cheap space may be available later if they think they can sell it to you now at the full rate.

Outdoor and transport

Poster advertisements range from crown size (about one-and-a-half times A3), used on some information panels; to double crown and quad crown posters located at places like bus shelters; to the 16-, 32-, or 48-sheet posters mounted on hoardings. Space is sold either 'line-by-line' (i.e. site by site) or, more commonly, in blocks of up to 800 sites, by month or half-month.

Compared to the ephemeral nature of most advertising, outdoor is a long-term medium, with posters benefiting from the repetition factor simply by virtue of remaining on the hoardings day-in, day-out. The planning and execution of a poster campaign takes some time, with printing and distribution alone typically taking a couple of months. Although the main expense, as always with advertising, will be hiring the space, production costs for poster advertising can be considerable, particularly with full-colour posters.

One other factor, apart from the cost, would seem to reserve outdoor advertising for the big league only. The majority of posters will be viewed at a distance by passers-by, whether on foot or in a vehicle, so the amount of copy they can carry is minimal. Many keep their copy to one headline, plus the advertiser's name or logo. This makes it very difficult to communicate effectively unless the advertiser already possesses high recognition or awareness among the audience, which few pressure groups will be able to do. With neither an obvious product to sell nor the opportunity to use a reply coupon, many groups would find it tough to get their message across and to prompt the audience into appropriate action. Those groups that do use outdoor advertising tend to be household name charities which give a telephone hotline number for donations and information.

One major exception to these constraints is transport advertising, where the audience, perhaps waiting for a train, will often have time to read advertising copy. Advertisements still will not be able to carry a coupon, but there is at least more opportunity for giving full contact details.

About 70% of available outdoor advertising space in the country is now controlled by a handful of big advertising contractors. These include the Allam Group, Maiden Outdoor, Mills and Allen, and More O'Ferrall. Maiden handles much of the advertising on train platforms and in mainline stations.

It may be possible to obtain free or heavily-discounted space if you approach the contractors directly, rather than go through a media buying agency, and stress your charitable or non-profit nature. For the contractors it provides a means of filling empty sites or covering other posters whose time has expired. The best times of year for this are probably August or January (indeed the whole first quarter) when business is at its slowest. The last two weeks in December may also be worth trying. Some contractors will allow charities to use unpopular sites if they just cover the costs of posting, which is about £50 a panel.

One other low-cost alternative, if you don't wish to resort to fly-posting, is just to book a handful of sites in the hope that you can turn the poster launch into a news event. The political parties now do this regularly at election time. With a pressure group it is unlikely that a new poster will be newsworthy enough by itself to win any press coverage, so it will have to be tied to a stunt or made unusually photogenic. Oxfam launched its 'Hungry for Change' campaign with a living poster featuring famous personalities; a similar approach has since been tried with homeless people sitting or sleeping in a specially constructed poster hoarding. For its advertisement protesting against cuts in the London fire services, the Association of London Authorities constructed a poster site that looked as if it had been half burnt down, smoke billowing out the back, with the headline: 'If they take away 12% of your fire service, what will be left?'

Television and radio

Television and radio are very difficult advertising media for campaigns to break into, due to one of those bizarre anomalies in our society that limits the freedom of speech of non-profit groups. Both free appeal slots and bought advertising space are, under specific conditions, open to charities wishing to publicise services or ask for money, but are largely debarred to groups (including charities) campaigning on issues. Winning editorial coverage on news programmes or documentaries is covered in the next chapter.

The BBC does not currently carry commercial advertising. The BBC's national broadcast appeals are made in special five-minute broadcasts on Radio 4 every Sunday morning, in 'The Week's Good Cause', and on BBC1 about once a month on early Sunday evening in the 'Lifeline' programme. Slots are only allocated to charities of national scope or significance which 'have attained or have a good prospect of attaining an established track record of charitable achievement'. There is a general, but not exclusive, social welfare emphasis.

A number of campaigning charities do secure BBC appeal slots: in 1998, for example, they included Maternity Alliance, the Terrence Higgins Trust, Public Concern at Work, Redress and the Rainforest Foundation. Appeal money raised varies from a couple of thousand pounds to over £50,000. There is now fierce competition among charities applying for appeal slots, which are allocated by the BBC Appeals Advisory Committee, meeting three times a year. The BBC will organise the programme production so, with nothing to lose, you might as well apply. Applications should be made about six months before a prospective appeal would be broadcast, to the Appeals Office (see appendix B).

The independent broadcasting industry is regulated by the Independent Television Commission (ITC) and the Radio Authority, in accordance with the statutory requirements of the Broadcasting Act 1990. As with the BBC, there are some free opportunities for broadcast appeals, and prospective groups should contact the individual broadcasting companies directly. The rules for television are a little different from those for radio.

Programmed appeal slots on television are only open to charities, or emergency appeals coordinated by a 'responsible public fund'. There are also Community Service Announcements (CSAs), which enable local voluntary and community organisations to publicise their services and which are transmitted free of charge between programmes. No appeals for funds are allowed during CSAs. They are not confined to charities and therefore are open to other kinds of non-profit group, but note that 'CSAs are not acceptable from bodies the objectives of which are wholly or mainly of a political nature ... CSAs should not show partiality in matters of political, industrial or religious controversy.'

The Radio Authority regulations are a little more relaxed in that appeal slots are not strictly confined to charities, but there is still an emphasis on respectability: 'Before appealing for funds, goods, or services on behalf of a charity or other body or giving editorial opportunities for a charity or body to describe its activities or appeal for funds, goods or services, Licence Holders [i.e. broadcasters] must ensure that the organisation concerned is either registered with the Charity Commission or that its *bona fides* is satisfactory.'

When it comes to bought advertising space, there are restrictions here too. 'Advertisements soliciting donations or

---

Restrictions on broadcast advertising

Politics, Industrial and Public Controversy

No advertisement may be inserted by or on behalf of any body whose objects are wholly or mainly of a political nature, and no advertisement may be directed towards any political end. No advertisement may have any relation to any industrial dispute. No advertisement may show partiality as respects matters of political or industrial controversy or relating to current public policy.

NOTES:
(i) The term 'political' here is used in a wider sense than 'party political'. The prohibition precludes, for example, issue campaigning for the purposes of influencing legislation or executive action by central or local government. Where there is a risk that advertising could breach this prohibition prospective advertisers are strongly advised to seek advance guidance from licensees before developing specific proposals.

(ii) The Broadcasting Act 1990 specifically exempts advertisements of a public service nature inserted by, or on behalf of, a government department from the prohibition of advertisements having 'any relation to any industrial dispute'.

ITC Code of Advertising Standards and Practice, Rule 10

promoting the needs or objects of UK bodies whose activities are financed wholly or mainly from donations' are only accepted from charities. In addition, advertisements for charities must 'handle with care and discretion matters likely to arouse strong emotions in the audience' and 'avoid presenting an exaggerated impression of the scale or nature of the social problem to which the work of the charity is addressed …' In practice, very few charities have bought commercial advertising space on television, largely because of the prohibitive cost.

Wider restrictions contained in the ITC code on advertising by political parties, trade unions or other pressure groups are quoted in the box opposite; very similar wording is used in the Radio Authority code.

Cinema

If you want to get your message across in moving pictures but cannot find a way around the regulations governing television coverage, or the cost, cinema advertising might provide the answer. The cinema is arguably the most impressive advertising medium of all, and is well-suited to targeting young people (18–24 year olds) who are the most frequent movie-goers.

Advertisements are always shown before the main feature and will be the same for every showing. The basic unit for buying space is one screen for one week, where the cost will depend on audience size, but most advertising space is sold in bigger packages by specialist agencies. Networked packages can get very expensive, but there are cheaper alternatives that could suit campaigns: Pearl and Dean, for example, have an Art Screen Package covering 56 screens round the country where a 30 second commercial can be shown for about £5,500 a week. Some cinemas have allowed charities to organise a collection after the advertisement is shown.

Evaluating advertising

The reason why the advertising budget is often the first thing to be cut when a company hits hard times is that the effect of advertising is very difficult to evaluate precisely. Even if responses can be traced back to individual advertisements or campaigns, this will take no account of the cumulative impact of publicity, from which advertising gains much of its potency. To pick just one example, research on broadcast appeals has shown that although factors such as the time of year and even audience size seem to have little effect on amounts of money raised, an appeal *is* more likely to be successful if it is organised as part of a wider publicity campaign on behalf of the organisation or cause concerned.

Initial donations received in response to display advertising rarely exceed the costs of the advertising: the real benefit comes from securing new supporters who can be persuaded by direct mail to contribute time and again in the future.

A system for keying and monitoring advertisements is essential to gain enough information for making decisions on the basis of past performance: continuing and improving successful approaches, and scrapping or varying unsuccessful ones. Keying is linked to the method of response. If the advertisement is one carrying a reply form (e.g. a leaflet), the simplest method is to print a different character in the corner of the form for every separate mailshot or method of distribution (printers are accustomed to being asked to do this). Completed replies are then logged so that you know what the response was from, say, the insert in *New Statesman* compared with the insert in *New Internationalist*. With advertisements that just carry a contact address (e.g. a poster) the key can be incorporated by varying the address slightly: using a different name or different set of initials for the addressee, for example, or creating fictitious departments such as Dept. A, Dept. B. For telephone replies, callers will have to be asked where they heard about the organisation from.

It is not easy to predict the response from new approaches. A display advertisement in the *Guardian* may seem like a dead cert at the time, but may turn out to be less cost-effective than a regular advertisement in *Social Work Today*. Successful advertising is based on varying your approaches, rigorously monitoring the response, and building on what works.

The advertising control system

Advertisements in non-broadcast media in the UK are regulated by the British Codes of Advertising and Sales Promotion. These make stipulations about the content of press, poster, direct mail, cinema, and other non-broadcast advertisements. See 'Television and radio' above for controls on advertising in broadcast media.

The Codes are supervised by the independent Advertising Standards Authority (ASA) to ensure that they operate in the public interest. Their principal concern is that advertisements should be 'legal, decent, honest and truthful', and members of the public are invited to complain to the ASA if they think particular advertisements do not match up.

The system is a self-regulatory or voluntary system agreed by the advertising industry. The Codes as such are therefore not enforceable by law, and the principal sanctions are public criticism by the ASA and ostracism by other bodies in the industry. For both advertisers who need space and agencies who need commission these sanctions can be serious: agency recognition, for example, requires acceptance of the Codes. For a small pressure group putting up posters in shop windows and on factory walls, however, they can be ignored. A group called the Committee of Advertising Practice (CAP) brings together trade and professional associations within the advertising industry to try and make sure the Codes are observed.

The Codes were amended in 1993 to bring advertisements dealing with issues or public policy, whether placed by charities, pressure groups, trade unions or corporate advertisers, within the requirements to be honest and truthful. In particular it obliges advertisers to have substantiation to support factual claims made within advertisements, which should be both accurate in their material details and truthful in the general impression created. The rules extend to advertisements placed by central or local government or by other advertisers on the subject of government policy, but not to advertisements by or about political parties. To what extent that is an unintentional smear on the integrity of our political parties, I do not know.

In its guidance for charities and pressure groups, the ASA notes: 'Charities often use graphic and shocking images to attract attention to their causes. The Codes permit the use of shock tactics where the subject matter justifies the use of such an approach.' This does not, however, give non-commercial advertisers 'carte blanche to offend'. In 1999, the ASA upheld a complaint about a poster by a Northern Ireland anti-abortion group with the headline 'Death Threat: Abortion Kills Babies', on the grounds that, given the political situation, the headline was insensitive and likely to cause serious or widespread offence. However, it refused to uphold a complaint from the Immigration Service Union about a Refugee Council advertisement on the subject of immigration officers and refugees that was headlined: 'Your chance to play God with someone else's life'.

In 1998, the ASA received a total of 310 complaints relating to 161 advertisements by charities and pressure groups. Of these, 94 were upheld, relating to 15 advertisements. Complaints are often made by other interest groups as well as members of the public. The Countryside Alliance complained in 1999 about a press advertisement against fox hunting by the International Fund for Animal Welfare; the ASA ruled that the claim that 10,000 foxhounds a year are shot because 'they're too old or too friendly to chase foxes' was unsubstantiated, but the claim that foxes were 'simply ripped apart' before death was demonstrably true. The CAP offers a free copy advice service to intending advertisers to help them avoid provoking complaints (or at least reduce the chances of a complaint being upheld).

Although the British Codes of Advertising and Sales Promotion are very liberal compared to the controls on broadcast media, individual advertising contractors may have their own house rules which are more restrictive.

Legal controls on advertising and publishing

In addition to the rules on the content of advertisements described above, which form a voluntary system of controls, there are also other restrictions which are enforceable in law. The bulk of these are part of civil law, and require legal proceedings to be taken by an aggrieved party, but the consequences are potentially much more serious than those of flouting codes like the British Codes of Advertising and Sales Promotion. Of particular importance is the law concerning plagiarism and defamation.

Copyright and passing off

If a substantial part of someone else's work, whether written or graphic, is reproduced in an advertisement or publication, there is a risk of being sued for breach of copyright. Pressure groups are unlikely to want to plagiarise material in order to exploit it commercially, but they might find themselves in the situation of reproducing material in order to make a point or pursue a purpose with which the copyright holder disagrees vehemently.

There is no simple quantitative test to define what is meant by 'substantial', but the mere use of a phrase or even a title from a work will not usually be sufficient to infringe the copyright (but see 'passing off' below). There is also no copyright in ideas, only in the concrete written or graphic form they take. To infringe copyright, reproduction has to be derivative rather than just coincidental: there would be no problem in publishing, say, a similar list of information to that in a copyright work if the information had been gathered by independent research.

In some instances unapproved reproduction may not infringe copyright even if it is substantial. The most significant of these are:

▼ *Fair dealing*. This covers the reproduction of reasonable extracts from a work for the purposes of criticism or review, reporting current events, or private study. Proper acknowledgement of the source must be given. Quite lengthy extracts can be used, but the use must be 'fair': only so much should be reproduced as is necessary for the permitted purpose. 'Fair', here, has nothing to do with being critically objective – you can be as scathing as you like.

▼ *Public interest*. Copyright will not be infringed if reproduction is held to be in the public interest; for example, if it serves to expose corrupt or unethical behaviour. A public interest defence may be appropriate in the case of a pressure group publishing leaked government documents.

Government documents are Crown or Parliamentary copyright. However, so long as the original is not used as camera-ready copy, the reproduction of substantial extracts from bills, Acts of Parliament and statutory instruments, as well as *Hansard*, is permitted without express authorisation. Acknowledgement is required. Reproducing substantial extracts (defined here as more than 5 per cent) from other parliamentary papers and any extracts from non-parliamentary papers will normally require permission.

When it comes to unauthorised publication of departmental memos, drafts and other government working papers there are laws other than copyright to fall foul of. Breach of confidence covers the disclosure of unpublished information where a duty of confidence exists, for example on the part of an employee, although here again public interest is a defence. Those who publish leaked or confidential information concerned with security and intelligence, defence, foreign affairs or crime may be found guilty of an offence under the Official Secrets Act.

The main thrust of copyright law, however, is the protection of property, and the courts may be reluctant to interfere unless the prospect of financial loss is involved. In their invaluable book *Media Law* (see appendix C), Geoffrey Robertson QC and Andrew Nicol quote an example from 1983:

> 'The Campaign for Nuclear Disarmament printed a pamphlet *30 Questions and Answers about CND*. On its cover the CND symbol was interwoven with a map of Britain. The Coalition for Peace Through Security, a group opposed to CND, produced a counter-publication, *30 Questions and Honest Answers About CND*. The design of the cover was very similar except that the CND symbol had been adapted to resemble a hammer and sickle. CND was refused an interlocutory injunction because it had suffered no financial loss and the judge was reluctant to restrain political controversy. *(Kennard v Lewis [1983] FSR 346.)*'

Finally, there is the common law claim of 'passing off', available to those whose commercial interests are damaged by others' works or products being passed off as their own. Big companies use it fiercely to protect their brand names, and pressure groups which ape their products in order to make a political point should take care to ensure that the name, packaging and circumstances of distribution are not sufficiently similar to the original to invite proceedings for passing off.

Defamation

The usual short-hand distinction between the two types of defamation, slander and libel, is that the former is spoken and the latter written. However, libel extends to cover other statements, even if spoken, that have a widespread or lasting existence, such as those made on television or radio programmes, with slander reserved for more transitory acts of defamation. The distinction matters because, with a few exceptions, slander unlike libel is only actionable if the plaintiff can prove that it has caused him financial loss.

Defamation is about damage to reputation. Statements are considered defamatory if they have the effect of lowering someone's standing in the eyes of respectable and reasonable people. Just publishing untruths about someone will not necessarily constitute defamation: to write, for example, that *x* was wearing a black shirt in the town square on Saturday might be untrue but it would not be libellous – unless, that is, the occasion happened to be a neo-Nazi rally. Common examples of libels are allegations of dishonesty, lawbreaking, infidelity or professional incompetence. The main pointers to help identify whether a particular statement may prompt a libel action are given in the box below.

Justification – showing that an allegation is substantially true – is an absolute defence to libel. There is even some give and take in the case of a number of connected allegations, if 'the words not proved to be true do not materially injure the plaintiff's reputation, having regard to the truth of the remaining charges' (Defamation Act 1952). Note that simply repeating a libel first published elsewhere, or inserting crafty phrases like 'it is rumoured that' or 'allegedly', will not make an untrue statement any less libellous.

The note to question 3b) in the box below refers to the defence of 'fair comment'. This defence will fail if the claimant can prove that the defendant was acting 'maliciously', in the technical legal sense of being dishonest or reckless with regard to the truth of the facts on

---

Is it libel?

A statement may lead to a successful action for libel if the answer to questions 1–4 below is in each case 'yes'.

1. Is the statement capable of carrying a defamatory meaning?
   Is it injurious to reputation, whether personal or professional?

2. Is the statement understood to refer to the potential claimant?
   Whether or not they are mentioned by name, and irrespective of the author's intention, will it be understood as referring to the potential claimant? If someone is part of a group that is the subject of a defamatory statement, she will only be able to sue if the group is small enough for the comment to reflect on her personally.

3. a) If a statement of fact, is it either incorrect or unprovable?
   The burden of proof falls on the publisher to demonstrate that 'facts' are true.

   or b) If a statement of opinion, are the facts on which the opinion is based incorrect?
   Opinions on matters of public interest, however eccentric or unbalanced, will not be libellous if they honestly refer to known facts. But expressions of opinion which do not make reference to the facts on which they are based are liable to be treated as assertions of fact themselves.

4. Has the statement been made known to at least one person other than the potential claimant?
   'Publication' is understood in this narrow sense. Successful proceedings for libel have been brought on account of statements made in press releases or in private letters to third parties.

which the opinion was based. So long as it is honestly derived, the opinion itself may be exaggerated or even spiteful.

The proceedings of some public occasions are 'privileged', which means that statements made at them or reports about them are protected from actions for defamation:

▼ Absolute privilege covers, *inter alia*, what politicians say in Parliament, official statements and reports made by ministers, and proceedings in court.

▼ Qualified privilege, which protects speakers or authors unless they act maliciously (in the sense defined above), extends to accurate reports of the above proceedings and to tribunals, company AGMs and other instances where honest complaints are made to a person in authority who has a duty to investigate them (e.g. an Ombudsman), or where people share information in which they have a mutual interest (e.g. an employment reference).

The political decisions made by politicians are almost by definition matters of legitimate public interest. With those who operate further from the centre of the public sphere, however, much greater care must be taken. Criticising the honesty or professional competence of a business person or local government officer, for example, is a tried and tested route to a libel writ.

Pressure groups targeting the commercial world, then, should beware, particularly as companies themselves can sue if an allegation damages their business reputation. Anti-fur group Lynx went into liquidation in 1993 after it was successfully sued by a mink farmer over allegations that mink were kept in unsuitable conditions. The award for damages came to £40,000, with Lynx also facing a £250,000 bill for costs. Two of the Lynx staff, including the director, were declared bankrupt.

You can be sued even if a libel was unintentional. However, in such a case you can limit any further liability by making an offer of amends: essentially a published correction and apology with an offer to pay legal costs and such compensation (if any) as may be agreed. The Lynx example also illustrates that a libeller will not be able to hide behind her organisation or employer. Both the organisation that publishes a libel and the individual author(s) or editor(s) are usually sued. Those who work for unincorporated bodies may find themselves at correspondingly greater financial risk, as the organisation's lack of corporate status means it cannot itself be sued.

And the risks are considerable. Defamation cases are tried in the High Court and claimants have the right to insist on trial by jury, rather than judge alone, both of which factors inflate costs considerably (although the Defamation Act 1996 introduced a welcome new procedure for summary disposal of a claim for defamation – planned to come into force in 2000 – with damages not exceeding £10,000, where the court holds either that the claimant has no realistic prospect of success, or that there is no realistic defence to the claim, and there is no other reason why the claim should be tried). The complexity of the law in this area means that trials tend to drag on, costs mounting further. The level of damages awarded by juries is also notoriously unpredictable, and at times out of all proportion to the injury suffered. The result is that libel proceedings are a form of redress in practice reserved for the rich and the corporate.

It is in the nature of campaigning that unpleasant facts have to be brought to light and responsibility for them pinned onto identifiable individuals. A basic grasp of the law will be of use to groups concerned about their liability in defamation, but should only emphasise the need to be sure of your facts and not publish what you don't know to be true and, in the event, can prove to be true. Quite beyond the issue of civil liability, such a policy will reap dividends for the credibility of a campaign.

6 Campaigning on the internet

The internet is probably the single most important new tool for campaigning to have appeared over the last decade and its potential is far from being fully exploited. Most campaigning is about exposing things that are wrong, publicising alternatives and building support for change. The internet has brought revolutionary advances to all these aspects of campaigning.

Providing estimates of internet usage is dangerous for any author, as the figures are likely to be out of date by the time the reader sees them. Internet traffic grew tenfold every year in the late 1990s and it is estimated that between a quarter and a third of European homes will have internet access in the first years of the new millennium. The World Trade Organisation estimated that by that time e-commerce (goods and services sold through the net) would top $300 billion a year.

This huge growth in the functions and use of the internet has been hailed by pundits as an information revolution, the most socially significant technological advance since the industrial revolution, only happening at many times the speed. Politicians proselytise about the 'information superhighway' and the power of the internet to transform everything from business to education.

However, despite what is often said, the key innovation brought by the internet is not an expansion in access to information (although it has to some degree achieved that). It is the internet's power to enable multi-directional communication between large numbers of disparate people, cheaply and almost instantaneously. For campaigners, that means that the net can be used to:

▼ locate and communicate with potential supporters or communities of interest all over the country or the world;

▼ mobilise supporters cheaply and very quickly;

▼ provide people with new and easy ways to become involved in a campaign;

▼ monitor or track events as they happen and update supporters;

▼ subvert censorship or other controls on publishing information, opening up the possibility of communication without borders.

The most successful advertising medium of all, it is often said, is word-of-mouth. People are most influenced not by what they read or see, but by what they are told by their family, friends or peers in the kitchen, the pub or the workplace. The really successful internet communicators are those who recognise the net's power to extend word-of-mouth into cyberspace.

Internet basics

Most readers of this book will probably already be internet users and can skip this section. But for those who are not already familiar with the net, the brief explanations below will be necessary for understanding what follows.

Getting started

The internet is basically an international network of computers set up to exchange information and all you need to get access to that network is a computer and a modem to connect you through your telephone line to an internet service provider. You can get some form of internet access from almost any computer, but to get reasonable performance you will need a computer with enough memory: any supplier will advise on current requirements. The development of Wireless Application Protocol also means that you can get limited internet access just from a mobile phone.

There are a large number of competing internet service providers (ISPs), including the big online services such as AOL (America Online) and Microsoft Network. The main criteria for deciding which to go for are performance (basically the speed with which you can access different chunks of information) and charges. Computer and internet magazines frequently test and compare different ISPs. Make sure you get one which has a local dial-up connection.

A full internet connection will include at least one e-mail account, access to the World Wide Web and to newsgroups. ISPs often charge a monthly or annual fee to provide internet access, sometimes with an initial set-up charge, although free trials are common. There are also a growing number of providers offering 'free' access, led by Freeserve which was established by the electronics retailer Dixons. These ISPs make their money through a cut on call charges and through advertising.

If you are wary of getting started, or have got online but still find it a bit confusing, you can always pop into a cybercafe and get the attendant to run you through the basics.

Surfing the web

The World Wide Web is the home of electronic publishing and most of it can be accessed free of charge. It is like a global library in which many of the books are continuously updated. Only these books – known as web sites – can also contain sound and moving pictures, can be read by thousands of people at the same time, and can often answer questions and handle transactions.

Your ISP will have provided you with a web browser such as Internet Explorer or Netscape Navigator. To access a web site all you have to do is type in its address or URL (Uniform Resource Locator). One part of the address, the domain type, should give you an indication of the type of organisation hosting the site, such as *org* for non-profit organisation, *com* for commercial organisation (*co* in the UK), *edu* for educational body (*ac* in the UK) and *gov* for government body. Some sites of general use to campaigners are listed in the box. If you don't know the address, or are just looking for information on a given topic, you can use a 'search engine' or directory like AltaVista, HotBot or Yahoo. These will give you a list of web sites matched with any word or phrase you type in. Most web sites will contain electronic links to other relevant sites.

Electronic mail

Electronic mail or e-mail is now so widely used that it hardly needs explanation. You can send e-mail down the road or halfway across the world almost instantaneously and for a fraction of the cost of traditional post. Documents, graphics and other electronic files can also be sent, simply by attaching them to an e-mail. Unlike traditional post, you can also access your mail from anywhere in the world, simply by logging on to an appropriate computer.

Newsgroups

Newsgroups are online discussion groups that function like public bulletin boards, where people can post notices, questions and comments and anyone can post replies. Newsgroups are located on a part of the internet called Usenet and they cover thousands of different subjects from censorship to medical politics to shortwave radio to feminism, as well as a huge array of hobbies and fan clubs. Despite their name, they are not about news, but if you want to foster debate on an issue or are looking for an elusive piece of information, you can post a question to an appropriate newsgroup. When the answers come, you have to use your judgement to distinguish the authoritative and erudite from the ill-formed or plain mad. Another part of the net houses 'chat rooms' or IRC (Internet Relay Chat) where discussions are conducted live.

Useful web sites

Monitoring the news

http://news.bbc.co.uk	Domestic and world news from the BBC, 'updated every minute'.
www.cnn.com	The best US-originated news site, covering global events.
www.the-times.co.uk	Carries the text of the *Times* newspaper from 2am every morning. See *www.newsunlimited. co.uk* for the *Guardian* and the *Observer, www. independent.co.uk* for the *Independent*, and *www.nytimes.com* for the *New York Times*.
www.pa.press.net	The news centre site for the Press Association, including breaking stories and other feeds for the UK media.
www.ecola.com	Provides listing and links to English-language newspapers worldwide. See also News Resource at *www.newo.com/news*

Politics and government

www.open.gov.uk	The main government site, providing links to government departments and hundreds of other governmental bodies.
www.parliament.uk	Covers parliamentary business in both the Commons and the Lords.
www.labour.org.uk *www.conservative-* *party.org.uk* *www.libdems.org.uk*	Welcome to spin doctor land.

International politics

www.cec.org.uk	Run by the UK office of the European Commission, this site includes contacts in EU institutions and a guide to other EU information resources.
www.undp.org	Extensive information and statistics on the UN's role in international affairs and development.
www.whitehouse.gov	A friendly welcome from the US president.
www.trytel.com/~aberdeen	Mailing addresses for every nation's leaders – 'with accessibility will come accountability ...'
www.stm.it/politic	A guide to international political resources on the net.

Activism

www.oneworld.net	A 'supersite' bringing together web sites managed by over 600 development organisations worldwide, with a news service, discussion fora and ongoing campaigns.
www.greennet.org.uk	Part of a global network designed for environment, peace and development groups, hosting web sites of over 300 members.
www.citizensconnection.net	Set up by campaigning organisation Common Purpose, this site is online from September 2000. It aims to be a forum for people to find out how to get involved in shaping their communities.

Research

www.ipl.org	'The first public library of the internet.'
www.bibliofind.com	With millions listed, this is now the best way to get out-of-print or used books.
www.lawrights.co.uk	Accessible guide to English law, concentrating on personal legal issues.

Publishing on the World Wide Web

Publishing your own web site on the internet enables you to attract new interest or support and also to update your existing contacts or supporters as regularly as you wish. Many internet users now see the web as their first port of call for information about almost anything, so having your own web site is now regarded as pretty essential for any self-respecting charity or pressure group.

Establishing a web site is surprising cheap and easy. At its simplest, it just involves converting your text into HTML (Hyper Text Markup Language) and then finding a space on the web to put it. There are now a range of HTML editing programmes available which automate much of the process of conversion (to see what HTML looks like, select 'View Source' from the browser menu when you are in any web page).

If you want to get your site noticed and revisited, however, it is worth investing in a good web designer. Many early sites resembled long leaflets or even books – text-heavy and with a narrative or linear structure – which are not very convenient in electronic format. An attractive and uncluttered appearance is obviously an asset, but most important of all is good sign-posting and navigation, so that visitors can find the information they want easily, move around and in and out of the site quickly, and you can steer them towards things you particularly want them to see.

Many ISPs now offer with a standard account enough web space to host a simple site. Alternatively, you can find a home in a virtual city at *www.geocities.com* and you don't even need to know HTML. But here again, if you really want people to remember your URL or address, you should go that bit further and have your own domain name. A URL with a long file path such as *www.geocities.com/hardtofind/9536/obscure.html* is hardly an aid to memory or easy access. By contrast, compare most of the URLs in the box above, which stop at the domain name. To register a domain name, contact your ISP or see *www.internic.net* or *www.netnames.com*

Unlike conventional forms of publicity such as leaflets, advertisements with response coupons, or hotlines, the volume of visitors or enquirers received by a web site does not have any automatic resource implications. You can go on receiving any number of visitors without ever having to reprint a leaflet or staff a response line. It is easy to install a hit counter (for details see *www.countmaster.com*) so that you can see how many people are 'hitting' or visiting your site.

To publicise your web site, register it first with all the main search engines or directories. Investigate other sites with similar themes or sites set up by sympathetic organisations and see whether you can set up reciprocal links so people can access your web site from theirs and *vice versa*. Announce the site in newsgroups on relevant subjects. And make sure your URL is listed on everything else you produce: letterhead, compliments slips, leaflets, advertisements, posters, business cards, merchandise, everywhere where your postal address is listed and more.

Real-time publishing and netcasting

Because a web site can be altered or supplemented easily at any time, it is an ideal medium to keep supporters updated or to keep campaigners or members of the public informed of fast-moving events. This monitoring or tracking capability of the net – virtual publishing in real time – can be of key importance in a range of campaign situations.

After the Bosnian war, the International Criminal Tribunal for the Former Yugoslavia indicted dozens of men suspected of war crimes and crimes against humanity. However, by 1997 the vast majority of them lived relatively openly in the Bosnian Serb Republic and other parts of the Former Yugoslavia, despite the presence of large numbers of UN peacekeeping forces, who seemed anxious not to provoke confrontation by carrying out arrests. Angered by UN inaction, human rights activists tracked the movements of 66 fugitives, supposedly in hiding. They posted a log or their whereabouts on the net, partly 'to mock and embarrass' those who pretended not to know where they were. Within two years, nearly half of the men indicted by the Tribunal had been brought to justice.

The flexibility of electronic publishing also adds a new edge to the cut and thrust of debate. A business supporter of the Tunisian authorities established a web site praising Tunisia's human rights record which he set up with an address which had the word 'amnesty' in the title. When Amnesty International discovered this new site in 1998 it was particularly concerned because its own web site, which detailed extensive human rights violations for which the Tunisian authorities were responsible, was blocked in Tunisia. So the human rights group set up a new site called 'Rhetoric vs Reality' at *www.amnesty.org/tunisia* which displayed the offending site within a frame which provided a running rebuttal of the claims made, juxtaposing the rhetoric of the official Tunisian line with the reality of the human rights situation in the country.

The development of webcam technology also means that it is relatively simple to relay events live through a web site. When a group of environmental protestors staged a sit-in in the London offices of Shell in 1999, the company quickly cut off the office phone lines and power supply. But using a digital camera, a laptop computer and a mobile phone, the protestors were still able to e-mail the media and to broadcast or 'netcast' the protest live on the internet.

Internet protest

Many of the most novel features of the internet are those which provide opportunities for interaction with visitors to a web site or automate processes or transactions which would otherwise be labour intensive.

Now that credit card payments and other transactions can be made securely on the net, perhaps the most obvious application for charities and pressure groups is the online handling of donations and membership subscriptions and renewals. With a strong appeal message and subscription forms all ready on your site, the web provides the most passive form of fundraising you can devise – and none the less effective for that.

But the interactive power of the net as a campaigning medium outdoes even its potential for raising money. The Environmental Defence Fund in the US pioneered a new form of electronically-assisted protest in 1998 with their web site *www.scorecard.org* The site contained a mass of scientific data on emissions and statistics on companies' pollution records, cross-referenced by geographical area, all easy to access and sort using the software provided. A visitor to the site could swiftly identify the top polluters in their area and then find a ready-made letter of protest for them to edit and fire off to the company's manager or the authorities. At one stroke, Scorecard placed the detailed, tailored information required for effective protest on the desktops of millions of potential activists. Environmental groups in the UK quickly set about copying the idea.

Simply providing the opportunity or the prompt for spontaneous interaction in the internet community – the millions of people who use the net every day – can be even more effective in spreading awareness and protest on the virtual grapevine. Perhaps the easiest way to do this is to set up a mailing list or a newsgroup on Usenet.

First check out and contribute to relevant existing mailing lists or newsgroups to raise interest – or better, get your supporters to do so. With current newsgroups numbering some 30,000 and counting, you should find several related to your field of work just through doing a search at *www.deja.com* You can also search mailing lists and other discussion fora at *www.liszt.com* or *www.reference.com*

The next obvious step is to start a mailing list on e-mail to circulate information, articles and views between those who are interested, and watch the list grow. For a list of any size, you will need to go through an automated list manager: ask your ISP or look at a service like *www.coollist.com* You will have to decide whether you are happy for messages to be relayed automatically or whether you are prepared to put in the time required to 'moderate' the list, or screen the messages before they are circulated. Note that you should never advertise merchandise for sale or appeal for donations through newsgroups or open mailing lists: you'll just be bombarded with complaints and abuse.

When the list is active enough, you can then start your own newsgroup. In the alternative newsgroups category, or alt. hierarchy as it is known, this is very straightforward and doesn't require clearance from anyone. Consult *news: alt.config* for advice. Be aware, however, that this is a naturally democratic forum and you won't be able to manage everything that is circulated or discussed.

One of the unique features of the internet is the ease with which it can pull together geographically disparate groups of people who share rare or unusual interests. For very specialist pressure groups, that can make all the difference to their supporter base. And for self-help or survivor groups, it can provide a life-transforming service.

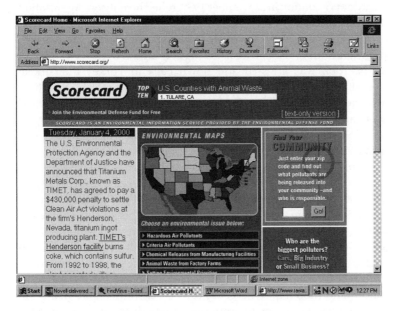

Mobilising

The hard slog of mobilising for big demonstrations or events has never been the same since the development of popular internet use. Spreading the word through e-mail lists, newsgroups and a web site gets the call out to receptive audiences cheaply and quickly, unlike the time-consuming, scattergun approach of leaflets and posters (it is also less likely to bring your plans to the early attention of those you are protesting against). Protests such as Reclaim the Streets and Critical Mass, which organise mass cycling actions to hold up urban traffic, have used the internet to mobilise successfully time and again. The Carnival Against Capital in the City of London in June 1999, and the big demonstrations against the World Trade Organisation in

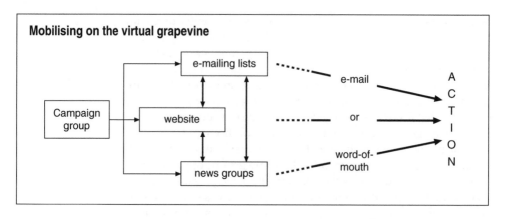

Mobilising on the virtual grapevine

Seattle and London in November 1999, relied heavily on organisation through the net.

In February 1999 Abdullah Öcalan, the leader of the Kurdish Workers' Party (PKK), who had sought refuge in the Greek embassy in Nairobi, was arrested and flown back to Turkey by Turkish security agents. In a simultaneous, coordinated protest which took the world by surprise, Kurdish demonstrators surrounded Greek and Kenyan embassies in some 20 countries. The Greek embassy in London was taken over by a group of 60 Kurds, while others staged protests from Moscow to Berlin, Stockholm to Jerusalem. Begun with a simple e-mail message to members of the Kurdish diaspora, thousands of supporters across Europe were mobilised within hours and protests coordinated over the following days through the internet.

It is in fact in international campaigning that the internet really comes into its own. Amnesty International's urgent action scheme exists to initiate immediate international protest when a human rights emergency occurs: when it is feared that a prisoner about to be tortured, for example, or a set of executions scheduled to take place. Information about the emergency can be transmitted via e-mail from the country of danger to Amnesty campaigners in London; once verified, it is e-mailed with details of how to protest to volunteer activists around the world. Suddenly the prison authorities or minister of justice are on the receiving end of e-mail messages, faxes, telegrams and letters from countries all over the world, showing they know what is happening to the prisoner(s) and asking for their human rights to be upheld. In about one third of cases, a positive outcome follows: for example, torture stops or a prisoner is released.

Mail-bombing and hacktivism

When protest e-mail arrives in sufficient quantities to disrupt the receiver's service, this is known as mail-bombing. Done systematically, it is a form of electronic picketing (see chapter 11) which can be employed against corporate nerve centres as well as government offices, although in practice the flexibility of the internet means that a corporate user with any technical skill will soon be able to sidestep the disruption.

But internet activists have gone one step further by adopting the techniques of hacking – getting through computer security systems – for political ends. One of the most popular types of action is to gain access to official web sites and then subvert the messages they carry.

In July 1998, two protest groups, Milworm and Ashtray Lumberjacks, targeted the world's nuclear powers with an organised mass hack of over 300 sites across the world, replacing selected web pages with a picture of a mushroom-shaped cloud and anti-nuclear statements.

During 1998 Indonesian government sites were repeatedly targeted by hackers either protesting against human rights abuses or calling for autonomy for Indonesian-occupied East Timor. However, human rights protestors do not hold the monopoly on such techniques and retaliation can lead to a full-scale information war or 'cyber-war'. In early 1999 disruptive hackers attacked the East Timorese top-level internet domain which had been established from Ireland by Nobel peace prize laureates and domain guardian Connect-Ireland in order to establish an East Timorese 'virtual nation'. Connect-Ireland was forced to shut down all its services for 24 hours while it upgraded its hardware and software to prevent a recurrence.

But perhaps the first international cyber-war was the one which raged over the peasant rebellion in Chiapas in southern Mexico. The Mexican finance ministry one day found the home page on its web site replaced with the face of historic revolutionary leader Emiliano Zapata. Even the web site of the Mexican president, Ernesto Zedillo, was disrupted, this time by a New York group called Electronic Disturbance Theatre which was out 'to demonstrate continued resistance to centuries of colonisation ...'

Communication without borders

Irritating though the Mexican government no doubt found such hacktivist protests, the real advantage the internet gave to Zapatista rebels in the Chiapas conflict was the simple power to communicate their experiences and arguments in the face of suppression by the authorities.

The Chiapas revolt began in 1994 at about the same time that the internet found mass potential with the invention of the first point-and-click web browser. By 1995, communiqués from sub-commandante Marcos posted onto the net were relaying an alternative version of events to the official Mexican one. The Zapatistas' views on economic exploitation and land reform were soon being debated by academics, commentators and other opposition movements in Mexico and around the world. Most importantly of all, the internet publication of testimony of torture, extra-judicial executions and other human rights abuses committed by Mexican forces and paramilitaries raised international support for the people of Chiapas and ensured that the Mexican authorities knew that the world was watching their activities.

The ease with which internet communication can breach or transcend both internal and external frontiers is a potentially definitive answer to governments which try to censor or suppress free speech. It also presents a major challenge to corporate dominance of the traditional media.

Particularly in Asia, from China to Indonesia to Burma, dissident groups were quick to recognise the internet as their best or only means of openly transmitting news and discussing political issues, both within their countries and with supporters or contacts internationally. When in Yugoslavia in 1996 the Serbian authorities closed down the independent B92 radio station in Belgrade, it simply switched to the internet and satellite broadcasting. The effect of the state action was to turn a local radio station into a focus for national and international dissent. Even in Saudi Arabia and Iran, governments have allowed limited internet access and the potential of the net to change society throughout the Middle East is huge.

Attempts to control this new freedom of expression have been varied and at times extreme. Internet user Lin Hai was sentenced to two years' imprisonment by a Shanghai court in 1999 for sending e-mail addresses to a dissident publication in the US. Burmese military intelligence is reported to have established a cyberwar centre to intercept or counter information circulated by pro-democracy groups. In Saudi Arabia, authorities have attempted to control internet usage by authorising a limited number of approved local ISPs with heavy use of 'firewalls' to block forbidden sites.

The difficulty for the censoring authorities is that, short of a total ban, it is practically impossible to control expression on the internet, particularly with the development of encryption or encoding technology (see below). And a dissident can always circumvent national controls altogether by dialling out of the country using a mobile phone to access the internet. Groups such as the Digital Freedom Network (*www.dfn.org*) monitor censorship on the net and campaign for free expression.

Multi-national corporations have also been made painfully aware of the net's ability to aid free expression. Fast-food corporation McDonald's spent years and some $10 million successfully suing two environmental activists for libel in the celebrated 'McLibel' case, yet

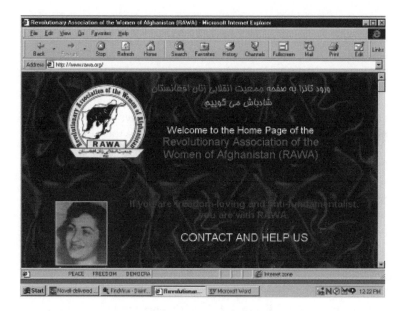

a web site (*www.mcspotlight.org*) continued for years afterwards to carry the text of the original leaflet that was ruled defamatory.

If an individual or an incorporated organisation publishes defamatory material on a web site they can be sued for libel (see chapter 5). Even if the actual publisher of a web site is hard to identify, the ISP could be pressured to remove the site or the offending material (under the Defamation Act 1996 an ISP has a defence if its dissemination of a libel is innocent, but once it has been made aware of the libel it can be held responsible too).

In practice, however, corporations are aware that pursuing the publisher or author of libellous material on the net may simply result in the material being published anonymously, or even repeatedly through different ISPs based abroad, and have been slow to sue. A number of multinationals that have been heavily criticised on the web, including Shell, Nike and Monsanto, as well as McDonald's, have responded by engaging in the debate and carrying on their own web sites an ethical defence of their business practices. Shell has even gone so far as to include links to the sites of its more respectable critics, such as Friends of the Earth and Greenpeace.

Security and encryption technology

Both the natural openness of internet communication, and its rapidly increasing effectiveness as a campaigning tool, mean that internet campaigners may attract the unwelcome attention of the authorities, particularly in countries where political expression is strictly controlled. There are, however, a number of ways to avoid exposure.

The advent of WAP (Wireless Application Protocol) makes it easy to connect to the internet just using a mobile phone or a wireless computer. This in itself will make it much harder for state authorities to monitor private internet usage, particularly if the net is accessed using an international connection.

Remailing services, which forward e-mail anonymously, have already existed for years, often used by people who want to contribute to mailing list discussions without revealing their identity. Specialist companies like Anonymizer (*www.anonymizer.com*) based in the US, have also developed anonymous web surfing and publishing services. During the Kosovo war in 1999, Anonymizer teamed up with the Electronic Frontier Foundation to create the Kosovo Privacy Project, which enabled dissidents inside Yugoslavia to e-mail and publish information on the internet anonymously and securely.

But the most important advance has probably been the development of encryption technology, enabling information to be transmitted through the internet securely in code. Powerful encryption software such as Pretty Good Privacy (*www.nai.com*) enables the simple generation of a set of public/private keys for encrypting and decrypting communications, and digital signatures for authenticating the identity of correspondents.

There are now a wide range of encryption packages available for downloading on the web. Althought the UK government is seeking to introduce powers to intercept communications and require compulsory access to encryption keys, the development of steganographic systems to hide encryption promises to keep the right to privacy alive. Human Rights Watch in the US noted that encryption was an important bulwark against violations of privacy in an age where computerisation and data banks enable the collection of huge amounts of personal information about individuals. More urgently, any dissident or human rights activist around the world equipped with a laptop computer and encryption software can circulate information with little danger of detection or retaliation. Political censorship may never recover.

7 Working with the media

The object perhaps is not so much to create public opinion, as to create an opinion about public opinion – WJM Mackenzie

Media coverage is a proxy for support. A statement in a letter or a slogan on a poster is an expression of someone's opinion; reported in a newspaper it becomes transformed into an expression of public opinion.

Newspapers and news programmes are consumed greedily by MPs, many of whom start the day with the *Today* programme on Radio 4 and end it with *Newsnight*. Enthusiastic councillors scan the local press to make sure they know about what is happening in their wards. In Whitehall, press cuttings for every news item covering issues of departmental relevance will be on the desk of a deputy secretary by 8.30 am. Ministers will be informed immediately by their private offices of anything significant that appears in the media. If something is reported it will get read, and politicians and officials know they will look stupid if they do not know about it.

The extent to which the mass media influence our society or merely reflect it has of course been debated for years by politicians, sociologists and the pundits themselves. But the key role of the media in relation to the boardrooms and chambers where policy is formulated in this country is not to swing decisions but to set the agenda. Whether the forum is national or local, public sector or private sector, the media have the power to force items on to an agenda, and in many cases to order the priorities for debate.

This chapter concentrates on gaining news and feature coverage in the press and on radio and television. Appeals, public service announcements and other 'soft slots' are covered in chapter 5.

Stories and angles

Stories are what journalists live and, occasionally, die for. They are interested in very little else. A pressure group will not start getting good coverage until it is able to feed them stories, rather than just publicising what it does in the hope that some of it will be of interest. You don't use the media: they use you.

There are really only two criteria for deciding what makes a good story: currency and reader interest. Other factors, from political importance to exclusivity to celebrity and scandal, are sub-sets of these two.

▼ *Currency*. News stories are about happenings and events, not process or argument. The existence of an appalling state of affairs is not news, although its revelation in a ministerial statement or a damning report may well be.

Different sections of the media will have varying benchmarks as to how recent an event must be to make it as news: unless it is a big story, broadcast news programmes may start to lose interest if the event is more than a few hours old; the daily papers will obviously consider things happening in the 24 hours before publication; weeklies and monthlies will often have a more relaxed interpretation of what constitutes news but may give priority to events that are fresher. Feature stories contain little news themselves but still have to be current, considering or illustrating the issues that are in the news.

▼ *Reader interest*. Each part of the media has a distinct idea of what will be of interest to its readers. Working with the specialist media it is thus particularly important to understand exactly who the readers are. In the general news media, reader interest broadly equates with what is known as 'public interest'.

Outsiders might have a good idea of what sort of events make the lead story on the television news, but are less likely to appreciate what will create interest at item six in the running order, or make it onto the inside pages of a newspaper, or be a good lead in a specialist journal. Giving priority to some news stories over others is a subjective and artificial process but developing a feeling for the decisions involved is essential to good media relations work, as is reading the publications and watching the programmes in which you hope to get coverage.

Stories generated by campaigning groups which most often make the national media are based on the publication of research reports, the leaking or exposure of government practices, the staging of stunts and demonstrations, and fundraising events and activities. In the local media the accent is on the last two of these, but there is also more scope for getting coverage just by issuing statements or condemnations. Journalists get particularly excited about public sector incompetence, consumer issues, fraud or dishonesty, and any kind of conflict – the more personalised the better.

Many of the general qualities good news stories possess are similar to those of popular fiction: drama, emotion, and a strong, simple plot. Any story that depends on the reader's grasp of complex financial or institutional relationships is unlikely to be used. Stories must be written for the non-expert reader (although the more specialist a publication is, the more knowledgeable its non-expert readers will be).

Campaigns often do centre on complex issues, however, that do not immediately present dramatic storylines. Here the skill will be in finding angles, or ways of approaching a specific event, that will appeal to different sections of the media. An example, based on real events, is given in the box below.

Finding the right angle

A human rights group commissions a report on El Salvador one year in the late eighties, which finds evidence of numerous specific instances of human rights abuse, although *under half the tally for previous years*. A press release headed

'THE HUMAN RIGHTS PARADOX': REPORT OF THE RIGHTSMONITOR INQUIRY PUBLISHED TODAY

is likely to get the work consigned to the very long and very dusty shelf on which most research reports permanently reside.

EL SALVADOR STARTS TO CLEAN UP ITS ACT

is a better story, but is not exactly the impression the group wishes to communicate.

FRESH EVIDENCE OF SALVADORAN TERROR

will certainly interest journalists on some of the national newspapers, but is unlikely to win much space because it is too similar to stories that have been run many times before. The story consequently rates low on news value and, being about a country a long way away that has little historical connection with the UK, fairly low on reader interest as well.

One fact buried away in the report, however, provides a fresh news angle and a link with a UK readership:

SALVADORAN MILITIA TRAINED AT SANDHURST

Leading on the story of a Salvadoran military cadet on a course at the Royal Military Academy, Sandhurst, the report stands a much better chance of securing good media coverage, and not just in the press: broadcast journalists can dash down the A3 to Camberley to obtain fresh pictures and interviews, even if it is just with someone from RightsMonitor standing outside the Academy's main gate. The story's potential for embarrassing the UK government is a very important bonus.

A different angle would need to be found for other local or specialist newspapers. (This is a good opportunity for involving local groups.)

MARIA'S FEAR FOR BROTHERS BACK HOME

This story, leading on the concern of a local resident, a Salvadoran refugee, for her family back in El Salvador, would probably be lapped up by a local paper. Coverage of this kind in local papers will get the main message of the report to thousands of people who would never see the story in the nationals.

The tabloid press is particularly creative about finding new or exciting angles in ostensibly sober stories. The Directory of Social Change regularly publishes a guide to charitable foundations which is press-released on publication with major trends highlighted. One year the quality press found little in it to write about, even as a filler, but it did make the lead story on the front page of the *Sun*. 'CLIFF GIVES £10,000 A WEEK TO CHARITY', screamed the headline, revealing what an enterprising reporter had discovered on page 145 about the work of the Cliff Richard Charitable Trust.

If you do not do so already, it is well worth reading the tabloids on occasion. They will provide an instant refresher course on how to dramatise stories and develop interesting angles, keeping things simple and always working up human interest appeal. Approach your own work with the eye of a *Mirror* reporter, and you will find the task of placing stories in the *quality* press much easier.

News and features

The basic distinction in media coverage, irrespective of medium, is that between news and features. These are compiled to widely differing timescales, usually by different sets of journalists, and their content is governed by distinct – sometimes conflicting – conventions. It follows that a campaign feeding stories or cooperating on them should be aware which kind of coverage is planned. Some of the main differences are described below.

Feature coverage is more varied than news in both content and format. Examples include:

▼ radio or television documentaries lasting anything from seven to 50 minutes;

▼ illustrated articles of 1,000 words upwards in magazines and colour supplements;

▼ interviews, investigations and background pieces in the second sections of newspapers or on the 'Living' page, women's page, education page, etc. (generally between 700 and 1500 words);

▼ comment and opinion pieces on a newspaper's 'op-ed' (= opposite the editorial) page.

Unlike news coverage, where the convention of objective and balanced reporting is paramount, features will often seek to highlight individual experience or opinion. Balance is achieved not within each story but through the juxtaposition of different stories on a page or programme or in a series.

A major news story will usually be covered by a number of programmes and newspapers simultaneously, although they will each try to develop exclusive angles. Features, however, are generally exclusive: editors are unlikely to be interested in a potential feature story unless they know that none of their competitors will be running it. It follows that you can news release widely in order to secure broad coverage, and some media may even pick up the story from other media, but you should only offer a feature story to, say, one daily broadsheet and one broadcaster at a time (there is certainly some scope for doubling up on print and broadcast, which are not in direct competition).

News coverage is almost always put together by an in-house team: everything that is printed or broadcast will have been produced by staff journalists. On a national newspaper the home news desk will receive press releases and gather in leads, and then assign them to its team of reporters. A typical day in the professional life of one such reporter, on the *Guardian*, is described in the box below. Specialist areas, like Parliament, health, or the law, are usually covered by special correspondents who are knowledgeable about their area and build up a network of contacts. The business desk will have its own small team

---

The reporter's day

A news reporter on the *Guardian* gives the following breakdown for a typical day.

10.00 am	Read newspapers on way to office.
10.30 am	Arrive in office, open post, follow up leads from day before, make telephone calls.
11.30 am	Allocated story or stories for the day by news desk.
12.00 – 4.00 pm	This is the main part of the day in which the bulk of news gathering is done. This may involve reporting live events, interviewing people in person and going to press conferences, or remaining in the office and working through the telephone and fax machine. (There is a minor copy deadline at about 3.00 pm for smaller stories or picture stories appearing on the inside pages of the paper.) One to two days a week will be spent travelling out of London to cover events.
4.00 pm	Return to office to write up story. Telephone calls to check facts or get last minute quotes.
6.00 pm	Main copy deadline. If on an out-of-town assignment, copy is either dictated to a copy-taker over the telephone, or sent by modem.
6.30 pm	Briefed by news desk on stories for next day, particularly if they involve events or press conferences taking place in the morning.
7.00 pm	Leave office. [Unless working on major news story to appear on the front or back pages of the paper, in which case:
8.00 pm	Final copy deadline.]
8.30 pm	Phone in to office to answer queries from sub-editors.

Notes: The best time to talk to a reporter or correspondent is first thing in the morning when they get into the office. They will be harder to get hold of after midday and by late afternoon they will be under pressure to file their copy.

of reporters. The foreign news desk relies on copy from its foreign correspondents and from the international news agencies.

The situation is similar for television and radio bulletins, although the fact that camera crews travel heavy, and at some expense, means that there is a greater attempt to plan ahead. Television news reporters will often find themselves competing with their colleagues in order to get a crew. Background footage and interviews are thus typically scheduled for a day or more in advance.

Once the copy has been filed, the reporter has little control over where it appears in the paper (if anywhere) and any cuts that are made. It is first knocked into shape by the sub-editors or 'subs', who check for accuracy, clarity and house style, and who cut text if necessary. This process is overseen by the news editor, who will also decide on the priority given to different stories.

In contrast to the news editor's relationship with the news team, a features editor will be dealing with input from a variety of different sources. Some of it will come from special features staff, some from news reporters who have the time to work on extended pieces, a little from guest contributors, and quite a lot from freelance journalists or producers. There has been a significant shift in recent years in the broadcast media towards more documentary programmes being bought in from independent producers or production companies.

The timescale by which feature coverage is put together is also markedly different. A newspaper feature may well be commissioned weeks in advance of publication (although often less), so if you intend to suggest a possible article to an editor or journalist you need to plan ahead. Send in a *news* release that far in advance, however, and the paper's news desk, where things start to look old after a few days, will probably ignore it. Considerably more notice is needed with the broadcast media.

Typical lead times for different media are given in the box opposite. These are necessarily simplified (a daily paper, for example, will have pages going off to print throughout the early part of the night) but serve as a guide for outside groups working with journalists and editors. The more leisurely pace of features coverage and the wider scope it gives for journalistic expression are conducive to striking up a closer relationship with features journalists.

Having stressed the differences between feature and news coverage, it is important to point out that there is a large grey area in which one merges into the other. Major national news stories will often be covered with background pieces run next to the reporting; the longer news programmes like *Channel 4 News*, *Newsnight*, and Radio 4's *Today* will run extended feature-type coverage near the back end of the programme; and newspaper feature editors often pride themselves on how newsy their pages are. Read, listen, watch, and get to know the individual styles and formats.

Lead times for major media

	Commission	Copy deadline	To bed
Press			
National daily paper			
news	12–36 hours	6 pm	9 pm
features	3–6 weeks	1–2 weeks	1 day
Sunday paper/weekly news magazine			
news section	2–6 days	Friday night	Sat. midday
colour supplement	3–8 weeks	2 weeks	1 week
Local paper (weekly)			
news	4–6 days	3 days	1 day
Glossy magazine (monthly)	3 months	2 months	1 month
Broadcast			
News bulletins	1–10 days	3–8 hours*	0–5 hours
Documentaries	2–4 months	2–4 weeks	1–2 weeks

* Unless live.

These are indicative lead times for the bulk of scheduled material. Most media will have special arrangements for 'breaking' stories: major news stories that come in after the normal deadlines.

News releases and launches

Issuing a press release or news release is the standard method for giving the media notice, usually in advance, of a story. Whether or not it prompts coverage will still depend almost entirely on how good the story or angle is; the function of the news release is just to get that story across as quickly and simply as possible.

Unlike most kinds of writing or narrative, which have an introduction, a middle and a conclusion, a news story makes as big a splash as possible immediately and then moves outwards in ripples from the centre. A news release should follow this format, starting with a terse, dynamic summary of the main story and following it with more layers of information, in decreasing order of importance. Trainee journalists are taught to ensure that their copy answers the basic questions: who, what, when, where and why.

An example of a classically structured news release is given in the box on page 139. Releases should be kept to just one side of A4 wherever possible, with any supporting material attached. If it does not fit on one page, print it single-sided on two sheets. Local papers or the trade press may use the text of the release itself as copy; for this reason releases were traditionally presented double-spaced with wide margins, ready for marking up. Ideally, it should be possible to cut from the bottom, paragraph by paragraph, with whatever remains (even if it is just the first paragraph) still making complete sense and getting across the main story. News copy is still often cut this way on newspapers.

Winning coverage from at least one in every two releases that you send out is a good target to aim at. Quite a lot of damage can be done to media relations if releases are constantly issued with non-stories, or stories that are not relevant to the journalists on the receiving end. It does not take long for an organisation to be identified as a time-waster and its notepaper recognised as a guarantee of irrelevance.

Generally speaking, news about your organisation itself – a new office, a change of director – will not be of interest to anyone except your supporters. News of your field – events whose primary impact will be confined to your existing contacts and their colleagues – should be released to the specialist press, but is unlikely to interest the national media unless the story is very big. Only news which clearly affects the wider world, the general public or a significant section of it, should you consider releasing to the nationals. On a big story, this may well involve working up different angles for specialist, local and national media, and issuing separate releases. If your mailings are currently structured so that the nationals get everything, you should re-assess your approach.

It is best to address news releases to individual journalists whenever possible: either those known to you, or special correspondents covering the relevant area. They can also be marked for the attention of the news editor, on a newspaper or journal, or the producer, in the case of a broadcast bulletin. Broadcast news bulletins also often have a forward planning team who can be sent releases about future events so that they can slot them into the production schedule. It is now possible to buy services such as Mediadisk or Targeter which provide on disk databases of media contacts, including specialist correspondents, which are regularly updated, but they will set you back upwards of £2,500 a year.

Timing and embargos

If a news release concerns something that has already happened it will be marked 'For immediate release'. If, on the other hand, it gives advance notice of an event it may be worth embargoing it. An embargo simply gives a time before which the story is not to be used. It enables you to coordinate publicity and also reassures the journalists that no-one will use the story before the set time. They have plenty of time in which to research, write or record their pieces, which can then only be published or broadcast once the embargo has elapsed.

An embargo usually takes the form of a bold line at the head of the news release: 'Embargo: Not to be used before [time] on [date].' If the release is tied in with an external event, like a speech, press launch, demonstration, etc., it should be embargoed for the time the event is to take place. The contents of the release are in effect conditional on the

WESSEX AGAINST POVERTY

2 The Market Square, Melchester MH14 5NL

Wednesday 16 March 1994
For immediate release

NEWS RELEASE

70-YEAR-OLD PENSIONER JAILED FOR NON-PAYMENT OF COUNCIL TAX

An old age pensioner has become the first person to be committed to prison for not paying his council tax. 70-year old John Smith was jailed today (16 March) by Wessex town magistrates after he told them he could not afford to pay the £242 a year bill.

John Smith was sentenced to 14 days imprisonment in the case brought by Wessex District Council. Mr Smith, who lives in a rented flat and suffers from arthritis, explained that he could not afford to keep both his whippet, Ginger, and pay his council tax.

The Reverend John Jones, vicar of Wessex St Giles, condemned the decision: "It is an outrage that our society should have to jail an old man whose only crime is his lack of means."

Sita Patel, chair of Wessex Against Poverty, added: "Mr Smith is a poor man who does not even own the flat on whose value his council tax is based. Wessex Council have today revealed the council tax for what it really is: the son of the poll tax."

ENDS

FURTHER INFORMATION:

Sita Patel, chair, Wessex Against Poverty, Tel: 0112–7843 (w), 0112–8735 (h)
Rev. John Jones, vicar of Wessex St Giles, Tel: 0112–8992

NOTES FOR EDITORS:

The council tax replaced the poll tax in April 1993. It is a roof tax, based on the value of an occupant's property rather than on ability to pay, regardless of whether the property is rented or owner-occupied.

Wessex Against Poverty was founded in 1989 to campaign against poverty and unfair taxation in the Wessex area. It organises a food cooperative and provides benefits advice to local people.

Notes:

1. Every news release should have a date, details of whom it was issued by, and contact name(s) and telephone number(s).

2. The body of the release is structured just like a news story. It could be cut from the bottom (in this case literally sentence by sentence) always leaving the main story intact.

3. News releases often contain a pithy quote from the issuer, or a supporter (the more respectable and distinguished the better). Journalists may use these directly, but more often will just read them as a taste of what is available. Note that the quotes are the only points in the news release where opinion is directly expressed: otherwise the text is kept objective.

event going ahead. For this reason, the media are often wary of news releases about demonstrations, which rarely go according to plan (it is probably better, in this instance, to aim for picture coverage: see below).

Where there is more flexibility about the timing of an embargo, for example with the publication of a piece of research or a leaked document, it is customary to lift an embargo at midnight, in order to catch the daily papers and early morning news bulletins. This effect can be achieved by leaving the embargo without a specific time, just a date, but some press officers like to make sure and put in a time of 00.01 hrs or 00.30 hrs.

A start of day embargo is attractive to daily newspapers because they know they are getting the news first. It also has the advantage of appealing to Radio 4's *Today*, which is by far the longest national news programme and from which other programmes will often pick up stories. On occasion, however, an embargo may be lifted at a different time of day, perhaps in order to give the story first to the evening news. (This is usually only worth it if you have a really big story or have arranged coverage in advance on a particular programme.)

The embargo date will also affect your chances of getting coverage. Some factors will be beyond your control, most significantly the weight of other news appearing on the same day. Many groups choose to publish whenever possible on a Monday, because that is generally the slackest day for news. Alternatively, tying in a release with major news of the moment can also prove successful: when a major government decision is imminent, for example, the media will be hungry for leaks or new angles on the story. The Directory of Social Change released a briefing on the legality of hospital closures a few days before the publication of a key government report on the future of hospitals in London: not only was it picked up by the media in the atmosphere of rumours and alarms preceding the report's publication, but the DSC got a second bite of the cherry when the report came out and the journalists needed comment and reaction. Finally, note that local television and radio will often run a local angle on a major news story the day after it breaks.

How far in advance an embargoed release should be mailed depends on the target medium. With the national press, it could be anything from one or two days up to a week; for the broadcast media, perhaps a little longer. Consult the commissioning lead times in the box in the last section for further guidance. News releases should really only be faxed if you have a breaking story.

Embargos are almost universally respected in the media, as it is a system which benefits the journalists as well as those seeking news coverage. Needless to say, once you have embargoed something, you are constrained by it just like anyone else. Any efforts by predatory journalists to persuade you to break an embargo just for them are best sternly resisted.

Press conferences

Once almost as common as the news release, news or press conferences are now thinner on the ground, confined to big stories or aimed at generating positive feature coverage rather than news. Life in modern journalism is pressured, and, as a general rule, a news reporter will not attend a press conference unless she already knows that she will be writing a goodly-sized piece on the subject.

As press conferences are so often poorly attended it is worth considering carefully what publicity benefits are likely to be gained from the exercise. If your story is clearly newsworthy, but deals with complex or frequently misunderstood issues, a personal forum in which to get it across might make all the difference; so too if your message partly depends on personality. In many cases, however, a press conference will have little to add to a simple news release, except expense.

If you are aiming for national news coverage, the conference needs to be in the morning, with 10.30 or 11.00 am being a popular start time (see 'The reporter's day' above). It should be kept short: 30 to 40 minutes is more than enough. It is also possible to run a press conference aimed at features writers and the specialist media, in which case there is more flexibility regarding time of day (but avoid Monday, when many journalists on the Sunday papers will be off). Rather like a short technical briefing, this sort of event may need to be a little longer but aimed at a smaller group. The specialist press briefing often works best when it relates to a major issue already in the news, and features writers can use it as a short cut to doing their homework.

Whatever sort of conference is planned, you need to send out personal invitations with a news release at least a few days in advance. Some press officers make a habit of ringing round a day or two before to check who is coming and gauge numbers, but this is unlikely to boost attendance unless the press officer has already established a strong professional relationship with individual journalists.

▼ Keep speeches short and to the point, with visual aids if possible and plenty of time for questions. Dispense with votes of thanks and congratulatory addresses from committee members who don't really understand the subject.

▼ Briefing material is very important. A good press pack might reiterate the key points made at the conference; supply the background evidence, figures, tables, etc., that are hard to communicate in a presentation; and give a short profile of your organisation and its credibility in the field. If you are launching a report, include a copy as well as a one-sheet summary of its main conclusions and recommendations.

▼ Ensure that there is adequate time, and space, after the formal proceedings for individual briefings over a drink or cup of coffee, photocalls, or recorded interviews (a separate room may be necessary).

Note that a good press conference is often a very small affair, involving perhaps just a dozen people. Try and reserve it exclusively for members of the press: they shouldn't have to struggle through the throng but should be given personal attention. If only two or three journalists turn up, sit them round a table, brief them well, let them ask questions to their heart's content, and the exercise will have been worthwhile.

Picture stories

Photographers follow the major home news of the day, but they also have stories of their own, where column inches are assigned according to picture quality rather than just news value. The development of the pressure group demonstration from a show of mass support to the small stunt with strong visual impact has been greatly influenced by the media's use of picture stories (see chapter 9). Other examples of common picture stories generated by campaigns include the animated poster (chapter 5), the protesting celebrity/old person/ child, the against-all-discrimination achiever, as well as the usual photogenic fare of bizarre and beautiful objects, wonders of modern technology or ancient history.

National newspapers have picture editors who can be press released with notice of photo opportunities. Photographers work alone and they appreciate flexibility about when they need to show up (with the exception, naturally, of one-off stunts, when it helps to keep to schedule). Information for the photo caption will probably come off the press release. For the local and specialist press, who are less fussy about using pictures that may be printed elsewhere, you can take your own photographs and mail these immediately after the event with a copy of the release.

With television the situation is a little different. Every story is in effect a picture story and camera crews are always accompanied by reporters. But good footage will make the difference between a story being transmitted or not, particularly late in the running order (at the front end of news bulletins, the nostrum that television is always picture-led starts to fall apart). If you are news releasing a story, make sure that any photogenic potential comes across strongly.

With television, the DIY alternative is also less of an option. Supplying your own footage in the form of a video news release would probably require hiring an experienced production company but is still unlikely to prove successful with the major TV channels unless the pictures are both exceptional and made available to one programme exclusively. The real potential for getting coverage through supplying video news releases and other types of ready-made footage comes with the digital revolution and the proliferation of cable and satellite channels. With a host of specialist audiences, hours of programming to fill and very limited budgets, the channels and production companies which work with them may be receptive to any ready-made solutions which make life easy for them.

The use of video news releases was pioneered by international campaigns and development agencies as a way of overcoming the problem of television not covering certain issues or parts of the world because actuality was too difficult or expensive to obtain. A Friends of the Earth video of the Pergau dam in Malaysia was shown widely on network news when a scandal erupted over the excessive amount of UK aid spent on the project and its link with arms deals. FoE only received an on-screen credit but they contributed to getting the story more coverage than it would otherwise have received, helping to stoke a major scandal.

Exclusives

A journalist's job is a curious mixture of looking over the shoulder to make sure that other journalists aren't getting better coverage, while constantly trying to steal a march on the competition by producing something new: a fresh angle, more in-depth coverage, a scoop. In fact the vast majority of exclusives are not the product of pure investigative journalism but are fed to journalists by outside groups or individuals.

The greatest scope for offering stories exclusively is on the features pages of the newspapers. This is particularly appropriate for stories that lack the immediacy needed for daily news, but which have a strong human interest angle or take a more in-depth look at current issues. The Sunday papers have the most extensive features coverage and in particular pride themselves on their publication of investigative articles which lay bare the scandals and injustices of the nation.

To offer a story to a newspaper you can talk either to the editor of the particular page(s) you are aiming at, or possibly to a staff writer or a regular freelancer, if you have dealt with them before. Approaching an editor, it is probably best to write in the first instance.

On a big event it is always worth trying to pre-arrange feature coverage to back up the news story. The story will be news released with an embargo as usual, but if they are given sufficient notice one newspaper may be happy to run a longer article as well, giving them better coverage than their rivals. This can also work well with radio and television, particularly if the embargo is timed to give one programme the first coverage (see above). Coordinating feature coverage, with its longer lead times, to coincide with news coverage is often something of a juggling act and calls for discipline on both sides to prevent the embargo falling apart.

Offering straight news exclusives to the print media is much less common. There is a lot to be said for the attitude that if one newspaper thinks the story is big enough to give it good coverage, then the others will too. One major exception is the publication of government leaks, where the need to keep a story quiet before publication to avoid an injunction favours striking a deal with just one newspaper. It may also be possible to extract promises of better coverage. Environmental campaigner Des Wilson describes with characteristic ebullience how he leaked an internal letter from the government's then Chief Medical Officer, Sir Henry Yellowlees, admitting that lead in petrol damages children's health – marching into the office of the editor of the *Times* and demanding both front page and op-ed coverage in return for the exclusive. Note that as a general rule, however, the media will never give a guarantee of coverage.

Contributing letters and articles

The easiest way for a campaign to get its views published in the national media, short of paying for advertising space, is through a letter to the editor. On any given day, letters from interest groups will probably make up a quarter of the letters pages of the broadsheet newspapers.

Letters are never published as a matter of course, even if they correct a factual inaccuracy that appeared in the paper, and the letters editor will always reserve the discretion to make cuts in any letter that is accepted. It is important to mark the letter 'For publication' and to give a daytime contact number for any necessary fact-checking or clarification. The chances of letters being published should go up if they:

▼ respond directly to something in the newspaper or, at least, in the news;

▼ have a distinguished signatory (the *Times'* letters page, in particular, is dominated by members of the great and the good);

▼ are short.

The average length of a published letter is about 170 words; it is very rare for over 400 words to be printed. Communicating just one point forcefully is a useful aim. If you are going to get letters published regularly it is important to establish trust in your accuracy and reliability.

Getting full length articles published is a lot more difficult. The vast majority of feature articles in newspapers, including comment pieces, are written by professional journalists, most of them on staff, although one or two papers have a regular slot for guest contributors of note. Others may commission occasional comment pieces from practitioners or experts in a given field.

In one respect campaigners are in a similar position to freelance journalists, submitting ideas for articles to an editor. It is useful to be able to show evidence of similar writing experience. Contributions from pressure groups, particularly from the director, are more welcome for opinion slots than for general feature journalism.

In any case, it is essential to contact the correct editor – on a national newspaper or major magazine there are several and there is rarely any system for allocating general approaches to the most appropriate person. There will be different editors for the op-ed page, living/health/women/etc. pages, as well as a features editor who has a general brief to oversee features coverage and possibly individual control over certain pages. On the multi-section Sundays, each section will have its own editor. With local papers and the smaller specialist journals or magazines, the overall editor can be addressed. *Willings Press Guide* and Macmillan's *Writer's Handbook* (see appendix C) both give details of senior editorial staff; for a newspaper, you can also get the names of relevant section editors from the switchboard.

Submitting unsolicited articles is by and large a waste of time. They may not even get read. Every editor will have a vision of the remit and style of her pages, the sort of writing that has appeared too often or that she wishes to encourage, as well as ideas for the future, and the likelihood that an unsolicited article echoes these concerns is slight. Potential articles need to be discussed and then commissioned. With new writers, editors often commission 'on spec', which means that no payment is made unless the article is accepted for publication.

Giving quotes and interviews

A major goal for any new pressure group is to build a profile and level of credibility that means the media will take the first step in approaching it for comment when a particular issue comes up in the news.

In print journalism the bulk of comment-gathering and short interviews are done over the telephone. It is often worth establishing whether the reporter just wants information or actually wants to quote you and, if so, see if you can agree a quote that they can use at the end of the conversation.

With both telephone and longer face-to-face interviews, it is generally accepted that the journalist will tidy up any quotes, correcting grammar and making a disjointed phrase into a full sentence if necessary. It is less accepted but not uncommon for them to go one step further and liven up the language. (It can be odd, knowing that what you said was 'We realised there was something wrong and asked the local authority for advice', when you see yourself quoted the next day saying 'We smelt a rat and called in the council'.) Straight misrepresentation is usually the product of misunderstanding rather than malice: the journalist does not appreciate why your position takes five minutes to explain and therefore misses something out or shifts the emphasis when he tries to condense it into ten words. If you have been misquoted on a substantive point, the best response is to write a letter for publication to the editor, correcting the mistake and reiterating your main point.

Radio and television news interviews fall into three distinct categories:

▼ *Recorded soundbites.* What the reporter is after here is just one or two pithy quotes, lasting anything from seven to about 20 seconds. The 'interview' may take up five or ten minutes of recording and be based on a standard question and answer format, but it is only those few seconds of talking head that will be broadcast. The reporter's questions are thus only there as a prompt: interviewees are usually free to say exactly what they want and if they fluff a line they can go back and start again. As the questions are not broadcast, anything said by the interviewee has to make sense on its own. Television soundbites are sometimes recorded in self-operating studios, or studios with just interviewee and camera, with the reporter on a telephone line.

▼ *Recorded questions and answers.* The recording set-up here is much the same, but the broadcast result will look like a conventional interview. There is more engagement between journalist and interviewee, and some of the questions may be broadcast as well. With television, note that as there is usually only one camera, trained on the interviewee during the session, the journalist has to be recorded separately afterwards, asking questions or just nodding attentively (these are known as 'noddies').

▼ *Live interviews.* Speed is the first thing people notice about doing a live interview. The interviewee is ushered into the studio, she does perhaps a straight three minutes on air and then is led out again. She has the opportunity to make, say, three or four points at most. It is part of the presenter's job on a live programme to ensure that interviews run smoothly without gaps, so do not worry about getting lost for words.

Having listened to endless combative interviews with politicians, it often comes as a surprise to realise that in most interview situations journalists are friendly and encouraging. Their principal concern is to make good radio or television, so it is in their interests to ensure that interviewees come across clearly and interestingly. On my first live experience on a radio station I was expecting to be grilled by a budding Jeremy Paxman and was a bit taken aback to be greeted by a good-natured 'So, tell us about the findings of your research.'

For any broadcast interview, whether live or pre-recorded, the journalist may well run through in advance the main questions that he is intending to ask. If there has been time to brief him about your position, he may even suggest the points it would be most effective for you to make.

In terms of your own preparation before an interview, it can be useful to note down the four or five questions that you think are most likely to come up, and get straight the two points that *you* really want to get across. Politicians often prepare a witty ten-second soundbite that they can deliver emphatically to the obliging microphone, knowing it will probably get used. If a journalist is recording an interview with a campaigner, however, she will usually try and get comments on a range of points, and the decision on which soundbite gets used will often depend mainly on how well it fits into the rest of the piece when it is finally put together.

In a live interview you actually have much more control: even if the interviewer is being difficult, at least you know that everything you say is being broadcast. The shortage of time and the need to keep your message as simple as possible means that it is sometimes useful to deflect a difficult question. There are many ways of doing this, as listening to any current affairs programme will demonstrate; the following are typical:

'That's really a marginal issue, what is of central importance is ...'

'That is a very interesting question, but we need to stress ...'

'You *say* that, but let's get back to the facts ...'

Don't overdo it. The received wisdom is that the practice of deflecting questions is now so commonplace that listeners rarely even notice, but I'm not so sure. Those politicians that have got it down to a fine art are also the ones that are often found by the public in attitude surveys to be the least credible.

A large part of how effectively interviewees comes across, particularly on television, depends not on what they say but on the general impression they create: sentences short and clear; any movements calm but emphatic; tone convinced, even passionate, but never ranting. It is very difficult to evaluate your own performance unless you make the effort to get hold of a copy of the programme in question and see or hear it for yourself.

A lot of the most important work in giving soundbites or an interview to radio or television is done away from the microphone. When a reporter first sets up his interviews by telephone, the story will often be quite nebulous in his mind: its exact shape is still to be worked out. The earlier that a particular interview takes place, the more chance there should be, both at the setting up stage and at the recording itself, for the interviewee to emphasise certain angles and downplay others and to suggest other interviewees. Many interviewees are too concerned with the microphone to exploit informally the knowledge advantage they have over the reporter in order to influence the final story.

That first telephone call from a reporter or producer will also be the time to get straight what the programme is and therefore what the audience is that you will be addressing, what the story is they are working on, how they see your input, who the other interviewees are, whether your comments are following a film on the issue and if so what it contains, etc. Apart from knowing what you are letting yourself in for, the information will enable you to gauge your input effectively.

Capturing the middle ground

1.

Mediator

Right-of-centre   Left-of-centre

Right-wing   Left-wing

This classic arrangement, loosely based on a parliamentary chamber, has become a norm for televised debates. The anchorperson or mediator in the centre is projected as impartial.

2.

Mediator

Independent?

Government

Opposition

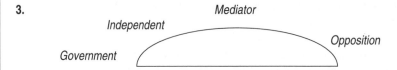

In this debate situation the independent spokesperson is projected as opposing government. If she is from a cause or group commonly associated with opposition politics, she will have to work extra hard to maintain an independent stance.

3.

Mediator

Independent

Opposition

Government

Here the independent spokesperson is in a much stronger position from which to attack government. With the centre ground against it as well as the official opposition, government is marginalised.

4.

Mediator

Opposition

Government

Independent?

On the fringe of the debate, the stakes are raised. The independent spokesperson may be able to project himself as detached from the party-political bickering, but risks coming across as being on the political extreme.

This information is especially valuable when considering your approach in a broadcast debate or roundtable discussion involving several contributors. In a sense, debates are always live because, although they are sometimes cut a little, you do not get a second chance. How you relate to the other contributors will be a determining factor in how you come across. Many debates, particularly on radio, are very good-natured and brusque interruptions are best avoided; on other occasions you will have to be forceful in order to make your point heard. Producers often like to set up contributors antagonistically and, unless the subject is completely apolitical, there will usually be an implicit political positioning in the arrangement. This is best illustrated visually (see box opposite) but is as pervasive on radio as it is on television. Simply the order in which contributors are invited to speak and how they are introduced may help to colour what they say.

One approach that is rarely ever attempted by campaigns in the social welfare field is to encourage members of their client group to speak on behalf of the campaign on radio and television. Broadcast debates are the province of the polite middle classes. Politicians are in fact warned not to appear with ordinary members of the public except in certain highly controlled situations, and for good reason: ordinary people will often not accept the niceties of rational debate but have a habit of ramming a point home repeatedly and speaking with a depth of personal experience that a politician cannot hope to match. It will probably be difficult to persuade producers to accept spokespeople of the rough-edged, non-urbane variety, but it may be worth the effort. After all, policy-makers should be able to justify their decisions to the people who really have to live with them.

Managing media relations

Sustaining effective media relations over any period of time is a symbiotic process. Some pressure groups realise that they need the media more than the media needs them, and therefore structure their press office so that it spends a lot of time giving journalists what they want. Once good relations have been established with journalists, the task of influencing the kind of coverage an issue gets, or even dealing with bad press, becomes much easier.

Apart from feeding the media stories, and giving quotes on demand, pressure groups can provide journalists with two other valuable kinds of information:

▼ *Summary briefings*. Journalists are, generally speaking, not experts and when they approach a new story they often have a problem getting simple, up-to-date background information to put them in the picture (the first three people they ring up all tell them it is highly complex and then go on at tedious length about a related issue). A short briefing summarising the main current facts with relevant figures is a godsend. The only problem is that reporters find it impracticable to keep many files, so it is important to send briefings at the time when they are likely to cover the subject.

▼ *Case-studies*. The media always need real-life cases to illustrate an issue, preferably where the people concerned are prepared to talk on the record, and will often look to a charity or pressure group to provide them. A particularly outrageous case may make a story in itself, but more often a journalist will be made aware of a problem in theory but then need real cases to back it up. (A television researcher's job partly consists of tasks like 'find a married couple with at least two children who live in a marginal constituency, voted Tory in the last election and have just had their home repossessed'.) Building up a list of clients or cases who would be able to talk to the media is a valuable resource for a press officer.

As with all dealings with the media, it is impossible to get any absolute guarantees as to how your material will be used. When passing on a case-name it is thus particularly important to ensure that the person's permission has been asked first and that they are aware of the publicity they are letting themselves in for. Particular care should be taken with the tabloids, where the tone of a story or the language used can easily vitiate any positive message in the story, and lead to the subject feeling degraded.

Occasionally parts of the media, newspapers in particular, can be persuaded to adopt a campaign for a few weeks or months if they think it will appeal to their readership. This partly depends on the personal predilections of key editors (a striking example is the support of the editor of the *Daily Mail* for the campaign for justice for Stephen Lawrence, murdered in a racist attack), but also on whether it is an issue on which the media judges the government to be vulnerable. With the Snowdrop campaign to ban firearms following the Dunblane massacre, a head of steam built up across the media which made action by the government inevitable.

Governments are in any case now much more media-conscious than they used to be. During the 1997 election campaign, the Labour Party famously developed a system of rapid rebuttal techniques with the help of its Excalibur database. The Labour government is developing a similar system in power, known as the Knowledge Network, which will provide ministers and their advisers with continually updated arguments, key facts, and rebuttal lines to promote government policies.

Although a lot has been said in recent years about the ability of political advisers to influence or 'spin' stories in the media, effective news management is not about twisting or responding to negative coverage so much as ensuring that the stories or issues covered are the ones which naturally favour your argument. During the long-running legal battle over the extradition of former Chilean leader Augusto Pinochet to face torture charges, the media, always hungry for a new story, soon turned to highlighting political clashes over the case or chasing allegations of partiality by politicians or judges. Rather than engaging in the acrimonious debate about Pinochet's political legacy, Amnesty International pursued a strategy of continually refocusing media coverage on Pinochet's alleged crimes, highlighting British citizens who were victims of torture or disappearance in Chile, flying over victims or their relatives to be interviewed by the media, or publishing testimony and statistics on what had happened under Pinochet's rule. Commentators continued to disagree about Pinochet's political or diplomatic importance, but no one was left who could credibly deny the horror of the crimes against humanity that had taken place in Chile – or the need for justice.

Handling bad press

Charities generally get quite a good press, not least because they are a useful resource that the media can draw on in questioning government policy. Non-charitable pressure groups are less likely to be

---

Government's media ploys

Releasing news at dead times

Bad or embarrassing news is released at a time when it is likely to get as little coverage as possible: on a Friday or over the weekend, or simultaneously with big events that will help push it out of sight. Another technique is to release news in a written answer to a Parliamentary Question (see chapter 14): by the time someone realises what has happened, often some days later, editors are wary of giving the story much space.

Leaks and hints

News of unpopular government decisions are often leaked out over a period of time so that when the formal announcement is finally made it sounds like old news. Leaks are something of an art in themselves; they are often used, particularly during the budget process, to gauge public reaction to different policy options and to lower expectations. Pressure groups have on occasion been used unawares as stooges to pass on a leak to the media.

Non-attributable briefings

The lobby correspondent system, managed by the Downing Street Press Office, enables central government to pass on major news on its own terms. One of the primary tools is the non-attributable briefing – elevated to heights of guile in the Thatcher era by Sir Bernard Ingham – in which government press officers will vouch for the reliability of a story without formally disclosing the source.

Welcoming bad news

Embarrassing figures, from economic indicators to hospital waiting lists, are often published with a news release stressing only the good news in them, in the hope that most journalists will be too ignorant or too lazy to work out the full story from the raw data.

Dirt briefing

Supposedly confined to the political parties, dirt briefing is the practice of releasing damaging information about opponents (one of those occasions when it is usually better to have the news reported without attribution). Often government will seek to discredit specific interest groups when talking to the media, usually by raising questions about the quality of their research, the depth of their support, or by suggesting that a group has a hidden agenda.

given the benefit of the doubt, and some causes have long suffered from a very negative or even hostile attitude from the media. On occasion this bias filters down into the language used in a report, without the reporter even being aware of it: 'management *offers*, union *demands*', etc.

The theory of crisis PR, or handling bad press, has been developed mainly by large corporations intent on keeping their markets sweet. One of its central principles is that, unless the source is impeccable, the media will be reluctant to run a story without any corroboration from inside the company or at least giving the company the chance to comment. Extinguish both information and controversy and most stories will be a damp squib. However, the institution with the greatest experience of dealing with bad press – which has in fact developed the management of hostile media into a fine art – is the government. Some of the techniques used by government media managers are described in the box overleaf: apart from providing some useful hints on handling bad press they should also be of help if you find yourself in a PR battle with government.

If you are dealing with bad press about a cause, rather than just an organisation, you will have to do more than just keep your head under the parapet. Generally the media does not react well to accusations of bias and there is little to be gained from complaining, unless it is a clear case of factual error (in which case the main opportunities for redress are a request for a published apology and retraction; a letter for publication to the editor; or, failing those, a complaint to the Press Complaints Commission or the Broadcasting Complaints Commission).

In the long term the best way to fight bad press about a cause is to feed the media positive stories or stories that reinforce your argument. For example in the field of industrial relations, where, arguably, coverage has displayed an anti-union bias for a number of years, groups like the Low Pay Unit have had considerable success in pushing stories about the pay and conditions that many workers suffer. Compiling figures on low pay nationally led to the Unit condemning Britain as 'the sweatshop of Europe'; documenting the situation in a number of specific companies enabled it to award one employer the title of 'Scrooge of the Year'. If a group manages to develop good media relations, that will be reflected in coverage of the cause as a whole, and *vice versa*. Reporters know not to bite the hand that feeds them.

8 Using the law

Magna Charta is such a fellow, that he will have no sovereign – Sir Edward Coke

Parliament, government and monarchy are the source of authority in our state, yet all three remain subservient to the law. The law's authority can be invoked to constrain government action, check abuse and generally make life difficult for those who govern.

Legal action against individuals, companies and public bodies can take the form of suing for damages, applying for an injunction or seeking another private remedy in the civil courts. Grounds for such action include breach of contract, negligence, assault, defamation and nuisance; indeed, any demonstrable infringement of a person's private legal rights. The scope for exerting pressure by legal action is enormous, although the complexity of the legal system means that it can only be covered in outline here.

Another way of challenging the decisions of public bodies which has become increasingly popular in the last two decades is the procedure known as judicial review. Since 1977 it has become a particularly effective tool with which to chip away at state power, whether exercised by government departments, statutory bodies or local authorities. In recent years the ambit of judicial review has expanded even further, and it is arguable that any body which exercises 'public functions' is now susceptible to judicial review. Much of the second half of this chapter is devoted to explaining how judicial review works and what it can achieve.

The importance of legal proceedings as a campaigning technique, however, stems not so much from the remedies that can be won in an individual case, but from the power of precedent. A scandalous practice may only have to be proved unlawful in one instance for it to be halted forever. A strong legal argument – in or out of court – can clarify rules, demolish the defence of the opposition and ensure that your target knows it is being watched closely.

The system of law sketched in this chapter is that of England and Wales (still referred to constitutionally as English law). Scotland and

Northern Ireland are separate jurisdictions, and space does not permit their description here.

The weight of the law

English law has two primary sources (although European legislation may now be considered a distinct third source). The first consists of statutes or Acts of Parliament and the mass of orders and regulations (collectively known as Statutory Instruments) that are made under them. There is also, however, the common law, which is not enshrined in legislation but has been built up by the courts over the centuries, with its origins in customs of the Middle Ages and before. While, broadly speaking, statute was primarily concerned with the relations between the state and its citizens and the common law concerned relations between individual citizens or citizens and their associations, in practice there is considerable overlap and both have come to affect each other.

The role of the judiciary is of central importance. Traditional legal theory has it that the courts do not make law but only interpret it, but interpretation is a creative process and judges will constantly be clarifying the meaning of statute as the dry words come up against the messy world of real people. Their role in the development of the common law is even more pronounced, as without legislation in a particular field the case law is all there is.

Legislation and case law together, then, provide the authority for the decisions made in court. They are not of equal authority. Subject to the scope of EC law, Parliament is sovereign and as such can legislate on any matter, even if it contradicts a basic principle of common law (e.g. a defendant's right to silence). Judges do not question statute, only what its meaning may be when applied to a particular case. Nor do they question the decisions made by courts higher than the one in which they are sitting: the rules of precedent establish that the decisions of higher courts on points of law are binding on all lower courts (a court will also generally be bound by its own previous decisions). Sitting in the High Court, for example, a judge will have no option but to follow the reasoning made a month before in a similar case by a judge in the Court of Appeal (unless, that is, she can distinguish the case before her as materially different).

Between 50 and 100 statutes are passed each year, although many simply consolidate or replace existing legislation. New statutes are available as soon as they are enacted from the Stationery Office, the government publisher; most libraries take the bound volumes which come out at the end of the year. Statutes frequently amend or refer to previous legislation, so lawyers tend to rely heavily on reference works like *Halsbury's Laws of England* which consolidate all the relevant legislation in a particular field.

Similarly, the pages of precedent are added to at an alarming rate by decisions made in new cases. These take the form of law reports, which summarise the facts of a particular case and the judgement. Case summaries are published regularly in most of the broadsheet newspapers (notably the *Times*) and in some specialist journals, but the most comprehensive selection is to be found in a number of special series of which the most authoritative is simply called *The Law Reports*. Legal textbooks will cite the well-known cluster of cases in any given field and these often form the starting point for further research. Digging around in case law is very much a scholarly quest. Although past cases frequently lose some significance as decisions are supplanted by legislation or new interpretations of the law, they may be rediscovered later for shedding light on a different point of law.

Law reformers often criticise the fact that the heavy emphasis on precedent in English law gives it an inherently conservative bias. This is, up to a point, unarguable and many judges will openly defend the legal system's affinity for the status quo, stating that the promotion of change in the law is something only Parliament is entitled to do. For the campaigner, however, this situation does present two significant advantages:

▼ government, too, is tied by legal precedent (although it can always promote new legislation, this is lengthy, resource-intensive and sometimes risky, and it will be avoided whenever possible);

▼ if you can show that legally you are in the right, then the weight of the establishment will for once be on your side.

Neither of these points should be underestimated. Discussing the great industrial struggles of her administration, Margaret Thatcher admitted: 'The criminal law on picketing ... had to be enforced by the police and the courts. Although the government would make it clear that the police enjoyed its moral support and would improve police equipment and training, the constitutional limits on us in this area were real and sometimes frustrating' (*The Downing Street Years*).

Outside the courts the frustrations continue. Time and again government is brought up short by its own lawyers or by outside groups pointing out that its plans would in some respect break the law – and government has to operate within the law just like anyone else. This was made devastatingly clear in 1993 when the House of Lords found the Home Secretary guilty of contempt of court for breaking a High Court injunction against deportation of an asylum seeker from Zaire. Lord Templeman commented that if the government's argument in the case had been upheld, it would 'establish the proposition that the executive obey the law as a matter of grace and not as a matter of necessity, a proposition which would reverse the result of the Civil

War'. The actions of government bodies have been described by every adjective under the sun, but the one that hurts the most is 'illegal'.

It is the law's independent authority, as well as its powers of investigation, which make critics of government habitually call for a public or 'judicial' inquiry in the wake of a disaster or scandal. Headed by an eminent judge or a QC, and with the power to summon witnesses, some public inquiries have consistently captured head-lines and deeply embarrassed or damaged public figures, including Lord Justice Butler-Sloss's inquiry into child abuse cases in Cleveland in 1988, Lord Justice Scott's methodical worm-can opening in the arms-to-Iraq case, and the Macpherson inquiry into the police handling of the racist murder of Stephen Lawrence.

The courts

The system of English law courts, with its different tiers and rights of appeal from some courts to others, often appears confusing. The diagram below illustrates how the main courts fit together and gives the titles of the judges or magistrates who sit in them.

The courts split roughly into two jurisdictions, one criminal and the other civil, although in some courts both types of case are heard. In a criminal case, the defendant or accused is prosecuted for an offence, usually by the state (in the form of the Crown Prosecution Service), and if found guilty is punished by the state. In a civil case, on the other hand, one individual or organisation (the claimant) will sue another (the defendant) on account of some private harm they have suffered. In most civil cases the proceedings will only be of immediate interest to the two parties involved, but the outcome may open the floodgates for a wave of similar litigation or it may force the defend-ant to behave differently to other people in the future. It is with this area of civil law that this chapter is primarily concerned.

The bulk of the work of magistrates' courts is concerned with summary criminal offences and with the inception of other criminal cases. They also hear some civil cases, principally in the areas of family law (child care orders, maintenance awards, etc.) and local administration (e.g. drinks and gaming licences; recovery of local taxes; appeals against certain local authority actions like the issue of notices under the Public Health Acts). Magistrates are neither law-yers nor judges (they undergo about two days' training) and, with a few exceptions, they work on a voluntary basis.

Small civil actions, however, are usually heard before a judge in the county court. This covers actions for breach of contract, negli-gence and so on, involving small claims for debt or damages. County courts also deal with a lot of landlord and tenant cases, with winding up companies and with certain other appeals against local authority decisions.

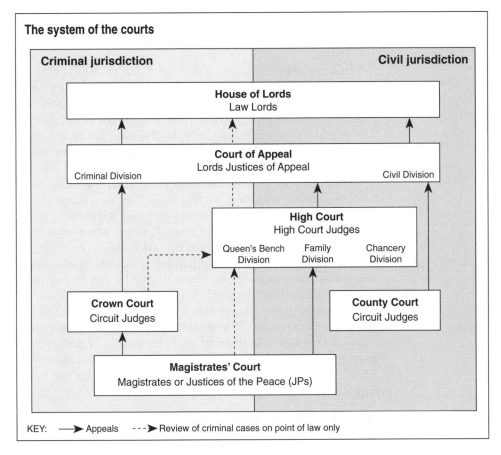

The system of the courts

Criminal jurisdiction — **Civil jurisdiction**

House of Lords — Law Lords

Court of Appeal — Lords Justices of Appeal — Criminal Division / Civil Division

High Court — High Court Judges — Queen's Bench Division / Family Division / Chancery Division

Crown Court — Circuit Judges

County Court — Circuit Judges

Magistrates' Court — Magistrates or Justices of the Peace (JPs)

KEY: ——▶ Appeals ---▶ Review of criminal cases on point of law only

Much pressure group litigation is started in the High Court, which hears the larger civil actions and those raising important points of law. Based in the Royal Courts of Justice in the Strand in London, but with regional outposts, it has three divisions (listed in increasing order of size):

▼ The Chancery Division deals with tax, wills and trusts, including actions for breach of trust. It is also the primary court for granting injunctions, which require someone to do or refrain from doing a specified act. Injunctions are often sought against pressure groups – preventing a demonstration or the publication of a leaked document, say – as well as by them: stopping a company discharging effluent into a river, for example.

▼ The Family Division hears major family cases as well as appeals from decisions of the magistrates' courts.

▼ The Queen's Bench Division deals with all the bigger breach of contract or tort proceedings (see below). It is the primary court responsible for judicial review of administrative action, issuing writs of *habeas corpus* (releasing individuals unlawfully detained), as well as hearing appeals on points of law from magistrates' courts.

Appeals from the judgements of the High Court or county courts are heard in the civil division of the Court of Appeal. Three judges sit in each case. The court rarely hears witnesses: it is all done with documents and lawyers. If an important point of law is at stake, then there is a further avenue of appeal to the House of Lords, where the case will be considered by five of the ten or so law lords. Commonly referred to as the highest court in the land, the House of Lords is in some respects inferior to the European Court in Luxembourg, which holds precedence in matters relating to EC law (see chapter 15).

The reality of proceedings in the civil courts differs markedly from the popular image of the English court, based as it is on reconstructions of criminal trials at the Old Bailey. Courtrooms are rarely crowded and, with some limited exceptions (most notably defamation cases), civil actions are not tried by jury but by judge alone. Civil law is considerably more technical than criminal law and is considered a greater intellectual challenge for the barristers. As a result, less time is spent on establishing facts and more on arguing points of law. Most significantly of all, the burden of proof in civil cases is different. Unlike the near certainty – 'beyond reasonable doubt' – that is needed to convict a criminal, civil cases are decided on the balance of probabilities.

Opportunities for legal action

The range of circumstances in which a campaign might further its cause by bringing a legal action is as wide as the law itself, but the examples cited below, all of which refer to actual cases, give some indication of what is possible.

The great majority of civil actions are brought in tort or for breach of contract. These are areas stemming from, and still dominated by, common law, but statute has intervened on occasion to clarify rights or to introduce new causes of action (so-called statutory torts). Tort is a word used in law to cover a diverse group of private or civil wrongs, including those illustrated below.

▼ *Negligence*. On a number of different occasions, victim support groups have sued for negligence the manufacturers or distributors of drugs which had harmful side effects. In the most famous case, the families who suffered from the drug Thalidomide won a settlement after 10 years of litigation and public pressure.

▼ *Nuisance*. A residents group brought an action for public nuisance against a local quarry, seeking an injunction to restrain the uncontrolled production of mineral dust which was making their lives a misery.

▼ *Assault.* After the Crown Prosecution Service failed to bring criminal charges against an alleged rapist, a pressure group helped the victim sue her attacker for assault and battery. (Note that the lesser burden of proof required in a civil action meant that the woman might have a strong case even if the CPS's decision not to prosecute was a reasonable one.)

▼ *Slander and libel.* See chapter 5 for examples.

▼ *False imprisonment.* A new firefighter sued her colleagues for false imprisonment, among other things, after she was tied to a ladder during a humiliating initiation ceremony.

If a tort has been committed, not just anyone can sue: only those whose rights have been infringed. Generally, the claimant must have personally suffered the wrong, whether financial, physical, propri-etorial, or damaging to reputation, as in an action for libel. With some torts, like public nuisance, a claimant will have to show 'special damage', or damage over and above that suffered by the public at large, in order to bring an action.

The role of a pressure group, then, will often consist of advising and supporting a claimant, rather than bringing the action in its own name. In some cases, a group may seek to acquire rights just to enable it to take legal action: an environmental group, for example, might purchase land by a river so that it could bring an action in private nuisance against a factory that was polluting the river water.

Both individuals and corporate bodies can be sued. As most civil actions are brought in order to seek damages, the decision to sue will often depend on whether the proposed defendant has enough money to make litigation worthwhile. Employers are vicariously liable for torts committed by their employees in the line of work, which usually ensures a sufficiently solvent defendant in the form of the company or employer concerned. Generally, consider who is the most appro-priate defendant: often there will be more than one.

Tort law has the effect of imposing a series of general obligations on all members of society, enforceable at the suit of a wronged party. However, particular individuals or companies can also voluntarily assume further specific obligations to each other in the form of a contract. Contractual obligations are enforceable only at the suit of one of the parties to the contract.

Consumer groups have supported a large number of breach of contract cases involving the supply of faulty or deficient goods, where the claimant is seeking compensatory damages. In some instances of breach of contract, as for example those involving intentional racial or sex discrimination, aggravated or exemplary damages may also be awarded. Other cases give further examples of what is possible:

▼ A junior hospital doctor took his employer, a health authority, to court arguing that a provision in his employment contract, which gave the authority the power to require him to work up to eighty hours a week, was subject to an implied term which limited the power in the interests of the health and safety of the doctor and his patients. Clarifying the terms of the contract, the Court of Appeal found in the doctor's favour.

▼ An order for specific performance was sought against a mining company to enforce its promise to restore a Pacific island to its former state after extensive phosphate mining.

▼ Both EC and UK law now enable the cancellation or rescission of contracts entered into through the heavy pressure techniques of door-to-door salespeople.

▼ In some instances, particularly in areas such as employment law, a claimant may have the option of suing for breach of contract or for a tort, or for both. The woman who suffered false imprisonment in the case cited above, for example, also sued the fire authority, as employer, for negligence and breach of contract.

Finally, it is worth saying a few things about the criminal law. New categories of criminal offence are created periodically and cover a huge range of things from inciting racial hatred (through the distribution of racist leaflets, for example) to persistent failure to submit company accounts to the Registrar of Companies. Offences can be reported to the police with any supporting evidence. If the police fail to take the matter further, or if on referral the Crown prosecutor decides not to prosecute, it is also possible to bring a private prosecution. However, offences which are particularly sensitive, for political or other reasons, may require the Attorney General's consent to be prosecuted and all private prosecutions can be terminated by the Attorney General.

The procedure in private prosecutions is much the same but the ramifications in terms of costs must always be considered: only if the defendant is convicted will there be even the possibility that he will be ordered to contribute to the costs of bringing the prosecution. Such costs can be considerable, particularly as serious offences carry the right of trial by jury. Private prosecutions are in fact rare as the chances of success are not great. In most cases where an offence has been committed and there is a victim, there will be open to the victim the alternative of bringing a civil action in tort, where the standard of proof is less exacting.

Bringing an action

If you think you have a case in law, but do not have a solicitor, where do you go? Citizens advice bureaux and legal advice centres may be able to provide initial guidance, but their legal expertise varies greatly – few have legally qualified staff although many receive some help from volunteer solicitors – and they tend to be most proficient in the fields of employment, housing, and some aspects of family law. At the very least, they should be able to direct an enquirer to an appropriate solicitor or specialist body.

The sixty or so law centres in the country, on the other hand, do have legally qualified staff and take on individual cases. They concentrate on helping less advantaged people and again are most practised in the fields noted above. The help of a law centre can be decisive for a local campaign on, say, tenants' rights or local authority services, which otherwise would not be able to afford proper legal representation. Addresses for law centres can be obtained from the Law Centres Federation (see appendix B). The Community Legal Service, a public service launched in April 2000, coordinates the funding of advice services to try and ensure that every community has access to legal advice providers of consistent quality.

Many solicitors now offer a fixed fee interview: up to half an hour's legal advice for a small sum. This should be enough to enable you to decide whether a case is worth pursuing further. Those solicitors offering fixed fee interviews are indicated in the Solicitors Regional Directory, which can be consulted in most local libraries. (This is not to be confused with the duty solicitor scheme, under which free legal advice is available round the clock to those questioned by the police about an offence.)

Legal resources available locally, however, may not have sufficient experience to give advice in many of the specialist fields in which pressure groups operate, particularly if they are seeking to use the law in an unusual or imaginative way. Other specialist non-profit bodies or umbrella bodies at national level are often the first port of call for informal help and advice in these situations. MIND, for example, the National Association for Mental Health, has extensive experience of advising on cases as well as providing representation. Unions and professional associations will often have built up considerable legal expertise, although it will obviously be weighted towards employment and related areas. Such organisations should certainly be able to put enquirers in touch with solicitors with relevant experience. If a difficult point of law is involved, a solicitor might suggest seeking counsel's opinion; that is, the advice of an experienced barrister on how the court is likely to react in this case.

Extra-legal tools, like letters of complaint and requests for compensation, will be more effective if they demonstrate a clear awareness of the relevant law. If the letter is from a solicitor, it will be taken that much more seriously. In many of the more well-trodden areas of litigation, protracted negotiations at this stage can deliver results, but if you are trying anything at all unusual, your solicitor will need to get a claim form issued to show that you are really serious. This also provides a good opportunity for publicity.

Civil procedure

A claim form is a document which effectively says 'see you in court'. It is issued by the court at the request of the claimant and is 'served' on the defendant, possibly by post but often in person. If the defendant is a company, it is delivered to the registered office or a place of business connected to the matter in issue. The claim form includes a concise statement of the nature of the claim and specifies the remedy that the claimant is seeking. Particulars of the claim must accompany the claim form or be served on the defendant within the next 14 days. The defendant either has to satisfy the claim or to file a defence, generally within 14 days of being served with the particulars of the claim.

A large proportion of claims are either not contested or are settled before they get to court. It is important to realise, particularly if you are bringing a case against a large corporation, that the decision whether or not to contest may be made on grounds other than just the merits of the individual case. With campaigning actions, a lot often depends on how much adverse publicity the defendant can expect to receive if the case goes to court. Conversely, a corporation may nearly always choose to contest a claim, simply to dissuade other people from making similar claims.

Contested cases are managed by the court, including identifying disputed issues at an early stage, fixing timetables, and disposing of cases summarily where they disclose no case or defence. In a process known as 'disclosure', the court can order that a party to the proceedings provides the other side with relevant documents, including documents that adversely affect their case, as well as those favourable to it. By this stage, each side will know most of the details of the other side's case, a factor which encourages early settlements.

Time, however, will also be on the side of a large corporation. Before the court's case management powers were boosted in 1999, a wait of two or three years before a case was listed for trial in the High Court was not uncommon. It is often in the interests of the corporation, with its permanent legal staff, to drag things out as long as possible. Pressure groups are typically ephemeral organisations and as the months or years go by they may no longer have the resources, the organisation or the will to continue. To this must be added the considerable emotional strain if campaigners are personally involved or at financial risk in the case.

Another factor encourages pre-trial settlements: as the trial approaches, costs start to escalate. In addition to the court costs and the fees of any expert witnesses, a barrister will have to be paid a brief fee to take on the case and then a retainer (or 'refresher' as it is known) for every day the trial continues. If it is a senior barrister or QC (Queen's Counsel), she will be accompanied by a junior, which means paying for two barristers plus the solicitor attending court. The fact that both parties' costs are usually awarded in favour of the winning party increases the stakes substantially. It is hardly surprising, then, that probably over a quarter of all negligence cases are settled at the eleventh hour, just before the parties enter the courtroom.

In negotiations in a civil case, the likely size of any damages awarded is in fact as important as the chances of winning. Calculations are further complicated by the mechanism of the payment into court, in which a defendant can pay a sum into court, usually the minimum that he thinks may be awarded in damages, without prejudicing the outcome of the trial (neither judge nor jury, if there is one, is made aware of the payment into court). If the claimant refuses to accept the sum as settlement of the claim and is subsequently awarded damages no greater than that sum, she will be liable for all the defendant's costs, and her own, roughly from the time of the payment in, which may well leave her worse off than when she started. There is more about costs at the end of this chapter.

The procedure sketched above is that of a claim for damages in the High Court, although many of the elements will be similar in other types of action. The court can act quickly if necessary: it is possible to obtain, for example, an interim injunction to prevent a party from doing something until the matter goes to trial; and the costs involved in such action are not great. In some instances, pressure groups who campaign on behalf of a large number of potential litigants may be able to save considerable costs by bringing a representative action. A group of shareholders, for example, may be able to sue the directors of a company in the name of the other shareholders, so long as their interests are the same.

In test cases, of course, the judgement is all important, but many other cases will never go to trial and the legal claim is effectively a means of applying pressure to ensure that rights are respected, to control the future behaviour of the defendant, or just to gain publicity. The amount of information required to be disclosed in civil proceedings can on occasion deliver some embarrassing revelations, and even if a case is not particularly strong in law it may still be worth bringing for the PR damage it can do to the campaign's target.

Suing the state

The examples considered so far in this chapter have mostly concerned private defendants, whether individuals or companies. It is also possible, however, to bring actions against government bodies, the police, or other statutory agencies.

Although it is not a universally applicable rule, there is a strong current in English law which holds that government bodies or officials are responsible for their actions to the same extent and in the same way as private citizens; that is, they are equally liable in tort, contract, etc. A property holder successfully sued a public authority which was acting on an invalid demolition order in destroying a building which did not have planning permission. A political activist sued law officers who entered his printing workshop and seized equipment and papers on the authority of a warrant incorrectly made out.

There are, however, significant limitations on when government bodies can be sued. The law imposes on such authorities a wide range of duties, for example, which they are obliged to perform but the execution of which may unavoidably result in others suffering nuisance or economic loss. An action for damages or an injunction would not be possible here (unless, perhaps, the duty was performed negligently). More generally, the courts have often proved reluctant to intervene unless an act by a public authority is both outside its statutory duties and outside the discretionary powers that it holds, i.e. the act is *ultra vires*. (The notion of *ultra vires* is explained further in the next section.) Furthermore, an action in tort for the negligent exercise of a statutory duty may only be arguable if the court can be persuaded that the statute was intended to create a right for individuals in the claimant's position that could be enforced by means of an action for damages.

Certain immunities and privileges in law are also held by the Crown (roughly defined as ministers of state and the central government departments for which they are responsible, but not other governmental bodies). These include the fact that the Crown is not liable in tort for a breach of statutory duty unless the duty also rests on people other than the Crown or its officers (i.e. the duty is not confined to the Crown); and that the Crown is not subject to any statutory obligation unless the statute in question expressly binds the Crown, but the Crown may take the benefit of any statutory provision even if it is not mentioned as a beneficiary.

But civil litigation against public authorities is an area of law that is developing constantly. There is even a tort that can only be committed by public officials, known as 'misfeasance in public office', which covers the intentional or malicious misuse of statutory powers. In some fields, litigation for common law torts is well-established – for example against the police – and can even lead to awards of exemplary damages. A black family sued the police for assault and battery, false imprisonment and malicious prosecution after the police forcibly entered their home, arrested them and prosecuted them on trumped-up charges. They won over £50,000 in damages.

Judicial review of administrative action

By far the most wide-ranging legal tool for challenging the actions of public bodies, however, and one that is growing all the time, is judicial review. In 1998, 1767 new applications for judicial review were dealt with by the court, and 636 applications were successful. That means that roughly twice a day someone managed to have a governmental decision overturned.

▼ The miners' unions challenged the peremptory decision by the President of the Board of Trade in 1992 to shut 31 coal mines with the loss of 30,000 jobs and obtained a declaration that the decision was unlawful.

▼ A local authority's resolution not to rehouse certain categories of homeless person was said to be unlawful; when exercising its powers to house homeless people it had to consider the circumstances of each case.

▼ Home Secretary Michael Howard was ruled in 1994 to have acted unlawfully and to have committed an 'abuse of power' when he cut compensation payments to the victims of violent crime by introducing a compensation scheme which was radically different from what Parliament had approved.

▼ The World Development Movement successfully challenged in 1995 the Foreign Secretary's decision to spend £234 million of overseas development funds on the Pergau dam project in Malaysia, a project that was deemed economically unsound by development officials but which was widely linked to UK arms sales to Malaysia.

▼ The prosecution and imprisonment of refugees forced to travel on false passports was ruled unlawful in 1999. The Crown Prosecution Service and Home Secretary Jack Straw were rebuked by the High Court for not having given 'the least thought' to their obligations under the UN Refugee Convention.

Judicial review is common in immigration cases and in cases involving eligibility for council housing or benefits. Unlike the civil actions described in the previous section, whose principal purpose is to compensate or halt the infringement of private rights, judicial review is concerned with the proper limits of public or state power, or, as it is sometimes put, the rights of citizens under public law. If a public body exceeds its powers or duties in coming to a decision, that decision can be quashed by a court as unlawful, whether or not private rights have been infringed.

The remedies available by way of judicial review are given in the box opposite. It is important to note that the supervisory jurisdiction of the High Court in judicial review is very different from the function of the appeal court: the court may quash an illegal decision but it cannot, as in an appeal, substitute its decision for the one quashed. The public body which made the original decision will usually be required to reconsider, and it may well create precisely the same outcome again (albeit by legal means this time). The effect of a successful challenge, therefore, may be merely to delay government action, or to scupper it completely.

The scope of judicial review

Almost all government bodies or officials are subject to judicial review, including government departments, executive agencies or fringe bodies, local authorities and health authorities. It is perhaps more accurate to say that it is the public functions undertaken, rather than the bodies themselves, which are the subject of judicial review. Thus a wide range of public functions performed by non-governmental bodies also come within the court's supervisory jurisdiction, for example the work of the Advertising Standards Authority, the British Pharmaceutical Industry's Code of Practice Committee, and various licensing bodies. This is a developing area, and there has been a tendency to increase the range of decisions subject to judicial review.

Although our doctrine of Parliamentary supremacy means that the creation of primary legislation by Parliament cannot be challenged in any court (subject to the effect of EC law), delegated or secondary legislation, in the form of orders or regulations drawn up

---

Remedies available under judicial review

Certiorari
The order of certiorari quashes, or deprives of legal effect, a decision that has already been made.

Prohibition
The order of prohibition lies to restrain illegal actions, i.e. it prevents a proposed decision from being made or acted upon.

Mandamus
This order compels a public body to do something. If a discretionary power is involved, mandamus can compel the body to exercise the power properly. The orders of certiorari and mandamus are sometimes sought together, first to quash an invalid decision and then to force the decision-making body to deal with the matter according to the law.

Declaration
A declaratory judgement simply sets out the legal position between parties in contention. It is particularly useful where more coercive remedies are inappropriate, against the Crown for example.

Injunction
The principal function of an injunction, to restrain illegal action, is very similar to that of the prohibition, but it has a wider application. In some cases an interim injunction will be the only available method of preventing a body taking action until the court has had time to rule on its legality. Unlike the order of prohibition, an injunction is also available against non-public bodies whose decisions are nevertheless subject to the rules of natural justice (see main text).

Notes
1. An action for damages can be joined to an application for a declaration or injunction, but only in cases where the plaintiff's private rights have been infringed.
2. One further, very specialised, remedy has extensive applications in immigration and civil liberties cases. The ancient writ of *habeas corpus* is used to secure the release of a person illegally detained.

by ministers under statutory powers, *is* subject to judicial review. So too, naturally, are administrative guidelines, codes of practice, etc.

As always, however, some areas of governmental decision-making slip through the net. Although the source of a power will not affect its reviewability, it has been argued that some powers exercised by the Crown (i.e. central government) are outside the scope of judicial review, including such minor matters as the making of international treaties, the appointment of ministers and the defence of the realm. This last is very important, as the government will often plead that a particular issue concerns national security and as such is non-justiciable, or unsuitable for review by the court. In 1985 the House of Lords ruled that the demands of national security relieved the government of any obligation to consult before banning union membership among employees at GCHQ, the government's intelligence headquarters.

The 'coercive' remedies of certiorari, prohibition and mandamus are generally not available against the Crown. The most appropriate remedy against the Crown is the declaration. It had long been established that injunctions were not obtainable against the Crown either, but, in a case cited earlier, the House of Lords found the Home Secretary guilty of contempt of court in 1993 for breaking a High Court injunction against deportation of an asylum seeker from Zaire. In one of the more important constitutional cases of the century, the Law Lords held that the courts can stop a minister taking action pending a court decision on its legality. It is not entirely clear following this judgement, however, in which cases the courts will now be prepared to award interim injunctions against the Crown.

The grounds for review

It was noted above that governmental bodies hold both duties, which they are required to perform, and discretionary powers, which they can choose to exercise or not. These may be conferred either by statute or by the common law. Acting outside of this authority is known as action *ultra vires* (literally, beyond powers) and is illegal.

But many of the decisions taken by government are highly complex; its powers are multiple and often ill-defined. What sort of behaviour will take a government body *ultra vires* and subject to control by judicial review? In the GCHQ case mentioned above, Lord Diplock classified such behaviour under three heads.

▼ *Illegality.* The concept of illegality is used here to cover not just deliberate breaches but also mistakes as to the applicable law. If, in coming to a decision, a legal rule is misstated, misinterpreted or misapplied, that may render the decision invalid, as may the failure to take notice of a rule that does apply. A council tenant was evicted from his one-room accommodation when his wife and children left their home in Bangladesh to join him, on the grounds that he had become homeless intentionally 'having deliberately arranged for his wife and children to leave [their Bangladeshi] accommodation which it would have been reasonable for them to continue to occupy'. The relevant statute, however, referred to accommodation 'which it would have been reasonable for [him] to continue to occupy' and the House of Lords duly quashed the council's decision.

▼ *Irrationality*. Many powers held by a public authority allow it considerable discretion, but if a decision taken is so extreme as to be irrational, it may still be *ultra vires*. An irrational decision in this context was famously defined as 'one so unreasonable that no reasonable authority could ever have come to it'. This is a tough test, and is an indication of the courts' reluctance to fetter public authorities' discretion, or to allow what are essentially policy decisions to be questioned in the courts. Acting on the basis of irrelevant considerations, or ignoring relevant ones, may take a decision down the path of irrationality. The making of a decision for some ulterior purpose, rather than the purpose of the power under which it was authorised, has also been considered grounds for intervention by the courts.

▼ *Procedural impropriety*. This covers instances where the decision-making process is at fault either because it seriously flouts statutory rules of procedure or because it breaches natural justice. The rules of natural justice require that a person should be given a fair hearing and that a decision-maker should not be biased (in the sense of self-interested, rather than politically motivated). Even if a set of procedural guidelines or a code of practice do not have the force of law, the fact that they exist might create a legitimate expectation that they should be followed, and not to do so may constitute a breach of natural justice.

Even the most powerful of authorities ignore proper procedure at their peril: in the first example cited in this section, it was the failure of Michael Heseltine and British Coal to implement a process of consultation and independent scrutiny before deciding to close the collieries which made their decisions unlawful. The miners' unions had a legitimate expectation that they would be consulted. The senior judge hearing the case further noted that the decision to deprive the unions and the workers of any independent scrutiny of the closure programme could properly be described as irrational.

Many statutes create a right of appeal from the decision of a public authority: a local authority closing order under the Housing Acts can be appealed against in the county court; a notice under the Public Health Acts in the magistrates' court. Social security and employment legislation create a number of statutory rights of appeal to the Social

Security Appeals Tribunals or Industrial Tribunals. Although the existence of a statutory appeal procedure does not automatically rule out the use of judicial review, if such a procedure does exist and has not been followed, a judicial review remedy may not be granted or an application for judicial review stayed while an appeal is pursued.

Procedure

Most judicial review actions (including all applications for the orders of certiorari, prohibition and mandamus) are brought through a procedure known as the 'application for judicial review', as laid down by Order 53 of the Rules of the Supreme Court. The procedure has two stages: an applicant first has to seek leave to apply and, if granted, can then go on to the hearing itself. The leave stage is relatively cheap, brief (if oral proceedings are deemed necessary they rarely last more than half an hour) and the success rate for being granted leave is around 60%.

Applications for judicial review have to be made promptly following the administrative decision or action that they seek to challenge. There is a maximum time-limit of three months within which to make the application; occasionally this may be extended, but an application should always be made as quickly as is practicable.

But the application for judicial review is not the only way of seeking judicial review of an administrative decision. In certain circumstances it is also possible to seek a declaration or an injunction by means of an ordinary civil action. Under this procedure there is no formal time-limit, there is no requirement to seek leave first, and the disclosure of documents (which is absent in an application for judicial review) can be an advantage in shedding some light on the opaque activities of the administration.

Initiating proceedings through an ordinary civil action, however, is only possible if the decision challenged has infringed a private law right, as well as a public law right. If governmental action is allegedly *ultra vires*, but has not affected the applicant's private law rights, an application for judicial review under Order 53 is the only method of proceeding. Exactly when it is appropriate to use each type of procedure is a difficult area, but the simplified diagram opposite covers the main points.

One great advantage of the application for judicial review is that the rules governing who is able to bring proceedings are much more relaxed than for ordinary civil actions. An applicant must have standing, or *locus standi*, but this means only that leave to apply for judicial review will not be granted unless the applicant has a 'sufficient interest' in the contested decision. Thus a journalist was found to have standing to challenge a policy of not disclosing the names of magistrates who try certain types of case; planning decisions can be challenged by the owners of neighbouring land; the holder of a

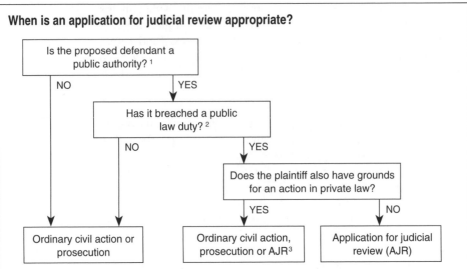

When is an application for judicial review appropriate?

Notes

1. This includes inferior courts and tribunals, as well as some clearly non-public bodies which are performing public functions, e.g., an industry self-regulatory body such as the Advertising Standards Authority.

2. That is, acted *ultra vires*, either through error of law, irrationality, or following improper procedure. This of course does not apply to an unlawful act carried out by the authority in a purely contractual or business – i.e. non-public – capacity, where an ordinary civil action or prosecution is the only course available.

3. Ordinary civil actions have certain advantages over applications for judicial review, including greater flexibility regarding remedies and the availability of an order for disclosure, which provides access to the other party's documentation. Where an application for judicial review is available, however, the courts may regard bringing an ordinary civil action as a misuse of procedure, unless the question of *ultra vires* is collateral (i.e. incidental to the main purpose of establishing civil liability).

'legitimate expectation' (as defined above) would have standing to challenge an action that thwarted that expectation.

But the notion of sufficient interest is a hazy one. While ratepayers have been held to have standing to challenge spending decisions by their local authorities, it is highly unlikely that someone will have standing to make an application for judicial review of a central government decision just because she is a taxpayer.

From the point of view of pressure groups, one of the breakthroughs of the standing rules introduced under Order 53 is that standing has been accorded to bodies acting in a representative capacity, although some kind of track record or a clear membership structure may be a help. Thus the Child Poverty Action Group was held by the court to have standing to challenge social security decisions, but the Rose Theatre Trust, set up just to campaign for the preservation of a theatre site, did not have standing to challenge decisions about the future of the site. Note that an unincorporated association cannot itself apply for judicial review; one of its members with sufficient interest must make the application.

When it was argued in court that Greenpeace did not have standing to apply for judicial review of the decision to commission THORP, the nuclear reprocessing plant at Sellafield, the judge took into account the fact that 2,500 of Greenpeace's members came from Cumbria. He concluded: 'I reject the argument that Greenpeace is a mere or meddlesome busybody or even an officious bystander. I regard the applicants as eminently respectable and responsible and their interest in the issues raised is sufficient for them to be granted *locus standi.*'

Much of the detailed law regarding judicial review is specific to particular fields, especially where, as in housing or immigration, judicial review has become a tried and tested technique. If you are contemplating seeking judicial review of an administrative action, it is essential to get experienced legal advice.

A body called the Public Law Project (see appendix B for address) aims to improve access to public law remedies and may be able to provide help to disadvantaged groups and other non-profits. Although it cannot underwrite litigation costs, the Project is able to take on judicial review cases, particularly in areas where the full potential of judicial review is yet to be explored. It has dealt with a wide variety of cases including those concerning education law, the powers of utilities regulators, civil rights and aspects of community care.

The Human Rights Act

The Human Rights Act 1998 has been described by the Home Secretary as the most significant statement of human rights in domestic law since the 1689 Bill of Rights. In force from October 2000, the Act will certainly have a huge impact on the law and provide a tool of considerable power to those fighting for social justice in the UK.

The Human Rights Act essentially makes directly enforceable in the UK the rights contained in the European Convention on Human Rights. The Convention rights concerned are listed in the box below. Instead of having to go to the European Court of Human Rights in Strasbourg (see chapter 15) to have these rights protected, people in the UK can now seek protection or remedy in their own courts.

Looking at former cases before the European Court of Human Rights provides a better understanding of what exercising the Convention rights means in practice. Courts and tribunals in the UK are specifically required to take into account the case law from Strasbourg when interpreting the Human Rights Act.

The proposed deportation of a Sikh separatist leader, for example, was found to violate article 3 because there was a real danger he would be tortured if returned to India. Refusing permission to enter the UK to a group of East African Asians who were citizens of the UK and colonies was found to amount to degrading treatment under the same article. A ban on homosexual people in the armed forces was held a violation of article 8, as was unregulated telephone-tapping. Both the distribution of political leaflets and the refusal to disclose journalistic sources have been protected under article 10. Article 11 has been held to protect the right to demonstrate as well as entailing the right to be protected from disruption by a violent counter-demonstration. Article 6 has generated more applications to Strasbourg than any other article, covering a range of issues from access to justice to admissibility of evidence. Only in one case has the Strasbourg court found – narrowly – a violation of article 2, when three IRA members were shot dead by the SAS in Gibraltar.

An internal government exercise undertaken before the Human Rights Act came into force to try and identify existing legislation and procedures that might conflict with the rights in the new Act produced a list eight pages long. The criminal justice system, the prison service, and the immigration system are all likely to see numerous challenges. The restrictions placed on charities' political activities might be challenged under article 10. The denial of education to children excluded from school might be challenged under article 2 of protocol 1. Some particular pieces of legislation are in for a torrid time: the Criminal Justice and Public Order Act 1994, for example, might see challenged its provisions on stop-and-search (under article 5), limitations to the right to silence (under article 6) and controls on trespassory protest (under articles 10 and 11).

In addition to the rights listed in the box, the UK government has indicated that it intends to amend the Human Rights Act to incorporate the further rights contained in Protocol 7 to the European Convention, once it has removed certain incompatibilites with domestic law. Protocol 7 contains procedural safeguards on the expulsion of aliens, a right to equality between spouses and certain fair trial rights, including the right to review of conviction or sentence in criminal cases, a prohibition on double jeopardy and the right to compensation for miscarriages of justice.

The responsibility of public authorities

Under the Human Rights Act it is unlawful for a public authority to act in a way which is incompatible with a Convention right. 'Act' here includes a failure to act. The provisions of the Human Rights Act must be applied in a such a way as to make the rights 'practical and effective' rather than 'theoretical and illusory', to quote a European Court judgement.

Public authorities include central government departments and agencies, local authorities, health authorities, immigration authorities, the police, courts and tribunals, as well as other public bodies. They also include bodies only certain of whose functions are of a public nature, for example a private security company managing a

The rights in the Human Rights Act

Article numbers refer to the articles of the European Convention on Human Rights and its Protocols which are incorporated in Schedule 1 of the Human Rights Act

Article 2   the right to life

Article 3   the right not to be subjected to torture or to inhuman or degrading treatment or punishment

Article 4   the right not to be held in slavery or servitude or required to perform forced or compulsory labour

Article 5   the right to liberty and security of person*

Article 6   the right to a fair trial

Article 7   the right not be punished through retrospective legislation

Article 8   the right to respect for private and family life, home and correspondence

Article 9   the right to freedom of thought, conscience and religion

Article 10   the right to freedom of expression, including the freedom to hold opinions and to receive and impart information and ideas

Article 11   the right to freedom of peaceful assembly and association, including the right to form and join trade unions

Article 12   the right to marry and found a family

Article 14   the right not to be discriminated against, in respect of any of the other rights and freedoms contained in the Convention, on any ground such as sex, race, colour, language, religion, political or other opinion, national or social origin, association with a national minority, property, birth or other status

Protocol 1

Article 1   the right to peaceful enjoyment of possessions

Article 2   the right to education+

Article 3   the right to free elections

Protocol 6

Article 1   the right not to be condemned to death or executed

* subject to UK government derogation concerning pre-trial detention under prevention of terrorism legislation

+ 'only so far as it is compatible with the provision of efficient instruction and training, and the avoidance of unreasonable public expenditure' (UK government reservation)

contracted-out prison, or a GP practice with both NHS and private patients. However, in the latter case such bodies will only be bound to act in a way compatible with Convention rights in respect of their *public* functions.

The way in which the responsibility of public authorities under the Human Rights Act is interpreted follows the approach of the European court and is markedly different from the standard public law approach described in the last section. Once a Convention right is engaged, there is a presumption that that right should be protected, and any restriction of that right by a public authority has to be prescribed by law and be 'proportionate to the legitimate aim pursued'.

Some rights are absolute and cannot be restricted in any circumstances, including the right to life and the rights not to be subjected to torture or held in slavery. Other rights, however, are subject to express limitations. For example, the full text of Article 8, the right to respect for private and family life, reads as follows:

'1. Everyone has the right to respect for his private and family life, his home and his correspondence.

'2. There shall be no interference by a public authority with the exercise of this right except such as is in accordance with the law and is necessary in a democratic society in the interests of national security, public safety or the economic well being of the country, for the prevention of disorder or crime, for the protection of health or morals, or for the protection of the rights and freedoms of others.'

The European Court recognised, in a leading case involving the UK, that 'inherent in the whole of the Convention is a search for the fair balance between the demands of the general interest of the community and the requirements of the protection of the individual's human rights'. In a case involving the monitoring of someone's correspondence, for example, the courts would seek this balance by asking whether the monitoring was prescribed by law (that is, whether it was legally regulated and the relevant rules were accessible to the people likely to be affected), whether it pursued one of the legitimate aims listed in the article above, and whether it was 'necessary in a democratic society' (this has been interpreted to mean both that it fulfils a 'pressing social need' and that the means employed are proportionate to that need). Unless all these criteria are fulfilled, the monitoring would be a violation of article 8.

Public authorities are not just required to refrain from acts which might breach Convention rights, they are also under a positive obligation to give effect to those rights. This might include, in some cases, ensuring that resources are made available to prevent breaches of rights (e.g. the provision of criminal legal aid) or ensuring there is an appropriate legal framework in place to protect rights, or effective regulation of private bodies. If pollution was violating the private and family life of local residents, for example, the responsible public authority would be required to ensure that it was stopped, even if the source was a private waste-treatment plant.

However, a public authority will not be acting unlawfully if under existing primary legislation it could not have acted differently. The authority will have to see whether the statute can be read or given effect in a way which is compatible with Convention rights, but if no such way exists it will still be bound by the existing law. Using the Human Rights Act to challenge legislation is described below.

Convention rights are not directly enforceable against private bodies such as individuals and private companies: private bodies cannot be sued for breach of a Convention right. However, they will be subject to an indirect or horizontal effect under the Human Rights Act, because of the fact that courts and tribunals (as public authorities themselves) are required to interpret the law so as to accord with Convention rights, even in litigation between private parties. A person who feels her rights have been violated by a private body, therefore, will either have to deploy the Human Rights Act arguments in court in relation to an existing private law cause of action, or find a public authority which has a positive obligation to protect her rights from violation by the private body.

Bringing a case under the Human Rights Act

If you think that one or more of your Convention rights have been, or are about to be, violated, you can bring legal proceedings, either by way of judicial review (see previous section) or by way of a civil action for breach of statutory duty. You can also rely on Convention rights as part of a defence in any criminal or civil proceedings against you.

Any person, group of individuals or non-governmental organisation can bring proceedings, but they must themselves be victims of the alleged violation. This means that they must be actually and directly affected by it, or at risk of being directly affected by it. Note that this is a more restrictive test of standing than the 'sufficient interest' test in judicial review. Charities and pressure groups will often therefore be in the position of supporting a claimant whose rights have been violated, but they will not be able themselves to bring proceedings under the Human Rights Act unless they or their members are victims.

Any court or tribunal can consider arguments under the Human Rights Act but legal proceedings brought under the Act will need to be made in the 'appropriate' court or tribunal, as determined by rules of court. The appropriate court for cases brought by way of judicial review will be the High Court. Proceedings need to be brought within one year of the alleged violation taking place or 'such longer period as the court or tribunal considers equitable', unless there is a stricter time limit applicable to the legal procedure in question (applications for judicial review, for example, will still need to be made within three months).

Where there has been a violation of a Convention right, the court or tribunal can award an appropriate remedy – such as the quashing of a decision, an injunction, or damages – so long as it is within its powers to grant such a remedy (a criminal court, for example, will not be able to award damages, but may grant a stay in proceedings, the exclusion of evidence, or the quashing of an indictment). An award of damages can only be granted if, taking into account all the circumstances of the case including any other remedy granted, the court is satisfied that the award is necessary to afford 'just satisfaction'. The principles applied by the European Court will have to be taken into account in any decision to award damages, which suggests that damages awarded for violation of Convention rights are likely to be modest.

Using the Human Rights Act to challenge legislation

Before the Human Rights Act was first introduced, there had been much discussion about whether it should 'entrench' rights by protecting them from future amendment or repeal or making them override other legislation, giving judges the power to strike down any law that was incompatible with them. In the event it was decided that in order to preserve Parliamentary sovereignty the Human Rights Act would not override other legislation, but that the courts should be required, as far as possible, to interpret all other existing and future legislation, as well as the common law, in a way which was compatible with the Convention rights. Whenever a minister introduces a new bill to Parliament, he is also required to make a statement confirming whether the provisions of the bill are compatible with Convention rights.

Where an existing piece of primary legislation cannot be interpreted in such a way as be compatible with Convention rights, the higher courts can make a 'declaration of incompatibility'. This in itself does not affect the validity or enforcement of the legislation, but it does enable the government to then follow a fast-track legislative procedure to remove the incompatibility. (The courts can, however, set aside subordinate or delegated legislation – that is, regulations made under an authority in primary legislation – if it is incompatible with Convention rights, unless the terms of the parent legislation itself make this impossible.)

Declarations of incompatibility are unlikely to be made often. The lower courts, where victims of an alleged rights violation will often go to seek relief, are not empowered to make such declarations and in the

High Court the cost of actions will probably be inflated by the fact that the Crown has a right to intervene in proceedings where the court is considering making a declaration incompatibility.

Once a declaration of incompatibility has been made, the government can make a remedial order to amend the legislation to bring it in line with Convention rights. A remedial order is a statutory instrument which requires a positive resolution of both Houses of Parliament after a 60-day period of consultation (in urgent cases, the order can take effect immediately but will expire after 120 days if not approved by Parliament).

It is important to note that the government is not actually required to take remedial action, although as a matter of policy the government has said that it 'almost certainly' will. The Lord Chancellor confirmed in the House of Lords that 'If a minister's prior assessment of compatibility ... is subsequently found by a declaration of incompatibility by the courts to have been mistaken, it is hard to see how a minister could withhold remedial action'.

However, the fact that there is no duty on government to amend legislation which is incompatible with the Human Rights Act, coupled with the fact that remedial orders will need to compete for Parliamentary time with other government business, means that the situation might well arise that legislation remains on the statute book which the courts have found to be in breach of Convention rights. In this eventuality, going to the European Court of Human Rights in Strasbourg will remain the only avenue of legal redress (see chapter 15).

From a campaigner's point of view, however, a clear judgement from the higher courts that a piece of legislation was in breach of basic human rights would potentially be a turning point in any campaign, and with the right publicity should create irresistible pressure for government action.

The Ombudsman

The Parliamentary Commissioner for Administration, most commonly referred to by the unreconstructed title of Ombudsman, investigates complaints about maladministration by central government. In theory, the role does not overlap with that of the courts – it does not cover, for example, cases where the complainant would be able to seek judicial review – but in practice the Parliamentary Commissioner has wide discretion over which complaints to investigate.

Complaints can be made about bias, neglect, arbitrariness, unfairness or other examples of maladministration by government departments or by a wide range of public bodies. The Inland Revenue and the Department of Social Security crop up most often as the subject of complaints. The Commissioner will not investigate policy

The investigators

The Parliamentary Commissioner for Administration
Scottish Parliamentary Commissioner
Welsh Administration Ombudsman
and *The Health Service Commissioners*
Millbank Tower
Millbank
London SW1P 4QP
Tel: 0845 015 4033

The Commission for Local Administration

21 Queen Anne's Gate
London SW1H 9BU
Tel: 020 7915 3210

Beverley House
17 Shipton Road
York YO30 5FZ
Tel: 01904 663200

The Oaks, Westwood Way
Westwood Business Park
Coventry CV4 8JB
Tel: 024 7669 5999

decisions just because the complainant happens to disagree with them politically.

Complaints have to be made through an MP; usually, but not necessarily, the local constituency MP. This should create few problems: it involves MPs in little work and is something they are asked to do only infrequently. Copies of all correspondence with the government body concerned should be attached to the complaint.

The Parliamentary Commissioner is only able to make recommendations and does not have the power to enforce them. The Commissioner's influence, however, should not be underestimated. It derives from unparalleled access to the records of the administration, which enables the Commissioner to get to the bottom of decisions made by individual civil servants and even ministers. As a distinguished judge, Lord Woolf, has explained: 'The Ombudsman's inquisitorial investigation, which is conducted at no cost to the member of the public who initiated the complaint, is much more searching than that of the court. I know from my period as Treasury [Junior] the dread with which his investigations are treated by government departments.'

More often than not, the Commissioner's recommendations are implemented. Even when, as in the investigation into the DTI's role in the collapse of Barlow Clowes, the findings are rejected by the government, the repercussions can still be momentous: in this case the investors received *ex gratia* payments from the government totalling £150 million. The ability to recommend payment of compensation is an example of the Commissioner's capacity to obtain redress in circumstances where the court is of no help.

In 1994 the Parliamentary Commissioner's role was expanded to include policing the new code of practice on open government. With double the budget and extra staff, the Commissioner's task is to improve public access to government information. A leaflet explaining how the code works is available from the Commissioner's office.

The Parliamentary Commissioner also holds the posts of Health Service Commissioner, Scottish Parliamentary Commissioner and Welsh Administration Ombudsman. There is also a Commission for Local Administration, which investigates complaints about local authorities. In this case, complaints can be made direct (or through a councillor in the case of local authority complaints), but the record of recommendations being implemented is much weaker. The Commission for Local Administration comprises three commissioners covering England (one covering Greater London, one covering East Anglia, the south and most of central England, and one covering Birmingham, Staffordshire, Shropshire, Cheshire, Derbyshire, Nottinghamshire, Lincolnshire and the north of England).

Under statute, the Commission for Local Administration is not able to investigate complaints about a local authority that affect all or most of the inhabitants in the authority's area. The effect of this is to take outside the Commission's remit the scrutiny of a wide range of policy decisions (another way of putting this is to say that the remit covers administrative, rather than political, action, although the distinction is clearly a difficult one). Although no such statutory provision binds the Parliamentary Commissioner for Administration, in practice a similar distinction is made: the Commissioner investigates only complaints regarding individuals or small groups who have been adversely affected by a decision.

Interestingly, the situation in Northern Ireland is a little different. Here there is an Assembly Ombudsman and a Commissioner for Complaints, who deals with local authorities; the Commissioner's findings can be backed up by damages or an injunction awarded in the county court. They are contactable by writing to the address in appendix B.

The costs of legal action

Aside from a lack of legal awareness or imagination, the biggest deterrent to taking legal action is the cost. Litigation is certainly not cheap, even if it is not always as expensive as many people think, their impressions gleaned from a handful of high profile libel or commercial cases. The streamlined procedure for making applications for judicial review, for example, means that such actions are relatively inexpensive by High Court standards.

Solicitors generally charge a stiff hourly rate and will not quote an all-in fee for handling litigation work, as the actual costs vary greatly depending on how the case goes, and this is difficult to predict. Most solicitors require sums on account as a case progresses. Experienced barristers charge more: the brief fee for a QC can amount to tens of thousands of pounds, depending on the complexity of the case. As if the mounting bills and the prospect of paying out a lot more if the case goes to trial were not enough, there is also the penalty that a losing party faces in terms of paying the opponent's costs.

Costs payable are made up of the winner's solicitor's and counsel's fees, witness fees and court fees. However, costs are generally awarded in the High Court on the 'standard' basis, meaning that only 'reasonable' costs can be recovered, so the amount claimed in costs may not be the same as the amount actually paid by the winner. In 1998 the average amount at which a bill of costs for actions in the Queen's Bench Division was allowed was over £21,000. Conditional fee ('no win, no fee') arrangements, under which lawyers receive an additional percentage of the fee if they win, but nothing if they lose, are increasingly available.

Damages awards in the UK tend to be modest compared with the US, and are based on what other judges have awarded in similar cases. (Damages in defamation cases are an exception, partly because they are awarded by juries rather than by judges, as in other cases, and partly because 'loss of reputation is an intangible form of harm.) Damages are essentially compensatory and aim to restore successful claimants to their 'pre-harm' position – insofar as this is possible through a financial award.

In some cases, support is available to help less well-off people both bring and defend actions. As part of the Community Legal Service, the Legal Services Commission itself provides services for people who qualify financially, mostly through accredited lawyers working under contract. This replaced the old civil legal aid scheme in 2000. Unlike legal aid, the new Community Legal Service Fund is not open-ended: a flexible funding code is used to assess whether there are other ways of dealing with, or funding, a particular case. Priority is given to cases involving issues of fundamental importance to those concerned (such as violence, the threat of homelessness, care of children, or adoption), and judicial review cases and others where there is a wider public interest. Litigants seeking to pursue most claims for money or damages are expected to finance them using conditional fee arrangements.

Support from the Community Legal Service Fund is only available to individuals; organisations such as pressure groups cannot themselves qualify. Finding a claimant who qualifies for support will often be the only way that pressure groups can afford to advance a test case.

Other sources of free help are few and far between; probably the largest single category consists of *ad hoc* advice and help from sympathetic lawyers. Some campaigns, particularly those on environmental or planning issues, have managed to get the local authority to join them in an action. Wealthy benefactors have in the past also supported both pressure groups and individuals who did not qualify for legal aid. Property developer Godfrey Bradman agreed to underwrite the legal costs of a large number of arthritis patients, suing for compensation for the side-effects they suffered from the drug Opren. A small organisation called the Free Representation Unit (see appendix B for address) provides free representation before tribunals for some people who do not have sufficient means.

The example of a former anti-apartheid campaigner demonstrates that litigation need not be a drain on resources, but can in fact be an effective means of fundraising. Richard Rocques raised enough money to stage his first play, *Looks like Freedom*, by repeatedly suing the police after he was unlawfully arrested during protests like picketing outside South Africa House and refusing to pay for South African goods in supermarkets. He explained in the *Guardian*: 'It became almost a regular pattern of protest, arrest, imprisonment, legal action, winning and then, after a long interval, compensation.' Payouts from these actions amounted to nearly £7,000, half of which went to the campaign and half to finance his play.

9 Demonstrations and stunts

¡No pasarán! – Spanish republican slogan

The demonstration is the most visible expression of people power. It is the muscle flexing of those who have neither money nor authority. From the Jarrow marches of the 1920s to the Aldermaston marches and Grosvenor Square demonstrations of the 1950s and 1960s to the great anti-poll tax and environmental demonstrations of the last decade, civil discontent has meant people on the streets.

The influence of the mass media, however, has radically altered the art of the demonstration. Small-scale, high impact stunts are now used to reach the huge audiences that a few column inches or broadcast seconds can bring. Highly visual, they pack at least as much media appeal as a mass demonstration, but at a fraction of the cost and effort.

But whatever the scale, in a society where most deeds are performed through words the demonstration is a conscious resort to the physical. Often confrontational, sometimes threatening, never less than embarrassing, the demonstrator is drawing a line that means 'no further'. Every effective demonstration, even the most good-natured, has in it the spirit of the barricade.

Regulation of demonstrations

Public order law draws a distinction between assemblies and processions. Police powers which cover both kinds of demonstration are described below and additional rules affecting processions only are dealt with in the next section. Most of the powers described are contained in the Public Order Act 1986. The sections of the Act empowering the police to impose conditions on demonstrations apply throughout Great Britain; the sections covering advance notice and banning orders regarding processions apply in England and Wales only, but similar rules exist in Scotland (for advice consult the Scottish Human Rights Centre – see appendix B for address).

Police conditions on demonstrations

A public assembly is a gathering of 20 or more people in a public place which is wholly or partly in the open air. Note that everything from a public meeting to a picket to a bus queue can fall within this definition. The police can impose conditions on a public assembly or any march or procession in a public place, if the senior police officer 'reasonably believes that

(a) it may result in serious public disorder, serious damage to property or serious disruption to the life of the community, or

(b) the purpose of the persons organising it is the intimidation of others ...' (Public Order Act 1986, Ss 12 & 14).

If so, conditions can be made as to the place at which an assembly is held, its maximum duration or the maximum number of people taking part, or, in the case of a procession, conditions including restrictions on the route or entry to specified public places. Conditions can be imposed either orally by the most senior officer present at the demonstration, or in advance in writing, in which case they should be from the chief constable (or Commissioner in London) or the assistant chief constable. Only such conditions can be made, however, as the officer believes are necessary to prevent the disorder, damage, disruption or intimidation.

Exactly what constitutes intimidation is not wholly clear. On the one hand, it is not just confined to the threat of personal violence; threats to property have also been interpreted by the courts as intimidatory. Threats can be implicit. On the other hand, merely creating embarrassment or discomfort for someone in order to put pressure on them, as in the case of most consumer pickets, would not be intimidation. This part of the Act was clearly designed to give the police greater power in controlling industrial picketing, particularly mass pickets, where the very numbers of people involved might be construed as intimidatory.

Serious public disorder or damage to property are more straightforward to recognise, although whether they are likely to result from any particular demonstration will of course be open to debate. The White Paper which preceded the Act cited the 'Stop the City' demonstrations of 1983–4 as an example of what was meant by 'serious disruption to the life of the community'.

It is worth reiterating that the Public Order Act powers to impose conditions on static demonstrations only cover those involving 20 or more people and do not include those in places not open to the air, for example in a railway station. (Note that the Criminal Justice and Public Order Act 1994 does give the police a power under certain conditions to place a ban on assemblies that trespass on private land: see chapter 10). However, the police also have a number of older statutory powers to prevent obstruction to streets and thoroughfares and these have been used, for example, to close off streets during a demonstration. These powers are widest in London and are not limited by the size of the demonstration. They were used against the 'Stop the City' demonstrations mentioned above. In addition, the police continue to possess common law powers to deal with or prevent a breach of the peace (see 'Trouble with the police' below).

In London, public assemblies and processions are prohibited in the vicinity of Westminster on days when Parliament is sitting (i.e. Monday to Friday except during a Parliamentary recess). Special arrangements should be made for mass lobbies of the House of Commons, covered in chapter 14.

Finally, many local areas have bye-laws which place restrictions on the holding of public meetings or assemblies in certain places like parks. A copy of the relevant bye-laws should be available from the local authority.

Marches or processions

Written notice in advance is required 'to hold a public procession intended

(a) to demonstrate support for or opposition to the views or actions of any person or body of persons,

(b) to publicise a cause or campaign, or

(c) to mark or commemorate an event,

unless it is not reasonably practicable to give any advance notice of the procession' (Public Order Act 1986, S.11). The three classes given cover just about every conceivable march or procession for campaigning purposes. Two types of procession *are* specifically excluded from the requirement to give notice: normal funeral processions and processions that are 'commonly or customarily held' in the area. This latter definition would cover the Durham Miners Gala, remembrance day parades or other events which have been held regularly in the same area, but not commemorative events which, although regular, have been held in different places in past years.

The notice must specify the date when the procession is to be held, the time when it is intended to start, the proposed route and the name and address of the organiser. It must be delivered to a police station, in the police area in which the procession is planned to start, by hand or by recorded delivery not less than six clear days beforehand; or, if that is not 'reasonably practicable', by hand as soon as is reasonably practicable. In Scotland, advance notice of processions must be made to the local authority as well as the police.

The references in the Act to what is or is not 'reasonably practicable' leave some latitude for spontaneous processions, such as a group of workers marching on the company offices when they receive news of unexpected redundancies. In most cases it will be possible to give at least some notice, even if not six clear days, bearing in mind that to fail to do so under the terms of the Act is an offence. Note that the prescribed form of notice is written notice, so someone should go to the police station with a letter rather than simply making a telephone call, if at all possible.

The information required by law to be given in the notice is minimal (see above) but the police may well ask for more in order to make adequate arrangements for the procession. In a few counties in England, local Acts of Parliament require the police to issue a code of practice governing street processions and these often call for more detailed information from the organisers (see box, overleaf, for example). The areas where this applies are Cheshire, Greater Manchester, the Isle of Wight and the West Midlands.

Marches of any size will usually require negotiating with the police regarding such matters as the route taken, assembly and finish points, stewarding and so on. The police will be concerned about natural obstacles on the route, such as difficult junctions, bottle-necks, sharp bends, etc, as well as potential flashpoints with those who can be expected to be opposed to the demonstration. Many towns have a long-established procession route which new marches will be encouraged to follow. The police are less likely to impose additional stringent conditions on a march if they feel comfortable with the route; on the other hand, a route may not be much good if it does not allow you to get near the object of your demonstration, whether it be the council offices or an embassy. In any case, keep an accurate note of any discussions with the police and what was agreed. Many organisers subsequently admit that the police, with their wealth of experience, turned out to be an invaluable help in planning a large demonstration.

If the chief officer of police believes that, 'because of particular circumstances existing in any district or part of a district', the powers to impose conditions on processions are not enough to prevent 'serious public disorder' resulting, he must apply to the local council for a prohibition order banning the holding of processions. The council may make the order, with or without modifications, with the consent of the Home Secretary. In London the discretion to make prohibition orders rests with the Police Commissioner, again with the Home Secretary's consent. This power to ban processions was in the main not new to the 1986 Act but had existed since the thirties.

Prohibition orders can be made to cover any period up to three months, although they are usually for a much shorter time. Following the Brixton riots in 1981, a blanket ban of 28 days was placed on processions (and was challenged by CND – see below). Prohibition orders can cover all public processions or any class of procession.

Information requested from organisers of processions or protest marches

1. Name of organisation
2. Reason for demonstration/march
3. Name, address and telephone number of organiser, or contact on organising committee
4. Place of assembly
5. Time, day and date of assembly
6. Parking facilities at start and end for those taking part in the procession
7. Name of person(s) who will be in charge at the assembly point
8. Time procession is to move off
9. Proposed route and final destination
10. Number and size of vehicles/floats in a mobile procession
11. Number of people expected to take part in the procession
    – Organiser's estimate
    – Police estimate*
12. Venue, name(s) of speakers and time of dispersal of any meeting to be held before or after the procession
13. Are any petitions to be delivered?
14. Has permission been granted for private property to be used in connection with procession (e.g. permission from local authority to use a park as an assembly area, etc.)?
15. Is any organisation likely to demonstrate in opposition?
16. Known militant organisations likely to support*
17. Number and identification of stewards for march
18. Will flags, banners, etc., be carried?
19. Name and location of person who may be consulted by the police should the occasion arise during the course of procession

*Note that the information sheet is to be completed by police personnel

Source: Greater Manchester Police

Commonly, the police impose a blanket ban but except a few classes of procession, usually those of a purely ceremonial or religious character. The prohibition can cover a whole district or just a specified part of it.

In general, however, bans are rare. The criteria for making a ban are much tighter than those covering the imposition of conditions, being restricted to the avoidance of serious public disorder, and the police are only able to consider a ban if they feel their powers to impose conditions are inadequate in the circumstances. The decision to make a ban, involving the consent of the Home Secretary, is made at a high level. Consequently, bans are only likely to be made in the case of highly provocative processions, where aggressive counter demonstrations are expected, or, as in the case of the ban cited above, where there is a recent history of serious public unrest.

Challenging regulation

It is worth noting that, notwithstanding what has been said above, permission as such is *not* required to hold a demonstration in this country. Although the police can use the extensive powers they do possess in order to make it difficult or pointless for a demonstration to go ahead, there is no permit requirement. Even regarding marches, the police cannot prohibit any particular march from taking place (as opposed to all marches or classes of marches). Back in the early sixties a class ban was put on processions organised by or on behalf of the Committee of 100, but nowadays the police appear to be too sensitive to allegations of partiality to link openly a ban to a particular group.

Organising counter demonstrations probably gives rise to the most problems, from the point of view of regulation. (Much of our public order law has developed as a response to openly provocative marches and demonstrations: the Public Order Act 1936, the predecessor to the 1986 Act, followed Sir Oswald Mosley's fascist marches in the East End of London.) The police often tend to operate what seems like a first-come, first-served policy, placing harsher conditions on the organisers of a counter demonstration in order to prevent dangerous encounters with the original march. In recent years this pattern is familiar from the clash of right-wing and anti-racist demonstrations.

The Public Order Act imposes criminal sanctions on those who defy police conditions or banning orders. An offence is committed by anyone who organises or takes part in a procession that he knows is prohibited, or who incites another to do so, or who knowingly fails to comply with a condition imposed on a procession or assembly by the police. A police constable in uniform can arrest without warrant anyone she reasonably suspects is committing such an offence. On summary conviction, offenders are liable to penalties of:

▼ for organisers and inciters, a maximum of three months imprisonment and/or a fine of up to £2,500

▼ for participants, a fine of up to £1,000.

It is a defence for someone to prove that failure to comply with a condition 'arose from circumstances beyond his control'. In the case of an organiser, this would involve proving not only that he did not directly authorise the breach but that he had also adequately briefed participants to prevent it from happening.

There is no statutory right of appeal against conditions imposed by the police on demonstrations or against banning orders on processions. The fact that a police officer must act 'reasonably' in deciding to impose conditions or a ban, however, means that the decision will

be amenable to judicial review (see chapter 8). If someone is prosecuted for flouting a condition or ban, showing that a police officer's
decision was not reasonable is a defence, albeit one hard to establish.
When the Campaign for Nuclear Disarmament challenged a blanket
ban imposed in 1981 in the wake of the Brixton riots, the court declined
to intervene even though the police evidence 'seemed meagre'.

All of which means that organisers are best off cooperating with
the police whenever possible. Police interest in a demonstration will
increase in proportion to its size. In contrast to processions, there is no
general requirement to give the police advance notice of a public
assembly, and whether or not you choose to do so will partly depend
on its size and duration: the larger and longer it is, the more risk there
will be that the police will act to disperse the assembly unless prior
arrangements have been made for maintaining order.

Organising mass demonstrations

The days are gone when it was enough simply to get a few people
together to stage a demonstration. To create an impact, demonstrators now have either to come up with something novel or to be present
in large numbers. The former kind of demonstration is covered under
'Stunts' below; the latter kind here. For the purposes of this section
'mass' does not necessarily mean absolutely huge but just refers to
those demonstrations where the impact comes principally from the
mass of people involved.

Organising mass events is a high-risk campaigning activity. It
requires extensive planning and preparation, considerable investment
in the form of equipment, insurance and publicity costs, and the
recruitment of a sizeable workforce for the event itself, yet there is no
way of guaranteeing a respectable turn-out. And the number of participants is really the only criterion by which success will be gauged.

There are many ways of displaying mass support which do not
involve supporters all having to be present on the same day at the
same place (letter-writing campaigns, for example) and if you have a
substantial membership, there is a lot to be said for not undermining
the strength of your own support by risking a poor turn-out at a
demonstration.

If it is national media coverage you are after, a stunt is a much surer
bet (see below). The handful of national demonstrations in recent years
that captured the imagination through their sheer size are in fact the
exception to a general rule: big demonstrations are essentially a local
technique. The people they impress most are those who are there, who
see them, whose lives are disrupted by them. 40,000 people can
congregate in London's West End and seem but a ripple in the tides of
the surging metropolis; 5,000 people get together in a small town and
the effect is devastating: everyone knows about it, no-one is unaffected.
Mosley was aware of it, just as anyone who has been on an anti-racist

demonstration in an inner-city borough is aware of it: demonstrating is a territorial activity.

To persuade people that they should spend a few hours on the streets on a particular day, the right occasion is needed. This could be:

▼ *An anniversary.* Peace groups have traditionally used Hiroshima day; the Troops Out movement often uses the anniversary of Bloody Sunday.

▼ *A vote or decision.* Very effective local demonstrations were held outside town halls up and down the country on the night each council met to set the first poll tax in early 1990. Campaigners for homosexual equality held a vigil outside the House of Commons on the night that MPs voted to lower the age of consent for gay men.

▼ *The visit or arrival of a key person.* Foreign dignitaries and government ministers are regularly met by handfuls of demonstrators, but security means that little advance notice is usually given, so a sizeable demonstration can be impressive. Local politicians or officials who are not used to it can be unnerved by demonstrations.

▼ *An existing demonstration.* A counter demonstration can draw a local community onto the streets like nothing else will, especially if territorial issues are involved.

Publicity can take the form of notices in newsletters, posters or handbills (for every ten bills handed out you will be lucky to get one person showing up on the day). The internet has transformed the art of mobilising for demonstrations (see chapter 6) but the main advertising medium for demonstrations is still word-of-mouth. Most demonstrations stand or fall on the work put in by a regular core of supporters. It rarely makes sense to advertise either to supporters or the press an estimate of the attendance in advance: unless it is quite high it will depress interest, yet if the event does not match the estimate it will be described as a failure.

With a march, publicity should whenever possible give details of the route to be followed. Once the march is underway, however, participants will naturally follow those in front. Do not underestimate the difficulty involved in controlling a large demonstration, especially if it is a march. Some police forces recommend a ratio of one steward to every fifty demonstrators. A few useful pointers on employing stewards can be picked up from the code of practice on demonstrations issued by some police forces (see box overleaf).

Many of the problems encountered in large marches stem from splinter groups or outside groups attempting to hijack the demonstration for their own ends. The head of the march is particularly vulnerable and needs to be stewarded with authority. Having a vehicle at the front helps (a loudspeaker van of the type politicians use for canvassing is ideal and this can double as a speakers' platform at the finishing point). But a sizeable splinter group can halt or deroute a march at any point, and to prevent it from doing so stewards must not only have command but also know the route well enough to spot what is going on at an early stage. There is really only one way of briefing stewards adequately: get them together a day or so beforehand so they meet each other, talk them through their duties and any eventualities, let them get used to using any equipment like walkie-talkies, and then *walk the route together*, no matter how well they think

---

Employment of stewards at demonstrations

'Stewards are essential in the organisation of any public event. However, it must be emphasised that a steward acts as a private person and cannot acquire or be delegated police powers or authority, nor any immunity from the law.

Organisation

When preparing for an event, organisers should determine how many stewards will be necessary and for what purposes they will be used. It is imperative that organisers retain control of their event and to this end a definite chain of command should be established whereby stewards are aware to whom they are responsible and can refer matters for decisions.

Identification

Stewards should be readily identifiable as such by all persons participating in the event. Previous experience has shown that wearing lapel badges alone does not achieve this purpose and that a distinctive shirt, jumper, coat or fluorescent waistcoat would be ideal and that such clothing be issued well in advance of the event.

Powers

Stewards should be clearly instructed that they are acting as private persons and their status does not confer any advantage in law nor allow them to act as police officers in any way. It is vital that they refer, immediately, to police any matters which are likely to lead to breaches of the law or public disorder and not become involved themselves.

The carrying of a weapon in any public place without lawful authority or reasonable excuse is prohibited by law. This includes the possession of such a weapon as a deterrent. Stewards must not carry or have with or near them any such weapons.

Duties

Stewards should confine themselves to acting on the instructions given by members of the organisation committee or on directions or advice received from police.

[There is] a possibility of police changing the route. Should the instructions given to the steward by those organising the event conflict with instructions given to the steward by the police officers on the scene, the steward should be reminded that should he persist in following the original instructions he might be in jeopardy of committing an offence of obstructing the police in the execution of their duty.

The use of tact and good humour cannot be overemphasised as it has the effect of defusing potentially difficult situations. People attending any event are likely to respond positively to organisers and their stewards who display the ability to control the event and guide the participants. The response is most likely to be achieved if stewards ensure that they give participants clear and accurate directions and advice which they can only do if properly and fully briefed themselves.'

From *Organisation of Public Events: Code of Practice*, Greater Manchester Police

they know it. Stewards are needed to accompany the march throughout the route, but there should be concentrations of stewards at the assembly point, the head of the march, and the finishing point and speakers' platform.

Much of running a successful demonstration is down to basic organisational skills. The information requested by the police listed on page 186 can serve as a useful checklist. A few points on banners and placards and stamping a visual identity on a demonstration are given in chapter 5. There are three other factors which have not been covered so far but do require careful consideration.

▼ *Equipment for amplification and communications.* Public address systems are notoriously unreliable (not least because parts of them tend to run away if they are not guarded) and adequate time needs to be set aside for setting up and testing them. Hand-held megaphones are only adequate for quite small demonstrations. For big marches, communication between the organisers and key stewards now tends to rely on mobile phones. Alternatively, you can use hand-held radios or walkie-talkies but a) people need to be trained how to use them and b) there should be a back-up method of communicating, e.g. runners, cyclists.

▼ *Insurance and first aid.* It is becoming increasingly difficult to find insurers prepared to cover one-off events like demonstrations and the cost is often prohibitive. Check that hired or borrowed equipment is already insured and that the policy will cover its use at your event (if it does not, paying the difference will be marginal compared to the cost of a one-off policy). Insurance to cover the third-party liability of the organisers (for unforeseen mishaps like a platform collapsing and injuring someone) will have to be arranged separately.

▼ *Fundraising.* From a fundraiser's point of view, a big demonstration is too good an opportunity to miss. A number of static collection points can be augmented by fundraisers in groups of at least two working through the participants as systematically as possible.

Trouble with the police

If you suspect there may be trouble with the police on a demonstration, there are a number of things that can be done in preparation. Demonstrators can be briefed about how to keep out of trouble and about their rights on arrest. A good way of doing this, particularly on a large demonstration where many people will just be turning up on the day, is to prepare 'bust cards' for handing out to participants (see chapter 10). Stewards, at the very least, should be aware of demonstrators' rights and alert at the sign of any trouble so they can witness what happens and record the ID numbers of police involved. This is both to guard against miscarriages of justice and, if necessary, enable complaints to be made against individual police officers.

Procedure in the police station, access to solicitors and notes about preparing defences are covered in the next chapter on direct action. There is a national organisation called Release which runs a 24-hour helpline providing emergency help and advice in cases of arrest. The number is 020 7603 8654.

In addition to their powers to regulate public assemblies and processions described above, the police have a number of more general public order powers to enable them to deal with disturbances. In particular, public order offences carry wide powers of arrest without a warrant. The main public order offences with which demonstrators have been charged are given in the box below. (Note that most convictions will result in a penalty considerably less than the maximum, which is reserved for the most serious version of the offence.)

Public order offences

Obstruction of the highway

Anyone who wilfully obstructs the free passage along a highway without lawful authority or excuse is guilty of the offence of obstructing the highway. It is a defence to show that the use of the highway was a reasonable one and this may be related to whether or not it was incidental to the accepted use of passing and repassing, whether the location was a regular place for meetings, or whether the obstruction created significant inconvenience. To be an offence, the obstruction must be wilful rather than just accidental. Police have a power of arrest without warrant, although anyone who was arrested without being warned first could count themselves unlucky. Enforcement is very uneven, but demonstrators have often been charged, including pickets stopping vehicles on the highway leading to a workplace. *Maximum penalty: £1,000 fine.*

Obstruction of the police in the execution of their duty

An offence is committed by anyone who resists or wilfully obstructs a police officer in the execution of his duty, or a person assisting a police officer in the execution of his duty. Arrests leading to a charge for this offence are often made when demonstrators do not comply with directions made by the police under their duty to preserve the peace (see main text). Maximum penalty: *one month imprisonment and/or £1,000 fine.*

Using or threatening violence when resisting or obstructing a police officer may lead to a charge of assaulting a police officer in the execution of his duty (although merely pulling away does not constitute an assault). *Maximum penalty: six months imprisonment and/or £5,000 fine.*

Offensive conduct

'A person is guilty of an offence if he–

(a) uses threatening, abusive or insulting words or behaviour, or disorderly behaviour, or

(b) displays any writing, sign or other visible representation which is threatening, abusive or insulting,

within the hearing or sight of a person likely to be caused harassment, alarm or distress thereby'
(Public Order Act 1986).

continued on next page

The stiff maximum penalties carried by the three most serious public order offences indicate the gravity with which they are taken. A number of demonstrators were charged either with riot, violent disorder or affray following the demonstration against the poll tax in Trafalgar Square in 1990, although in many cases they were acquitted due to lack of evidence.

Traditionally, the only uses of the street or highway which were clearly sanctioned in law were to pass and repass along it, or reasonable associated uses such as stopping to talk to friends or standing in a queue outside a shop. In an important case in 1999, the court confirmed that 'the public has the right to use the highway for peaceful and usual activities, including peaceful assembly, which are consistent with the primary right to use it for passage and repassage'. However, any use deemed unreasonable, or which may constitute an obstruction, will result in the police asking you to move on.

---

continued:

The scope of this offence is very wide and it has already been used often against pickets. The writing referred to in (b) may be that on a placard or banner, or a slogan on a wall. The power of arrest associated with the offence requires the police to issue a warning first. *Maximum penalty: £1,000 fine.*

Causing fear or provocation of violence

This offence consists of the use of threatening, abusive or insulting words or behaviour, or the distribution or display of writing or signs, towards another person with intent to make him fear violence, to provoke violence by or against him or another, or so that he is likely to expect violence. *Maximum penalty: six months imprisonment and/or £5,000 fine.*

Affray, violent disorder and riot

These three offences all have in common the use or threat of unlawful violence in situations which would cause a person of reasonable firmness present at the scene to fear for his personal safety. This person is hypothetical (no such person need be actually present at the scene) and serves as a measure of the violence employed: *if* he were present, would what he witnessed cause him to fear that he was in danger?

▼ A person is guilty of **affray** if he uses or threatens unlawful violence towards another and his conduct is such as would cause a person of reasonable firmness present at the scene to fear for his personal safety. *Maximum penalty: three years imprisonment and/or a fine.*

▼ A person is guilty of **violent disorder** if he uses or threatens violence where three or more people are together using or threatening violence and their conduct (taken together) is such as would cause a person of reasonable firmness present at the scene to fear for his personal safety. *Maximum penalty: five years imprisonment and/or a fine.*

▼ A person is guilty of **riot** if he uses violence where 12 or more people are together using or threatening violence for a common purpose and their conduct (taken together) is such as would cause a person of reasonable firmness present at the scene to fear for his personal safety. *Maximum penalty: ten years imprisonment and/or a fine.*

But some of the police powers which have in the past seemed most arbitrary to demonstrators are those associated with the duty of the police to prevent breaches of the peace. A breach of the peace is not defined in statute but has been authoritatively described in the Court of Appeal in the following terms:

> '... there is a breach of the peace whenever harm is actually done or is likely to be done to a person or in his presence to his property or a person is in fear of being so harmed ...'

In England and Wales a breach of the peace is not in itself an offence (unlike in Scotland) but the police have the power to disperse, detain or arrest people committing an actual breach of the peace *or who are reasonably believed to be about to commit an imminent breach of the peace.* It is this category of anticipated breaches which it is particularly difficult to be clear about.

The anticipated breach of the peace must be both real (rather than remote) and imminent, but this is a matter for the judgement of the police on the scene. During the miners' strike, a group of picketing miners were stopped while travelling on the M1 motorway and directed to turn back, the police officer in charge having reason to believe that there would be a breach of the peace if they continued (there were several collieries in the area). The courts have generally proved reluctant to question the judgement of police officers on the ground even when, as here, their powers of anticipation bordered on the psychic. However, in 1999 a hunt protestor received an award of £3,500 in damages against a police force who arrested him on the way to a hunt. He successfully argued that he was simply walking on a country lane, half a mile from where the hunt was taking place, and the court ruled that the arresting officer could not lawfully have anticipated a breach of the peace.

A person arrested for a breach of the peace may be charged later with a substantive offence, but commonly they will be brought before magistrates to be bound over. This is not a conviction; the person makes an undertaking to keep the peace for a specified period, often with a sum of money as surety.

The rights of demonstrators have been significantly bolstered by the Human Rights Act 1998, in force from October 2000. The Act introduces for the first time a statutory right of freedom of peaceful assembly (see chapter 8).

Picketing

The criminal law on picketing is essentially the same as that for other kinds of demonstration, if enforced a little more readily (by the end of the 1984/5 miners' strike, over 10,000 criminal charges had been brought). This is particularly apparent in the use of police powers to prevent breaches of the peace. The Code of Practice on picketing, issued by the Secretary of State under statute, points out:

> 'It is for the police to decide, taking into account all the circumstances, whether the number of pickets at any particular place is likely to lead to a breach of the peace. If a picket does not leave the picket line when asked to do so by the police, he is liable to be arrested for obstruction either of the highway or of a police officer in the execution of his duty if the obstruction is such as to cause, or be likely to cause, a breach of the peace.'

The well-publicised changes to the law on industrial picketing that occurred during the eighties were changes to the *civil* law. As such they can only be enforced in practice if employers, or in some cases other employees, are prepared to take legal action. Broadly speaking, the wide immunity from civil actions that trade unions had previously enjoyed was stripped away. A residuary immunity does remain, however, covering peaceful picketing in furtherance of a trade dispute at a picket's own place of work, set out in the so-called peaceful picketing exemption (see box). The exemption clearly does *not* cover most secondary picketing, that is, picketing by union members or supporters at a place of work other than their own.

An employer can seek an injunction in the court to prevent or restrict secondary picketing or other picketing that does not fall within the terms of the exemption. (Breaching an injunction will make pickets and their union liable to be fined, heavily, and may lead to sequestration of union assets.)

How in practice the courts have interpreted the limits of the immunity conferred by the exemption cannot be deduced easily from the actual words and there is a confusing overlap between the civil and criminal law. Picketing in large numbers, particularly in such a way as to form a physical barrier, suggests something more than peaceful persuasion and will not fall within the exemption. Following the Code of Practice on picketing, the civil court has in the past limited the number of pickets at a workplace entrance to six.

Section 241 of the Trade Union and Labour Relations (Consolidation) Act 1992 makes it an offence to 'watch or beset' the house or workplace of others, or to

---

The peaceful picketing exemption

Section 220(1) of the Trade Union and Labour Relations (Consolidation) Act 1992 provides that:

'It is lawful for a person in contemplation or furtherance of a trade dispute to attend –

(a) at or near his own place of work; or

(b) if he is an official of a trade union, at or near the place of work of a member of that union whom he is accompanying and whom he represents

for the purpose only of peacefully obtaining or communicating information, or peacefully persuading any person to work or abstain from working.'

The effect of the exemption is to make picketing *which falls within this description* immune from civil actions and from prosecution for 'watching and besetting'. Note that the exemption does not confer any immunity from the general criminal law.

persistently follow them, in order to compel them to do something. Although this has actually been an offence since 1875, it has rarely been used. (It does have some relevance to certain direct action techniques like personal harassment and is covered in more detail in chapter 10.) The courts have held that pickets operating within the terms of the peaceful picketing exemption are immune to prosecution under this measure.

The peaceful picketing exemption only refers to industrial disputes and does not cover consumer picketing, e.g. a pressure group picketing outside a high-street shop. Furthermore, consumer pickets will often be situated in busy streets which makes it more likely that they will be obstructing the highway; shopkeepers may be particularly swift in seeking an injunction to prevent a demonstration interfering with their trade. Consumer picketing is certainly possible, however: anti-apartheid campaigners maintained a picket, on and off, outside South Africa House for many years. Some ideas for getting round the legal problems are given in the section on consumer action in chapter 11.

Stunts

A stunt is a type of demonstration which is concept-led, designed for maximum visual impact and (usually) small-scale. Stunts hold a number of advantages over conventional mass demonstrations:

▼ they provide better photo opportunities and consequently more chance of media coverage;

▼ they can be planned in advance to occur at an exact time and place;

▼ there are fewer people to organise and there is less chance of things getting out of control and people being arrested;

▼ they provide an opportunity to do something different and distinctive.

Stunts are, at least in part, aimed at the media, and making them a success involves careful liaison with photo desks or camera crews and thorough briefing of journalists (see chapter 7). From the media's point of view, stunts are particularly attractive in the off-seasons for news (e.g. in August) and are a good way for a group to keep itself in the public eye when not much else is going on.

It is useless trying to categorise stunts as the range of what is possible is limited only by the imagination, and many of the most effective stunts are those which work by adapting individual circumstances. The following ten examples shocked and entertained in their time:

1. In 1907 members of the Women's Social and Political Union campaigning for votes for women chained themselves to railings in Downing Street and to a statue in the lobby of the House of

Commons. The action demonstrated their determination and at the same time provided a neat symbol for the bondage of women in political life.

2. Students at Tulane University in 1972 sought a way of protesting at the Vietnam war during a planned speech by George Bush, the then US representative to the UN. Advice from veteran activist Saul Alinsky suggested to them an unusually effective protest which would not put them in danger of being expelled from the University. Dressing up as members of the Klu Klux Klan, they applauded vigorously every time Bush said anything in favour of the Vietnam war and waved placards saying 'The KKK supports Bush'.

3. When Marlon Brando was awarded an Oscar for his performance in *The Godfather*, he sent a Native American to the ceremony to refuse the award on his behalf in protest at the treatment of Native American groups.

4. When Barclays Bank invested over £6 million in South African Defence Bonds in the seventies, the Anti-Apartheid Movement arranged for two people to dress up in South African military uniform and parade outside the City headquarters of Barclays.

5. While the Ideal Home exhibition was playing at Olympia, Brent Housing Action Campaign threw open a local hostel as Brent's 'ideal home' to publicise the appalling state of hostels for the homeless. The Campaign made up a brochure, held conducted tours and handed out tea on the moss-covered concrete patio outside. The day attracted about a thousand people, including a local MP who went on to become Minister of Housing.

6. Friends of the Earth dumped 10,000 empty bottles on the doorstep of Schweppes Ltd. to highlight the need for companies to produce returnable bottles. The action echoed that of the Committee of 100 in 1961 who dumped hundreds of milk bottles with 'Danger – Radio-active' stamped on them outside the Soviet embassy to protest at nuclear tests.

7. A local anti-poll tax union in Scotland delivered a huge summary warrant to the offices of the local bailiffs to protest at the distraint of people's goods for non-payment of poll-tax. The warrant resembled the thousands that had been pushed through the letter-boxes of non-payers.

8. The anti-fur lobby persuaded a group of supermodels to do a photo shoot wearing nothing except a banner saying 'I'd rather wear nothing than wear fur'. The stunt's success was partly measured in its wide coverage in fashion magazines the world over, with millions of consumers getting the message that it was sexy to be anti-fur.

9. Members of the Women's Action Coalition in New York celebrated Mother's Day by marching a drum corps into Grand Central Station with a huge banner declaring '$30 Billion Owed Mothers in Child Support'.

10. Greenpeace brought attention to the estimated world death toll from increased discharges from the THORP nuclear reprocessing plant at Sellafield by having 600 protestors wearing skull masks 'drop dead' outside Downing Street.

If a stunt involves an element of performance, this should be rehearsed in advance to make sure that when the time comes people play their allotted roles without hesitation.

An element of humour is a useful asset, but campaign stunts are very different from fundraising stunts or sponsored events where people are often encouraged to be as silly or foolhardy as possible. There should always be a direct relation between the stunt and the subject of the protest, ideally one – bearing in mind those photo stories – that is comprehensible in snapshot. Having your own photographer taking pictures should ensure at least some coverage in the local or specialist press, even if no other journalist turns up. If you can take advantage of an occasion when you know the press is going to be out in force (e.g. stunts 2. and 3. above), so much the better.

10 Direct action

Justice, that dwells with the gods below, knows no such law – Sophocles, *Antigone*

The argument of the broken window pane is the most valuable argument in modern politics – Emmeline Pankhurst

Most of this book is about pressure. Whether it be seeking publicity in order to shape public opinion, or influencing policy-makers through lobbying, the techniques described ultimately depend on the actions of others to achieve change.

But there is an alternative. If a tax is unfair or creates severe hardship, don't pay it. If a group of tenants is about to be unjustly evicted, occupy the building. If an industrial waste pipe is discharging effluent into the sea, block it up.

Such direct actions, impressive though they may be, rarely secure permanent change. But in disturbing the *status quo* and establishing in its place, however briefly, an alternative, they can prove that change is not only possible but within our grasp. As a means of demonstrating the determination of campaigners and raising the confidence of supporters, direct action cannot be matched.

The distinction between some forms of direct action, like civil disobedience, and the demonstrations and stunts described in the last chapter is not a clear one. Much of what is commonly referred to as direct action – sit-downs, strikes – is in essence demonstrative: it too is a tool of pressure. Frequently sliding into illegality, it can be seen as a protest sufficiently radical in form to question not just the policy or decision in dispute but the very authority of those who govern.

Throughout modern times direct actions have been successful in breaking through seemingly impenetrable barriers to change. The greatest political U-turn of the last decade, the abandonment of the poll tax, was prompted by mass, often spontaneous, direct action. From women's suffrage to Indian independence to the struggle against the poll tax, history bears testimony to its power: direct action, gateway to the impossible.

Gandhi and non-violent resistance

It is not that easy talking about direct action as a technique, because many of its most celebrated practitioners have looked on it more as a way of life. It is, first of all, civil action – an alternative to the military option of armed resistance – and therefore usually non-violent. Revolutionary activists who advocated not seizing the reins of power but unilaterally setting up an alternative conceived of a form of action that was at once exemplary and an end in itself. The most famous, and perhaps the greatest, exponent of such an approach was M K Gandhi.

Gandhi was not the first to view non-violent resistance as an ideal, but he was probably the first to make it the cornerstone of an entire philosophy. Gandhi saw non-violence or *ahimsa* (literally, 'non-killing') as an immutable, positive force, and he coined the term *satyagraha* (literally, 'holding-to-truth') to denote the practical application of *ahimsa* as appropriate to our own age of mass exploitation and violence.

Adopting ancient Indic practices like boycotts and fasting, Gandhi successfully employed *satyagraha* in numerous campaigns throughout his life: in an eight-year struggle against the colour bar and indenture laws in South Africa; in campaigns against tariff-barriers in Viramgam, forced labour in Kaira and discrimination against untouchables in Vykom and Tamilnad; as well as in campaigns on the road to India's independence.

Gandhi identified four distinct fields of operation for non-violence – to quell communal strife, to meet external aggression, to counter illegitimate authority and, pre-eminently, to act between members of a family or institution – and evolved five basic methods of substituting non-violence for violence in *satyagraha*:

'1. In civil disobedience one accepts the penalty of law, usually imprisonment, possibly attachment of property.

2. In civil resistance and non-cooperation one refuses the benefits of cooperation with the evil person or system. A type of non-cooperation involves giving more than is unjustly demanded.

3. In *hijrat* (migration) one gives up home and land.

4. In fasting one denies the flesh, senses and mind.

5. In non-violent resistance or defence unto death without retaliation, one gives life.' (William Borman, *Gandhi and Non-violence*)

Satyagraha, then, is not easy. Its influence is achieved as much by spiritual discipline and self-mortification (*yajna*) as by external action, or rather, each is achieved through the other. Many of the techniques involve drawing the enmity of others onto oneself. Through an ideal of truthful, non-violent conduct, the body of the satyagrahi is held, as it were, on trust for the purpose of reform. If it is pure, however, this 'non-violence of the strong' lays claim to astonishing effects. In the case of Gandhi himself, his mere presence on the scene of communal riots in Calcutta and Delhi in 1947–8 was observed to halt the shooting and to still large crowds.

Some of the principal axioms of *satyagraha* are given in the box below. These are taken out of context, with some apologies, because the theory rejects any over-arching strategy, arguing that each campaign is unique and, more fundamentally, advocating detachment (*anasakti*) from material ends. The aim is not to upset or seize power but to transform human relationships. In a characteristic passage, Gandhi points out: 'Of course there must be organised resistance to organised evil. The difficulty arises when the organisers of *satyagraha* try to imitate the organisers of evil ... The way of organising forces of good must be opposite to the evil way.'

Much can clearly be learnt from Gandhi even if his whole philosophy is not accepted. As with other practitioners of direct action since (see below) great emphasis in his thinking is placed on the social dynamics of the community, however large or small. Gandhi's

---

Gandhi's non-violent action or *satyagraha*

a) Non-violence implies as complete a self-purification as is humanly possible.

b) Person for person the strength of non-violence is in exact proportion to the ability, not the will, of the non-violent person to inflict violence.

c) Non-violence is without exception superior to violence, as the power at the disposal of a non-violent person is always greater than it would be if that person were violent.

d) There is no such thing as defeat in non-violence. The end of violence is surest defeat.

e) The ultimate end of non-violence is surest victory – if such a term may be used in non-violence. In reality where there is no sense of defeat, there is no sense of victory.

From M K Gandhi, *Non-violence in Peace and War*, Vol I

It is not any single isolated act which can be called *satyagraha* apart from the spirit behind it.

Public opinion is the most potent instrument of *satyagraha*.

Non-violent actions ought not to be taken up without careful elimination of all coercive intent, even that which may be misinterpreted as coercive. [Gandhi condemned hunger strikes – as opposed to penitential fasting – on these grounds.]

The isolation of and attack on evil called for in non-violent action will necessarily bring material reaction: this is neutralised by non-retaliation.

In true non-violence of the strong, the same strength used to gain the result should suffice to retain the gains.

A unique property of *satyagraha* is that it can harm the user alone if the cause turns out to have been unjust.

Even violence is preferable to cowardice or non-violence through weakness.

Adapted from Borman, *Gandhi and Non-violence*, (State University of New York, 1986)

approach is perhaps most valuable when planning civil disobedience, where, confronted with the overwhelmingly superior power of the state, protestors have little to gain unless they possess a moral advantage which can be clearly recognised.

Civil disobedience

In chapter 9 on demonstrations it was broadly assumed that trouble with the law should be avoided wherever possible. On certain occasions, however, groups deliberately engage in rule-breaking, and that may include law-breaking, in order to challenge those in authority. This is civil disobedience.

Sit-downs and obstruction

One of the most familiar forms of civil disobedience is the sit-down, where a group of protestors sit down or lie down on the ground, either to obstruct some activity or simply to indicate their refusal to disperse. On a street or pavement this will constitute the offence of obstruction of the highway; protestors who persist even after being instructed by the police to move on will also be obstructing the police in the execution of their duty (see chapter 9). Some considerable nerve and self-control is required to carry on from this point, particularly if the police handle people roughly: if you thrash about or threaten violence when being carried or dragged away, it may result in the much more serious charge of assaulting the police in the execution of their duty. The presence of a few older and more respectable-looking people can help to calm down both fellow protestors and the police.

Ideally, the sit-down demonstrates that feeling about an issue is so strong that citizens are prepared to suspend their ordinary duty of obedience to the law; if the police react, it also displays the state publicly taking repressive measures in order to enforce the opposite point of view. But to create both these impressions the action must be peaceful and it must be linked as closely as possible with the issue itself, whether through the location chosen or the identity of the protestors. After a private member's bill to strengthen disabled people's rights was talked out of Parliament by the government in 1994, disabled protestors sat down or parked themselves outside the House of Commons, some even chaining themselves to buses. Media coverage was very sympathetic.

A standard form of protest in the late sixties, sit-downs and associated actions were dramatically revived in the nineties by activist green groups. Beginning with a prolonged battle over the construction of the M3 motorway through Twyford Down outside Winchester, and emboldened by a victory in 1993 when the government cancelled another planned road through Oxleas Wood in south London, a programme of protest campsites, sit-downs and other civil disobedience spread to numerous sites across the country, including Yeovil,

Wymondham near Norwich, and Wanstead in north London. The removal of protestors from sites is made much more difficult by their chaining themselves to bulldozers, trees or other objects. This enables the non-violent protest to be dragged out considerably, while giving the media plenty of opportunity to take pictures.

Although eventually unsuccessful, the Twyford Down protest cost the M3 development some £1.9 million in delays. Plans to sue 76 protestors for that amount were abandoned by the Department of Transport after the legal action was condemned in Parliament as a waste of money. Together the road protests led to a rethink of the government's entire road-building programme.

The Twyford Down protest was strengthened by informal alliances with local Conservatives, and the radical-traditionalist axis has become a feature of other protests since. A turning point in the Oxleas Wood case was reached when the British Road Federation decided to withdraw its support for the new road and called on the Department of Transport to compromise. The Federation's assistant director was quoted in the *Independent on Sunday*, saying: 'Politicians would find the levels of protest unacceptable'.

Occupations and trespass

Occupation of buildings is a natural extension of the sit-down protest, particularly if the buildings themselves are partly the subject of the dispute. In the campaign against the construction of the M11 link road in Wanstead, 300 protestors occupied a handful of houses due for demolition. It took some 600 police and bailiffs painstakingly to evict them all, many of them having secured themselves in ingenious ways to the fabric of the buildings. They then moved on to occupy other houses further up the route.

Housing or homelessness campaigns have often staged occupations. One of the most famous occurred in 1974 when the massive Centrepoint office building in London, which had stood empty for ten years, was occupied by 70 people over a weekend. They scaffolded across the lower part of the entrance to prevent anyone else from getting in, and a crowd of several thousand had gathered by the time they came out.

In the past, occupations and other forms of trespass were largely a matter for the civil rather than the criminal law. The Criminal Law Act 1977 did create a summary offence of using or threatening violence for the purpose of entry. The offence depends on there being someone else present on the premises at the time opposed to the entry, and is rarely prosecuted. The Act also created the offence of trespassing on a foreign mission. Property used for defence purposes may also be protected under the Official Secrets Acts, or under bye-laws such as the RAF Greenham Common bye-laws 1985. But in the case of most property, no offence was committed by a trespasser if her entry to the property was peaceful (e.g. if there was no-one present on the property) and no damage was done.

The Criminal Justice and Public Order Act 1994, however, criminalised trespass significantly. The offences in the Act which are of most relevance to pressure groups are given in the box below. Protestors demonstrating about the effect the new law would have on squatters' rights occupied Artillery Mansions in London's Victoria Street, a huge residential block owned by the government that had stood empty for years.

A significant range of direct action which had proved successful in the past was criminalised by the Act, including some of the activities of hunt saboteurs who have caused a growing number of fox-hunts to be abandoned. The provisions for prohibiting trespassory assemblies encompass both protest demonstrations and the sort of meetings held at sites of ritual significance. Government estimates

---

The criminalisation of trespass

The Criminal Justice and Public Order Act 1994 created a number of new offences relating to trespass. The following are of particular relevance to pressure groups.

Aggravated trespass

This offence is committed by someone, trespassing on land in the open air, who tries to intimidate, obstruct or disrupt people engaged in a lawful activity. The senior police officer present may also direct people to leave the land if she believes that they have committed, are committing or intend to commit aggravated trespass.

Trespassory assemblies

A chief officer of police who reasonably believes that an assembly of 20 or more people will be held on land in the open air and

a) is likely to take place without the permission of the occupier, and

b) may result in serious disruption to the life of the community or damage to a site of historical, architectural, archaeological or scientific importance

may apply for an order prohibiting the holding of all trespassory assemblies for a period of not more than four days. To organise or take part in a prohibited assembly, or incite others to do so, is a criminal offence.

Failure to comply with interim possession orders

This applies where an interim possession order has been made in respect of premises unlawfully occupied. It is an offence for a person who is subject to such an order to fail to leave the premises concerned within 24 hours, or to enter the premises again as a trespasser within one year.

The Act also created further powers to remove unauthorised campers from land and to remove certain trespassers on land who are present with the purpose of residing there.

in 1994 suggested that enforcing the provisions on aggravated trespass would require 60 special police operations a year in England and
Wales and a further 24 in Scotland; in practice, however, the police
have found their new powers unwieldy to use and there have been
relatively few prosecutions.

Many of our current public rights of way in the countryside
were secured through organised mass trespass by ramblers in the
thirties. To the extent that such peaceful direct action was successful
in establishing new rights of way as well as confirming ancient rights,
it too if carried out today would be subject to criminal sanction under
the Act.

Non-cooperation and non-payment

The techniques considered so far in this chapter require the campaigner to seize the initiative in taking principled action, often at
some risk to herself. Because of the effort and sacrifice involved, only
a committed minority of people are likely ever to take part in such
interventions.

But some of the policies campaigners may find themselves opposing, particularly government policies, require the active cooperation of a large section of the population. Official policies from the
possession of a television licence to the completion of a tax return to
the proposed requirement to carry a national identity card place a
duty of action on the citizen. The more widespread such duties are,
the more vulnerable they are to non-compliance. It is, after all, much
simpler to persuade someone, or to make it easy for someone, to do
nothing than it is to talk him into throwing himself in front of a
bulldozer or a whaler's harpoon.

Even in very difficult campaigns, like those against military
conscription, the force of inertia has proved a great advantage. The
movement against the Vietnam war draft began with scattered instances of individuals refusing the draft on principle, but soon
broadened to include those who did not really see why they should
go to war, or those who just thought they could get away with it. The
resistance of a vocal minority, publicised through stunts such as the
public burning of draft cards, and a growing awareness of the imperfect
and unfair nature of the draft selection criteria, suggested to a large
proportion of young Americans the option of doing nothing or making
their excuses to the draft board. This option was bolstered and legiti-
mated by the wide dissemination of books such as Kupferberg's *1001
Ways to Beat the Draft*. Local support groups helped to reassure young
men that draft resistance was neither cowardly nor un-American.

The readiness to attract free-riders to the cause was also a key
element in building resistance to the community charge or poll tax in
Britain. Anti-poll tax activists were quick to promote non-payment of
the tax for whatever motive, and the movement's most famous slogan

– 'Can't pay? Won't pay!' – justified non-payment whether people could afford the tax or not.

It was often overlooked in subsequent political posturing that the community charge was a policy defeated through mass non-cooperation. The Thatcher government had pushed through policies in the face of popular opposition before, and it did so with the poll tax, first in Scotland in 1989 and then a year later in England and Wales. Despite their doubts, councils of every political colour implemented the tax.

But nearly one in five people in Scotland liable for the tax did not pay in the first year; by the second year, it was over one in three. In England and Wales the Audit Commission reported that by January 1991 non-payment was running at 27% in metropolitan district councils, 18% in the shires, 23% in outer London boroughs and 34% in inner London. The size of future poll tax bills had to be jacked up to compensate for the lost revenue and the cost of chasing defaulters. At near £400, the average bill set for 1991 was double the amount politicians had envisaged when the tax was first planned; billions had to be spent by central government in 'transitional relief'. A week before its abolition was announced in March 1991, Prime Minister John Major admitted that the poll tax was unenforceable: *17 million people* had either not paid or were in serious arrears.

A local authority had to go to extraordinary lengths to recover the community charge when faced by simple inaction on the part of non-payers (assuming, of course, that they had registered in the first place). The original bill, information leaflets and rebate form would be followed by a reminder, then a further letter giving seven or 14 days' notice to pay. Most councils followed this with another letter threatening legal action. The next step was to issue a summons, and if court proceedings went the authority's way, a liability order was served on the non-payer. Realising the vast number of summonses issued, and the limited amount of court time available for hearing local authority business, hundreds of local anti-poll tax unions up and down the country worked to persuade non-payers to turn up in court and argue their case. Delaying tactics meant that often only a fraction of the cases could be heard.

Six months, seven letters and a court case later, the council was finally able to take action against the non-payer. All the available options – wage arrestment, benefit deduction, distraint of goods and further legal action to commit people to prison – presented problems. The third option was widely chosen, but bailiffs proved much less effective than they had been in chasing up defaulters under the old rates system. Both the number of non-payers involved and a new awareness of their rights conspired to ensure that few people were intimidated into paying up or even letting the bailiffs into their house. In most cases the bailiff's threats were ignored just like every other communication about the poll tax had been. The councils, meanwhile, were only too aware that the costs of recovering unpaid tax often exceeded the amounts owed.

Whatever they thought personally of the ethics of the non-payers, or of the demonstrators and rioters on the streets, the inhabitants of Whitehall realised that the poll tax had raised the spectre of a Britain that was ungovernable. No administration can ignore that and survive. The poll tax had to go.

Some of the lessons gleaned from movements such as those against the poll tax and the Vietnam War draft are summarised in the box right. Much will depend on the possible sanctions that could be applied by the state (or other target) to try and break non-cooperation. The extent to which the target quickly has to resort to crudely coercive methods is an indication of the strength of the campaigners' position.

Most administrative systems depend on only having to deal with a small proportion of problem cases. Once that proportion rises above a certain level, they become unworkable. What the campaigner has to do is to ensure that people feel easy and happy about doing nothing.

The conditions for non-cooperation

The inertia factor

If active cooperation is needed from ordinary citizens for a policy to work, then inertia will work against the success of the policy. The more effort or sacrifice required from the citizen, the greater the inertia factor.

The free-rider factor

If levels of non-cooperation rise to a certain point, large numbers of free-riders with little commitment to the actual cause will be attracted to jump on the bandwagon. It helps if the justification for non-cooperation is widely drawn.

The unenforceability factor

Enforcement of a policy usually requires both adequate information on individual cases of default and the legal or *de facto* power to apply sanctions. Either of these may be difficult to obtain, or the enforcement methods available may be complex to apply, or seen as politically inappropriate.

Sabotage and monkey-wrenching

Sabotage has been a central weapon of armed resistance movements throughout history; its use by the French Resistance in World War Two and by the Umkhonto We Sizwe wing of the African National Congress provides but two recent examples. Some IRA bombing campaigns, particularly in the City of London, were also aimed as much at economic sabotage as at terrorising the population.

A big problem with employing sabotage, then, is its strong association with violence. Damaging vehicles or machinery may actually make them dangerous and liable to injure someone (in any case, the target will often claim that was the saboteur's intention). Chemicals, explosives and incendiaries also carry risks for the untrained user. On a smaller scale, the criminal damage favoured by the suffragettes, like smashing windows, was a striking form of civil disobedience at the time, but would probably be dismissed now as mindless vandalism.

But green activists, once again, have successfully pioneered a non-violent form of sabotage with wide application in today's world. Ecotage, or monkey-wrenching, is aimed at pushing back the timber, mining and other environmentally-destructive industries in the US by putting a spanner in their works. Developed partly by a militant group called Earth First!, techniques include:

▼ tree-spiking: driving long nails into the trunks of condemned trees to ruin chainsaw or sawmill blades (the nails do not harm the trees and, driven home, become invisible);

▼ plugging waste discharge pipes, usually with sandbags and quick-drying cement, so that the waste oozes back into the plant (or, in the case of an unfinished block of flats, all over the new carpets);

▼ pulling up survey stakes or flags to hinder developers;

▼ disabling bulldozers and other vehicles by methods, such as putting sand in the oil, which are hard to detect but will perma-nently damage the engine within a couple of days;

▼ spiking dirt roads and paths with short metal rods to close them to vehicles.

Some of these actions will be more applicable in the UK than others, but perhaps monkey-wrenching's greatest innovation is to have built up and publicised a series of very simple techniques which can be used by anyone with environmental sympathies, whether working alone or with a group. Employed systematically, or by enough people, they are capable of causing untold expense and delay to the target, and the only element of danger involved is the beating the monkey-wrencher risks if she is caught by security guards.

The monkey-wrencher's bible is a book called *Ecodefense: A Field Guide to Monkey-wrenching*, edited by Dave Foreman and Bill Haywood. In addition to detailed guidance on a host of different methods of sabotage, there is a long section on security and avoiding detection, with the whole prefaced by a standard disclaimer noting that the book is for entertainment purposes only. It is certainly entertaining, as well as ambitious: the epilogue is headed 'How to sink whalers and driftnetters'. The 1993 edition of *Ecodefense* was published by Abbzug Press, Chico, California, at $20; a handful of specialist bookshops may stock it in the UK.

Environmental groups in the UK have used sabotage on occasion, perhaps most notably in the destruction of genetically-modified crops used in trials. When Greenpeace was involved in one such action it invited the media along to watch, so as to draw as much publicity as possible to the issue.

In the urban environment, sabotage does not have nature on its side in the way that it does in rural areas. Confronted with the security surrounding corporate offices or installations, the would-be saboteur is in much the same position as any thief or burglar. Putting things through company letterboxes is ineffective as a means of protest and is easily dismissed as vandalism. Nevertheless, there have been some examples of successful urban sabotage by activists, for example by the

Chicago Fox, who in a series of daylight 'raids' dumped raw sewage onto the office carpets of corporate polluters.

Clearly the Achilles' heel of the modern office lies in its computer and communications systems. Computer hacking, or accessing computer networks through telephone lines, opens up numerous possibilities. 'Hacktivism' and electronic picketing are described in Chapters 6 and 11.

Under new legislation going through Parliament in 2000, the criminal penalties faced by saboteurs could become very serious indeed. The Terrorism Bill seeks to extend the definition of terrorism to the 'use or threat, for the purpose of advancing a political, religious or ideological cause, of action which involves serious violence against any person or property'. Although it does not create a specific offence of terrorism itself, the bill does create an offence of 'directing terrorism' and associated offences. It also makes it an offence in Britain to incite others to commit violence abroad.

In response to concerns over the inclusion of violence against property in the definition of terrorism, and the wide range of activities that might be covered, the Home Secretary has stated: 'The new definition will not catch the vast majority of so-called domestic activist groups which exist in this country today ... This Bill is not intended to, nor will it, threaten in any way the right peacefully to demonstrate. It is not designed to be used in situations where demonstrations turn unaccountably ugly.' Whether it might be used against activists who, for example, destroy GM crops would ultimately be for the courts to decide. The Home Secretary did indicate, however, that the bill might be used to target animal liberation activists who have engaged in acts which have resulted in serious violence to individuals.

Pressurising individuals

Much of the coercive force from successful direct actions comes from making individuals in positions of power personally accountable for their behaviour. Normally, the responsibility for repressive decisions lies with a number of people, and with the system of which they are a part, which makes it easy for individuals to hide behind a professional facade: 'That decision wasn't made by me, it was made by the board', 'If I don't do it, somebody else will', 'That's just the way things are in this business', and so on. By focusing attention on particular sites of action and pinning the blame on individuals, a campaigner can make power-holders accountable, not just professionally but morally, to their community, friends and family.

'Outing', or the practice by some gay activists of exposing the homosexuality of public figures, is a controversial example. After the House of Commons rejected a move to bring the age of consent for homosexuals in line with that for heterosexuals, activists threatened to out those allegedly gay MPs who had voted against the measure,

Personal coercion

'A person commits an offence who, with a view to compelling another person to abstain from doing or to do any act which such other person has a legal right to do or to abstain from doing, wrongfully and without legal authority:–

(a) uses violence to or intimidates that person or his wife or children, or injures his property; or

(b) persistently follows that person about from place to place; or

(c) hides any tools, clothes or other property owned or used by that person, or deprives him of or hinders him in the use thereof; or

(d) watches or besets the house or other place where that person resides, works, carries on business, or happens to be, or the approach to any such house or place; or

(e) follows that person with two or more other persons in a disorderly manner through any street or road.'

Trade Union and Labour Relations (Consolidation) Act 1992, Section 241

in order to expose their hypocrisy and pressure them into taking a more liberal stance.

Such publicity stunts would seem to make more sense, however, if the exposed activity is one which the campaign is trying to censure: waste-dumping or arms-dealing, for example. People are often not aware that their neighbour, fellow church-goer or golf-club member is an arms dealer, and might well ask him to explain himself if it was brought to their attention. At a time when public tolerance of arms dealing is declining, publicising the names and photographs of dealers in their local community could prove surprisingly effective.

Personalising issues does lead a campaign into greater danger of being sued for defamation. Extra care must be taken that any allegations made are supported with evidence, and that in their enthusiasm protestors do not go beyond the facts. Read the section on libel in chapter 5.

Beyond simple publicity, personal pressure techniques include 'ghosting' or 'haunting', following individuals with placards or banners, or demonstrating outside their home or place of work. This is an extreme form of the sort of stunt described in the last chapter, involving a high embarrassment or nuisance factor. Most actions of this kind are strictly illegal, by virtue of section 241 of the Trade Union and Labour Relations (Consolidation) Act 1992 which aims at halting the measures taken by trade unionists against scabs or strike-breakers. The relevant section is given in the box left.

Prosecutions under this section are summary only, but note that the use of violence – completely unjustified and counter-productive in any case – will lay the perpetrator open to more serious charges. Picketing at one's own place of work in furtherance of a trade dispute is exempt from the watching and besetting charge (see chapter 9). Prosecutions under the Act are in fact very rare, with police more likely in the first instance to use their powers to prevent breaches of the peace. In practice, a lot of the activity described under sub-sections (b) to (e) is quite difficult to control or police, particularly if it is short-lived.

The Protection from Harassment Act 1997 was introduced to deal with stalkers, but there have also been attempts to use it against campaigners. The Act makes it an offence for a person to pursue a course of conduct which he knows or ought to know amounts to harassment of another person. Injunctions against anticipated harassment have been obtained against protestors under the Act, although this will not prevent a reasonable level of protest at an appropriate distance. However, when members of the British Union for the Abolition of Vivisection were accused of harassment for protesting outside an animal laboratory, the High Court judge threw out the case, stating '[The Act] was clearly not intended by Parliament to be used to clamp down on the rights of political protest and public demonstration, which are so much part of our democratic tradition'.

Outside trade disputes or corporate actions, ghosting or personal picketing has been employed to great effect in a wide variety of situations where the target was susceptible to the social embarrassment caused. In Gandhi's 1928 Bardoli campaign, protestors would shadow officials everywhere, throughout the day. In both the US and the UK, tenants groups have picketed the homes and clubs of slum landlords – often just the threat of having their activities so publicly exposed to their respectable friends was enough to win concessions.

Getting arrested and being sued

Getting arrested is something of an occupational hazard for practitioners of direct action. Most arrests do not require a warrant. Public order offences generally carry a power of arrest by a constable in uniform; the police can also detain or arrest people under their powers to prevent a breach of the peace (see chapter 9).

For those less serious offences which are not defined as 'arrestable', the suspect will usually receive a summons to appear before a court on a given date. However, under the Police and Criminal Evidence Act 1984, the police can make an arrest in relation to *any* offence if they do not know the suspect's name or have reasonable grounds for doubting that he has given his real name, if the suspect has failed to give a satisfactory address for the service of a summons or if the police have reasonable grounds for doubting whether an address given is satisfactory.

The civil rights group Liberty publishes some useful materials which explain people's rights on being arrested and in police custody, as well as general advice on trouble with the police.

A police officer making an arrest is required to inform you that you are under arrest, state the grounds for the arrest and caution you. Only such force may be used in making an arrest as is reasonable in the circumstances: in the case of a completely non-violent protestor who makes no attempt to escape, this means no force at all. If you are asked to accompany a police officer to the station, ask whether you are under arrest and for which offence. 'Helping the police with their enquiries' is a term used to denote voluntary attendance at a police station: you are at liberty to leave at any time, unless placed under arrest.

A police officer can search you on arrest if there are reasonable grounds for believing that you may present a danger to someone, including yourself, or may have concealed anything which might be evidence relating to an offence or might be used to assist escape. No search can be carried out in public which involves more than the removal of gloves, an outer coat or jacket.

The custody officer at the police station, usually a police sergeant, must determine whether there is enough evidence to charge you. This should happen as soon as is practicable.

▼ If the evidence is insufficient, you must be released unless there are reasonable grounds for believing that detention is necessary to secure or preserve evidence relating to the offence for which you were arrested, or to obtain evidence by questioning.

▼ If the evidence is sufficient to charge you, you should be charged and then released. You can only be detained if your name and address are not known or doubted, or if it is necessary to prevent harm to yourself or others, damage to property, interference with the investigation or the administration of justice, or to ensure your attendance at court.

The custody officer should inform you of your rights under arrest and allow you to look at a copy of the code of practice on detention. If you have not been charged, your detention in custody must be reviewed within the first six hours, and periodically thereafter, by a police inspector or more senior officer, and the reason for continued detention recorded in the custody report. The standard maximum period of detention without charge is 24 hours, although this can be extended a further 12 hours in serious cases. Beyond that time, further detention has to be authorised by a magistrates' court.

You have a right to free legal advice from a solicitor and a right to inform someone, like a friend or relative, of your detention. Since 1986, when the relevant provisions of the Police and Criminal Evidence Act came into force, duty solicitors have been available on a 24-hour basis to attend police stations. The advice is paid for by legal aid. It is generally best not to answer questions or make a statement until you have seen a solicitor.

A personal search can be carried out by a police officer of the same sex as you. If this involves more than the removal of outer clothing it is known as a strip search and can only be carried out in the presence of a police officer of the same sex. No-one can be present whose presence is unnecessary. The reasons for a strip search and the result should be recorded on the custody record.

Complaints about the conduct of particular police officers can be made at a local station or to the chief constable of the relevant police force (in London, the Metropolitan Police Commissioner). They can also be submitted to the Police Complaints Authority (see appendix

B). If your complaint is serious, it is worth getting some legal advice first, if only from a Citizens Advice Bureau. In cases of unlawful arrest, imprisonment or assault, a civil action can also be brought against the police (see chapter 8).

Many protestors are deterred from taking direct action for fear of acquiring a criminal record. A conviction may damage a person's chances of getting a job, or affect their eligibility for insurance or credit facilities. After a set 'rehabilitation period', however, certain sentences become spent, which means that for most purposes they need no longer be disclosed. (But note that any criminal conviction may bar you from certain professions, e.g. becoming a lawyer, for life.) A non-violent demonstrator hauled before magistrates for the first time may be bound over to keep the peace or given a conditional discharge, which will become spent in one year or when the bind-over ceases, whichever is the later. But a fine on conviction or a community service order carry rehabilitation periods of five years, and a sentence of up to six months imprisonment a rehabilitation period of seven years.

More detailed information about police powers and people's rights when in custody is available from Liberty. A group called Release also provides emergency advice in cases of arrest. (See appendix B for addresses.)

If an act of civil disobedience is planned, everyone involved should be briefed about their legal rights beforehand and what they should expect if approached or arrested by the police. Apart from anything else, talking this through will mean that people are less likely to panic and the situation grow out of control. If the protest is expected to include supporters or sympathisers turning up on the day, 'bust cards' can be prepared for handing out, giving basic advice and information on the law and dealing with the police.

Some members of the protest group should refrain from taking any part in the action, but be briefed to act as observers, recording the identities of police officers involved in any incidents and getting the names and addresses of witnesses if there are instances of police provocation or brutality. In many cases, observers will turn out to be superfluous, but if trouble does develop the information they can collate can be invaluable in helping to prepare a defence for protestors that are charged. Take care if you intend to video the proceedings, as the police may well use the film in evidence.

Even small demonstrations can involve a lot of things going on at the same time, and experience has shown that the police can sometimes take a rough and ready approach to what they record in police statements. Being able to provide an accurate chronology of events, with details of the individuals involved at a given place and time, and backed up by credible witnesses, should go a long way to preventing any miscarriages of justice.

Civil proceedings

If a direct action takes place on private property, interferes with property or the conduct of business, or otherwise affects the private rights of an individual or a company, it may also provoke legal action. What happens when civil proceedings are brought is described in chapter 8. Both individuals and incorporated pressure groups or charitable companies can be sued.

The target may seek damages or an injunction to prevent further direct action from taking place. If you defy an injunction by persisting with activity which falls within the terms of the injunction you will be guilty of contempt of court. This is a criminal offence and can result in severe penalties. When Arthur Scargill and the National Union of Mineworkers were found in contempt of court during the miners' strike, they were fined £1,000 and £200,000 respectively.

A civil action cannot be brought against an unincorporated association in its own name, however, as it has no legal identity. Many very small pressure groups fall into this category (see chapter 1). Although the members of such an association can still be sued as individuals, the difficulties involved in proceeding against the group as a whole do blunt the effectiveness of the civil law in restraining direct action. The identities of most members of a group will probably be unknown to the intending claimant.

In certain circumstances it may be possible for a claimant to bring a representative action against an unincorporated pressure group, that is, suing one or more named members on behalf of all the other members of the group. A fur company was thus able to obtain an injunction against one named defendant on behalf of the members of Animal Aid, even though the other members were unknown. This will not work, however, if not all the members of the group are held to have the same interest in the legal proceedings. Some members of Lincolnshire and Nottinghamshire Against Nuclear Dumping (LAND) had interfered with the surveying of a site to be used by UK Nirex Ltd. for disposing radioactive waste. The court held that a representative action was not suitable as many of LAND's members would not consider breaking the law in any form and their interests therefore clearly diverged from those of other potential defendants (cited in Warburton, *Unincorporated Associations*, Sweet & Maxwell, 1992).

Much direct action in the UK has been carried out by unincorporated associations of activists. Few assets are held in common and many of the individuals concerned may be eligible for legal aid. Once a group gets to a certain size, becomes incorporated and acquires some money, it has much more to lose from legal action. The most appropriate structure for widespread direct action is thus probably a loose network of local unincorporated groups, like the anti-poll tax unions. Many direct action cells of green activists were formed across the country in the nineties in order to fight road-building schemes. Linked mainly by e-mail, they constituted a large but flexible body of people ready to rush to protest sites at short notice.

Entryism and insider actions

Because it uses radical techniques to challenge the existing order, the assumption is often made that direct action is action by outsiders, by those marginalised by society or those on the periphery of conventional political debates. This need not be so. In fact some of the most successful 'direct' techniques are those deployed by people already placed within government, companies or other institutions.

Perhaps the most notorious example of this type of action is entryism. A practice associated with the Trotskyite left, entryism involves positioning your own supporters to enter other more mainstream organisations or parties in order to radicalise them. Using other organisations as hosts, the entryist group can gain influence much more quickly than if it had to build its own power base from scratch. Depending on strategic requirements, entryists fall into two main types:

▼ *the agitator*: fostering discontent and winning converts as she goes along, the agitator seeks to establish a conscious and expanding faction within the host organisation;

▼ *the sleeper*: keeping his politics largely to himself, the sleeper may use his position to gain information but waits until a key occasion or opportunity to take the traditionalists by surprise and declare his support for radical change.

A policy of entryism was employed by the Militant Tendency to gain control of a number of local Labour parties during the eighties.

Such high-profile examples, however, and the somewhat arcane language of entryism, draw attention away from what is in fact quite a widespread set of techniques. The growing number of secondments and exchanges between business and government, for example, accomplish many of the same goals: enabling the business case to be made inside government, keeping the business community directly informed of new measures or developments, ensuring that more and more business methods are adopted by government.

Entryism aside, the possibility of exercising leverage *from inside* the target institutions should not be dismissed lightly. As a means of getting your way, declaring total war on your enemies is a considerably less reliable method than making friends with some of them. (Even in cases of appalling oppression, such as occupation by a foreign army, resistors have on occasion been able to avoid the worst by befriending and assimilating enemy forces.)

One particular danger of rejecting any bridge between yourself and your target is that it ignores the opportunity to take advantage of schisms within the target institution. No group of people of any size is entirely homogeneous, and there will always be differences of opinion or approach between them. In campaigns against companies or local government, sections of the workforce and their unions have often proved useful allies. The field of professional interests and professional ethics is particularly fertile for sowing discord. Some civil servants have recently broken ranks in exasperation at the politicisation of their role; doctors and dentists have proved surprisingly militant when their own interests and professional judgement have been threatened by health reforms.

The potential strength of insider support should not be underestimated just because it has to take a more cautious or low-key form than outside support. One of the key elements of the anti-poll tax movement was the large numbers of local government officers who did not strike or resign, but who complained, and delayed, and whose deliberate inefficiency enabled many more people to avoid paying the tax.

Tactics for direct action

Once the campaigner ceases to confine her imagination to the conventional round of publicity, lobbying and demonstrating, the options for action are endless. The box on pp218–219 gives 100 different ideas for actions, based on what other people have actually done; these can be adapted, combined or added to.

In very many cases, however, the power of an action will not depend so much on what is done as on the target's reaction to what is done. This lies behind most acts of civil disobedience and is at the heart of Gandhi's theory of non-violent resistance. But it is also apparent in political scandals from Watergate to Westland: great centres of power brought to their knees not by their policies or practices but by their reactions when placed under unaccustomed pressure. Greenpeace was born in the horror which greeted pictures of an anti-nuclear protestor being beaten up in the South Pacific; it gained mass support a decade later when its flagship, the Rainbow Warrior, was revealed to have been sunk by French agents. The imprisonment of poll tax defaulters or the distraint of their goods hardened popular opposition against the tax.

Direct actions are provocative, literally, in order to start a dialogue of reaction and counter-reaction which leads the target onto unfamiliar, and therefore dangerous, territory. The use of unconventional or non-establishment methods will mean that when confronted with them the establishment will cry dirty, but will still have to keep its own behaviour above board. This, of course, is unfair, and the more frustrating and unfair it seems, the easier it is for the target to be drawn into making a mistake and acting illegally or unprofessionally, from which it has so much more to lose than you do.

Campaign strategy in these circumstances may well have to be improvised, but there exists the chance of making major gains. The US community organiser Saul Alinsky developed a series of rules to serve as a guide for radical actions (see box below). These are particularly useful in thinking beyond the rationale for individual actions to the management of a direct action campaign over time.

A word of warning to finish. The fact that many direct actions are aimed at breaking society's own rules means that they require more, not less, control or regulation on the part of the campaigner. The choice to take such action should be submitted to the sort of hard-headed analysis detailed in part 4 of this book, but with a heightened awareness of the level of risk involved. If extreme methods are employed in non-crisis situations, or situations where alternative solutions are clearly available, many potential and existing supporters could be alienated. Breaking the law also raises the stakes considerably. The price of a failed campaign technique is usually limited to wasted effort and loss of morale; the consequences of direct action gone wrong can be much worse.

Alinsky's rules

1. Power is not only what you have but what the enemy thinks you have.
2. Never go outside the experience of your people.
3. Wherever possible go outside the experience of the enemy.
4. Make the enemy live up to their own book of rules.
5. Ridicule is man's most potent weapon.
6. A good tactic is one that your people enjoy.
7. A tactic that drags on too long becomes a drag.
8. Keep the pressure on, with different tactics and actions.
9. The threat is usually more terrifying than the thing itself.
10. The major premise for tactics is the development of operations that will maintain a constant pressure upon the opposition.
11. If you push a negative hard and deep enough, it will break through into its counterside [i.e. rebound on the enemy].
12. The price of a successful attack is a constructive alternative.
13. Pick the target, freeze it, personalise it, and polarise it.

Saul D Alinsky, *Rules for Radicals*

---

100 ideas for actions

Protest actions (symbolic actions)

1. Refusal of assembly to disperse
2. Sit-down
3. Bodily interjection (e.g. protestors placing themselves between whalers and their prey)
4. Bodily obstruction (e.g. protestors chained to, or lying in front of, bulldozers)
5. Trespass into closed areas (e.g. a military base)
6. Airborne 'invasion' (flying protest balloons or airships over target)
7. Occupations
8. Inviting arrest/imprisonment
9. Sit-in (attendance at private or restricted facilities, e.g. a park or club)
10. Stand-in (joining queues at targeted shops or services to dissuade other custom)
11. Ride-in (use of restricted or segregated transport, e.g. on trains, buses)
12. Pray-in (attendance at services of religious institutions opposed to change)
13. Return of waste products (returning dumped waste to the dumper or manufacturer)
14. Heckling
15. Mail bombing
16. Guerilla theatre (theatre that involves the bystander or even the target: Jerry Rubin threw dollar bills onto the dealing floor of the New York Stock Exchange to show how the stockbrokers scrabbled like animals to get hold of the money)
17. Public burning of papers (e.g. poll tax bills), flags, etc.
18. Protest strip
19. Graffiti
20. Defacing signs or advertisements
21. Adoption of new signs or names (e.g. renaming a street or institution in defiance of authority)
22. Refusal to collaborate with government bodies
23. Declining government awards or appointments
24. Boycott of elections
25. Hunger strike
26. Penitential (satyagrahic) fast

Social actions

27. Ghosting (persistent following of individuals)
28. Publicising individual's activities
29. Social boycott (e.g. refusal to converse or trade with particular individuals)
30. Ostracism (radical form of social boycott)
31. Denial of sexual relations (classically, a women's protest against their warmongering males)
32. Excommunication
33. Boycott of meetings, events or lectures
34. Group silence (e.g. refusal of audience to question or applaud)
35. Walk-out
36. Picketing
37. Breaking social taboos
38. Socialising with outcasts
39. Harbouring fugitives
40. Sanctuary (use of sacred building to harbour individuals, e.g. those threatened with deportation)

Boycotts and strikes

41. Consumers' boycott of goods
42. Consumers' boycott of producer
43. Withholding of rent
44. Refusal to pay tax
45. Refusal to pay debts or charges
46. Withdrawal of bank deposits
47. Retailers' boycott
48. Blacking of goods by suppliers
49. Blacking of raw materials by workers
50. Demonstration strike (short strike to demonstrate power and build solidarity)
51. Go-slow
52. Work-to-rule (a form of go-slow in which all rules and regulations in the workplace are meticulously observed)

53. Coordinated reporting sick
54. Overtime strike
55. Selective strike (withdrawal of labour on selected activities)
56. Detailed strike (strike joined by individual workers or units one-by-one)
57. Bumper strike (striking firms in an industry one-by-one to expose them to competition by rivals)
58. Wildcat or lightning strikes
59. Lock-up or stay-in strike
60. Reverse strike (e.g. carrying out public works unpaid in order to draw attention to need)
61. Personal strike (individual refusal to obey orders, e.g. by a prisoner)
62. *Hartal* (cessation of economic activity for limited periods in protest by entire community)
63. General strike (strike by workers across industry; main tenet of revolutionary syndicalism)

Non-cooperation and obstruction: actions by outsiders

64. Overloading facilities or services
65. Overloading administrative systems
66. Slow or cumbersome compliance with regulations
67. Stalling by customers (e.g. by drawing out or complicating routine transactions)
68. Breaking bad laws on principle (e.g. non-payment of poll tax)
69. Covert breaking of bad laws (e.g. non-registration for poll tax)
70. Publishing secret material
71. Disclosing secret identities (e.g. of security agents)
72. Tracking (e.g. following military or nuclear deployments)
73. Forgery of letters, etc.
74. Breaking official boycotts/blockades
75. Refusal to recognise appointed officials
76. Non-cooperation with police, bailiffs, etc.
77. Removal of street signs, door numbers, etc. (as carried out by populations under occupation to fool security forces)
78. Closure of roads
79. Infiltration of institutions with spies or saboteurs
80. Electronic picketing or hacktivism
81. Spoiling or contamination of goods (e.g. with ink or other dye)
82. Monkey-wrenching (see main text)
83. Liberating animals in traps or laboratories

Non-cooperation and obstruction: actions by insiders

84. Refusal to perform selected actions (e.g. officials refusing to proceed against poll tax defaulters; cf. selective strikes)
85. Failure to pass on information/instructions
86. Deliberate inefficiency
87. Industrial sabotage (sabotage of plant by workers)
88. Non-cooperation by juries (e.g. refusal to find guilty)
89. Non-cooperation or mutiny by security forces
90. Non-cooperation by government units (e.g. local authorities in budget setting)

Positive direct action

91. Non-retaliation
92. Entryism
93. Alternative radio/newspapers
94. Alternative schools/colleges
95. Selective patronage (positive buying/investment)
96. Alternative economic bodies (e.g. cooperatives, non-profits, 'green' companies)
97. Alternative economies (e.g. local exchange trading schemes, black markets)
98. Suspending specified regulations within community (e.g. property rights in commune)
99. Selective refusal of entry to area (e.g. nuclear-free zones)
100. Alternative community with independent sovereign government

Sources: Gene Sharp, *The Politics of Nonviolent Action* (Porter Sargent, Boston, 1985); author's own sources.

Part 3
Targets

11   Companies

The customer is always right

To say that policy-making, both here and abroad, is dominated by the interests of large private corporations has become a commonplace. It would certainly be foolish to underestimate the power of multinational capital. Few people, however, realise how vulnerable individual companies are, and how fragile their hold on power.

In fact, compared to the meagre controls on our elected representatives in government and in particular on civil servants, the controls on companies' behaviour are considerable and continuous. In addition to the mass of company law that regulates what companies can do and ensures that detailed information on what they do actually do is open to public scrutiny, companies are vulnerable to actions by the groups listed below. Concerted action by any one of these groups can place the existing management of a company at risk, and in the case of all but the first two groups, may well endanger the future of the company itself.

▼ *Directors*. Company directors can be ousted at any time by their fellow directors or by major financial backers. A glance at the business press will show how frequent such boardroom revolutions are.

▼ *Shareholders*. Company law gives formidable powers to shareholders, including approving the appointment of new directors, the ability to have directors removed, putting resolutions for vote at general meetings, calling extraordinary general meetings, taking legal action against directors and, ultimately, selling the share capital and with it control of the company.

▼ *Sources of finance*. In addition to the existing shareholders, companies need to keep other sources of money sweet, including bankers, bond-holders and other creditors, and potential shareholders represented by the company's standing in the City. There is also the income from parent or associated companies: the growing complexity of corporate links and multinational structures can be a source of weakness if one link in the chain fails and begins to drain cash from the structure.

▼ *Suppliers*. If a company's suppliers of raw materials or services encounter problems, this can quickly translate to problems at the company itself, particularly if alternative suppliers are hard to come by.

▼ *Competitors*. Of all the groups listed here, competitor companies are the only ones that companies traditionally regard as the enemy.

▼ *Employees*. To the last sentence should have been added: with the possible exception, in some cases, of the unions. In fact most companies don't expect organised pressure from their employees and will be at pains to diffuse it.

▼ *Consumers*. The fate of any company will always land in the hands of its customers. Corporate profit margins and cash flow are such that in many cases even a relatively small decline in sales can spell disaster.

It is through consumer action, particularly by environmentalists, that most of the recent successes in campaigning against companies have taken place. Much of this depends on an appreciation of how companies respond to the old corporate clichés about the primacy of the profit motive and the customer always being right. Many companies, for example, have been persuaded to adopt ethical practices or 'environmentally friendly' practices in the belief that it will give them a competitive advantage in the marketplace.

Pressure groups often criticise companies for being exclusively profit-oriented, for putting business above their employees or business above society. To be successful, however, pressure groups must first understand companies as *businesses*: where a company's market is, who the competitors are, where the principal threats lie, where the money comes from, where the company sees its opportunities.

The structure and environment of the modern company

In contrast to the companies limited by guarantee described in chapter 1, profit-making companies are limited by shares. This means that the liability of the members, or the shareholders, is limited to the value of the shares they hold (if a company goes down with huge debts, the shareholders lose their investment but nothing else).

Companies are most frequently divided into two kinds: public and private. Public companies have a share capital of at least £50,000, call themselves 'public limited companies' in their memorandum of association and have 'Plc' written after their name. Nearly all the big household name companies are public. All other companies are private and carry 'Limited' or 'Ltd.' after their name.

Influence Map 1: Environment of the modern company

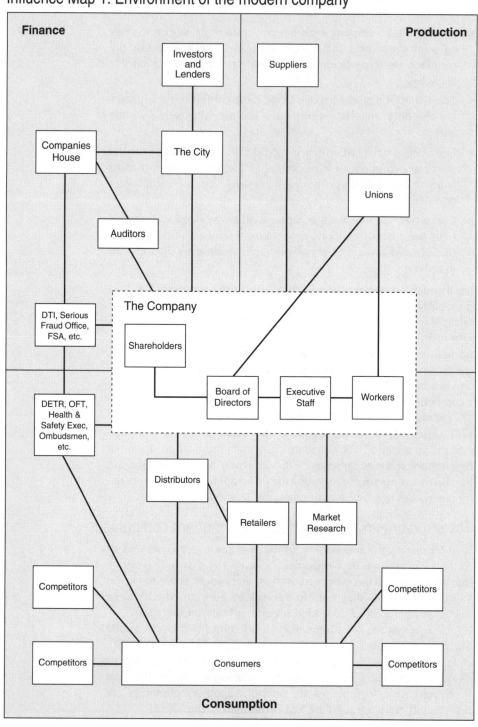

In fact, the vast majority of companies, including all small companies, are private. The equity or shares in a private company will be controlled by an individual, a family or other closely knit group of people (generally the same people who set the company up in the first place, usually with just some savings and a bank loan.). Private companies are not able to advertise their shares for sale to the public, and therefore will not be listed on the stock exchange, and their articles of association often place restrictions on the ability of shareholders to transfer shares. The person or people that own the business and those that run it are generally one and the same (although there may be 'sleeping partners' who hold part of the share capital but play no part in the day-to-day running of the company). Control over the company is thus tight, shareholder action is not an option, and the company is unlikely to be very susceptible to public opinion, unless it is on a matter directly affecting its customers' behaviour.

Once it has reached a certain size, a company may acquire public status to enable it to raise money by issuing shares to the public. This is generally done to fund expansion, but it may also be a way for the owner(s) to raise cash for themselves by releasing some of their investment in the company. Companies are usually floated on the Stock Exchange at the same time (but note that not all public companies have a Stock Exchange listing). A minimum of 25% of a company's share capital must be put on the market for its shares to be listed or quoted on the Stock Exchange, and the company has to abide by the Exchange's rules, contained in the so-called 'yellow book'. In addition to the main market, there is also a junior market, known as the AIM or Alternative Investment Market, on which the shares of younger companies can be traded.

Once there is a market in the company's shares, the directors cannot control who becomes a shareholder. The interests of the management and certain groups of shareholders may also begin to diverge, as for example if the company becomes the subject of a takeover bid by another company.

Exactly how closely a company's management and its shareholders are identified will depend on how the share capital is divided. When a company first comes to the market the founder(s) will frequently hold onto a majority of the shares and continue to run the company, but as time goes on, the company grows and more shares are issued, this shareholding is often diluted. Issuing non-voting shares in addition to ordinary voting shares can enable the founder(s) to keep control even if they only retain a minority of the share capital. As well as issuing equity, companies also borrow money from banks and other investors by issuing bonds, or debentures. Bondholders can constitute another strong source of pressure on the boardroom.

So long as a company remains solvent, however, the board of directors will always be the centre of corporate power. In addition to controlling the business itself, the directors of larger companies will be able to draw readily on the corporate panoply of lawyers, bankers, public relations consultants and other advisers.

The executive directors of a company are its top managers. Many larger companies also have non-executive directors, who are not involved in the day-to-day running of the company, but are paid a salary and have a place on the board like the executive directors, bringing to the board outside experience and, in theory, a more detached or independent viewpoint. It is often argued (for example by the Cadbury committee on corporate governance) that part of the role of a non-executive director is to monitor the performance of the board, acting as a watchdog for the interests of the shareholders. This suggests that on certain issues the non-executive directors may provide a more fruitful channel for approaching the board. However, it should be borne in mind that the non-executives are generally chosen by the executive directors, have their access to company information controlled by them, often have other business links with them, and are, in any case, in a minority. Tiny Rowland once notoriously described non-executive directors as 'decorations on a Christmas tree'.

In addition to the Stock Exchange, a number of supervisory bodies nurture, regulate and police the corporate jungle, including the Department of Trade and Industry, Companies House, the Serious Fraud Office, the Bank of England and the Financial Services Authority. The key link between an individual company and the supervisory regime is the company's auditors, external accountants who check the books and report on whether the annual accounts present a true and fair picture of the company's affairs. The auditors should, in theory, be able to provide the first indication if something is amiss financially.

Business operations

Companies on the stock market are conventionally divided into a number of different sectors, depending on the sort of business they undertake. The classification most often used by professional investors is that followed by the FTSE Actuaries indices, which divide the top companies into 35 sectors such as Construction, Media, Insurance, Property, etc.; the newspapers list share prices under a slightly simpler classification. Note that companies within the same sector may still be very dissimilar, certainly servicing diverse markets and maybe operating not just one but several businesses.

Most large companies will in fact own a number of subsidiary companies, each operating or controlling a distinct business. In the case of a conglomerate like BAT, with interests ranging from tobacco to financial services, the subsidiaries may appear to have little in common and do operate with considerable autonomy, with only major financial decisions being taken at the centre. In the case of a major multinational, the ownership structure may be extremely complex with literally hundreds of subsidiary and associated companies spread across several countries (one reason why fraud, even on such a spectacular scale as with the international bank BCCI, can continue so long undiscovered).

The operations of most companies are quite compact, however, and even the big conglomerates are best understood (at least initially) as simply a collection of different businesses. Once you have targeted a particular business, get to know the product(s) or services it sells, the pattern of suppliers and distributors, and the size and variety of its market, for this knowledge will affect your choice of approach. If the business is supplying goods or services to other companies rather than direct to consumers, for example, this will limit the capacity for organising consumer action.

Some parts of a business are likely to be more profitable than others. The performance of the larger companies is monitored by armies of analysts in the City, who want the information for making investment decisions, and their opinions will be indirectly reflected in the movement of share prices. Factors like gearing, or the proportion of borrowings to equity capital, can also communicate a lot about a company's overall financial health. However, even if a company is very healthy, compiling a risk profile of its business can be invaluable in indicating where that company will be most vulnerable to pressure. Some of the most common sources of risk are listed in the box.

Common risk factors in business

▼ *Profit margin* – The higher the turnover compared to profit, the greater the level of risk. This factor is particularly acute in capital intensive businesses, where up-front investment is required and fluctuating capacity is harder to manage. If a high volume of sales is needed to break even, or maintain profitability, then a business will be particularly vulnerable to slides in demand.

▼ *Time* – Risk increases with the length of time between investment and return. This factor is prominent in businesses with a long production cycle, or which require high spend on research and development.

▼ *Competition* – The more competitive the market, the harder it is to retain market share (but completely new markets can be pretty tough, too).

▼ *Reliance on individual contracts* – Here everything can stand or fall on the signing of just one or two contracts (very common in the defence industry). Note that this can to apply to contracts with suppliers as well as customers. A particular variant is the awarding of franchises.

▼ *Disruption* – Some businesses are particularly vulnerable to interruption, for a range of different reasons: they may involve produce or raw materials which spoil quickly, they may provide services whose continuity or reliability is regarded as essential, or they may simply find it very hard to recover lost market ground.

The need for business sensitivity in campaigning is amply illustrated on the grand scale by comparing the two most significant industrial actions since the war: the miners' strikes of 1972–4, that helped bring down the government, and the 1984–5 miners' strike. The eighties strike was much longer and more determined, yet, by the standard of the actions in the seventies, hugely unsuccessful. The point was that when the Saltley Coke Depot was closed by over 12,000 secondary pickets in early 1972, the action was more than symbolic: it demonstrated beyond doubt that the miners had it in their power to sever the lifeline of the entire economy – the great nationalised industries included.

By 1984 things had changed. Some of the changes were legal, in the restrictions on secondary picketing, others political: a special Whitehall committee had existed since 1981 to advise on such strategies as stockpiling coal at power stations to withstand a long strike. But the biggest change was in the position of the coal industry itself. Coal was now only one of the major sources of energy open to British industry, and coal imported from abroad was looking increasingly competitive. The timing of the strike, starting when winter's end was already in sight, further weakened the miners' economic position. So when the full force of the strike hit, the government was able to announce – just – that it was business as usual.

Sources of information on companies

The requirements of company law and the hunger of the market both ensure that an abundance of information is available on companies.

Every company, public or private, is required under the Companies Acts to make an annual return to Companies House. Information contained in company returns is listed in the box overleaf, and is accessible to the public. Note that the Companies House register also holds details on overseas companies which trade in the UK, although the exact information required to be filed varies slightly. See chapter 4 for details on using information held at Companies House.

Most public companies publish annual reports which should be obtainable through a telephone call to head office. It hardly needs saying that they are a PR job. They will, however, contain a useful summary of the activities of the company and its main subsidiaries, as well as the summarised annual accounts, and so might save you going through Companies House.

At their simplest, annual accounts will comprise four elements: the directors' and auditors' reports, the profit and loss account (detailing income, expenditure and any profits for the year), the balance sheet (summarising assets and liabilities at year end) and the notes to the accounts. Note that accounting standards still allow companies considerable leeway in the way they present their finances, which means that individual figures are always vulnerable to massage, and that includes the so-called 'bottom line': the profit figures.

If a company is being floated on the market it has to issue a prospectus, which contains considerably more information on matters such as the company's future plans and prospects, its business history, its parent, subsidiary or associated companies, as well as full details on the offer itself and what the money raised will be used for.

The easiest way to obtain basic information on companies is through the Companies House web site (*www.companies-house.gov.uk*) or CD-ROM, which contains general details on approximately one million companies, including those in liquidation or receivership. There are also commercial services which search and summarise information from Companies House and other official registers; for example the Disclosure Information Centre operated by Primark (see appendix B).

Information contained in companies' annual returns

- Address of registered office
- Principal business activities
- Location of register of members and register of debenture holders (these are usually held at the registered office and under the Companies Act 1985 should be made available there for public inspection)
- Company type (e.g. public limited company)
- Name and address of company secretary
- Names and addresses of directors with details of other directorships
- Details of the issued share capital
- List of members (shareholders) with details of shares held

Although companies are obliged by law to file their annual returns promptly and the Stock Exchange requires listed companies to publish interim results, this information will always be a few months out-of-date. The business sections of the newspapers and the specialist business press and trade journals are a good source of current information, although the newspapers in particular tend to concentrate on just the bigger companies. There are also the other business information services listed in chapter 4.

There are a number of standard reference works which give summary information on companies and the people that run them. Some of the most useful are listed in the box opposite; these should all be available in a good reference library. There are a range of trade directories which cover individual industry sectors. Published market research also tends to be organised by trade and can provide valuable information on companies' activities; see chapter 4.

One of the most secretive industries, defence, is documented in great detail by Jane's Information Group (see appendix B). *Jane's Defence Weekly* is well-known but the company also publishes a range of other newsletters, market reports and yearbooks on specific parts of the defence industry here and abroad (these can get very expensive).

The sources listed above were developed primarily for the purposes of financial regulation or for providing business-to-business information. They can therefore be annoyingly uninformative when

---

Business directories

Who Owns Whom
The guide to over 100,000 subsidiary companies and who owns them. Volume One lists alphabetically by parent, Volume Two by subsidiary. Published by Dun & Bradstreet.

Macmillan Stock Exchange Yearbook
Names, addresses, directors and summary financial information on the 4,000 companies listed on the London Stock Exchange.

Macmillan Unquoted Companies
Similar information on 20,000 unlisted companies. Very useful.

Kelly's Industrial Directory
Perhaps the best known of a number of business-to-business directories, giving details of companies providing goods and services to other companies.

Directory of Directors
This is a guide to who runs whom. Volume One lists alphabetically some 60,000 individual directors of major companies; Volume Two lists by company. Published by Reed Business Information.

Who's Who in the City
Potted biographies of the pinstripe brigade.

---

it comes to details of a company's employment practices or its environmental record. However, a number of research-oriented groups have been set up to plug just such gaps.

The Ethical Investment Research Service (EIRIS – see appendix B) holds information on computer about companies on the FT All-Share Index, covering issues such as military purchases, tobacco, production of CFCs, etc. One of EIRIS' main functions is to screen investment portfolios, producing an individually tailored list of companies acceptable to the ethical concerns of a particular investor (see below).

The Directory of Social Change (DSC – see appendix B) also publishes information on corporate social responsibility, including a *Guide to UK Company Giving*, which lists the community affairs commitments of over 500 top companies, and *Corporate Citizen*, a journal published three times a year.

Other pressure groups can also prove a very useful source of information on companies, ranging from those that target companies generally, like some of the environmental groups, to those that are concerned with particular industries or groups of companies, like the Campaign Against the Arms Trade. Labour Research (see appendix B) is an independent group supported by the trade unions which produces regular reports investigating companies' activities, including their support of the Conservative Party.

If more conventional methods fail, it is worth noting that companies' reliance on the market always makes them vulnerable to casual inquiries. According to the newspapers, industrial espionage – one company spying on another for commercial advantage – is on the increase, particularly in high-tech industries. There are certainly a growing number of corporate intelligence consultants who carry out low-key intelligence or security work for companies. The central technique used, contrary to popular suspicion, is neither computer hacking nor bugging devices but the pretext telephone call. Posing as a potential customer or supplier can produce interesting results.

Shareholder action

Becoming a shareholder in a market-quoted company is easy and cheap. Shares can be bought through shareholders or through the share-dealing services now operated by high street banks. They vary in price from a few pence to a few pounds, although minimum brokering charges will add £20 to £30 to the bill. You only need one ordinary share to acquire the rights of a shareholder or member of the company. These rights are laid out in the box opposite.

Although shareholders' rights are extensive, to be really effective they have to be exercised collectively. The company is, after all, a highly democratic structure (in theory at least) and the Companies Acts construe it mainly as a self-regulating structure, with directors elected by shareholders and directly answerable to them. Craig MacKenzie makes the point succinctly in the *Shareholder Action Handbook* (New Consumer; 1993): 'When big companies collapse, or experience considerable financial difficulty, the common shareholder reaction is to complain loudly "the regulators" have failed to do their job. Shareholders conveniently forget that, in the eyes of the law, they are the primary regulators of companies.'

Like many democratic mechanisms, however, corporate democracy is much abused and open to hijack by a small group of people. Successful shareholder action is largely about turning individual shareholders and the social interest into the hijackers rather than the hijacked. There are numerous opportunities for a small group of shareholders to have an impact on a company far greater than that represented by the number of shares they own.

One such clutch of opportunities derive from the fact that shareholder dissent is still comparatively rare in this country, so directors are likely to treat it seriously if it does occur. Persistent, informed letter-writing and tough questioning at AGMs fall into this category. Tone is important. Approaches should be polite, as objective as possible, and of an appearance that the target would regard as respectable. Rather like many MPs, directors will pay considerable regard to what they see as the 'legitimate' concerns of their own constituents, but are apt to dismiss outside influence or dissenters they think have been put up to it. Rather than all arriving in similar format on campaign headed paper, letters may be more effective if they appear to come from individual shareholders, on ordinary writing paper, even if some of them then allude to the existence of the campaign.

If a letter from a shareholder merely expresses protest at corporate practices, it would probably get a response, but it will have gone no further than the PR department and the reply will be written in appropriate PR-speak. Detailed requests for specific information on what the company is doing in a particular area are likely to be more useful; at the very least they should result in the same questions being repeated within the company and the feeling spreading that the

---

Shareholders' rights

The holders of ordinary voting shares

▼ have the right to receive the directors' annual report and audited accounts

▼ have the right to attend AGMs and other general meetings of the company

▼ have the right to put resolutions for vote at general meetings*

▼ have the right to vote on the appointment of directors and on any other resolutions put before the meeting

▼ have the right to remove or dismiss directors*

▼ have the right to call annual or extraordinary general meetings if the directors fail to do so*

▼ have the right to sue on behalf of the company individual directors who are in breach of their duties or act *ultra vires*

▼ are protected from being 'unfairly prejudiced' by the actions of directors or other members of the company.

* Requires collective action by shareholders. See main text.

A company's articles of association will often stipulate the manner in which rights should be exercised and may also confer rights additional to those listed above.

---

company's behaviour is being closely watched. They may even elicit some new information, although two or three attempts may be necessary.

The tendency for companies to try and stage their AGMs as a slick public relations exercise means that a little well-organised dissent here can also go a long way in embarrassing management, particularly if the press are present. Persistent questioning from anti-apartheid or environmental campaigners has occupied more than half the time at certain company AGMs in the past, pushing other business to one side, and doing much the same to their press coverage. Companies' fear of having their expensive PR efforts derailed can lead them to agree concessions with pressure groups: in 1990 Shell consented to set aside half an hour at its AGM for a debate on the company's involvement in South Africa. Other techniques used to sway media coverage have included stunts and photo opportunities at AGMs (Greenpeace set off recorded messages about damages to the ozone layer at an ICI AGM) and the production of alternative annual reports detailing the less attractive side of corporate activity, with even a mock board meeting of famous supporters.

Putting down resolutions

Most of the resolutions put before an AGM are concerned with routine matters such as the adoption of the annual report, appointment of auditors and re-election of directors, and a few protest votes are unlikely to raise more than an eyebrow. To be effective, formal dissent generally requires collective action by a more substantial shareholder grouping.

To put a resolution before an AGM, for example, shareholders must not only lodge a copy of the resolution with the company before the meeting but must also ensure that it is circulated to other share-holders; for a public company that means in practice requiring the company itself to circulate the resolution. The Companies Act 1985 stipulates that a company is obliged, on pain of committing an offence, to circulate a resolution together with a supporting statement of up to 1,000 words if it receives a written requisition supported by either shareholders holding at least five per cent of the voting rights, or by at least 100 shareholders who have each paid an average of £100 for their shares. The shareholders have to pay the circulation costs and the requisition must be received at least six weeks before the date of the AGM, or longer if the resolution concerned is one requiring special notice, such as one calling for the dismissal of a director or auditor.

Getting together a shareholder bloc of sufficient size to propose a resolution is thus a formidable task for a small pressure group and can take months of work. Social action resolutions are consequently very rare in the UK. In the US, where the threshold for pushing a shareholder resolution onto the agenda is significantly lower, hun-dreds of dissenting resolutions are proposed every year, and they provide a tantalising glimpse of what might be possible here. Resolu-tions are regularly put forward proposing changes in corporate environmental or industrial relations policy, criticising the compe-tence of directors, seeking the availability of information on aspects of the company's work, or calling for the dismissal of a particular director or the appointment of a new one.

Any of these resolutions could be proposed at AGMs in the UK, their content subject only to the provisions of a company's articles of association. Although the organisational problems are considerable, they are hardly insurmountable. As many of the companies that pressure groups target are very large, it would generally be easier to find, or create, 100 shareholders who have paid in total £10,000 for their shares than to win over institutional investors who can deliver five per cent of the company's voting rights. The £10,000 is, of course, not an expense but an investment. Taking such action might trans-form the image of a group from that of a bunch of outsiders making a nuisance at the AGM into a genuine dissident shareholder grouping with which management might be prepared – or forced – to bargain. The US experience has shown that although social action resolutions are hardly ever won on the vote, the threat of putting one down is often enough to force a concession in corporate policy.

Ordinary resolutions require only a simple majority vote to be passed. Most resolutions at AGMs are passed by a show of hands, on a one member one vote basis. As only a tiny proportion of a company's shareholders generally bother to turn up at an AGM, you might think that decisions are at the mercy of an organised lobby, but management are protected by the fact that a written ballot can always be called instead of a show of hands, or even after one has taken place, and here voting power will depend on the size of shareholding.

Shareholder proxies

Yet the degree of control directors have over an AGM is considerably greater than even this suggests. Their secret weapon is the proxy system, which in effect functions rather like the trade union block vote. Any shareholders not attending an AGM can elect to appoint a proxy in their place on the proxy form distributed with the notice and agenda of the meeting. The proxy can then attend the meeting to vote on their behalf. The standard procedure, however, is for shareholders just to assign their votes to the company chair. The company directors thus manage the proceedings at the AGM, choose who can ask questions, put down most if not all of the resolutions and control the majority of votes!

However, proxies can be used to work against management as well as in its favour, with a shareholder action group soliciting the proxy votes of other shareholders. As with raising shareholder support in order to put down a resolution, this is straightforward in theory but tricky to pull off on any significant scale.

A glance at the members' register of most big companies at Companies House will show that the majority of shares are held not by individuals or even by other companies, but by the big investing institutions like pension funds and insurance firms. The money these institutions invest is of course that represented by the pension or life assurance schemes of millions of individuals up and down the country. The trustees of pension funds are susceptible to pressure for two reasons:

▼ the funds they control are actually held on trust for the benefit of pension scheme members, so they should be receptive to the wishes of those members;

▼ assigning their proxies to support social responsibility actions involves no financial charge on their funds and therefore does not conflict with their trustee obligations (in fact, it could be argued that on occasion it aids their discharge).

The most noteworthy attempts at harnessing shareholder voting power for social ends have concentrated on winning the proxies, or indeed in-person support, of institutions like pension funds, churches and universities.

One organisation which coordinates shareholder action on social issues is called Pensions and Investment Research Consultants

(PIRC – see appendix B). In 1997 it succeeded in bringing a resolution to the Shell AGM, asking for the company's environmental and human rights records to be reviewed and responsibility for them to be assigned to someone at board level. The resolution was co-sponsored by PIRC's client pension funds and the Ecumenical Council for Corporate Responsibility, between them getting the 100 shareholders required.

The background to the resolution was an ongoing dialogue between Shell and human rights and environmental groups, including an analysis of the company's acknowledged failings in its operations in Nigeria. PIRC raised support for the resolution in the City, running a special investment briefing. By the time of the poll (which managed to muster nearly 20% in votes in favour together with abstentions) Shell had bowed to the pressure and accepted the main points in the resolution.

Employee action

Compared to the other kinds of action described in this chapter, which are building in strength and sophistication, employee action is seriously in decline. Most action taken by, or on behalf of, employees is coordinated by trades unions, which suffered numerous set-backs under the Thatcher administration. Union power has never really recovered from the following:

▼ *Decline of manufacturing industry.* The traditional power base of the unions, manufacturing industry has undergone a rapid and probably irreversible decline in the UK.

▼ *Difficulty of organising modern workers.* Post-Fordist patterns in production, such as industrial decentralisation and the evolution of leaner units of production, the growth of the private service sector (with its historically low rate of unionisation), and the proliferation of temporary or part-time jobs, all lead to workplaces which are harder to organise. Solidarity and peer-group pressure are weaker among smaller, isolated groups of workers.

▼ *Anti-union legislation.* A quintet of Employment Acts in the Thatcher years whittled away at the closed shop and union recognition, implemented extensive voting reform including the use of secret ballots, outlawed much secondary action and ended protection from dismissal for striking workers. Potentially the most cutting of the reforms, however, were those that limited the immunity of unions and their members from civil actions for damages that could be taken by employers or other interested parties. This led to moves such as the sequestration of NUM funds during the 1984/5 miners' strike.

Agitate, educate, organise

▼ Dissatisfaction is spread in the workforce by the pinpointing of injustices or elaboration of grievances, and apathy or resignation countered by examples of other workplaces where a better deal has been won.

▼ Workers are educated in how management benefits from current arrangements, how those arrangements are not the only possible alternative and how they can be changed.

▼ Finally, workers join together to build the structures to force change.

Much of this legislation was a reaction to perceived union militancy. Union strength has ultimately tended to rely on one sanction, namely the withdrawal of labour, whether it be removal of goodwill work (the 'work to rule'), the partial withdrawal of labour (e.g. an overtime ban), the obstruction of others' labour (blacking) or a full strike. The central problem faced by unions in employing this sanction, ironically, is that it is not militant enough: it will always be expected to stop short of inflicting permanent damage on a company which provides employment to union members. This community of interest between employees and employer has been consistently exploited by management, particularly in the case of industrial action aimed at saving jobs. It has also made unions in the past poor allies of outside pressure groups agitating on environmental or other non-industrial issues.

At the same time there is, for any social activist, also something enduringly seductive about what can be described as the classic model of union development, encapsulated in the old Fabian slogan: 'Agitate, educate, organise' (see box). It remains an exemplary formula for any pressure group looking to build popular support.

A potential turning point in trade union campaigning came in 1994 with the brilliant campaign run by the Union of Communication Workers (UCW) against the privatisation of the Royal Mail. Instead of persuading its members to stage mass demonstrations or go on strike, the union used altogether more effective tactics:

▼ postal workers targeted the constituencies of government backbenchers to raise public concern over the threat privatisation presented to sub post offices;

▼ the union obtained a legal opinion that government measures to protect sub post offices after privatisation would contravene EC competition law;

▼ a study was commissioned from London Economics, a respected research consultancy, that concluded that it was possible to marry public ownership of the post office with greater commercial freedom.

Successfully publicising the economic case against privatisation marked a clear departure from many trade union campaigns in the past, but perhaps the most interesting aspect of the campaign was the fact that the UCW used its members 'as ambassadors rather than as strikers' (in the words of political columnist Peter Kellner), organising door-to-door leafleting and raising support among local voluntary and community groups in the target constituencies.

Taking campaigns outside the workplace certainly increases the range of tools available to unions considerably. As in the case of the UCW above, this can involve adopting the techniques of the modern pressure group that are described throughout this book. To the extent that such techniques relieve unions' reliance on strike action, they might paradoxically also help them to regain respectability as bargaining partners.

An important corollary of such a development might be wider alliances between unions and pressure groups. Outside industrial relations, unions will always make the strongest advocates or most valuable allies in fields where their members have professional expertise. Its doctor members make the British Medical Association, for example, the most powerful health pressure group in the country.

A trade-off could be imagined where a pressure group would benefit from a union's mass support and bargaining strength within a company, while the union drew on the group's ability to coordinate consumer campaigns. Loose alliances of this nature have already existed on issues, such as foreign investment, where there was a shared interest between the labour movement and human rights campaigners. An unincorporated arms-length pressure group may be of particular use in undertaking radical operations, bearing in mind the difficulty of bringing representative actions against such groups (see chapter 10).

Consumer action

Consumer action is about the market, but it is not just about buying. It is also about not buying and about using the privileged status of consumer to question, complicate and, if necessary, discredit the behaviour of companies. It is about targeting action where it hurts most: sales. Finally, and perhaps most importantly, it is about exploiting the vicious competition that exists in the market for social ends.

The field in which consumer action operates is the entire bottom half of influence map 1. At its most devastating when consisting of marginal measures that affect corporate competitiveness, consumer action is the campaigner's answer to the supply-side revolution that gripped the private sector in the 1980s.

One of the oldest examples of such action, indeed of any organised campaigning, is the consumer boycott. Governments have used it for centuries as the ultimate in trade tariffs. Merchants in New England boycotted British goods over the Stamp Act in the mid-eighteenth century; nearly two hundred years later, Gandhi led India into a boycott of British cloth. In 1993 an era ended when over 30 years of consumer boycotts of South African goods finally came to a halt.

If a boycott or other economic sanction is enforced by a state, it will have considerable power, but can a consumer-led boycott ever be more than a gesture? When the anti-apartheid boycott was at its height between 1985 and 1989, South Africa's share of the UK imported fruit market fell from 11% to 8%, according to research by the Anti-Apartheid Movement. After 1989, market share rose again to 10%. Whatever economic pressure the boycott was able to bring was clearly secondary to its role in mustering and managing support for the anti-apartheid cause among the general public. Possessing a mechanism which enables individual supporters and sympathisers to take concrete action, repeatedly, in their everyday lives is a valuable asset for any campaign.

Predicting beforehand the likely success of a boycott is notoriously tricky. However, the box opposite gives some questions which should help to evaluate whether a boycott would be an appropriate technique. They illustrate the general point that any form of campaigning involving companies, but particularly consumer action, requires a keen appreciation of market factors.

In the late eighties there developed out of the boycott an alternative, and altogether mightier, consumer technique. Friends of the Earth launched a campaign against the use of ozone-depleting chlorofluorocarbons (CFCs), publishing a pamphlet, 'The Aerosol Connection', which listed CFC-free areas. FoE campaigners could hardly have realised the full extent of the idea's potential. Helped by the high political and media profile afforded to the issue, customers started abandoning CFC products in droves. What made it possible was the ready availability of alternative products that customers could turn to which did not involve the production of CFCs.

What happened was a market squeeze. Companies quickly saw that the campaign provided them with an opportunity, something that could give them a competitive advantage, and aggressively marketed CFC-free sprays and other products. The market for conventional aerosols shrank dramatically and producers were forced to move away from CFC-oriented products in order to survive. Here was social action operating not against the market, but through it, by harnessing positive consumer power.

The environmental movement provides other examples of this process, albeit on a less spectacular scale, with the endorsement of biodegradable detergents and lead-free petrol. There is no reason why it should not work with campaigns in other areas, although they may not present as readily the combination of strong product-issue identification and marketable alternatives. Beauty Without Cruelty and other groups have had some success with the promotion of non-animal tested cosmetics.

Although a pressure group can set the ball rolling and activate a market squeeze, it should be clear that the real power in the technique comes not from the group, nor from the reactions of the targeted company, but from the activities of competitor companies which smell blood. The collective muscle of these competitors will normally outweigh that of the target several times over. This reinforces the importance in corporate campaigning of isolating companies, of literally picking them off one at a time, not just so that your attack can be as concentrated as possible but, more importantly, so that you will be effectively joined by other companies looking to exploit the temporary weakness of a competitor.

Market squeezes can happen very quickly indeed. In the 1999 campaign against genetically-modified foods, the right conditions were established with the publication of research highlighting the potential dangers of genetic modification and the creation of emotive labels like 'Frankenstein food'. The big supermarket chains which had yet to introduce GM foods immediately saw their competitive advantage: before long, Britain's supermarkets were in a headlong rush to proclaim themselves GM free.

Once a company begins to attach social or environmental claims to its products, with or without the specific endorsement of a campaigning group, it lays itself open to increased outside pressure. Bogus or exaggerated claims can be referred to the Advertising

---

Will a boycott work?

1. *Does the product have a monopoly, or quasi-monopoly?*
   The closer a product comes to enjoying a monopoly position in the market, the harder it becomes to make any impact at all with a consumer boycott. This is particularly the case with necessities; nobody is going to boycott their local water company.

2. *How competitive is the product?*
   More generally, the competitiveness of the product will indicate the extent to which its sales are at risk of diversion. Those with a big price advantage, for example, will be more resistant to a boycott (although this is less marked with luxury goods than with staples).

3. *Is the issue closely identified with the product?*
   The ideal situation, boycott-wise, is when the product *is* the issue (e.g. fur coats). If there is little obvious connection between them (e.g. instant coffee and bottle-feeding in developing countries) it will be harder to make the action take root. There are similar problems with targeting more than one product (the anti-Nestlé campaign blacklisted over 60).

4. *To what extent is the boycott enforceable?*
   Campaign coordination and peer group pressure may give you the edge in tight-knit communities, like workplaces or college campuses.

5. *How close is the target market for the product to the target audience for the campaign?*
   Among the most successful of the anti-apartheid actions were those aimed at Barclays Bank and spearheaded by students – a key target group for a high street bank.

Standards Authority, trading standards officers in local authorities or, in some cases, to the Office of Fair Trading. Alternatively, a company's claims can be publicly exposed as inaccurate, or merely hypocritical in that although strictly true they are not matched by the rest of the company's behaviour.

In all such cases, accurate research is paramount. Of all the major pressure group targets, companies and business people are by far the most litigious (see chapter 5). Genuine complaints made to regulators or supervisory authorities are privileged under defamation law, but they will cut little ice unless they are able to provide specific instances of abuse, preferably with documentary evidence. The National Consumer Council (see appendix B) has information on some of the main regulatory bodies which have a duty to consider, and act upon, consumer complaints against companies.

Corporate disruption

Traditionally, direct disruption of company activities has been concentrated in the workplace, where the law still provides some protection to workers taking action in furtherance of a lawful trade dispute. In the high street, however, the police have considerable powers to compel demonstrators to disperse or to arrest them for obstruction of the highway (see chapter 9). This is unfortunate, as a little militancy here goes a long way. A company's sensitivity about its public image, mentioned above as particularly apparent at the AGM, is even more pronounced in the retail arena. In fact, point-of-sale is where the public relations veneer is at its most polished, and most brittle.

Sales staff have to give potential customers the benefit of the doubt. This simple fact provides the opportunity for a number of highly disruptive but non-confrontational techniques that are very difficult to control under the law. Pioneered by American civil rights activists in the sixties, when they were dubbed 'shop-ins' or 'mill-ins', these involve groups of protesters entering shops or offices and quietly standing in the till queues, occupying counters as though they were shopping, asking endless questions of the sales staff, or, if present in sufficient numbers, just milling around for hours. The effect on sales is potentially dramatic, especially on, say, the last Saturday before Christmas.

Retail disruption is particularly easy with businesses operating customer services. Take the example of a group protesting at a building society's practice of 'red lining' depressed areas – districts where it refuses to lend. Each of the society's branches has the capacity to interview perhaps 20 prospective mortgagees each week, at an hour an interview. It would only take 20 people, working a morning each, to tie up every branch in the town for an entire week. What could be more civilised? – a protest by appointment, simple to

Influence Map 2: Secondary targets

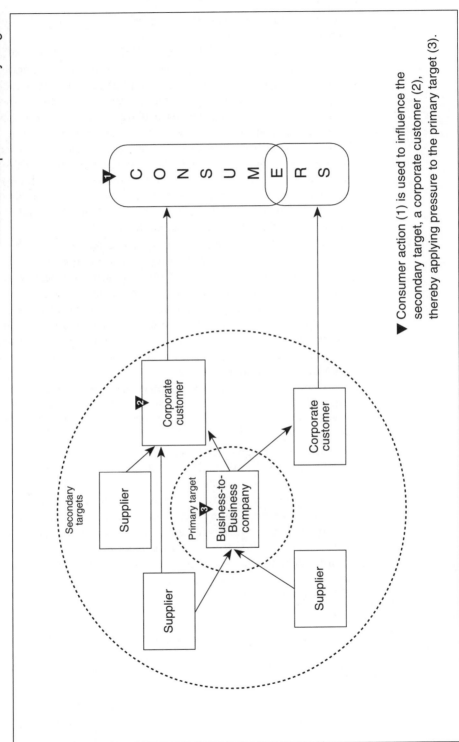

▶ Consumer action (1) is used to influence the secondary target, a corporate customer (2), thereby applying pressure to the primary target (3).

execute, with a clear message: if you're not prepared to lend every-where, then you'll lend nowhere.

Everyday technology enables non-confrontational disruption to be extended effortlessly into the very nerve centres of corporate life. Usually known as electronic picketing (one of the earliest practitioners was the Canadian Communication Workers union), the practice of tying up telephone, telex and particularly fax lines can bring head office to its knees in just a few hours. Many numbers will not be publicly listed; an internal directory or some pretext telephone calls will give the numbers used by senior management, the chair's office, etc. The aim is blanket coverage of key communications lines for a short period when management is most busy or vulnerable. The development of e-mail bombing and hacktivism has extended this technique to the internet (see chapter 6).

One of the advantages of electronic picketing is that it can be used with almost any company, although it will be more efficacious if combined with other measures. Consumer actions generally have a bias towards companies operating in the consumer field, as opposed to those in the capital sector which are supplying raw materials, products or services to other companies rather than direct to the public. In this latter case, it may be appropriate to consider action against secondary targets: suppliers or, more probably, corporate customers (see influence map 2).

Companies resent fighting another company's battles. Few will allow their businesses to be damaged by what they see as the PR problems of their partners. That resentment will rebound onto the primary target.

Many campaigns seek to harness consumer power by targeting retailers as well as manufacturers. But the success of secondary action will depend, as always, on the economic relationships involved. A secondary target will stand by its business partner for as long as it remains in its financial interests to do so, and no longer. Through secondary action you may not immediately be able to cut the volume of sales of your primary target, but the action could push up their costs or force them to offer discounts, and that may be all the pressure you need.

12   Local authorities

At local level, the building blocks of power are small. Wards, departments, committees and boards are all made up of identifiable individuals, each with their own idiosyncrasies and their own interests to which the lobbyist can appeal.

All lobbying involves understanding and using two basic elements: the people and the system. Of the two, local authority lobbying is relatively people-centred. Senior officers and chairpeople wield an effective discretion that most national civil servants and even ministers – cogs in a complex machine – could only dream of. Local bosses are close to power.

That power is, however, strictly limited. An appreciation of how the limits apply will not only save time, but can be turned to advantage.

Which council?

The first step in lobbying on a local issue is to identify which of the authorities commonly referred to as 'the council' is actually responsible for it. In many areas of the UK there are two or even three levels or tiers of local government, each with its distinct functions and responsibilities. The table overleaf shows how the major responsibilities are carved up.

There are two basic patterns. If you live in Scotland, Wales, London or one of the English metropolitan areas, most of the functions of local government are undertaken by a unitary authority (in metropolitan areas, usually known as a borough council), with only a few services, such as fire and police, coordinated over a wider area by joint boards or authorities. The metropolitan areas are Tyne and Wear, Greater Manchester, Merseyside, South Yorkshire, West Yorkshire, and the West Midlands. Following local government reorganisation in the late 1990s, unitary authorities were also created in some other parts of England.

In the rest of England, there are two major tiers of local government which split responsibilities between them: the larger county

Local authority responsibilities	County councils	District councils	Unitary authorities, including London and metropolitan boroughs	Joint bodies
Strategic planning	●		●	
Local planning		●	●	
Housing		●	●	
Roads	●		●	
Traffic	●		●	
Social services	●		●	
Voluntary sector liaison/grants	●	●	●	●
Education	●		●	
Libraries	●		●	
Leisure and amenities		●	●	
Tourism and entertainments		●	●	
Environmental health		●	●	
Refuse collection		●	●	
Refuse disposal	●			●
Consumer protection	●		●	
Electoral registration		●	●	
Fire	●			●

Northern Ireland
Many of the functions undertaken by local government in the rest of the UK are coordinated in Northern Ireland by the Northern Ireland Assembly and associated quangos, with the 26 district councils in Northern Ireland assuming a lesser role, dealing mainly with environmental health, leisure, and refuse collection and disposal.

councils and the smaller district councils. The situation in Northern Ireland is rather different: see note to the table.

A number of standard activities, not shown on the table, are undertaken by most authorities. These include public relations, tourism, the promotion of equal opportunities and a host of diverse regulatory and licensing functions. Most kinds of authority also hold some responsibility for promoting economic development. Relationships with voluntary or non-profit groups, including the award of grants, are similarly common with every kind of authority. Which local authority is most relevant to the work of a particular group will depend on the type of service and the geographical area covered.

There are exceptions to the conventional patterns of local government responsibilities around the country. Among the most widespread of these are those created by agency or contracted relationships. District councils, for example, may undertake some of the functions of the county council on an agency basis. Private companies or non-profit groups may run services under contract to a council, including many that were previously undertaken by the council's own direct service organisation or other department. In all these examples, the organisation actually running the service will be different from the authority which holds the principal responsibility for providing the service and to which the main avenue of recourse still lies.

In some parts of England and Wales, typically in country towns or villages, there is further tier of authority at the very local level: the parish council. Known as community councils in Wales (and in some towns, rather confusingly, as town councils), parish councils have limited powers, mainly in the environment and recreation area. They may be responsible for village halls, greens and playing fields, allotments, cemeteries and car parks, street signs and lighting, and so on. They must also be consulted on local planning applications. Larger parishes have an elected council; the smaller ones can be run by a twice-yearly meeting of all registered electors in the parish.

How the council works

Local authorities are run by a group of locally-elected representatives known as councillors or members of the authority. Elections for county councils, London boroughs and the Welsh and Scottish unitary authorities are held once every four years. For district councils, either one third of the council is elected in each of the intervening three years (the 'thirds rule') or the whole council comes up for election once every four years (the 'all-in, all-out' system), generally a year or two after any county council elections. Councillors are not salaried, but are paid attendance and other allowances; most of them have other jobs, separate from their council duties. The great majority of councillors are members of a political party and operate on the council in party groupings.

Salaried staff known as officers are employed by the council in order to advise it and enable it to implement its policies. In practice, most of the work of running the local authority is delegated to officers. Senior officers have management responsibilities for many hundreds of staff and will often have pursued a career in local government. But however powerful they may be and however important their titles may sound – chief executive, director of social services, etc. – it is important to remember that they are the agents of the council and it is the council that is ultimately responsible for making decisions. The role of officers is non-political, and it is not unknown for them to mutter under their breath about how political fighting on the council is preventing them from doing their job properly.

The distinction between the role of councillors and officers is reflected in the structure of the local authority (see influence map 3). The administration of the authority's work is split into a number of departments, broadly corresponding to the different functions listed in the table at the start of this chapter. Main departments are headed by a chief officer, often known as a director. However, overall policy for the work of a service department and major individual issues will be tackled by the corresponding committee of councillors, meeting periodically. (Note that the chief officer is not a member of that committee, although she will attend its meetings and liaise closely with the chair.) Thus the housing committee and its subcommittees will develop the council's detailed policy on, for example, residential lettings, partly based on the recommendations made by the director of housing and his staff. Once the policy has been approved by full council, the officers in the housing department, led by the director of housing, will put it into practice: talking to the public, administering the letting of flats and houses, handling the day-to-day management of the housing stock, liaising with tenants' groups, etc.

In addition to the service departments there are a number of central departments that deal with matters such as finance and accounts, personnel, and legal services to the authority. The head of the paid staff in a local authority usually now carries the title of chief executive (formerly, town or county clerk) and the chief executive's department has a key administrative role in coordinating the policy work of the council as well as providing clerks to the council's committees. Units like women's units, racial equality units and grants units, if they exist in a particular local authority, are also usually found in the chief executive's department.

In many authorities, the chief executive also holds the post of monitoring officer. A post introduced under the Local Government and Housing Act 1989, the monitoring officer is a kind of internal whistle-blower, ensuring that decisions or actions taken by the authority do not break the law or constitute improper practice or

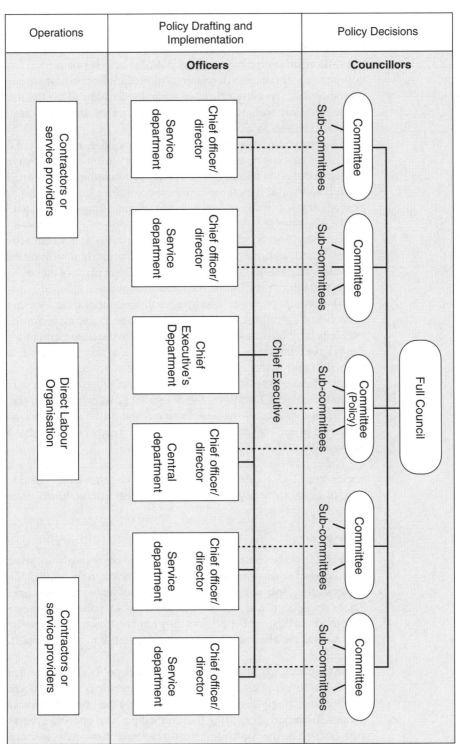

Influence Map 3: Structure of a local authority

Operations	Policy Drafting and Implementation	Policy Decisions
	Officers	**Councillors**

Contractors or service providers

Chief officer/ director — Service department

Sub-committees — Committee

Chief officer/ director — Service department

Sub-committees — Committee

Direct Labour Organisation

Chief Executive's Department

Chief Executive

Sub-committees — Committee (Policy)

Full Council

Chief officer/ director — Central department

Sub-committees

Chief officer/ director — Service department

Sub-committees — Committee

Contractors or service providers

Chief officer/ director — Service department

Sub-committees — Committee

maladministration. The role of monitoring officer may be held by a chief officer other than the chief executive, but it cannot be held by the treasurer or director of finance. Another introduction of the Act is the imposition of restrictions on the political activity of senior local government officers. Senior officers, political advisers to party groups on the council, and any officer earning above point 44 on the local authority salary scale who speaks on behalf of the authority cannot stand for election as a councillor.

Council committee meetings are held in cycles, with each main committee meeting once in a cycle. Cycles vary in length from council to council but often take about six weeks, culminating in a meeting of the full council at which the different committee decisions are approved (or not, as the case may be). All these meetings are open to the public. The timetable is worked out for a year ahead, with a break in the summer. One committee, usually known as the policy committee or policy and resources committee, has a particularly important role in deliberating the main policies and expenditure plans of the council and is usually chaired by the leader of the council.

The amount of power held by a committee varies from council to council and committee to committee. On some matters a committee may only be able to make recommendations to the council; on others, it may have what are called 'delegated powers' to take decisions in the council's name. Most committees also have subcommittees to consider particular aspects of their work, some of whom will also have delegated powers. Details on the delegated powers held by specific committees, and rules on how business should be conducted, are contained in each council's standing orders, a copy of which should be available to the public.

Note, however, that no body, not even the full council, ever begins from a clean slate with regards to policy-making. The decisions of a local authority always have to fall within its statutory duties and powers (see below).

Political control

Most councils are controlled by one political party or group, which has managed to win an absolute majority of seats on the council. The leader of the controlling group then becomes leader of the council. Places on council committees are allocated to political groups in proportion to the number of seats they hold on the council. Committees will nearly always be chaired by a member of the controlling group.

In familiar party fashion, members of each political group will get together before council and committee meetings, in private, to decide policy and strategy. Larger groups elect one of their number to act as whip, with the job of ensuring that councillors turn up to meetings to vote. So long as the controlling group has a clear majority, it should therefore always be able to push through its main policies. Party control extends deep into an authority through its dominance of committees and by virtue of the close working relationship between committee chairs and chief officers.

Political power in the authority is centred on the leader's office. (In big authorities this may be supplemented by a whip's office; the major parties also have paid political assistants.) As well as heading their party group, the leader of the council is the council's principal spokesperson and usually takes a hands-on role in the strategic management of the authority. In contrast to the leader of the council, the office of mayor (in county councils, the council chair) is mainly formal or ceremonial.

If no political party controls a majority of council seats, the result is what is known as a hung council. Some parties will have more seats than others, but if any one party seeks to assert control it can always be out-voted by the combined forces of the opposition. In some cases, parties may be able to form pacts or coalitions which deliver them the required majority and give some political stability to the council. In others, the situation will be more fluid, with the chairing of committees rotated between parties from one meeting the next. In such situations officers will strive to secure agreed working practices from the parties, so the authority's work can progress.

Hung councils often have more than their fair share of political drama. Voting arithmetic becomes all-important, the whipping gets intense, and if power is evenly balanced on a vote at full council, the mayor may even be required to abandon her lofty position of impartiality and deliver the casting vote. Hung councils are more common in areas of the country where there is a strong third party, or significant numbers of independent councillors who have not been elected on a party ticket.

For lobbyists, the election of a hung council has important consequences. Attention will no longer be concentrated on just the controlling group, but will have to be paid to each of the main parties. Fewer committee decisions will be passed on the nod at full council, with consequently more effort needed to lobby and brief councillors for the debate at full council meetings. In theory, a hung council increases the potential for influence from outside groups, just as it boosts the influence of the smaller parties, but realising that potential requires a lot of hard work.

Sources of information on local authorities

Local authorities present less of an access problem than the other major targets considered in this book. Most of an authority's business (as opposed to that of the parties) is transacted in public, and agenda, working papers and minutes should all be available in advance, if not always as early as one might wish.

The bible of information on local authorities is the *Municipal Yearbook*, published every year in two volumes. The first volume covers local government by function, outlining the work and structure of authorities in education, housing, social services and so on, with the responsibilities of officers. The second volume lists all the local authorities in the UK, with the names of senior officers, the names and addresses of all councillors and composition of council committees. Good libraries should stock a copy of the *Yearbook*, but it is available at £173 (plus postage) from Newman Books (see appendix C).

The best source of information on the work of any particular local authority is the authority's own offices, usually known as the town hall or county hall. If you are unsure who might hold the information you want, telephone the chief executive's department first. The main local library will also have copies of the summons for meetings of the full council, which contains the agenda for the meeting and the minutes of all committee meetings held in the current cycle. It will also usually hold copies of local bye-laws.

Public rights to information on council business were extended significantly under the Local Government (Access to Information) Act 1985 and some of the main ones are summarised in the box below.

Public access to local authority information

Under the Local Government (Access to Information) Act 1985 a member of the public has the right to:

▼ attend meetings of the council, its committees and subcommittees (except during discussion of exempt business: see below)

▼ be given at least three days' notice of such meetings

▼ inspect the agendas, minutes and reports for meetings (and for any past meetings going back six years)

▼ inspect background (internal) papers used to compile reports for meetings and the list of all such papers (and those related to meetings going back four years)

▼ be informed of the reason for their exclusion from any council meeting while an item of exempt business is being discussed, and be able to see a written summary of the discussion in the minutes

▼ know specific powers of the council that have been delegated to officers, and the titles of the officer(s) who can exercise them.

Exempt information under the Act includes information relating to particular council employees or tenants, particular recipients of council services or aid, or the care of a particular child; commercially sensitive information on council contracts or that relating to the business affairs of a particular person; labour relations matters; and legal communications relating to the council and matters concerning the prevention or prosecution of crime.

Most documents, including agendas, minutes and reports, should be supplied to you free, but councils are able to charge a 'reasonable fee' to cover the supply of copies of background or internal papers, and in a few cases have charged excessive amounts. If an officer refuses to send you information which you are entitled to see, make a complaint. Councillors hold additional rights of access to council papers and could be approached if you are having trouble getting hold of something.

Influencing councillors and officers

Notwithstanding what was said above about political control on policy-making, much of the work of a local authority concerns practical problems and in coming to decisions political factors often do *not* predominate. Councillors' proximity to local people, and their responsibility for providing services to them, mean that good administration rather than good politics is the usual goal (in contrast, perhaps, to our representatives in the House of Commons).

In addition to the councillors present at committee meetings there will be a number of officers to brief and advise them. There may also be co-opted onto a committee outside experts or practitioners, or representatives of service users such as council tenants. Co-opted members can participate in discussions, but not vote. Furthermore, councils may have a range of working parties or advisory committees which exist to make recommendations on specific issues to one of the main council committees. Membership of working parties includes councillors but is usually drawn from the wider community, and their meetings may well not be open to the public. All in all, the involvement of such a wide range of people means that council decisions can be well-informed – as well as ensuring that party politics is frequently eclipsed by neighbourhood or organisational politics.

Officers

The first contact made with a local authority on any given issue will nearly always be with an officer. If you do not know which officer is dealing with the issue, write to the head of the department or, failing that, to the chief executive, asking for your enquiry to be referred to the appropriate department and for you to be informed who will deal with it. Try and establish as early as possible when any decisions will be made on the issue, who will make them (that is, which committee or officer) and how they will be made. Is the authority consulting with interested parties or the wider public? Will there be a chance to appeal against decisions?

Depending on the issue involved, a letter to the appropriate officer outlining your concerns and bringing his attention to relevant facts will often be taken into account in recommendations he makes to councillors. On small matters like specific complaints over services it may even resolve the issue to your satisfaction. On a policy matter, any input you make will be much more effective if it considers existing draft proposals or policy papers, so study the papers from previous meetings when the issue was discussed and ask whether anything has been produced since that you could usefully comment on. The officer will be preoccupied with the administrative aspect of the issue: What does your approach involve? Will there be any repercussions? What resources are required? Is it within the authority's legal powers to do it? Will it work?

The ideal scenario in local authority lobbying is to brief officers regularly so that they back your case and the relevant committee just approves their recommendations. If it is an ongoing matter of local authority responsibility you may over time be co-opted onto an advisory committee where your input can be formalised. On issues of any magnitude, however, convincing officers will rarely be enough, as it is the committee(s) and the council which have to make the decision and they may reject what is recommended to them.

Councillors

Many officers' recommendations *are* accepted in committee with little discussion, but it is dangerous to predict which ones will and will not be accepted, especially if you are not familiar with the personalities and dynamics of the particular committee. In practice, then, you would usually be well-advised to follow the issue on its journey through the committee mill, until it is finally approved at full council, briefing and securing the backing of relevant councillors on the way. Do not wait until the full council meeting to start trying to influence the result: with most councils, particularly those with a strong controlling group, the committees are where the bulk of decisions are generated.

The formal decision-making process is illustrated in influence map 4, taking the example of a grant award to a voluntary group. (Further information on local authority grants is given in chapter 3.)

Councillors are at once representatives of a particular ward or county division, committee members who deliberate specific administrative decisions, and politicians, in that they represent a political party. All of these roles present points of access to an outsider, but the first is privileged. As a committee member or politician, a councillor may say that she has to balance the interests of different sections of the community, but it is always her unequivocal duty to represent the interests of people in her ward. It is usually fine to contact councillors at their home address, or you can write to them care of the local authority.

When briefing councillors, a basically apolitical approach is still preferable, if it is possible. Ensure that what you say is based on facts,

Influence Map 4: Lobbying for a grant

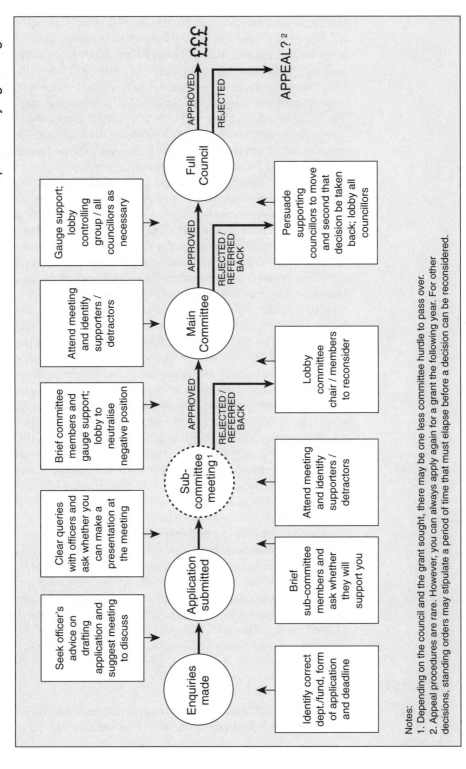

Notes:
1. Depending on the council and the grant sought, there may be one less committee hurdle to pass over.
2. Appeal procedures are rare. However, you can always apply again for a grant the following year. For other decisions, standing orders may stipulate a period of time that must elapse before a decision can be reconsidered.

and argue your case on its merits. Be aware that most councillors will not know the background to the issue or have papers to hand in the same way as officers, and will need filling in. More generally, relationships built up with councillors over time will prove the most valuable, so try and involve them in your work: invite them to address a meeting of your supporters, for example. As politicians, councillors like being loved, and few will resist the temptation to say positive things about you that they know will please the audience – and that you can hold them to in the future. Early evenings are best, as most councillors will be at their own jobs during the day.

Particular attention should be paid to the chair(s) and vice-chair(s) of relevant committees and, on major issues, to the leader of the council. Meetings can be sought with either. These people are very busy, however, and it is important to make your approach at a level that is appropriate to the size of the issue. A committee chair in a big authority, for example, is unlikely to be stirred by a grant application from one voluntary organisation. The right level of the councillor hierarchy to approach is a matter of judgement, as it will vary with the type of authority and the particular committee in question, but looking at a recent committee agenda will give you a feel for its work. The chair will be preoccupied with the broad outcome of the major items on the agenda; on other matters, you may be better off initially talking to one or two committee members from the controlling group.

Committees and meetings of the full council can also be formally lobbied through petitions and deputations. Rules governing the presentation of petitions and the admittance of deputations to address committee meetings are usually included in a council's standing orders. These vary from council to council and should be consulted before you organise anything. Petitions will normally be presented at a meeting by a councillor. On the whole their effect is limited, unless they succeed in demonstrating consensus among the particular local people affected by a decision or issue.

Pressure of time means that councils rarely agree to receive deputations from outside groups at meetings, but if you do get the chance it can be a good opportunity to make your case in person and deal with questions or objections. Write to the chief executive asking whether the council will consider receiving a deputation, outlining the issue and the number of local people affected. A deputation is only as effective as the people involved, so choose spokespeople who can present your case clearly and briefly and who include those personally affected.

Political pressure

If the softly-softly, officer-friendly approach does not work, or if your case is being blocked politically, it will be necessary to try stronger tactics. The temptation at this juncture is often to cry foul and publicly denounce the controlling party, but this is only one possible approach (emotionally satisfying though it may be) and another may be more likely to yield results. Most decisions have a political, an administrative and a legal aspect, and which to apply pressure to may depend on where the blockage lies or on how a particular decision was reached. The main alternatives are set out in the box below, although there is clearly overlap between them.

The larger political parties on a council will often have different factions within them. If the controlling group is ostensibly opposed to your point of view, this may not reflect the opinion of everyone in the party and it can be worth exploring whether a dissident faction is prepared to take up your case. They are unlikely to go as far as to vote against the party line, but they may well put pressure on the leadership to think again or compromise. This approach stands a much better chance if your campaign is not on an issue strongly split on party lines.

With councils where there is only a small majority, an alternative is to target councillors from the controlling group who represent marginal wards. The ward is not only the principal responsibility of the councillor, it is also his Achilles' heel: few councillors will be prepared openly to defend a policy if they know that doing so may result in them losing their seat at the next election. Through the local press, supportive councillors and letters from residents, put pressure on councillors from marginal wards to declare their stance.

Applying appropriate pressure

POLITICAL	ADMINISTRATIVE	LEGAL
Who decides?	**How is/was it done?**	**On what authority is/was it done?**
How can they be influenced?	Is the procedure improper or unfair?	Is the action *ultra vires*, negligent, or does it break any contractual obligation?
Depending on the nature and scope of the issue, lobby: • the relevant ward councillor(s) • members of the relevant committee • members of the controlling group, or the full council	Complaint to: a) officer concerned b) chief executive and/or councillors Refer matter to: • District Auditor • Ombudsman	Exercise statutory rights of appeal Litigation

If you decide to engage in this sort of political pressure, however, great care must be taken during election periods. Under section 75 of the Representation of the People Act 1983:

'No expenses shall, with a view to promoting or procuring the election of a candidate at an election, be incurred by any person other than the candidate, his election agent and persons authorised in writing by the election agent on account:

(a) of holding public meetings or organising any public display; or

(b) of issuing advertisements, circulars or publications; or

(c) of otherwise presenting to the electors the candidate or his views or the extent or nature of his backing or disparaging another candidate.'

Failure to comply is a criminal offence. The section covers negative campaigning against a particular candidate as well as positive campaigning in favour of one. The major exception is that the section does not restrict anything published in a newspaper or other periodical, which would include a regular newsletter published by a voluntary group (but would *not* include a one-off 'election special'). The restrictions apply to elections for MPs and MEPs as well as local council elections. Remember that the restrictions only apply during the few weeks of the actual election period.

Administrative and legal pressure

If one political group has a genuinely strong grip on a council, however, and is opposed to your campaign, lobbying will never be very productive. In this situation, the only practical alternative is to put administrative or legal pressure on the authority. To do this effectively, it helps to know a little about how local authorities work and the legal basis for their actions. Just disagreeing with a decision or action on political grounds will not be enough.

Local authorities must always act within the powers conferred on them by law. They are also obliged to perform a wide variety of duties, written in statute, that range from the very general (such as the duty on education authorities to provide schools for children) to the more specific (such as the duty periodically to review rents for council housing). If an authority breaches its duties or otherwise acts outside of its statutory powers – that is, if it acts *ultra vires* – it can be challenged in the courts. A local authority must also abide by the general law and honour legal contracts just like anybody else. Litigation against local authorities can take the form of an application for judicial review or a private civil action, both of which are described in detail in chapter 8.

But local authorities are also required to abide by their own rules. If, for example, in coming to a decision an authority breaches its standing rules, this may in itself be sufficient grounds for challenge. Members of the public are also entitled to expect that a local authority should act reasonably promptly, that they should be treated fairly by the authority and that they should receive a reply to their letters. If the authority fails in this regard, and a direct complaint does not solve the problem, they can ask their councillor to refer the matter to the relevant Commissioner for Local Administration, generally known as the local 'ombudsman' (see chapter 8). Matters investigated by the local commissioners cover most local authority activities, with the two largest categories being housing and planning decisions, such as failure to carry out repairs to council housing or unfair treatment of an application for planning permission.

Inefficient or illegal expenditure by a local authority can be reported to the district auditor. As just about every council activity involves some expenditure, the scope of this form of redress is wider than it might at first seem. It can be a useful method of bringing pressure to bear on issues which do not affect you directly (other than, perhaps, as a local taxpayer) but about which you feel strongly. The use of audit is discussed in more detail later.

Finally, many of the duties which local authorities hold require them to consult the opinions of local people in coming to specific decisions. Town planning provides a good example of this. Representations from local people can be made to a district or unitary council when it draws up its local plan covering development and land use in the district or a particular area. Before it is adopted, the council must make it available for public inspection and advertise the fact. If there are public objections to the plan, a public inquiry must be held, conducted by someone appointed by the Secretary of State, giving objectors the chance to make their case. Individual applications for planning permission and the resulting decisions also have to be publicised, and there is an avenue of appeal to the Secretary of State, which in cases of public objection leads to a public inquiry.

Many appeal procedures exist in relation to other local authority functions, from the licensing of old people's homes to the compulsory purchase of land for road developments. It is important to discover from the local authority whether there is an avenue of appeal, or the opportunity to make representations, on the issue on which you are working, and to exercise the right before or during other campaign action. Authorities have argued, often justifiably, that relative silence from the public at formal consultation or appeal procedures implied consent.

Finance and audit

The financing of local government, always a controversial subject, underwent a series of fundamental changes in the 1980s and 1990s, from rate-capping, through the poll tax and the council tax, to the sale of council housing and introduction of higher charges for many services. From the campaigner's point of view, the biggest change was the relative shift in control over local financing and expenditure from the councils themselves to central government.

Councils now have remarkably little discretion over their overall spending limits and what discretion there remains lies mainly in a downward direction – facilitating cuts, but not increases. Where the councils still have great power is in setting priorities within financial limits.

Capital expenditure on buildings, plant and infrastructure projects like new roads is financed largely from borrowing, either from a government source such as the Public Works Loans Board or from the issue of bonds, up to a credit approval limit set by central government. Some spending relating to specific programmes benefits from central government or EU subsidy.

A local authority has four main sources of income, aside from receipts from the sale of capital assets. These are central government grants, the business rate, the council tax on individual local authority residents and the fees charged to users of services. Local authorities have no direct control over the first two. The main government grant, the revenue support grant, is based on a standard spending assessment (SSA), which is the government's calculation of the level of expenditure needed by the authority to provide a nationally standard level of service. Business rates are set and pooled centrally, and then distributed to authorities. In fact local authorities now only receive about 20% of their income from local taxation.

Councils are in principle able to set their own levels of council tax but they must keep below an upper limit set by central government, or they will be 'capped'. Where there are two tiers of government in England and Wales, council tax is collected on behalf of both by district councils, which then hand part of it over in a levy to the county council. As the amount levied will vary from county to county, this is in practice a further constraint faced by districts in setting council tax levels.

Detailed financial information on a local authority is available to the public. This includes the estimates, which set out expenditure plans for the coming year, and the annual accounts. Estimates are drawn up in draft form in the autumn to be placed before each committee of the council. For the annual accounts, the deadline for publication is the end of the calendar year.

Questions and objections to the auditor

The job of the auditor is to give an independent assessment of whether the accounts present a fair picture of the authority's finances, and of the general financial standing of the authority, the adequacy of financial and management control, as well as the performance and value for money of particular services. To carry out this task the auditor has access to the complete financial records of the authority and can require officers to produce further explanation. In England and Wales auditors are appointed by the Audit Commission, either from its own district audit service or from private firms of accountants.

The auditor appoints a date when local authority electors can ask questions about the accounts and make any formal objections to them. (The date is advertised but not very widely; find out from the authority's finance or treasurer's department when it is likely to be.) For 15 working days before that date there is a public right to inspect the accounts to be audited and 'all books, deeds, contracts, bills, vouchers and receipts relating to them'. Notice of an objection should be made in writing first.

Close scrutiny of the accounts and working papers may yield interesting information to flesh out the bones of an objection. As well as detailed figures on specific items of expenditure, you can compare actual spending to budget, and inspect the terms under which financial transactions were made. Anything bearing on the objection should be brought to the attention of the auditor together with other evidence you may have. Given the constraints on time and the difficulty of knowing exactly what to look for and where, it is highly unlikely that you would be able to make a conclusive case, but that does not necessarily matter. The auditor can dismiss objections as invalid (for example if they are merely frivolous or vexatious) but if there is something in them, the auditor will use her inquisitorial powers to investigate further.

Reporting the results of audit takes three main forms:

▼ The **audit opinion** gives the auditor's view on the accuracy and fairness of local authority financial statements.

▼ A **management letter** is prepared for the members of the authority, summarising significant matters that have arisen from the audit. Under section 11 of the Audit Commission Act 1998 the letter may contain written recommendations that the authority must consider at a meeting of the full council and to which it must respond publicly.

▼ Should the auditor uncover serious problems at the authority, he may decide to issue a **public interest report** under section 8 of the Audit Commission Act. At every audit, the auditor is under a duty to consider whether this is necessary. During the 1998/99 audit year 21 such reports were issued, compared to 19 the year before.

Notably, the auditor has the power to recommend in serious cases that individual councillors or officers be surcharged, that is, made personally liable for money lost to the authority as a result of their recklessness or wilful misconduct.

A large part of the auditor's job is to match finance with performance and about 30% of the audit effort is focused on assessing value for money. Whereas her expertise and powers of access to information make her the expert on the financial side, members of the public or interest groups who actually live with local authority services may have a more realistic idea of performance: Is a service efficient? What does it actually achieve? Does it justify the amount of money spent on it? Even with the introduction of specific performance indicators, an auditor's view of performance is necessarily a limited one and it will be dominated by whether or not the books appear sound. Auditors will not take an opinion on the political policies of a council, but they do rely heavily on the public to bring issues of concern to their attention, whether they relate to efficiency, performance or probity.

And auditors' reports can certainly have bite. Following a four-year inquiry into the 'designated sales' policy of Westminster City Council in the late eighties, the district auditor concluded in 1994 that boarding up homes which fell vacant in marginal wards so that they could be sold to owner-occupiers – more likely to vote Tory – rather than be relet to council tenants, was a 'disgraceful and improper' action, as well as 'unlawful'. His report recommended that six councillors and officers should be surcharged a total of £21 million to pay for the losses to the authority. This included £13 million from selling the properties at a discount to market value, as well as the costs of providing bed-and-breakfast accommodation to homeless families while boarded up properties lay empty. The courts cleared the councillors and officers involved of wilful misconduct in 1999, but the district auditor appealed the decision to the House of Lords. The district auditor's inquiry was originally prompted by an objection from a local GP. Doing his rounds of patients in Bayswater, Dr Richard Stone had noticed steel shutters placed over properties and suspected that the council's policies were creating more homeless people than they were housing.

Local MPs

Members of Parliament have no formal influence on the local authority in which their constituency is situated, but they can make effective advocates on local issues. Their involvement is particularly useful for mobilising press coverage.

Channelling a complaint through an MP may possibly cause it to be handled with greater care and attention by officers. MPs can always bring attention in Parliament to a constituent's problems, for example by putting questions to ministers with relevant responsibility for the matter. This certainly will make officers sit up and take notice, particularly as departmental civil servants advising the minister will want to know the facts of the case. Information on parliamentary techniques and contacting MPs is given in chapter 14.

Spare a thought also for prospective parliamentary candidates, who are often looking for local issues to champion. Both their time and their enthusiasm may be greater than that of the sitting MP. Beware, however, of allowing your issue to be turned into a party political football: whereas the principal role of the MP is to represent constituents, prospective parliamentary candidates are seen to represent only their party.

Contractors and service providing agencies

A growing range of council services are now provided not by the council's own employees or its direct labour organisation, but by outside agencies working under contract to the council. These may include both commercial companies and charities or non-profit groups.

Some services, like refuse collection, catering, and maintenance of parks and grounds, must be put out to competitive tender by the local authority. The contract is awarded to the company that can deliver the specified level of service at the lowest price. But other areas of local authority work are being contracted out by choice, including some advice services and social services. The concept of 'best value' has now been introduced to replace compulsory competitive tendering. Under a duty to obtain 'best value', councils will produce annual performance plans, setting out their achievements, their plans and targets for the future, and their priorities in selecting services for review.

The use of agencies has considerable repercussions for those looking to influence services. The provider agency or contractor, controlling the front-line of service delivery, is clearly in a position of some power. While the local authority will specify exactly what is required from the service, in negotiation with the contractor, many operational decisions as to how the service is actually run will be at the contractor's discretion.

Influence map 5 plots some of the main features and countervailing pressures in this new triangular relationship between authorities, contractors and the consumers or users of services. It is based (very loosely) on a model prepared by the Audit Commission and suggests a level of sophistication in monitoring and feedback procedures that is probably beyond that currently exhibited by most contracted-out services.

Charities providing services under contract to local authorities may find restrictions, real or imagined, placed on their freedom to campaign on local authority issues. (In some cases these are very real, taking the form of conditions included in the contract.) In many ways the situation is similar to that of any campaigning group with a major paymaster. It must, however, be weighed against the fact that the charity, now working in partnership with the authority, is in a much better position to influence the development of the authority's services, both those carried out by the charity itself and those provided by others.

Influence Map 5: Influencing contracted-out services

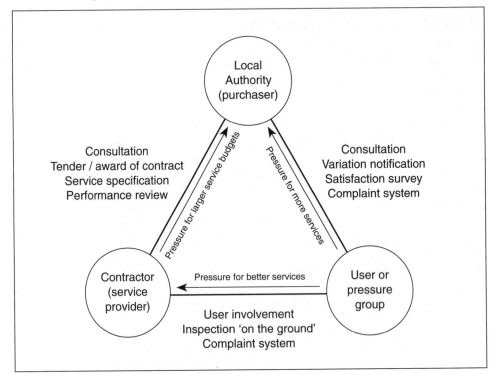

13 Government and Whitehall

Les princes commandent aux peuples, et l'intérêt commande aux princes –
Duke of Rohan

This chapter is about the executive: that part of government which initiates and implements policy. The dominance of the executive in the modern system of government is such that it has become synonymous with government itself, and if power can be said to be centred anywhere in our complex and interconnected society, then it is on the Prime Minister, ministers and the 'permanent government' of civil servants that support them.

Why, then, do pressure groups spend so much time lobbying MPs in Parliament? There are a number of reasons: democratic instincts and the parliamentary tradition in which we are schooled both point to the House of Commons as the natural seat of government; it is the job of our elected representatives to take account of our views and they expect to be lobbied; and Parliament, where ministers are grilled and the political parties draw verbal swords, is the most visible facet of government, whereas the work of Cabinet committees and government departments is cloaked in obsessive secrecy. Finally, and perhaps most importantly, Parliament is where the formal stages of the legislative process take place.

Yet the role of Parliament is ultimately confined to monitoring, approving or questioning the actions of the executive. This – vital – role is covered in the next chapter. For the moment it should suffice to note that the amount of successful legislation initiated by individual MPs is tiny, and that, providing the governing party has a reasonable majority, no bill will be enacted which cannot command the support of government. In addition, many decisions that will be of concern to pressure groups and that affect thousands of people may never even be discussed in Parliament. For professional campaigners, the executive is *the* target.

The central core of government

The components of executive government can be grouped into three main parts, although policy is the product not so much of the institutions themselves as of the relations between them:

▼ the Prime Minister and the Prime Minister's Office;

▼ Cabinet;

▼ Whitehall, or the network of departments and agencies run by civil servants, with ministers at their head.

How these parts interact is sketched out in influence map 6.

Cabinet is, in constitutional terms, the ultimate decision-making body in the country. It consists of the Prime Minister and the 20 or so most senior ministers, in practice including at least one from each of the principal government departments (see box on page 267). The composition of Cabinet can change to adapt to circumstances; currently the only department with two Cabinet ministers is the Treasury.

Full Cabinet normally meets once a week on a Thursday, and deals with major strategic policy issues, the business of the moment in Parliament or the public arena, assorted crises as they come up, as well as knotty interdepartmental problems that have proved incapable of resolution at a lower level. It is beyond the reach of the ordinary lobbyist; Cabinet is the body ministers themselves have to lobby.

Most policy decisions in particular areas, however, are made by the 150 or so Cabinet committees. As with the full Cabinet, their business is secret. The membership and terms of reference of the main committees are now generally made public although their system of nomenclature, based on initials, is appropriately cryptic. There are basically three kinds of Cabinet committee:

▼ Main (standing) committees, covering major policy areas, some with subcommittees. HS, for example, covers home and social affairs, and DOP is concerned with defence and overseas policy. Subcommittees of HS include HS(H) (health strategy), HS(D) (drug misuse) and HS(W) (women's issues).

▼ *Ad hoc* committees or miscellaneous groups, which usually carry the prefix MISC and some of which may only meet a few times. MISC 6, for example, was set up to develop policy on biotechnology and genetic modification.

▼ Both of the above kinds of committee consist solely of ministers. There are also official committees, that is those made up of civil servants, which shadow ministerial committees, preparing the ground, particularly on administrative matters.

It is difficult to lobby something whose business is officially secret, so attempts to influence a Cabinet committee will have to be confined to lobbying individual ministers or civil servants. Just knowing that a

Influence Map 6: Central government

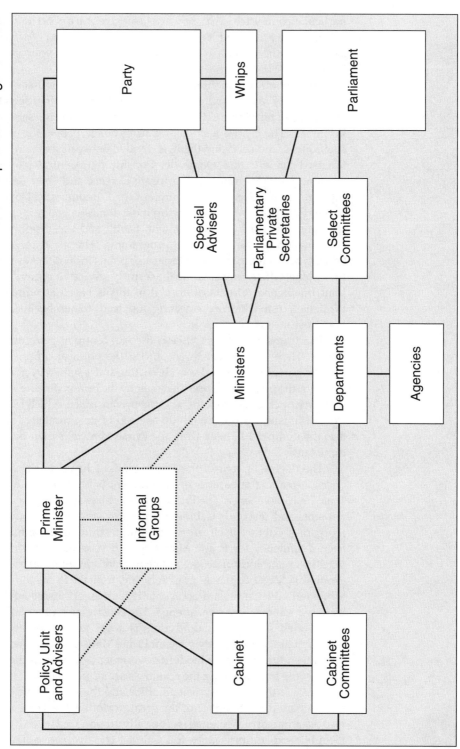

particular committee exists, however, can give you a good indication of the priority afforded its subject, and if you get wind of when an issue is on the agenda it could help the timing of your general lobbying.

The smooth functioning of Cabinet and its committees is the responsibility of the Cabinet Office, headed by the Cabinet Secretary (and Head of the Home Civil Service), the most senior civil servant in Whitehall. The central task of preparing policy papers for cabinet committees, and servicing them, is divided between six main secretariats: Economic and Domestic; Constitution; Central (covering machinery of government); European; Defence and Overseas; and Intelligence and Security. The remit of the Economic and Domestic Secretariat is very wide, lapping up most domestic policy including environment and local government, health and social policy and coordination of the legislative programme. The existence of the Security and Intelligence Secretariat also points to another key role of the Cabinet Office: coordinating the security services and running the Joint Intelligence Organisation. All of this is based at number 70 Whitehall, from where a connecting door leads to number 10 Downing Street.

The Prime Minister's Office is the real centre of governmental power. There are in fact three offices: the political office, which handles party business and speech-writing and is staffed by non-civil servants; the press office, presided over by the Prime Minister's press secretary or chief spin doctor; and the private office, which runs the Prime Minister's professional life as head of government. There is also the number 10 Policy Unit, the Prime Minister's own personal think tank.

The degree of control the Prime Minister has over the central decision-making apparatus of government is limited only by personal time and energy. The Prime Minister hires and fires ministers, appoints and disbands Cabinet committees, and has the power to reorganise Cabinet itself. In recent administrations there has also been a tendency for Prime Ministers to bypass the constitutional machinery and formulate key policy decisions in informal or *ad hoc* groups made up of officials, ministers, staff from the Prime Minister's office and policy unit, and occasionally high-level outside advisers, usually from business or academia. The construction of an 'alternative Whitehall' of personal advisers is a key feature of the more presidential style adopted by recent Prime Ministers and it looks set to be an enduring facet of modern government – as well as the most direct route to influencing the country's senior politician.

Outside the Prime Minister's office and the Cabinet office, the government department with the greatest clout is the Treasury. Its grip over the rest of Whitehall is especially pronounced when it comes to public expenditure: only full Cabinet can override a Treasury decision on a spending matter. A combination of intellectual superiority and weariness at being continuously lobbied by other departments makes Treasury officials a daunting breed to have to deal with.

The way in which government ministers have to approach the Treasury cap-in-hand is a good illustration of two general principles: firstly, that decisions of any significance are never taken by a department acting in isolation, but will always involve other departments with an interest; and secondly, that the *administrative* constraints under which the individual parts of government labour nearly always outweigh *political* constraints (although, unlike the latter, they are rarely appreciated by outsiders). Work promoting the interests of women, for example, is sponsored by the Women's Unit in the Cabinet Office, but actively involves most other major departments. Even a relatively minor issue, like the arrangements for distributing money from the National Lottery to charities, pulls in the Home Office, the Treasury, the Department of Culture, Media and Sport, and the Scottish, Welsh and Northern Ireland Offices.

As well as identifying all the key players on an issue, the would-be government lobbyist will thus also have to develop a sensitivity to the administrative environment. This is especially so because civil servants are unlikely to complain about the internal problems they face. The constitutional doctrine of collective Cabinet responsibility (see box right) extends, albeit in diluted form, over the whole edifice of government, encouraging departments to present a more united front to outsiders than is in fact often the case. Needless to say, it also makes a conveniently imposing facade for the individual civil servant to hide behind.

Sources of information

The fact that the major decisions on how our country is run are made not in the public arena of Parliament but behind the closed doors of Whitehall and Downing Street means that obtaining accurate

---

Membership of the Cabinet

Prime Minister

Deputy Prime Minister and Secretary of State for the Environment, Transport and the Regions

Chancellor of the Exchequer

Chief Secretary to the Treasury

Secretary of State for Foreign and Commonwealth Affairs

Secretary of State for the Home Department

Lord President of the Council and Leader of the House of Commons

Lord Privy Seal and Leader of the House of Lords (and Minister for Women)

Lord Chancellor (the head of the legal system)

Chancellor of the Duchy of Lancaster and Minister for the Cabinet Office

Secretary of State for International Development

Minister of Agriculture, Fisheries and Food

Secretary of State for Defence

Secretary of State for Education and Employment

Secretary of State for Health

Secretary of State for Culture, Media and Sport

Secretary of State for Northern Ireland

Secretary of State for Scotland

Secretary of State for Social Security

Secretary of State for Trade and Industry

Secretary of State for Wales

As at February 2000

information on the workings of government is as difficult as it is important.

The central reference work, the *Civil Service Yearbook*, is published by government itself. Produced annually, it contains details of the responsibilities of every government department (except the secret ones like MI5 and MI6) by division and major branch, with contact names and numbers of civil servants. There is similar information for government agencies, royal households and the Palace of Westminster. It is still not always easy to find the right corner of Whitehall for your concerns, but the *Civil Service Yearbook* is the best aid available and its steady growth in size over the years marks the dogged progress towards open government. The *Yearbook* is available from the Stationery Office.

Another Stationery Office publication, *Public Bodies*, gives only sketchy information on the wide range of non-departmental public bodies and government agencies. The *List of Ministerial Responsibilities*, produced by the Cabinet Office, is the definitive guide to the current field of responsibility of each government department, bearing in mind that these often shift after ministerial reshuffles. *Vacher's Parliamentary Companion* (see chapter 14) also covers ministerial responsibilities as well as listing membership of the main Cabinet committees.

Two fictions of government

1. Collective Responsibility of Cabinet

    Government policy is decided in Cabinet and is binding on all members of the government. A new policy announced by an individual minister is the policy of HM government; the policies of HM government are supported by individual ministers as their own.

In practice, major policy decisions are made by the Prime Minister and/or small groups of ministers, often in committees of the Cabinet, with more detailed policy filled in by individual ministers and their departments. Disagreements between ministers are naturally not uncommon, and in severe cases will crack the façade of collective responsibility (e.g. on the issue of strategic arms control). Ministers will effectively lobby Cabinet in order to advance the cause of their department – or their career.

2. Ministerial Responsibility

    Ministers are responsible for every decision taken by their departments. Civil servants are accountable to ministers and ministers are accountable to Parliament and, through Parliament, to the people.

In practice, departments are managed by senior civil servants – the Whitehall 'mandarins' – and hundreds of policy decisions are routinely taken by civil servants, often at a mid-level of seniority (i.e. grades 5–7). Ministers have neither the time to take every decision nor the professional expertise. They will, however, be personally involved in decisions of political or strategic importance, and may have to carry the can for decisions made by their civil servants in the line of duty (in the extreme case, being forced to resign).

The Stationery Office now also produces the *Whitehall Companion*. Its departmental plans give a clearer picture of the chain of command in the higher civil service than the *Civil Service Yearbook*, but it lacks the detail at the crucial branch level. The principal Cabinet committees and subcommittees are listed, but the main feature of the book is the potted biographies of senior civil servants, including all those at director level and above. Details of all these publications can be found in appendix C.

There is now extensive information on both government departments and public bodies available on the internet. *www.open.gov.uk* is the best way in.

The other major source of information on the inner workings of the executive are the diaries of ex-ministers. The publication of ministers' memoirs has become more common in recent years, including those of Thatcher, Major and several of their chancellors of the exchequer, but few are half as honest or revealing about the curious bunch of people who purport to run the country as the diaries of the late Alan Clark, a former minister of defence. It is worth browsing through these, if only to cheer you up after an hour of being passed around the departmental telephone system.

Departments, ministers and officials

Central government departments are hierarchies of influence that always seem at one remove from the actual exercise of power. The reason for this is the constitutional distinction between the politicians and those who serve them; between the ministers who formally wield power as members of the government and the hierarchy of non-political civil servants or officials who exist to advise and support them. The distinction is fundamental to the role of the British civil service and its upshot is that ministers are very visible and very busy, while officials are classically reserved in judgement and self-effacing in style.

The ministerial diary commitments are genuinely onerous. In addition to the time-consuming work of Cabinet committees, a senior minister will have a lengthy round of public engagements as well as being required regularly in Parliament to answer parliamentary questions, speak in adjournment debates, attend standing committees and vote when needed by the whips, to say nothing of leaving some time for constituency work. And that is before the main job as minister of a department begins. There is a danger that ministers' departmental work is consigned to the red boxes of papers that they plough through, bleary-eyed, late at night, and hurried colloquies with top officials at which ready-made decisions are given a stamp of approval.

If anything, the situation is even worse than this suggests. The average length of time that a minister will stay in office is about two years, often much less. How long does it take to get up to speed in a new job? What if that job happens to include reorganising the whole of the educational system, or the National Health Service? In practice, unless they are very determined, or very stupid, ministers rely heavily on the advice produced by their departments.

The layout of the Department for Education and Employment is given for illustration in influence map 7 (each department is a little different but the map gives the basic structure around which they are all built). The senior minister will usually have the title 'Secretary of State' and will be a member of Cabinet. Although the Secretary of State has overall responsibility for the department there may also be one, two or three Ministers of State who will have line responsibility for broad areas of policy, and possibly a similar number of Parliamentary Under-Secretaries, the most junior kind of minister. There may also be one or more non-departmental public bodies or agencies which are formally accountable to the Secretary of State.

Officials

Following a recent restructuring of the senior civil service, the job titles and grades of senior civil servants are no longer uniform across departments. This can make understanding the structure, or who is in charge, somewhat baffling for outsiders, particularly as the old system of grades and titles is still commonly referred to. The main posts at the top of the civil service pyramid are as follows, with the former grades in brackets for ease of reference:

▼ *Permanent Secretary* (former grade 1). The civil service head of a department, and the official who will have most influence with the Secretary of State.

▼ *Director General* or *Director* (former grade 2, deputy secretary). In charge of a directorate or directorate-general, covering one of the main areas of departmental responsibility. In a complex department like the Department of the Environment, Transport and the Regions (DETR), there are a number of directorates-general handling areas such as environmental protection; housing, construction, regeneration and countryside; local and regional government; and planning, roads and local transport.

▼ *Director* or *Head of Division* (former grade 3, under secretary). In charge of a division or directorate. Divisions tend to cover more defined, cohesive areas of responsibility, e.g. housing (DETR), public health (Department of Health). In executive or operational areas, posts of this seniority are generally called Chief Executive.

▼ *Assistant Director* or *Head* (former grade 5, assistant secretary). In charge of a branch, unit or sometimes division. At this level the remit is specialised enough to enable much of the real graft of policy work to take place.

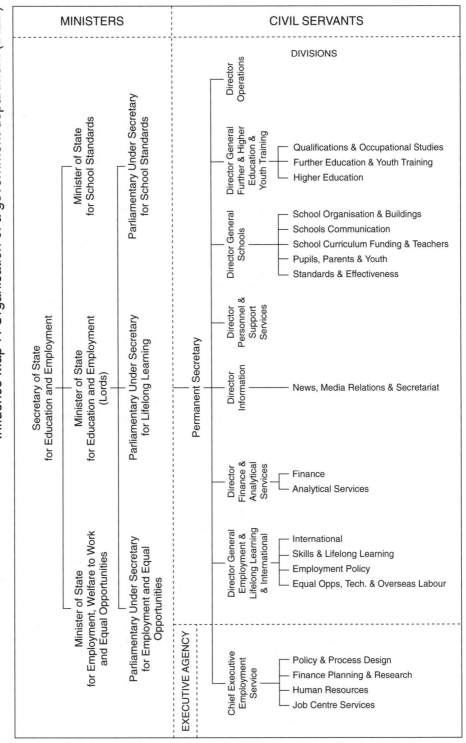

Influence Map 7: Organisation of a government department (DfEE)

MINISTERS

- Secretary of State for Education and Employment
  - Minister of State for Education and Employment (Lords)
  - Minister of State for School Standards
    - Parliamentary Under Secretary for School Standards
  - Parliamentary Under Secretary for Lifelong Learning
  - Minister of State for Employment, Welfare to Work and Equal Opportunities
    - Parliamentary Under Secretary for Employment and Equal Opportunities

CIVIL SERVANTS

DIVISIONS

- Permanent Secretary
  - Director Operations
  - Director General Further & Higher Education & Youth Training
    - Qualifications & Occupational Studies
    - Further Education & Youth Training
    - Higher Education
  - Director General Schools
    - School Organisation & Buildings
    - Schools Communication
    - School Curriculum Funding & Teachers
    - Pupils, Parents & Youth
    - Standards & Effectiveness
  - Director Personnel & Support Services
  - Director Information
    - News, Media Relations & Secretariat
  - Director Finance & Analytical Services
    - Finance
    - Analytical Services
  - Director General Employment & Lifelong Learning & International
    - International
    - Skills & Lifelong Learning
    - Employment Policy
    - Equal Opps, Tech. & Overseas Labour

EXECUTIVE AGENCY

- Chief Executive Employment Service
  - Policy & Process Design
  - Finance Planning & Research
  - Human Resources
  - Job Centre Services

▼   *Principal* (grade 7). With their own area of responsibility within a branch or unit, principals will usually be the main initial point of contact with interest groups, and will act as a filter for outside policy input.

These posts form the elite of the civil service administrative and managerial class, and below them there are a huge number of executive and clerical officers. The exact responsibilities will vary depending on circumstances. In many cases a Senior Executive Officer (SEO) will be performing the same sort of tasks as those given above for a principal; in provincial offices, they can be responsible for over 100 operational staff.

Officials at the very top have areas of responsibility of comparable magnitude to ministers, with similar problems of overload. From the lobbyist's point of view, then, directors and heads of branch or unit (grades 3–7) are the primary target. A head of branch is junior enough to get stuck into detailed policy work, but senior enough usually to benefit from direct access to the minister. They will be responsible for most of the work involved in putting a new bill together and keeping it together while it goes through Parliament, and they often work very hard.

Most successful Whitehall lobbying is in fact built on good relations at branch level. If government needs to know what the likely consequences of a new measure will be on those affected, how a specific policy goal can be best achieved in practice, or what the most efficient structure for a new operation might be, it is to the grade 5's team that the work will probably go. If you can feed in your evidence and concerns at this level, preferably on a regular basis, they may well influence what comes out at the end. Conversely, it can be a waste of time trying to develop relations with officials much below principal grade; they will probably need to obtain clearance from their superiors even to send you certain information.

It is an important part of a civil servant's job to be aware of the views of major interest groups in their field and to take account of them in the advice given to ministers (which is not the same as agreeing with them). This might involve consultation, formal or informal, receiving lobbies, or simply gauging the likely spread of interests across a particular subject or issue and representing them in the department and more broadly in Whitehall. The process goes under the general name of sponsorship. Thus, for example, the Department for International Development is the sponsoring department for third world aid; wildlife and the countryside is sponsored by a division in the Department of the Environment, Transport and the Regions. In any one case the interest groups involved might include the professions, employers' associations, trade unions, manufacturers, the City, the churches, the military, or whoever else is relevant to the work in question. The civil service tends to treat charities and pressure groups, despite their largely disinterested or altruistic nature, as representing vested interests like any others.

The Whitehall village also has its own interests. Officials of the administrative class are still nearly always career civil servants. Serving the minister might be their *raison d'être*, but their official superiors will be the dominant presence in their professional lives. The emphasis is placed on quiet competence, on ensuring that the government machine runs smoothly without any hitches, whether in the form of policy U-turns, administrative fiascos, or embarrassing revelations in Parliament or the media. This is why relations with outsiders are so important: as career administrators rather than specialists, officials rely on interest groups in the areas they sponsor to alert them to new developments, to the unforeseen consequences of new policies, or to representations that are going to be made in the public arena.

What do civil servants spend their time doing? Firstly, they administer. The civil service used to be notorious for its lack of attention to good management but this has largely changed due to the reforms of the last 15 years. It has always administered a host of rules and regulations in almost every area of national life, as well as operations of daunting size: the benefits system, the tax system, the NHS, the economy. Now, every department across Whitehall has drawn up a Public Service Agreement specifying the targets and outputs which it is committed to delivering.

Secondly, they advise. Much of what officials do is directed towards advising ministers, although as we have seen, a good part of this 'advice' will be automatically accepted.

But the civil service activity *par excellence* is drafting. Policy papers, regulations, ministerial statements, answers to parliamentary questions, speeches, reports, legislation: all will go through a number of drafts. Classically, these move up the hierarchy for amendment and approval at successive levels, before being presented to ministers and finally adopted. The process of refinement is horizontal as well as vertical: drafts will be circulated to other departments with an interest and interdepartmental negotiation will help fashion the end product. The process takes considerable time, consumes volumes of paper,

---

What civil servants want from interest groups

▼ Specialist briefings, concise and in layperson's language, on issues affecting their work.

▼ Evidence of how measures are affecting, or will affect, your clients or those you represent.

▼ Evidence of the reaction of different groups or members of the public to particular measures.

▼ Advance warning of any major campaign action. (Whether or not you choose to give such warning may depend on whether you want a considered response from government or are just seeking to embarrass the minister.)

▼ Practical proposals, with details of cost implications, for improving particular measures or solving administrative problems.

and leaves scope for measures to be introduced (perhaps on your instigation), removed, or simply refined out of existence. For the lobbyist, it is important to try and be brought into the drafting process as early as possible, and to continue monitoring successive drafts and applying pressure if necessary.

As measures are considered by top civil servants and ministers, political and strategic considerations may start to edge out good administration as the primary influence on policy-making. This will be especially true of issues which divide along party political lines or of measures which, although not highly politicised themselves, require political will to succeed, e.g. those involving significant public expenditure or those which offend a major interest group. Civil servants of course are not supposed to make political decisions, but they would not be doing their job if their advice did not take account of political realities. They will naturally also be influenced by what they think ministers are likely to accept.

Influencing the minister

Getting your message across to ministers directly will involve either meeting them or influencing one of their personal advisers. A surprising number of approaches by outsiders are actually addressed to the wrong minister: if in doubt check in the *List of Ministerial Responsibilities* or ask officials in the department. A meeting is probably not worthwhile if you just want to put your side of the case. This is better done through officials, as described above, and if officials feel you are going over their heads they are more likely to marginalise what you have to say. If you want to reinforce the case you have already made to officials, if you are seeking a ministerial commitment or, exceptionally, if you have some reason for believing that a minister will be more sympathetic to your case than the officials, then a meeting could be useful. Note that the relevant officials will be present at any meeting, however, and will have briefed the minister beforehand, so clear the ground with them first whenever possible.

Unless you are the chief executive of a major organisation, any letters you write to ministers will probably not be answered by them personally but will be passed down to the relevant civil servant for reply. Requests for meetings are also likely to be declined. In both cases, getting a sympathetic MP to make the approach for you should do the trick (if it is a local matter this should be the constituency MP). Replies to MPs' letters will always be signed by a minister, and this is the easiest way to get a ministerial response on the record. Most MPs will be happy to let you draft the letter for them (see chapter 14 on approaching MPs). Although it is the MP and the minister who are formally corresponding, in fact it is you and the civil servants who are communicating with each other.

Ministers will always agree to see an MP, time-permitting, and will usually consent to you being there as well. Good preparation is essential. As the MP will be leading your delegation, he has to be well-briefed. You should also carefully brief the minister, through her civil servants, in order that she will be able to give you a considered reply. Keep the talking on your side concise, encouraging the minister to comment, prepare probing questions and, if appropriate, see whether she is prepared to make any kind of commitment. The date and time of the meeting will be allocated by the diary secretary in the minister's private office. An alternative is to invite the minister to address a function, opening or conference you are organising; in this case plan well in advance, get the diary secretary to give you two or three dates on which the minister is relatively free and then invite her in writing, allowing her to choose which of the dates is most convenient.

The size of the minister's office will depend on her seniority. The three most important figures in the entourage of a senior minister are:

▼ *Principal private secretary.* Although the permanent secretary is the most powerful official in a department, the principal private secretary will be the official closest to the minister: usually relatively junior in grade but omnipresent, and vital for deciding who gains access to the minister.

▼ *Parliamentary private secretary.* The PPS is an MP who acts as the minister's eyes and ears in Parliament. PPSs are considered the most junior members of government, although they are not actually on the government payroll. They may be worth contacting if it is on an issue relevant to parliamentary support for the minister's policy.

▼ *Special adviser.* Not a civil servant but an outsider brought in by an individual minister, the special adviser can be a political fixer, speech writer, policy adviser or a combination of these. They are mavericks within Whitehall, and their influence with their respective ministers – as well as their relationship with civil servants – varies wildly. There is more on special advisers below.

In most cases ministers and officials should be regarded as one target and care taken not to alienate the officials, but to work through them. As in all campaigning, however, it is important to be alive to those occasions when the interests of different parts of the target are not the same.

If you feel that, despite having a strong, well-researched case, civil servants are consistently marginalising you, you will need to put pressure on the department. Classically, this is done in Parliament or through the media. Just a little such pressure will sometimes work wonders: civil servants know that dealing directly with outside groups involves them in considerably less work and stress than having to brief ministers to deal with the same issues in the glare of the public eye.

Favourite Whitehall ploys

1. *No response at all.*

   This is probably Whitehall's single most common reaction to initial communications from outsiders – and its most devastating. Check that you have written to the most appropriate person and follow up your first letter with a polite reminder by letter or telephone. If you still have no luck, get your MP to forward a copy of your letter or write on your behalf.

2. *'Thank you for your useful communication; your information/views will be taken into account.'*

   This, in one form or another, is another frequent response. It may simply confirm receipt of your submission on a consultation document. In other cases it will be worth following up to get some feedback or to request a meeting. It illustrates the general point that civil servants will avoid committing themselves whenever possible and that you should always structure what you say in order to invite a proper response: lobby by question, not by assertion.

3. *'Thank you for your letter; it has been passed to – [Grade 7 official] for a reply.'*

   This is a likely response if you follow up your letter to a minister. It is not a snub, merely a polite lesson in how the department works. You probably would have been better off writing direct to the official.

4. *'It is no use talking to me about that, that is for the minister(s) to decide.'*

   This is the civil servant invoking the constitutional doctrine of ministerial responsibility. Try asking: a) when ministers are likely to consider the issue; b) how ministerial thinking is progressing; c) whether there is any briefing or other input you can make that they would find useful in advising ministers.

5. *'That issue is not being considered at the moment'* or *'That will only be considered after the committee report is published/bill is enacted/review is completed.'*

   This may be true and it may be worth biding your time, but if you wait as long as the official suggests it will almost certainly be too late. Departments closely monitor committees of inquiry and develop their response as they progress; work begins on the content of secondary legislation while the primary legislation is still going through Parliament.

6. *'I'm afraid that has already been decided'* or *'I'm afraid that is government policy.'*

   This is almost certainly true, but don't be browbeaten into giving up. Try and establish if the policy is being reviewed in the future or when the next piece of legislation affecting the whole area is planned. If you are really trying to reverse a tenet of government policy, it will require considerable pressure outside Whitehall as well as within it.

The spin doctors

The number of special advisers in government proliferated under the Blair administration. They are generally referred to as spin doctors by the media, for their PR role in presenting government policies and news in such a way as to make their minister look good. However, although the stereotype is of a young, aggressive media manipulator, special advisers are as often experienced party hacks or professional policy wonks. They should certainly be quick to see what can make a particular issue publicly or politically sensitive.

For the lobbyist, the key thing to note is that unlike the apolitical civil servants, special advisers owe their allegiance – and their prefer-ment – to their minister personally. This means that they are one of the best ways of getting an alternative case put to the minister if the department's officials are strongly pushing one line, or if there is some friction between ministers and officials. This situation will be more common after a reshuffle or a general election, when the minister is new. Special advisers are often a bit paranoid about being left off departmental circulation lists for information, and should welcome good briefings. They can also occasionally be useful in getting swift access to a minister.

But special advisers really come into their own when there is a policy conflict *between* departments. If you are working on an issue where there is significant or potential ministerial conflict, talk to the special advisers in the departments sympathetic to your line, who may discreetly welcome you raising the heat on the issue. They are certainly not above briefing the media against other ministers, on a non-attributable basis of course, if they see a potential advantage for their own minister. They are naturally also a good source of leaks.

Special advisers can, however, be a bit obsessed by what is in the newspapers this week rather than how policy will be implemented over the next year. The way in which the role of special advisers has developed is in fact one of the symptoms of short-termism in government.

How are new policies created?

The legislative process is usually described in textbooks as starting with the first reading of a bill in Parliament and ending with the bill receiving Royal Assent and becoming an Act. In fact, this is less than half of it, and generally the least important half. It is covered in the next chapter.

By the time a bill reaches the stage of publication and first reading, its main measures will already be in place. As likely as not some of those measures will then be amended by Parliament, but the basic structure will remain. The process, similarly, does not end at the completion of a bill's parliamentary stages and its coming onto the statute book. Many details still have to be worked out, often in the form of regulations or secondary legislation (also referred to as delegated legislation, as the power of ministers to draw it up will be contained in the main Act).

Influence map 8 illustrates some of the major policy inputs in the creation of a new piece of legislation. The major parties start internal talks on what will be in their election manifestos about 18 months beforehand. Party research departments, ministers and special advis-ers all provide possible channels to influencing the manifesto.

Influence Map 8: The creation of legislation

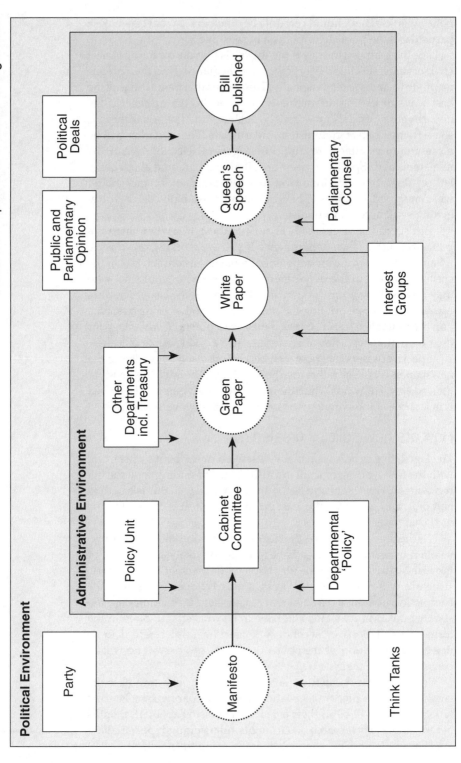

A policy commitment in a party's election manifesto will have been forged in a highly politicised environment. If the party gains power, that policy will suddenly enter the cold light of administrative reality. From now on its progress will be steered by the ministers and officials in the relevant department. Civil servants in the department will have already taken a view on whether the policy was practicable, whether it needed modification or whether it would be better off being quietly shelved. Other forces in government, such as the Downing Street Policy Unit, commissioned directly by the Prime Minister, may contribute new ideas, significantly unencumbered by departmental interests. At this stage everything is still unformed and could take a number of different directions.

The time it takes to firm up a policy varies greatly, depending partly on its priority in a heavy government workload. A number of decisions will be taken, probably at Cabinet committee level; other departments with an interest will take a view, including the Treasury with its assessment of economic implications. By the time a green or white paper is published, the form of the future legislation is already quite clear.

Green and white papers both set out legislative proposals publicly and will be directly responded to by a wide range of interested groups. Such exercises in consultation are a common technique in British government. Often prospective legislation will not go through the green paper stage, which is more consultative. White papers are a statement not so much of what a government is thinking of doing as what it intends to do, and are less subject to change. (The colour of green and white papers, incidentally, does not have to live up to their names.)

A draft bill will be drawn up, incorporating any modifications prompted by the white paper responses, and once it is approved by Cabinet committee it will go to parliamentary counsel, the government's legislative draftspeople, to be turned into workable law. Alterations at this late stage may include deals between government and interest groups, between the interests of different departments, and perhaps some compromise with strong expressions of public opinion and the concerns of government backbenchers in Parliament. If space is found for it in the parliamentary timetable, the bill can then be published. Most major bills will be first announced in the Queen's speech that opens each session of Parliament.

A lot of new legislative proposals never appear in a manifesto and the original ideas for legislation could in theory spring from any of the sources of influence described above, including the department's own officials. (Civil service policy is one of those things in government that does not officially exist but is nonetheless a force to be reckoned with.) Officials at the former Department of Transport, for example, were long convinced of the value of introducing compulsory seat-belt wearing before they finally found a political master prepared to put it into effect.

Most of the elements present in the creation of legislation will be there in the formulation of any kind of policy, although often in a less formal way: the forced marriage of political and administrative concerns, the influence of groups both within government and outside it. The earlier you can enter the process of making policy, the better. If your briefing dominates the thinking of the departmental principal, or the bright spark in the Cabinet Office or Policy Unit, who is tasked with writing the original policy papers, then if the policy itself survives between a third and two thirds of your ideas may survive too. That level of influence is unthinkable if your first input is a response to a consultation paper. In the case of legislation, the publication of the bill marks a further point of no return: from here on it becomes a matter of departmental honour to resist attempts to violate the bill's integrity.

Once a bill is enacted, the policy environment is rather different, with fewer players involved. The formulation of regulations under an Act is very much the job of officials. The political heavyweights will have long turned their attention to more pressing matters, and even junior ministers tend to see it as very much an administrative matter. Parliamentary scrutiny is minimal, with regulations brought into force in the form of Statutory Instruments: delegated legislation which Parliament has to approve but cannot amend. SIs are frequently used for setting levels of benefit and other financial limits, as they will need to be changed over time, or for detailed rules too specialised or unwieldy to be dealt with in primary legislation.

The detailed content of regulations, which must be within the powers given under the Act, will thus be largely left up to officials and any interest groups with the stamina to continue making representations. The bargaining power which such groups still have at this point stems from the officials' own interest in producing regulations which work and which will secure compliance.

Authority, integrity, neutrality

It is worth making a few comments about the tone of negotiations with Whitehall and the sort of approach that is most likely to be taken seriously.

From the uses civil servants have for interest groups described above, it should be clear that it helps to be considered an authority in your field. In the case of the bigger charities, this will partly derive from their experience and value as service providers: it is hardly surprising that some of the major aid agencies have a close relationship with the Department for International Development. In other instances, Whitehall will look to pressure groups as a voice, or a litmus paper, for the reactions of sections of society which do not have the organisation or the political clout to defend their own interests. Department of Social Security dialogue with the Child Poverty Action Group is an example. But authority gained this way can also prove fragile: Margaret Thatcher once notoriously dismissed CPAG with the words 'They haven't got any troops'.

Reasoned argument backed by hard facts is vital. One of the fathers of the modern civil service, R B Haldane, wrote a line which encapsulates the rational detachment that serves as a Whitehall ideal: ' ...in the sphere of civil government the duty of investigation and thought, as preliminary to action, might with great advantage be more definitely recognised.' Even when this fine ideal is over-ridden by political imperatives, fact and argument remain the politicians' primary tools. In her autobiography, *The Downing Street Years*, Thatcher reveals how a file of dodgy evidence was enough to enable her to swing British support behind the butcher military in El Salvador:

> '... the Assistant Secretary for European Affairs, Lawrence Eagleburger, had come to Britain and other European capitals to show us a dossier of evidence substantiating the US claim that arms from Cuba, acting as a surrogate for the Soviet Union, were pouring into El Salvador to support the revolution against the pro-western, if undoubtedly unsavoury, government there. There was still some difference of view about whether the threat was as serious as the US claimed. But the evidence which we now saw made it easier to express support for the American objectives in the region and to resist the pressure from other lobbies ... I warned of the danger of losing the propaganda war on El Salvador – the reporting was very one-sided.'

Much of what central government actually does takes the form of creating, implementing and enforcing law, so a basic grasp of the law covering your area of work is very useful. You don't have to be a lawyer – few civil servants are – but the classic legal strengths are worth cultivating: targeted research, mastery of a brief, strong advocacy, and an air of respectability.

Information is often circulated within Whitehall on a strict 'need-to-know' basis (you only get it if you need it to act on) and the work of government generally is carried out in an atmosphere of cosy confidentiality which is at odds with the loud, publicity-hungry approach of many pressure groups. Such groups may consequently be regarded with suspicion. If you arrange a meeting with a minister, his officials will brief him beforehand on your organisation, how credible they think it is, how trustworthy, and that will help determine how freely he is prepared to talk with you. A group's access to information will be curtailed if it is felt that it will use it to embarrass the government.

This, of course, is a no-win situation – you are only given access if you can be trusted not to make use of it – and every group will have to decide for itself when it is worth toeing the line and when it is better off going public, even if that may sour relations with a department for some time. Working for Amnesty International, I was once publicly told off by the Foreign Secretary for daring to criticise aspects of the Labour government's ethical foreign policy: 'If Amnesty International want to improve human rights, they should support the government's work in promoting human rights, rather than criticising ...' I was also once told by Ann Widdecombe, then a junior minister in the DSS, that some of the most effective lobbies she had received were those that no-one else got to hear about. (Well she would say that ...) Whichever alternative is chosen, it rarely pays to be anything other than honest in dealings with government, and to act with integrity.

As the representative of a particular interest, you will never be seen as impartial by Whitehall, but you should be at pains to ensure that your cause is regarded as politically neutral. If possible avoid any situation which will encourage it to be seen as a party-political matter, and certainly refrain from associating it with the Opposition or Opposition rhetoric; that would be inviting ministers to reject it emphatically. Politically astute they may well be, but civil servants tend to behave as if they considered party politics rather vulgar: making a partisan comment in a meeting produces a reaction not unlike farting at a vicar's tea party.

Public expenditure and the Treasury

One of the most striking features of modern government is the steely grip the Treasury now has over all government spending. Budgetary control has been tightening ever since the late fifties, but since the seventies there has also been a move away from treating public expenditure as an investment in the economy towards regarding it primarily as a net drain on the resources of government and, by association, the country.

Keeping the lid on government spending is the preoccupation of a dry band of officials in Whitehall, formally presided over by the Treasury's number two minister, the Chief Secretary. Their hand was further strengthened by an innovation of the Thatcher years: the customary bilateral negotiations between the Treasury and each department on spending were supplemented by a series of discussions in Cabinet committee, thus bringing departmental budgets under scrutiny from ministers in other departments. Just how much is at stake for the politicians involved may be gleaned from the fact that during the evolution of this committee it was dubbed the Star Chamber, after the Tudor court responsible for interrogating enemies of the king.

Treasury control is not limited to the government's annual budgetary cycle. The effective veto held by the Treasury on spending matters in ordinary Cabinet committees has already been noted. The Treasury is also in the unique position of having its own officials in every spending department, keeping an eye on public expenditure. In fact, every decision taken by a department that has significant spending implications will involve the Treasury. If Whitehall is where elected politicians first have to reconcile their vision with the administrative and financial constraints of the real world, then the Treasury is where Whitehall itself is brought face to face with reality.

The annual expenditure round has now been merged into one unified Budget in the spring, covering both tax and spending. Chancellor of the Exchequer Gordon Brown also introduced a pre-budget report or 'green budget' in November ('green' in the sense of consultative rather than environmentally friendly) to gauge public opinion on planned Budget changes.

The Treasury receives a large number of submissions from outside groups prior to the Budget, arguing for measures such as extensions of tax reliefs or rises in benefit levels. Individually, such submissions will have little effect on decisions regarding general levels of budgeted spending and other macro-economic considerations, but they may help a particular measure get added as an option to the list of 'minor starts'. It is worth getting a submission in early, so that it can be considered for the pre-budget report. By this time Cabinet will already have approved the Treasury's overall control total for public expenditure in the Budget.

In the Budget, spending plans for each government department within the control total will be announced for the next three years. (Figures for the second and third years will of course be revised in the next Budget.)

Although the supply of money for public expenditure has to be approved by Parliament, this is largely a formal process, with little opportunity for serious challenge. Parliament votes for money from the Consolidated Fund to be appropriated for certain broad purposes. The permanent secretary in each department, as accounting officer for the parliamentary vote, is responsible for ensuring that the money is actually spent on the purposes for which it was voted.

Within those broad constraints, a department does exercise considerable discretion over the spending of money voted to it, especially as regards the award of contracts or grants.

The more devolved the spending decisions, in fact, the more scope there probably is for an outside lobby to influence them. As with any submission to government on an expenditure-related matter, proposals to a spending department should be rigorously costed, with an indication of how they could be financed, whether from an existing fund or from new measures. Although your figures will not command the same credibility as those of, say, the Treasury, they may well reveal unexpected costs or opportunities that the department, with its less specific knowledge of the area, had not taken into account. Treasury officials take an especial delight in pointing to the wider economic repercussions of any proposed measure, so it is important to be able to show that repercussions will be limited, or of a positive nature.

A certain amount of buck-passing goes on between departments, and this has to be handled carefully by the outsider. John Biffen MP, a former Chief Secretary, advises that if an official tells you that the Treasury is blocking something, find out from the Treasury who actually has the spending discretion.

When it comes to lobbying against threatened cuts, a strong economic case for retaining the expenditure is often supplemented by pressure groups with a warning of the strong political price that would be incurred by going ahead with the cuts – a form of blackmail, in effect. The department knows that if the group has nothing to lose it will gain as much publicity as possible for the cuts and try and maximise public resentment and disillusion with the government. The embarrassment factor is to be found lurking behind many a government spending decision. It was spectacularly evident in the swings and roundabouts of threatened hospital closures in London following the NHS reforms. A reserve fund is always kept for dealing with contingencies, although it is naturally not well-publicised.

The reverse of the embarrassment factor is the feel-good factor that a government will try to cultivate before an election. Chancellors will allow public expenditure to expand and it is a good time to try and win concessions.

Finally, one practice that pressure groups often fail to notice is under-spending. A significant proportion of departmental funds or budgets will end the year under-spent. Although departments, like any organisation, need to under-spend a bit here and there in order to balance those budgets that go over-spent, the management controls will be concentrated on limiting the latter. Government bodies generally will find it more difficult to resist pressure to spend up. Local authority associations took this principle one step further in 1993 when they campaigned on the millions in assistance for depressed areas from the European structural funds that the UK government had forgone by failing to make matching grants.

Devolved government in Scotland and Wales

From 1 July 1999 significant governmental power in the UK was devolved to the Scottish Executive and Scottish Parliament and to the National Assembly for Wales. Politicians and lobbyists alike in those countries have been jockeying for position, seeing how many government functions they can control or influence and realising at the same time that quite a lot of power is still exercised in Whitehall and Westminster.

One political difference between the new devolved institutions and Westminster that is immediately apparent is the negligible standing of the Conservative Party. Labour, the nationalist parties and the Liberal Democrats are the political forces to be reckoned with. The use of proportional representation to elect the Scottish Parliament and Welsh Assembly also increases the likelihood of power-sharing and the political compromises that go with it.

The Scottish Executive and Parliament

The Scottish government, known as the Scottish Executive, is led by the First Minister who appoints a cabinet of ministers to develop policy and legislative proposals in the areas of devolved responsibility. These 'devolved matters' are defined in the Scotland Act 1998 and are summarised in the box below, together with the 'reserved matters' on which the Scottish Parliament cannot legislate.

Note, however, that under a process known as executive devolution the Scottish Executive can by order be given responsibility for certain functions (for example, the making of appointments) in areas in which the power to make primary legislation is reserved to Westminster. Although the Parliament in Westminster, as the sovereign parliament of the United Kingdom, retains the power to legislate on any matter in Scotland, in practice it is expected that it will not legislate on devolved matters without the consent of the Scottish Parliament.

The Scottish Executive and Parliament are also responsible for allocating the budget or block grant made available to Scotland from the Treasury. In addition, they have the power to raise or lower the basic rate of income tax in Scotland by up to three pence in the pound, although notably the Executive agreed that it would not use its tax-varying powers in the first Parliament.

Many of the general lobbying techniques used for Whitehall and Westminster also apply naturally to the Scottish Executive and Parliament. However, certain features specific to the system in Scotland are worth noting.

When the Scottish Executive wishes to introduce a bill it must be accompanied by a policy memorandum setting out:

▼ the bill's policy objectives;

▼ consideration of any alternative approaches;

▼ details of consultation exercises and their outcome;

▼ assessments of the bill's effects, if any, on equal opportunities, human rights, islands communities, local government, sustainable development and any other matter which the Executive considers relevant.

The usual parliamentary process for a bill consists of three stages: an initial consideration of its general principles, both by parliamentary committee (which may take evidence) and by the full Parliament; secondly, scrutiny of the details of the bill in committee; and thirdly, final consideration of the bill and decision to pass or reject it by the Parliament.

The importance of committee work is a general feature of the Scottish Parliament. 'Mandatory committees' include the Equal Opportunities Committee, Public Petitions Committee and Standards Committee; subject committees deal with a particular subject or area of public policy. Committees can consider executive policy, administration and finances, proposals for legislation in the Scottish Parliament, as well as UK or European legislative proposals. Committees can also initiate Scottish legislation themselves. They can invite evidence and witnesses.

Committees are made up of between five and fifteen Members of the Scottish Parliament (MSPs), chaired by a convenor, with the membership reflecting the party strengths in the Parliament. Meetings can take place anywhere in Scotland and are normally held in public. In addition to scrutinising the Executive in committees, MSPs can raise issues in the Scottish Parliament through oral and written questions and by giving notice of or moving a motion.

The Scottish Executive has already shown its appetite for pursuing different policies from the UK government in the fields of student loans and freedom of information. Policy is naturally likely to vary much more at times when the parties leading the respective governments are different.

Although there is a clear distinction between devolved and reserved matters in law, in practice there is considerable overlap. Liaison between the officials in Whitehall and in Scotland is governed by a concordat or non-statutory agreement, but

---

Devolution in Scotland

Devolved matters, or areas on which the Scottish Executive and Parliament can develop policy and legislate, include:

▼ health services

▼ social work services

▼ local government

▼ education and training

▼ housing

▼ planning and roads

▼ economic development and assistance

▼ tourism

▼ law and order (police, courts, lawyers)

▼ environment

▼ farming, fishing and forestry

▼ the arts and sport

Reserved matters, which remain the responsibility of the UK Parliament at Westminster, include:

▼ the constitution

▼ foreign policy

▼ defence

▼ national security

▼ immigration and nationality

▼ financial and economic matters

▼ trade, industry and energy policy

▼ railways

▼ employment

▼ social security benefits

▼ abortion, genetics, surrogacy, medicines

▼ equal opportunities

detailed working practices will take some time to bed down. A joint ministerial committee exists to enable Scottish ministers to be involved in the UK government's consideration of reserved matters which impact on their devolved responsibilities. It will be interesting to watch how the relationship shakes out on major policy issues – with regard to Europe, for example – in the early years of devolution.

The National Assembly for Wales

Under the Government of Wales Act 1998, the National Assembly for Wales has the power to develop and implement policies in specified areas, allocating the funds made available to Wales from the Treasury. The main areas concerned are listed in the box right.

Unlike the Scottish Parliament, however, the Welsh Assembly does not have the power to pass primary legislation. The Secretary of State for Wales will continue to be responsible for taking through the UK Parliament provisions in primary legislation which relate to Wales, although he will consult and debate with the Welsh Assembly in doing so.

> **Devolution in Wales**
>
> The Welsh Assembly is responsible for developing and implementing policy regarding:
>
> - Agriculture
> - Economic development
> - Education and training
> - The environment
> - Health services
> - Heritage and culture
> - Housing
> - Industry
> - Local government
> - Social services
> - Sport and recreation
> - Tourism
> - Town and country planning
> - Transport and highways
> - Water and flood defence
> - The Welsh language

In practice, though, the Welsh Assembly and its Cabinet have responsibility for a very wide area of policy-making, from setting the National Curriculum in Wales, to NHS funding, to implementing policies on care in the community. To enable it to implement such policies, the Assembly does have the ability to make Statutory Instruments, or delegated legislation under the Government of Wales Act.

The Assembly's 60 members once again do a lot of their work in committees. In addition to a number of subject committees, which shadow the areas of responsibility of the Cabinet members, there are also four regional committees which represent the interests of their localities and are responsible for conveying issues of local concern to the Assembly. Most committee meetings take place in public.

Quangos and agencies

This chapter has concentrated on the work of ministers and officials in departments, the engine rooms of government policy-making. However, more and more of the work of central government is now being hived off into public bodies on the Whitehall fringe.

Known variously as government agencies, quangos (quasi-autonomous non-governmental organisations), or non-departmental public bodies, these vary from executive bodies such as health authorities or the Housing Corporation, to regulatory or monitoring bodies such as the Equal Opportunities Commission or the Health and Safety Executive, to quasi-judicial bodies such as the Parliamentary Commissioner for Administration or the Social Security Appeals Tribunals. Many will fulfil a range of functions: the Charity Commission, for example, is part regulator, part judicial body. More examples of public bodies listed in the box give an indication of the huge range that these bodies cover.

The Next Steps programme, launched in the late eighties, sought to float off many more government operations that had previously been administered directly by departments. By 1999, three quarters of civil service staff had moved to working in executive agencies, a quiet revolution in British government of which few members of the public are aware. Executive agencies, mostly dealing with the service provision functions of government, are headed by a chief executive who is directly accountable to the minister, within the terms of the agency's published framework document. The professed aim of Next Steps was to foster business-like virtues of competition and financial efficiency.

Government by quango, however, has other important consequences. Sir Patrick Nairne, a former permanent secretary at the then Department of Health and Social Security, once stressed to me how convenient it was to have government functions performed by outside agencies: 'The advantage for government is that people can't ask questions in the House'. Although most quangos are directly funded by government and are required to make an annual report to the relevant Secretary of State, questions in Parliament on the work of a quango are often just referred to its chief executive. And unlike local authorities, which are controlled by elected councillors,

---

The quango explosion

The following are just a few of the government agencies or quangos now in existence:

- ▼ Arts Council
- ▼ Commission for Racial Equality
- ▼ Countryside Commission
- ▼ Economic and Social Research Council
- ▼ Equal Opportunities Commission
- ▼ Health Education Authority
- ▼ Housing Corporation
- ▼ Medical Research Council
- ▼ Monopolies and Mergers Commission
- ▼ Office of Fair Trading
- ▼ Parole Board for England and Wales
- ▼ Police Complaints Authority
- ▼ Rural Development Commission
- ▼ Women's National Commission

Executive agencies established since 1989 under the Next Steps programme include:

- ▼ Companies House
- ▼ Defence Intelligence and Security Centre
- ▼ Employment Service
- ▼ Insolvency Service
- ▼ Land Registry
- ▼ Medicines Control Agency
- ▼ Ordnance Survey
- ▼ Planning Inspectorate
- ▼ Rate Collection Agency (NI)
- ▼ Social Security Benefits Agency
- ▼ UK Passport Agency
- ▼ Veterinary Laboratories Agency

quangos are usually managed by boards directly appointed by government.

In the mid-1990s, Home Secretary Michael Howard famously attempted to shield himself from responsibility for failures in prison security, including high-profile jail breaks, by insisting that they were an 'operational' matter, and therefore the responsibility of the Prison Service, rather than a 'policy' matter that fell to ministers. The director-general of the Prison Service was forced to resign but Howard's position remained intact, if shaken.

Most ministers would now be too embarrassed to echo explicitly Howard's distinction between policy and operations, but will often fall back onto a version of that distinction all the same, acknowledging that they make policy but effectively passing responsibility for the unfortunate effects of that policy to an outside body. The distinction also obscures the obvious fact that within their areas of responsibility agencies are developing policy all the time, the details of which the sponsoring department may not even be aware of.

In order to negotiate this difficult area it is important to understand what the agency's responsibility and powers are under law, as stated in its governing statute, framework document, etc. This will help establish what it does have the power to do itself, as well as those decisions which are beyond its remit and remain the responsibility of the sponsoring department.

When the National Lottery Charities Board was first set up, it was sometimes lobbied to fund types of organisation that it was actually barred from supporting by primary legislation. Conversely, when the Board was asked to support areas of work which did fall within its discretion it sometimes responded, so long as the case was well-argued and could not be dismissed simply as the complaint of an organisation unsuccessful in securing a grant.

With political accountability so weak, other methods have to be found to pressurise quangos or agencies. For many, the potential Achilles' heel is their need for a workable relationship with the professions or their non-government partners. Thus health authorities have to get on with the medical professions; the Charity Commission needs to secure cooperation from the massed ranks of charities. Quangos have to listen to interest groups not just as a sounding board, but as partners. In this respect, the less politicised atmosphere in which quangos operate can be an advantage: less interference from the politicians, fewer political consequences if there is a shift in policy.

Formal challenge to agency rule, deflected on the parliamentary floor, can still be made through the audit system or through the courts. Scrutiny of how agencies spend their money has been strengthened, with not just probity but also efficiency or value-for-money assessed by the National Audit Office (for central government), the Audit Commission (for local government) and further investigated by the Public Accounts Committee of the House of Commons (see next chapter). More generally, agency decisions are open to legal challenge through the judicial review process (see chapter 8).

Finally, the media has shown a readiness to get to grips with quango culture, with damaging exposés on the work of the Child Support Agency, utility regulators and the UK Passport Agency, among others. Although bad press on an agency will reflect less on government than bad press on a department, agencies are not accustomed to the constant stream of invective to which government is subjected in a democratic society, and may thus feel it all the more keenly. In such situations the minister may wash her hands of the matter in public but be quick to lean on the agency's chief executive in private.

However, the distancing of more and more parts of government from parliamentary scrutiny is a worrying trend. How that scrutiny works, and just how effective it can be, is described in the next chapter.

14 Parliament

Parliamentarianism – that is, public permission to choose between five basic political opinions – Nietzsche

Parliament is the formal arena for challenging government policy. The many conflicting interests which government has to accommodate and appease in order to govern are at their most dangerous when powerfully represented in Parliament.

Parliament also holds the supreme legislative authority in our state, even if, as we saw in the last chapter, the opportunities for introducing new legislation or substantially amending government legislation in the parliamentary chamber are often overestimated. But victory in a parliamentary campaign can prove especially satisfying, yielding not just a concession or a change in policy, but a new law.

Compromise is a constant feature of parliamentary lobbying. You will have to compromise with the personal attitudes of the MPs with whom you work, compromise with the views of other factions you need to neutralise or get on board, compromise with the very mechanisms and antiquated customs in which every argument has to be dressed. (One visit to the Palace of Westminster is enough to show how the tradition of dead generations weighs like a nightmare on the minds of the living.)

Few people are experts at parliamentary procedure, MPs included. You can certainly be very effective without becoming an expert, particularly if you are sensitive to the advice of experienced MPs on what is likely to work best.

Conversely, a few lobbyists find themselves seduced by Parliament and its quaint procedure, and end up treating it almost as an end in itself. It should be remembered that, whether the objective is just to raise an issue or is something more ambitious, nearly every parliamentary technique is in some way or other aimed at the 80 or so MPs and peers who hold executive power, forming the government.

Working with MPs and peers

Members of Parliament only have time to work on, or actively represent, a small number of issues, and even these often only in a limited way. In addition to their constituency mail, MPs are sent reams of material from companies, pressure groups, unions and many other groups representing particular interests. Most of this inevitably ends up in the waste bin, much of it without being looked at.

There are three subject areas on which you can write to MPs and be reasonably assured of getting their attention:

a) constituency matters;

b) matters relating to one of their posts, e.g. as a party spokesperson or as a member of a parliamentary committee;

c) one of their special interests, which often relate to their professional or extra-parliamentary activities.

Information on posts held by both MPs and peers, and their special interests, is given in a number of different reference works (see box overleaf). Some of these may indicate the stance taken on an issue; if not, further research through parliamentary debates in *Hansard* is required. Reading through past debates on your subject will show which MPs or peers contributed, and what they said.

In practice b) and c) overlap considerably, particularly as an MP's career advances. For example, Joan Ruddock MP, ex-chair of CND and a former Parliamentary Under Secretary of State for Women, has her special interests listed in *Dod* as 'Foreign Affairs, Transport, Environment, Women'. Until 1997 Ms Ruddock was frontbench spokesperson for environmental protection, and before that spokesperson on Home Affairs, and she has sponsored a private member's bill on fly-tipping.

Identifying the interests of individual MPs has also become easier with the growing number of all-party groups. These are loose groupings of both MPs and peers with an interest in a given subject, who come together to draw attention to an issue, discuss developments and coordinate pressure. The range of subjects covered by all-party groups is very wide; those listed in the box on page 295 are an arbitrary selection. There are also all-party groups on dozens of different countries or regions around the world.

Membership of all-party groups is informal and often fluid. Some groups become defunct as interest wanes on an issue, or lie dormant until they are revived by a fresh intake of MPs or by current events. For most groups, the names of the chair and secretary, at least, should be available from the House of Commons Public Information Office (see 'Sources of information' right). Many all-party groups have close relationships with interest groups and may even have been established at the instigation of an outside organisation. A few are backed

Sources of information on politicians and Parliament

On the politicians

Dod's Parliamentary Companion

Published every year, Dod contains biographical details of MPs and peers with photographs, constituency lists and some other useful information about Parliament. There is an index of MPs and peers by political interests, which is useful, but comes from information supplied by the MPs themselves, so treat it as a first step only.

Available from Vacher Dod Publishing Ltd.

Vacher's Parliamentary Companion

This appears four times a year and contains up-to-date lists of MPs, peers, ministers, opposition front-benchers, committees, ministerial responsibilities, etc., plus some information on parliamentary procedure.

Price: £11.50 a copy or £32 for a year's subscription, from Vacher Dod Publishing.

Parliamentary Profiles by Andrew Roth

Famous for the scathing comments, Roth is actually most useful for the information it gives on what MPs have done: concise details on political career, key speeches made and stances taken on particular issues, quotes, voting record, etc. Published in four volumes, this is the best source of information on MPs, but expensive (£150 the set).

Available from Parliamentary Profile Services Ltd.

Register of Members' Interests

MPs are required to register interests they may have, as follows: remunerated directorships; employment or offices; trades or professions; the names of relevant clients; financial sponsorships; overseas visits; payments from abroad; substantial property holdings; and declarable shareholdings. Incomplete, but worth a look.

Available from the Stationery Office.

On Parliament

Hansard

The official verbatim report of everything that is said in Parliament, plus the answers to written parliamentary questions. There is one for both the Commons and the Lords and they are published every day, covering the events of the day before. There is also a standing committee *Hansard*.

Available from the Stationery Office.

House of Commons Weekly Information Bulletin

Published on Saturdays, the *Bulletin* contains details of the previous week's work and the events of the coming week for the House of Commons, as well as information on the progress of bills, standing committees and select committees (incl. membership), green and white papers, forthcoming business in the Lords, etc.

Price: £1.50, annual subscription £53.50. Available from the Stationery Office.

continued overleaf

The House Magazine

Weekly details of current and forthcoming work of both the Commons and the Lords, also information on progress of legislation, Commons committees, etc. Each issue usually has a number of articles by politicians and others on a particular subject. Widely read by MPs.

Price: £345 a year. Parliamentary Communications Ltd.

Vote Bundle

The Vote or Vote Bundle is the daily collection of working papers for the House of Commons, including the order of business, standing committee papers, notices of questions and EDMs. These can be picked up at the Parliamentary Bookshop if you are going into the House; otherwise, the information in the *Weekly Information Bulletin* should suffice for most purposes. The Vote Bundle is very expensive to get every sitting day – an alternative is to employ a parliamentary consultant to monitor this and other material for you and alert you to anything relevant.

Erskine May

Or, to give its full title, 'Erskine May's Treatise on the Law, Privileges, Proceedings and Usage of Parliament', which gives a better idea of the character of the thing. The bible on how things are done, and what can be done, in Parliament. For the initiated.

Published by Butterworths.

The *House of Commons Public Information Office* (020 7219 4272) and the *House of Lords Journal and Information Office* (020 7219 3107) will answer telephone queries from the public on most things, including government and opposition appointments, membership of committees and groups, progress of bills, etc.

POLIS

The Parliamentary On-Line Information System now provides a way of speedily accessing that elusive parliamentary statement. It is the only easy way of getting a full list of the MPs who have signed a particular early day motion. POLIS is very expensive to subscribe to, but the Commons Public Information Office has access to it, as do MPs through the House of Commons library, so you could ask either to get a POLIS trawl done for you.

Parliamentary website

Detailed information on parliamentary activity can now be accessed promptly on the world wide web at *www.parliament.uk* In addition to guidance on procedures, the site contains the full text of current issues of *Hansard* and the *Weekly Information Bulletin*, as well as other publications.

(See appendix B for publishers' addresses.)

up by outside resources and expertise. The clerk of the All-Party Parliamentary Group on Penal Affairs is a member of staff at NACRO, the National Association for the Care and Resettlement of Offenders, and the All-Party Group on Charities and the Voluntary Sector is serviced by the National Council for Voluntary Organisations. If an all-party group exists on an issue related to your work, it will be a useful initial point of contact.

But the first job of every MP is to represent his constituents. Unlike other correspondence, constituency mail is virtually guaranteed to receive attention and some kind of a reply. Constituents should always be given a hearing, and this applies not just to constituents' individual problems, but also to their concerns over wider policy issues.

Typically, an MP will have a constituency surgery or advice session once a week or once a fortnight, probably on a Saturday. Non-London MPs tend to travel down to Westminster on Monday morning, staying there until Thursday afternoon, and then spend Friday and Saturday in the constituency, unless there is any parliamentary business of pressing interest on the Friday for which they are persuaded to stay in Westminster.

Most of the time MPs are best contacted initially by letter to the House of Commons, London SW1A 0AA (see next section). You can suggest a meeting, if you think it will be useful, in which case offer to come to the House at a time when it is convenient, and stress that it will take no more than ten or 15 minutes of their time. Many informal meetings take place in one of the cafés or bars in the Palace of Westminster.

Telephone contact is easier than is often supposed: most MPs have modest office space and secretarial back-up at Westminster and if you ring the main House of Commons line, 020 7219 3000, and give the name of the MP, you will be put through. Usually a secretary will answer and take a message, occasionally it will be the MP herself. Often, however, there will be nobody in and you will have to leave a short message with the (very good) message service. MPs spend a lot of time wandering between the Commons chamber, committee or group meetings and appointments or receptions in or around the Palace of Westminster,

---

All-party groups

Current all-party groups include those on:

- ▼ AIDS
- ▼ Animal Welfare
- ▼ Cycling
- ▼ Disablement
- ▼ Housing Cooperatives
- ▼ Human Rights
- ▼ Insurance and Financial Services
- ▼ Mental Health
- ▼ Parenting
- ▼ Road Passenger Transport
- ▼ Scotch Whisky Industry (popular)
- ▼ Solvent Abuse
- ▼ Tourism
- ▼ Youth Affairs

- ▼ Argentina
- ▼ Belgium
- ▼ Cambodia
- ▼ Canada
- ▼ Euro–Arab Cooperation
- ▼ Germany
- ▼ Gibraltar
- ▼ Kashmir
- ▼ Poland
- ▼ Russia
- ▼ South Africa
- ▼ Yemen

---

so while it is difficult to get them in the office, they will usually receive a message quite quickly. Late afternoons and evenings are often a good time to catch them.

If a constituent or lobbyist wants to see an MP urgently, he can just turn up any time when Parliament is sitting, go through St Stephen's entrance and fill out a green card in central lobby. The green card will be passed to the MP, if she can be found, and if she has time she might come to see her visitor. It is a bit of a hit-and-miss affair: it's advisable to telephone first in order to make an appointment, or to find out when the MP might be available. Constituents are better served attending the MP's constituency surgery. Once again, it is worth trying to make an appointment beforehand.

The best relationships with MPs are partnerships, in which there is mutual benefit. As with many people in positions of influence, lobbying MPs requires the 'Kennedy approach': ask not what they can do for you, ask what you can do for them.

Apart from having many demands on their time and attention, MPs are generally badly resourced and lack specialist support. At the same time, they are frequently required to become instant experts on different topics, and have complex and wide-ranging information needs. This is where you come in. Many MPs rely on charities and pressure groups for specialist information and support, as well as for a range of other 'services'.

What you can do for MPs

1. *Information*. Information about the issue(s) on which you work, if it is relevant to forthcoming legislation, to the news of the moment, or to the MP's own work, can be invaluable to a politician as can suggesting possible lines of argument to support a case. Information provided should be concise and demonstrably accurate.

2. *Reduction of their workload*. Some of the bigger pressure groups loan a member of staff to be an MP's research assistant for a period of time. This eases the MP's workload while providing excellent training for the staff member as well as access to the Houses of Parliament. On a more realistic level for smaller groups, most backbench MPs would find it hard to conduct a parliamentary campaign without the specialist support and advice of a lobbyist.

3. *Opportunities to star at Westminster*. Backbench MPs, particularly new ones, are on the lookout for chances to make their mark in Parliament. You can help by providing them with incisive parliamentary questions to ask, suggesting subjects for adjournment debates or drafting 10-minute rule bills that they can present.

4. *Publicity*. MPs crave good publicity. Getting involved with your cause can provide this, particularly at local level, where their participation in some activity will provide a photo opportunity for the local press.

5. *Raising their profile*. All of this enables MPs to raise their profile, whether in Parliament, in the constituency, or with the public at large. Such image-building can be vital to continued electoral success and to their political career.

What MPs can do for you

1. *Information*. Answers to written parliamentary questions can provide detailed information that would otherwise be unobtainable. Letters to a minister should always elicit a response from the minister herself if sent by an MP. (Letters from ordinary mortals are usually replied to by departmental civil servants.)

2. *Supporting your cause in Parliament.* MPs can table early day motions, ask PQs, introduce new bills, back your case in committees and, of course, vote the right way.

3. *Other parliamentary services.* Friendly MPs can perform a number of other useful services, such as booking rooms in the Palace of Westminster for receptions or meetings with other MPs, or passing on relevant briefings or copies of papers they get free.

4. *Publicity.* Support from MPs should get you good publicity at local level, and might help to get national coverage for larger campaigns, particularly if coordinated round an appropriate stunt.

5. *Political influence.* Backbench MPs, with rare exceptions, are relatively powerless as individuals in Parliament, but they may have very good access to senior figures in their party and can combine to apply strong political pressure. On a local level, MPs can have considerable direct influence with councillors, local business people or community leaders.

Note how similar the two lists above are, especially as regards information and publicity. The most productive and long-term partnerships with MPs are often those where your needs and their needs can interlock in a way which is mutually beneficial.

For a local campaign, showing that you have the backing of the local MP can be an important factor in your chances of success. For national campaigns, the token support of a number of MPs can still be impressive, although it is important to ensure that the support is cross-party if at all possible. The more senior your supporters, the better. Ideally, you would be able to demonstrate both wide-ranging support (across the parties) and depth of support (a large number of supporters in Parliament).

Many of the above points also apply to members of the House of Lords. But there are important differences. Peers will generally have more time than MPs, and they don't have to cope with the demands and pressures of constituencies and the electoral process. They are less disciplined by their parties. On the other hand, many peers are at the end of their careers and their ambition and energies can be correspondingly less intense. They are also even more poorly resourced than MPs. For pressure groups, then, peers have certain advantages and disadvantages compared to MPs. They might have more free time and be politically more independent, but they often present fewer points of access and, for publicity purposes, seem further from the centre of power.

Letters and briefs

There are 659 MPs and the occasion will hardly ever arise when you need to write to all of them, or even most of them. Stick to those where your message is related to their constituency, job or stated interests and you will save a lot of time and postage (note that any more than two letters delivered by hand to the House of Commons will not be accepted unless they are stamped).

Following House of Lords reform in 2000 (see below) there are now some 665 peers. You can write to peers at the House of Lords if they are still regular attenders; otherwise write to their home addresses (usually given in *Who's Who*). The House of Lords will redirect mail.

Many letters to MPs from pressure groups are wasted because the recipient does not know what is expected of him. Ask something concrete of the MP, whether it is to add his name to an early day motion, to be present in the House for a division, or to meet you in person.

Letters should be concise; if you wish to include detailed argument on an issue, or the text of a suggested PQ or an amendment to a bill, put that on a separate sheet. Never photocopy letters: photocopied circulars might as well be addressed to the trash can, because that is where they will go.

Some of the most effective campaigning letters are not those written on behalf of a pressure group but those from individuals written to their own local MP. Your individual supporters or members are a powerful resource in this respect. There is a convention that letters MPs receive from individuals outside their own constituency are passed to the relevant local MP (except, of course, if the letter concerns something directly related to the MP's own work). Letters from their own constituents, however, will be read and heeded.

Many MPs still gauge the strength of public opinion on an issue by how many letters they receive on the subject from their constituents. This fact is surprisingly under-exploited by pressure groups in the UK. The ubiquitous pre-printed form letters or postcards, which the individual just has to sign and send off, are very much less effective. Alternatively, just asking supporters to 'Write to your MP' rarely results in more than one or two unfocused attempts: few people know who their MP is, or will take the initiative to find out.

In the United States, by contrast, organising individual members and volunteers to write to their representatives is a major element in congressional lobbying. The process is known as 'getting out the grassroots'. The aim is a stream of individually-written letters from concerned constituents arriving at key times in the progress of legislation. The steps involved in running this kind of legislative network of volunteers are described in the box opposite. An important by-product of a legislative network is the galvanisation of local members, who are tasked with something valuable to do other than fundraising.

Briefs are information papers on a given subject, used to provide MPs and peers with the information they need to act for you. Briefs should live up to their name. One to two sides of A4 should suffice for most purposes. They should be factual and should keep to the specific issue on which you want the MP to act, and not stray off the point. Avoid using jargon which would be unfamiliar to those not working in the field. Briefs are not only for convincing MPs of your case, but also for them to use to convince others. If the brief is good and the MP is pressed for time or imagination, you might even have your words quoted *verbatim* in the House and recorded for posterity in *Hansard*. If there is strong or well-publicised opposition to your case, you need to mention how the main arguments can be refuted.

Briefing papers can certainly be photocopied and sent to more than one MP, but should be accompanied by a personalised letter, specifying what is requested of the MP. You can even vary the briefs

---

Getting out the grassroots

Running a legislative network of members/volunteers

1. Identify the MPs whom you need to target. These might include members of the relevant standing committee, government backbenchers who are waverers or are broadly sympathetic to your aims and other MPs who need pressuring and reminding to make sure they deliver their vote.

2. Recruit members or supporters living in the relevant constituencies who are prepared to commit themselves to writing letters or contacting their MP at short notice. Those who already have contact with their MP or are influential members of the community are particularly valuable. If you have a local group structure, find a linchpin person in each constituency who will help in the recruitment and organising of network volunteers.

3. Set up a database or mailing list (or segment your existing members database) so that you can communicate with network volunteers swiftly, ideally by constituency. It is possible to task your constituency organisers with contacting their own set of volunteers, but it is much safer to organise mailings centrally.

4. As soon as action is required, send out a legislative alert to all members of the network. This will need to:
   - state clearly that urgent action is required;
   - give the name and address of the relevant constituency MP and possibly a few biographical details;
   - outline briefly the legislative measure, the argument, and what the MP should be asked to do;
   - give a deadline by which the volunteer has to write.

   Encourage network members to say what they think, to give any local examples that come to mind and to report back if they receive an interesting response. Emphasise that only a very short letter is required. If a really big issue comes up, you can send out a 'priority alert', rather like a three-line whip.

5. After an alert has gone out, telephone network members to check that they have written, or encourage them to do so. This is time-consuming and quite expensive, but it will boost considerably the number of letters written.

6. Report back to network members on the result and thank them for their efforts. If you are lobbying on a big piece of legislation and sending out regular alerts, the feedback could be incorporated on the back of the next alert.

you send out, employing arguments that you think will have most weight according to the parties/groupings to which the different MPs belong. Take care, however, not to give out conflicting information, or to set up MPs against each other. If you are working closely with an MP on a campaign, discuss with her the briefings you intend to use and always keep her informed of what you do. Make an MP look silly in Parliament, and you will never be forgiven.

Political dynamics of the House

The House of Commons is the showpiece of our wonderful democracy and it is important to realise from the start that it is stitched up. Business in the House is carefully controlled by the two main parties, who plan in advance the major items that are debated and who are well aware of their respective parliamentary strengths, notwithstanding the aggressive jostling for position. In terms of implementing policy, the government party is very nearly all-powerful – Austin Mitchell characterises the role of the opposition as 'heckling a steamroller'. Since 1979, for example, the government has been defeated in only 12 divisions on the floor of the House of Commons.

Business is controlled and party discipline enforced by the whips, MPs appointed by their party to keep their colleagues in line and get out the vote. 'The whip' is also the name given to the sheet issued to MPs by their party whips every Thursday, detailing business for the following week and when they are required to be present for a division (that is, a vote). The number of times a debate is underlined on the whip indicates how important it is that MPs attend:

▼ three-line whip: a division will take place and attendance is essential;

▼ two-line whip: attendance is necessary, unless the MP is let off by the whips;

▼ one-line whip: a division is unlikely to take place and attendance is only requested.

Permission to be absent is usually granted under the pairing system, in which one MP pairs off with another MP from an opposing party, enabling both to be absent for the division. Division bells that ring through the Palace of Westminster alert MPs to when a division is about to take place.

The whips from different parties coordinate forthcoming business through the Speaker and the office of the government chief whip, commonly referred to as 'the usual channels'.

Why do MPs obey the whip? Firstly, as they control attendance, the whips can make life very difficult for MPs who stray out of line, greatly curtailing their free time. Equally importantly, the whips are the eyes and ears of the parliamentary party, always present in the House of Commons or in standing committees. Their recommendations are vital for the award of government or opposition posts, particularly in the early stages of a political career. On the government side, the whips also coordinate the support which ensures that some legislative measures succeed and others fail, so their cooperation is key for an MP pushing an amendment or a piece of private member's legislation. Disobedience is expensive.

If backbench MPs do vote against the whip, it may be because the interests of their constituents conflict with party policy, or because it is an issue on which they feel particularly strongly. They may also want to send a message to the party bosses. In any case, dissent will usually be cleared with the whips first.

Both the two main parties have a number of party groups or backbench groups. These cover subjects roughly corresponding to government departments (e.g. defence, health, etc.), regions of the country and a few other subjects. Backbench groups enable MPs to consider party policy in a given field and to influence their frontbench colleagues. They occasionally invite outside groups to come and speak. There are also plenary groups: Labour has meetings of the Parliamentary Labour Party and the Conservatives have the 1922 Committee of all Tory backbenchers. PLP meetings are attended by frontbenchers, but in the case of both parties these meetings represent the most powerful organised expression of backbench feeling. Thus with a Conservative government, the chair of the 1922 Committee is the most influential backbencher in the House.

The government can always count on its 'payroll vote', which comprises ministers, their parliamentary private secretaries (who are not, incidentally, paid), and the whips themselves. As the opposition parties can usually be counted on to vote against the government, particularly on a contentious issue, the key group for parliamentary lobbyists are backbenchers of the government party. The smaller the government's majority in the House of Commons, the more powerful government backbenchers become, although the more pressure they will be under to toe the party line.

The importance of the size of the government majority can easily be demonstrated by looking at the number of government defeats in recent Parliaments. In the 1987–1992 Parliament, when the government majority averaged about 100, there was only one government defeat in a division on the floor of the House of Commons (this, notably, occurred on a new clause to the NHS and Community Care Bill concerning social security benefits in residential homes, an issue of intense concern to charities and pressure groups). In the next Parliament, the Conservative government, its majority reduced to 14, suffered nine defeats. The Labour government which came to power in 1997 with a majority of 179 has never experienced a defeat, whereas the last Labour government in 1974–9, with a majority averaging just four, suffered some 42 defeats.

Influence Map 9: The House of Commons

Can usually be expected to vote with the opposition, but are consistently marginalised by both main parties. Their importance increases as the government majority declines; with a negligible government majority, the minority parties hold the balance of power. Individual MPs useful for raising issues.

Collectively hold the casting vote in every division. May rebel against government policy in order to win concessions but have too much at stake to press their opposition consistently. Always a very heterogenous group: some left-wing, some right-wing; some hungry for power, others beyond political ambition and more independent.

Minority Parties

Government Backbenchers

Opposition Backbenchers

Shadow Ministers / Opposition Spokespeople

Ministers

Parliamentary Private Secretaries

Whips

Whips

Useful for raising issues. More independent than the opposition frontbench and less inclined to turn every issue into a party-political football. Distanced from both power and preferment, some individuals have chosen to become highly effective campaigners on particular issues, making use of their insider access to politicians.

Mobilise and coordinate opposition to government policy. (But rarely sign early day motions, unless put down by opposition frontbench itself.) Tendency to transform something into a party-political issue and kill its chance of parliamentary success. May form the next government...

The government 'payroll' vote. Do not sign early day motions, ask parliamentary questions, etc.

But headline defeats on the floor of the House are only the most visible aspect of a much larger spectrum of parliamentary dissent. Defeats in standing committee (see under 'Lobbying on government bills') are more common, where detailed legislative measures are discussed and where the much smaller size of the forum makes turning a vote much easier. Most government setbacks, however, are not the result of an actual vote but are occasioned by sustained pressure and even threats from government backbenchers and the opposition parties, leading to a negotiated compromise.

The government will make a concession to backbench feeling in order to show responsiveness and to secure support for the main thrust of its policy. It may agree, in return for immediate backing, to reconsider an issue in the future or undertake to resolve the problem using its executive powers. All the time the whips will be calculating the parliamentary arithmetic, making sure they have enough votes to push on the government's legislative programme.

Such political horse-trading provides the lobbyist with numerous opportunities, bearing in mind the difficulty of actually defeating the government in a division. The lobbyist's aim is thus not generally to win enough votes to make a majority, but to raise enough strength of feeling among government backbenchers and by building alliances to give an issue real bargaining power. Different issues will call for different alliances among MPs, but influence map 9 indicates which are the more important parliamentary targets.

The golden rule of parliamentary lobbying is to pursue an all-party approach wherever possible. The arithmetic dictates that the government can never be defeated, or will never feel seriously threatened, unless the opposition parties and enough government backbenchers vote together. This makes it necessary to advance an issue in a way which will find supporters across the parties.

Some issues may already be so strongly divided on party lines as to make an all-party approach impossible, but such issues are more rare than is generally supposed. With a small government majority, a splinter group of backbenchers, often motivated by constituency interests, is all that is required.

House of Lords

The political dynamics of the House of Lords are different from those of the Commons in a number of important respects:

▼ *Non-elected members*. As they are not elected, members of the House of Lords do not have to worry about keeping their seat, nor about representing constituents. The primary route for influencing individual MPs, the constituency, is thus not present in the Lords; peers do not rely on their party to get them re-elected; and there is not the same incentive to embrace populist policies.

▼ *Weaker party control*. Not only do they have security of tenure, but peers are less ambitious than MPs and there are fewer government or opposition jobs in the Lords with which they can be tempted by their respective parties.

▼ *Importance of cross-benchers*. The balance of power in the House of Lords is held by independent peers, called cross-benchers, who are not allied to a political party. Like many peers, they do not always respond well to heavy lobbying, but if present in sufficient numbers their vote is often decisive.

The House of Lords, then, is politically less fixed than the Commons, and the parliamentary arithmetic is rather different. Party strengths in the Lords in 2000 are given in the box below. Following House of Lords reform in 1999, there are now only 92 hereditary peers, compared to 543 life peers (including law lords) and 26 bishops. Ex-members of the House of Commons are good first targets for lobbyists, as they are likely to be more active, more politically astute, and rate higher on the publicity stakes.

A Royal Commission on further reform of the House of Lords, chaired by Lord Wakeham, proposed in 2000 an upper House of some 550 members, of whom the majority would be appointed by a new independent committee and the minority would be elected on a regional basis. The remaining hereditary peers would go, but seats allocated to religious leaders would be broadened to include faiths other than the Church of England. The proposed reforms are unlikely to be implemented before 2004 at the earliest.

The overall importance of the Lords for lobbyists is roughly proportional to the size of the government majority in the House of Commons. During the Thatcher years when the Tories held a big majority, giving them a degree of immunity to pressure in the Commons, many lobbyists spent more time on the House of Lords as the last refuge of dissent. Interest in the Lords waned after 1992 when the government majority in the Commons shrank dramatically but then rose again when Blair came to power in 1997 with a huge Labour majority. In 2000 the Lords inflicted a stunning defeat on the Blair government when they backed a cross-party amendment to the Criminal Justice (Mode of Trial) Bill, effectively killing the bill and its plans to restrict the right to trial by jury.

Political composition of the House of Lords

	Life peers	Hereditary peers	Bishops	Total
Conservative	180	52	0	232
Labour	177	4	0	181
Liberal Democrat	49	5	0	54
Cross-bench/other	137	31	26	194

The figures do not include 4 life peers on leave of absence.

Source: *House of Lords 2000*

Raising issues in Parliament

Many opportunities exist for raising issues in the Houses of Parliament, enabling MPs and peers to bring matters to public notice, to extract information from the government or simply to embarrass or pressure ministers. Some of these only take place on paper, others when the House is nearly empty: to make the most of such opportunities, therefore, you will need to coordinate a little extra-parliamentary publicity, promptly releasing details of what happens to the press, informing your supporters, and using any quotes obtained in documents or research. MPs, if they are sharp, appreciate this fact and should be keen to work with organisations who can deliver publicity for them.

Parliamentary questions

Parliamentary questions are put by MPs to government ministers, and they come in two basic types: questions for written answer and questions for oral answer. The rules governing how written and oral questions should be put down, or tabled, are much the same, but their functions are very different.

▼ *Written questions* are designed to elicit information from the government. The answer appears at the back of *Hansard* and may, if necessary, take up several columns in providing figures or other information. The information can of course be used subsequently to embarrass the government. Questions will not be answered if the information is not available, or if acquiring it would result in 'disproportionate cost' (see chapter 4 for more details).

▼ *Oral questions* are designed to call ministers to account, or embarrass them, on the floor of the House. MPs use them to make political points. They are not appropriate for eliciting detailed information, which would prove cumbersome to recite in Parliament. The opportunity to ask a supplementary question, of which the minister will have no forewarning, is particularly useful for putting on the pressure and extracting admissions from government.

Parliamentary questions have to be tabled in advance by MPs at the House of Commons table office. MPs are limited to asking two oral questions a day, but there is no limit on written questions. Some 40,000 questions are now tabled a year, and MPs will usually agree readily to table questions on behalf of constituents and outside groups to whom they are sympathetic.

Questions will not be accepted unless they follow the correct format and satisfy a number of rules, although the clerks at the table office will advise MPs and help them amend questions drafted incorrectly. Questions must concern a matter for which a government department holds responsibility and must be addressed to the senior minister in that department. Every parliamentary question therefore begins 'To ask ...', followed by the title of the department's senior minister, usually a Secretary of State (see example in the box overleaf). If an MP seeks information which concerns the work of more than one department, separate questions have to be tabled for each department. Some subjects are blocked; these include matters of national security and those dealing with commercially sensitive information.

A parliamentary question must seek information or press for action and should be based in fact. It should not just ask for the minister's opinion. Nor should it attempt to give information or to express the opinion of the questioner. However, while these rules are strictly applied to the questions that go down on the order paper, they are often ignored by the time the MP gets up to ask a supplementary.

Written questions normally receive a reply in *Hansard* within about a week. Departmental instincts still often lean towards being economical with information, so if a reply is unsatisfactory it may be worth trying again, varying the terms of the question (see box for example). At the least, this will indicate to the department that someone is taking a real interest in the subject.

Oral questions are answered in the House of Commons for about an hour every day, except Friday, starting after prayers at 2.30pm on Monday to Wednesday and at 11.30am on Thursday. It is the turn of a different department to answer questions each day, with a rota ensuring that each department comes up about once a month. Although questions must be formally addressed to the senior minister, the ministers from a major department will usually share the task of answering questions between them.

As many more oral questions are tabled than there is time to answer, to stand a chance of having his question answered an MP must table it at the earliest possible time, which is exactly two weeks (ten sitting days) before the next date assigned to the relevant department. Questions tabled on that day go into what is known as 'the shuffle' (or the 'five o'clock shuffle', after the time it takes place) with only the first 15–20 or so questions drawn out likely to have time to be answered. In the House, after the minister has read out a prepared reply to the question on the order paper, the MP gets a chance to ask one supplementary, which has to be on the same subject or a related matter. The Speaker may then call other MPs to ask further supplementaries, often favouring MPs with a known interest or expertise in the subject. If several questions have been tabled on the same topic, they may be taken together, with each MP being called in turn to ask a supplementary question.

The best-known variant of question time, Prime Minister's questions, is actually a little different. The Prime Minister answers questions for 30 minutes once a week, at 3.00pm on Wednesdays. As questions relating to subjects covered by a government department should be properly addressed to the senior departmental minister,

MPs have had to develop a way of posing admissible questions related to government business which are nevertheless the exclusive concern of the Prime Minister. Consequently, most questions addressed to the Prime Minister are very similar – asking him to list his engagements for a given day – with the 'real' question coming in the supplementary. This has the added advantage of not requiring an MP to disclose what she wishes to grill the Prime Minister about until the last moment, enabling her to pick a highly topical subject. The reliance on such a quaint convention has been criticised by reformers, who also complain that Prime Minister's question time has become largely an opportunity for political point-scoring. Although fun to watch and undoubtedly a test of the PM's nerve, it is now rarely a very effective mechanism for holding the executive accountable.

Early day motions

Although often overestimated by lobbyists, early day motions are a useful way of getting MPs formally to record their support for an issue. An EDM is a motion put down for debate on 'an early day' by one or more MPs. In normal practice the day never arrives and EDMs are never debated, but they are printed with the names of supporting MPs on the notice paper, or 'blues', part of the daily vote bundle.

> ### Written PQs: if at first you don't succeed …
>
> *27 May 1993*
> NHS Equipment
> **Mr Hutton:** To ask the Secretary of State for Health what estimate she has of the volume of NHS equipment purchased by voluntary local subscriptions in each of the last five years in (a) cash terms and (b) in constant 1993 prices.
> **Mr Sackville:** Information exactly as requested is not available centrally.
>
> *14 June 1993*
> **Mr Hutton:** To ask the Secretary of State for Health what information she has on the value of donated equipment (a) held by NHS trusts and health authorities at 31 March 1992 and (b) acquired by NHS trusts and health authorities over the preceding year.
> **Mr Sackville:** The summarised accounts of health authorities and of national health service trusts in England for 1991–92 show the total net book values of equipment acquired through donations at 31 March 1992 as £91 million and £28.3 million respectively …
> Source: *Hansard*

An EDM is tabled by an MP handing in the text of the motion to the table office with the names of any other sponsoring MPs. Motions cannot be more than one sentence long, although they are often a very long sentence. They must begin with the word 'That' (usually 'That this House' etc.). Otherwise there are few restrictions on the content of EDMs, which may range from criticism of a government decision to a call for an issue to be given a full debate, from censuring the human rights record of a foreign regime to congratulating a sports team on its performance. In 1979 the opposition, led by Margaret Thatcher, sponsored an EDM which proved ominous for one half of the Commons: 'That this House has no confidence in Her Majesty's Government'.

An EDM is usually first printed in the notice paper the day after it is tabled. For the first two weeks afterwards, it will be reprinted every time more MPs add their names to it, but subsequently only on Thursdays. If no new signatories are added, the EDM lies dormant until the end of the parliamentary session, when, like all EDMs, it falls.

The names of up to six original sponsors are reprinted every time with the motion, as well as the names of new signatories that day. A number printed next to the motion gives the total of MPs who have supported it. As well as supporting the motion, MPs can also amend it–sometimes reversing the thrust of the original motion–and recruit supporters for the amendment. Amendments are printed separately, immediately below the original motion, so that new signatories can be added to each. The fact that the notice paper is cluttered with EDMs on subjects from the trite to the tragic, liberally amended by other MPs, and that none of them is ever likely be acted upon, has led to EDMs being dismissed as 'House of Commons graffiti'.

An early day motion

197   *FIRST AID IN SCHOOLS*   **10:12:90**

Mr Neil Thorne
Mr Donald Anderson
Mr Matthew Taylor
Mr John Wheeler
Mr Tom Cox
Mr Ken Maginnis

* 66

Mr Ronnie Fearn	Sir Nicholas Bonsor	Mr Vivian Bendall
Mr Alex Carlile	Mr Sydney Bidwell	Mr Robin Corbett
Mr Dennis Canavan	Mr Paul Flynn	Mr Patrick Cormack
Sir John Farr	Mr Eric Illsley	Mr Jacques Arnold
Mr Alex Eadie	Mr Roger Gale	

That this House commends the recently revised Approved Code of Practice which followed the Health and Safety (First Aid) Regulations 1981 (Health and Safety at Work etc Act 1974) and which now requires that every employer of more than 50 people should ensure the on site availability of a qualified first aider and believes the same requirement should apply to children in schools; moreover recognises the value of teaching first or emergency aid in schools; applauds the initiative of the St John Ambulance in issuing its publication Emergency Aid in Schools which, accompanied by a video, shows how children can be taught a basic course between the ages of 10 and 15 years so that they are competent in assessing emergency situations, restarting breathing and circulation, dealing with bleeding, shock and unconsciousness especially resulting from drug or solvent abuse and burns and scalds and so qualifying for the St John Ambulance Three Cross Emergency Aid Award; and congratulates the six children who this year received the St John Ambulance's Robert Balchin Award for putting those skills to the best possible use by saving or attempting to save life.

Source: Parliamentary copyright

EDMs will sometimes be sponsored by one of the opposition parties, or factions within a party, in which case they are only likely to win support from one side of the House. For pressure groups, however, it is nearly always more useful to try and get an all-party EDM tabled. You can then try and get as many MPs as possible to sign the motion, in order to demonstrate the depth of support for the issue. If you are asking an MP to support an EDM, make sure you give the EDM's number, which will enable it to be identified quickly, or else a copy of it from the notice paper.

The original choice of sponsors, whose names will go down before the motion on the notice paper, is very important. You will need to find six MPs from across the parties who are respected by their colleagues and who will, ideally, help you recruit signatories. Getting over one hundred signatures is difficult; getting two hundred is exceptional. The few EDMs since 1980 that have attracted over three hundred signatures include those on civil rights for disabled people, road traffic reduction, the merchant navy, pardons for executed soldiers, and children in prostitution and pornography. The EDM given in the box above eventually pulled in a phenomenal 413 signatories; it is quoted as it appeared in the notice paper one day when it had so far mustered 66 supporters.

Adjournment debates

Adjournment debates provide a rare opportunity to get a minister to talk on the record about a specific issue for as long as 15 minutes. There is usually one adjournment debate at close of business on every sitting day, lasting half an hour. The MP kicks off, outlining her concerns, and then the minister replies. The debate usually ends simply with the MP getting a chance to come back and then the minister concluding, but this may vary, with contributions brought in from other MPs if there is time. On occasion, with the debate taking place late at night or in the early hours of the morning, there will literally be no other MPs in the chamber. There is no division.

MPs apply for adjournment debates to the Speaker's office by Wednesday evening and the debates for the following week, decided by ballot, are announced the following day (one adjournment debate a week is actually allocated by the Speaker, rather than by ballot). Some MPs apply automatically every week.

The one significant limitation on content is that the debate cannot be used to press for legislation. It is best, however, to choose quite a limited subject, so that the minister can be pinned down, and the subject must clearly be one for which a government minister carries responsibility. MPs sometimes use adjournment debates to raise constituency issues.

It is important to realise, particularly if you are dealing with an inexperienced MP, that it is not the MP's speech which you have to try and influence, but that of the minister. It is quite hard for the minister to speak on an issue for as long as 15 minutes and not say something of substance; it is also difficult to be relentlessly negative for that time and still appear reasonable. The minister, therefore, may well be drawn into making a concession, even if it is just a expression of sympathy with part of your aims which you can then quote subsequently. It is often a good idea to brief the minister's office on the background to the issue, so that the debate is as constructive as possible, but discuss this with your MP and keep him informed of what you do.

A succession of timed adjournment debates or private members' debates are also now held on Tuesday and Wednesday mornings in Westminster Hall. Once again, these are allocated by ballot.

Other opportunities

There are numerous other opportunities for the astute lobbyist or politician to raise an issue in Parliament. Some of these occur with little notice and may only be exploitable in practice if you have already established a good relationship with an MP or peer. Ask your supporters in Parliament for their advice on how you can get your concerns on the agenda.

▼ *Ministerial statements*
Ministers often make statements in the House, reporting to Parliament a government decision on anything from the financing of local authorities to the future of hospitals in London. MPs get the chance to ask questions. Every Thursday the Leader of the House, a Cabinet minister, makes a statement listing the next week's business in the Commons, followed by what are known as business questions. These are very wide-ranging, with MPs bringing up almost any issue in the context of what is being, or should be, debated the following week, although the Leader of the House is often studiously non-committal in reply.

▼ *Points of order*
If a matter is very urgent, an MP can bring it up when the House is full under pretext of raising a point of order, or he can seek an emergency debate. Both types of intervention are usually given short shrift by the Speaker.

▼ *Private notice questions*
An MP can also raise an urgent matter by seeking to ask a private notice question at the close of question time on any given day. The MP has to apply to the Speaker before noon and the department concerned is immediately informed. PNQs are only allowed if the matter is genuinely urgent and of public importance, such as the wreck of an oil tanker or an outbreak of violence.

▼ *Starred questions (Lords)*

The House of Lords has its own version of many of the procedures described so far in this section. Of particular note is the starred question. This is similar to an oral question in the Commons, but it is addressed to the government as a whole rather than to an individual minister, and the supplementary questions and replies tend to go on for longer. On average it is also easier to get a starred question asked, partly because there is no departmental rota so questions concerning the work of different departments can be taken on the same day.

▼ *Presentation bills and ten-minute-rule bills*

A very important opportunity exists for MPs to promote legislative ideas by presenting draft bills or introducing bills under the ten-minute rule. These are varieties of private members' legislation and are covered in the relevant section below.

Finally, something should be said about two techniques for raising issues which hark back to the campaigning methods of yesteryear: petitions and mass lobbies.

A petition can be presented to Parliament by an MP when the House is sitting. There is no chance to have a debate, or even make a speech, but if the MP decides to present the petition formally, she can read out in the chamber what the petition is for. Parliamentary petitions must be specifically (and respectfully) addressed to the House of Commons; many follow the traditional wording, as laid out in the box overleaf.

The petition must be handwritten and not typed, printed or photocopied. If the signatures go on to more than one sheet, the 'prayer' of the petition (that is, the paragraph beginning 'Wherefore') should be repeated at the top of each sheet; on these subsequent sheets the prayer can be printed or photocopied. Everybody signing the petition must write their address after their signature. Before going out and getting signatures, it is a good idea to check with the clerk of public petitions in the House of Commons journal office that a draft petition is likely to be acceptable for presentation. After it has been presented, the petition will receive a reply from the relevant minister, printed in 'Votes and Proceedings', part of the Vote Bundle.

Collecting endless signatures for a petition may have spin-offs in terms of consciousness-raising or fundraising, but it is barely noticed in the House and carries little clout with government departments. It is a lot of effort for little parliamentary effect.

Much the same could be said of the mass lobby. Although demonstrations or marches cannot take place in or around Westminster on days when Parliament is sitting, a large number of people can turn up at the same time to lobby their MPs on the same issue. Such mass lobbies can only take place while the House is actually sitting

Traditional wording for petitions to Parliament

To the Honourable the Commons of the United Kingdom of Great Britain and Northern Ireland in Parliament assembled.

The Humble Petition of [*insert description of petitioner(s)*],
Sheweth
    That [*describe circumstances for which attention is sought*].

Wherefore your Petitioner(s) pray(s) that your honourable House [*insert aim of petition*].

And your Petitioner(s), as in duty bound, will ever pray, &c.

After these words, signatures and addresses only should follow, and nothing else.

(after 2.30pm Mondays and Tuesdays, 9.30am Wednesdays and Fridays and 11.30am on Thursdays). All lobbyists must go through the standard security check at St Stephen's entrance. The Sergeant at Arms' office estimates that over the course of a mass lobby up to a thousand people can be admitted to Central Lobby to try and see their MPs, and a further thousand can have meetings with MPs in the Grand Committee Room or the interview rooms off Westminster Hall (note that these rooms can only be booked by an MP).

If your members or supporters come from different areas, involving them in a mass lobby can help them feel less isolated and closer to the centre of the action. Making their own case to their representative in Parliament can also be an empowering experience for marginalised groups. On a different note, some of the most effective mass lobbies of recent years have involved groups of disabled people, where the very difficulty of coordinating wheelchair access to the Palace of Westminster pushed the message home.

But mass lobbies can also lead to intense irritation. Invariably many people will not be able to see their MP because he is busy on parliamentary business or not even in Westminster that afternoon, or the time they know their MP is free will pass while they are still waiting in the queue (it is worthwhile for lobbyists to inform their MP in advance that they are coming and to make sure he will be around, but inadvisable to make actual appointments). Mass lobbies are often organised around a piece of legislation going through Parliament, but if there is a debate on at the time of the lobby many key MPs will be in the Commons chamber waiting to speak.

If you are thinking of organising a big lobby, get in touch with Police Operations at the Palace of Westminster (020 7219 6882) who will be able to tell you whether anyone else is planning anything that day, and to send you a leaflet on arrangements for mass lobbies. This gives the basic rules and provides useful advice. Organisers of mass lobbies also need to inform the special events office at Charing Cross police station (020 7321 7524).

Lobbying on government bills

The genesis of a piece of government legislation was described in the last chapter. By the time it is first considered by Parliament a bill is already at quite an advanced stage.

Major bills will be announced in the Queen's speech, with which each parliamentary year, or session, begins, usually in November. The various stages through which the bill then progresses, until it finally receives Royal Assent and becomes law, are displayed in influence map 10 (note that this begins where influence map 8 leaves off). To pass into law and become an Act of Parliament, a public bill must complete all its parliamentary stages in the same session in which it was introduced. This rule creates a considerable pressure of time which, with the increasing size of governments' legislative programmes, means that the strongest tactic of the parliamentary opposition is simply to delay. Minor concessions can be won in exchange for enabling debate on a bill to progress.

The first reading of a bill is a purely formal occasion, with no opportunity for debate, but it marks the stage at which the bill will be first published (occasionally the government now publishes a bill in draft form first, for consultation purposes). All bills are available from the Stationery Office. In the printed copy of a bill, the text and the contents list, or 'Arrangement of clauses', are preceded by an explanatory and financial memorandum, which provides a brief explanation of what each clause in the bill is intended to do. The financial memorandum notes the financial implications for government resources of particular measures and can be a useful indication of the size of scope of a measure.

Second reading follows in ten days or so (the date can be easily gleaned from newspapers or from the *Weekly Information Bulletin*). The debate at second reading covers the principles of the bill, including what it does and does not contain, but will not cover detailed discussion of individual measures. In addition to briefing relevant MPs and encouraging supportive ones to raise your concerns in the debate, send copies of briefing material to the House of Commons library, where MPs often go to seek information. Speaking in the second reading debate will also increase the chances of an MP being chosen as a key player in the next stage of the bill's progress: committee.

Committee

The standing committees which consider bills are standing in name only, since their membership changes with each new bill. MPs are formally appointed to them by what is known as the committee of selection, but in practice the whips play a major role. Party strength in committee reflects that in the House of Commons as a whole. Standing committees always include a minister from the department sponsoring the legislation, an opposition front-bencher and the ubiquitous whips. Committees considering government bills usually meet on Tuesday and Thursday mornings, with further sittings added if more time is needed. The names of committee members will often be announced the Thursday before the committee first meets.

Influence Map 10: Passage of a government bill through Parliament

Government	Parliament	Interest Groups
After much hard work, officials take a breather	Bill published	Confirm major concerns with allies, decide lobbying priorities
Government whips ascertain backbench reaction to bill and marshall support	- HOUSE OF COMMONS **Second Reading** *Debate on principle of bill, followed by division*	Brief sympathetic MPs and those with an interest in the issue(s)
Officials produce amendments to close loop-holes and tighten drafting	**Committee Stage** *Standing committee of 18 or more MPs consider bill in detail, voting on amendments*	Brief committee members; decide on major lines of amendment
Government makes concessions, often by agreeing to redraft opposition amendments and table them itself		Brief members to table amendments; attend meetings / Clarify detailed concerns with officials
Government reverses some defeats suffered in Committee	**Report Stage and Third Reading** *In Report, further amendments to the revised bill are considered on floor of the House. Third Reading is either a formality or consists of a short general debate on content of the bill as a whole; division possible*	Push further amendments; ask MPs to talk to whips
	- HOUSE OF LORDS **Second Reading** *Similar to Commons; but division rare*	
Similar to Commons, perhaps with more effort to brief – and pressurise – peers not of the government party	**Committee Stage** *Detailed amendments considered in 'committee of the whole House'* **Report Stage** *Similar to Commons*	Similar to Commons, but with special attention to crossbench peers; possibility of getting major amendments passed on 'conscience' issues
	Third Reading and Passing *Brief debate in which amendments may be considered and voted on. Followed by short debate on motion 'That the bill do now pass' (often a formality)*	
Government may reverse some defeats suffered in the Lords	- HOUSE OF COMMONS / LORDS **Commons consider Lords amendments** *Commons consider amendments by Lords; if the Commons reverse or amend them, the Lords then consider the Commons amendments, until both Houses agree the text*	
Officials draft regulations under the Act, often in consultation with outside groups	**Royal Assent** *The bill becomes an Act and passes into law* **Statutory Instruments passed** *Debate possible on motion to annul or approve SIs; no opportunity to table amendments*	Talk to officials; respond to consultation drafts

Standing committees meet in public session and it is worth attending one or two to get the feel of how they work. The public galleries in committee rooms are small, so on a major bill you will need to be there early.

Amendments tabled by members of the committee are selected for debate by the chair, a senior MP chosen from the Speaker's panel whose role is impartial. Amendments can seek to add, alter or delete words from the text of the bill, or even add whole new clauses, so long as they are broadly within the scope of the bill's long title (i.e. the passage on the bill that begins 'A bill to …'). Normal procedure is for amendments to be considered clause by clause, in order, followed by consideration of new clauses and then of any schedules to the bill. The chair may decide to group some amendments for discussion together.

When briefing MPs to table amendments it is customary to quote the clause number, page number and line number. Put each suggested amendment on a separate page with a brief explanation of the point of the amendment. Use the language of the bill itself to guide you in drafting amendments, but don't worry unduly about the finer points of phraseology: if an amendment is accepted by government, it will probably be redrafted by the government's parliamentary counsel to knock it into shape.

Committee provides the best opportunity for outside groups to alter a bill in Parliament. Government backbenchers are still the primary target for lobbyists, but the size of committee means that not many of them have to be turned to start putting real pressure on the government. However, although many more government defeats are sustained in committee than on the floor of the House, government will have the power to reverse them when the bill returns to the Commons chamber for its later stages. Tactics at committee stage are therefore often geared towards pushing the minister to accept minor amendments or make concessions. Many amendments will not be pressed to a division, but will be withdrawn by the promoting MP having extracted clarification from the minister or an undertaking to redraft or consider the matter again.

Major or complex bills can spend several weeks in committee. If things drag on too long, particularly if the opposition are filibustering, the government may introduce a timetable motion, or guillotine, on the floor of the House which limits further debate on the bill to a set timetable.

Report and final stages

At report stage the whole House considers the reworked bill as amended in committee, and debates further amendments. At this stage most of the amendments selected for debate by the Speaker will be government amendments, some of them tabled following undertakings made by the minister in committee. Amendments debated in committee cannot be reintroduced at report. Some lobbyists wait until report to table major amendments, where the resulting publicity will be much greater, but this is a dangerous strategy as their amendments may well not even be selected for debate. Third reading, usually following immediately after, rarely provides opportunities for lobbyists and may be just a formality.

Leaving the Commons, the bill then goes through the same stages in the House of Lords. The main differences are that committee stage is taken on the floor of the House and that amendments can be tabled at third reading. In recent years their Lordships have been prepared to alter major bills significantly, in fields such as education or criminal justice, passing amendments of a scope not acceptable in the government-dominated Commons. However, their revisions will always be considered again by the House of Commons, until the two Houses agree a text. As the cries of 'Unconstitutional' get louder, the government can put great pressure on the Lords to compromise. Note that the Lords is not able to consider money measures or those that involve taxation.

Some politically uncontentious bills, or those of a very technical nature, start their life in the Lords, later progressing to the Commons (otherwise the stages are exactly the same as normal). Such bills are denoted by '(H.L.)' after the title. The bill which became the Charities Act 1992 is one example.

Once the bill receives Royal Assent and becomes an Act of Parliament, the numbered parts of the Act are no longer known as clauses and sub-clauses, but become sections and sub-sections. Delegated legislation, or regulations introduced under an authority given in the Act, are drafted by civil servants (see chapter 13). It is at this drafting stage that regulations can be seriously influenced by outside groups: once the regulations or orders go before Parliament in the form of Statutory Instruments the chances of affecting them are negligible.

Private members' bills

Individual backbench MPs may also sponsor new legislation in Parliament. Private members' bills, as they are known, come in three types: ten minute rule bills, presentation bills and, most importantly, ballot bills. (Note that private members' bills are another form of *public* bill; *private* bills are those which give powers to, or regulate the conduct of, particular organisations or individuals, usually private or statutory corporations, or local authorities.)

Ten minute rule bills and presentation bills stand practically no chance of ever being passed and are simply a means of drawing attention to an issue or enabling new legislative ideas to be discussed in Parliament. Under the ten minute rule, an MP speaks for ten minutes seeking leave to introduce a bill, followed by a speech of the same length by another MP opposing the motion. Ten minute rule bills get a prime parliamentary slot, on Tuesday and Wednesday afternoons following question time when the House – and the press gallery – are quite full.

Ten minute rule bill places are made available to MPs on a first-come, first-served basis, with the lucky MP being the one who is first outside the Public Bill Office at 10 am exactly three weeks before the day when she hopes to seek leave to introduce her bill. MPs often arrive at dawn or even sleep outside the office all night in order to try and secure their place. Whether this is a very grown up way of allocating parliamentary time you will have to decide for yourself, but at least it makes a change from the customary lottery for deciding between private members.

The reason why MPs are prepared to go to such lengths is that ten minute rule bills can attract a lot of attention, both inside Parliament and outside. They regularly feature in the national news, particularly if the parliamentary day has otherwise been rather pedestrian. The fact that they are ostensibly about introducing legislation helps to arouse interest in the media and among the general public.

This last point is also true of presentation bills. Any MP is able formally to present a bill and have it printed, although the chances of it being debated are negligible. But presenting a bill in this way, or introducing one under the ten minute rule, enables an MP to have it reported in the local or even national press that he introduced a bill in Parliament. Most press articles will contain the give-away phrase 'the bill is unlikely to succeed due to lack of parliamentary time' but the great majority of the public will fail to realise that the whole thing is really just a publicity stunt. I have never understood whether the journalists concerned fail to realise it too or are happy to collude in pulling the wool over the eyes of their readers, but either way the MP, and the cause, get their publicity.

Very occasionally, a completely non-controversial measure will be introduced as a presentation bill, which with government and all-party backing may pass into law (for this to happen, however, not even one MP can object). Presentation and ten minute rule bills may also be reintroduced in a subsequent session as a serious attempt at legislation in the form of a ballot bill (see overleaf), in which case the ten minute rule debate, if adroitly handled, will have been a useful test of the parliamentary water, and a spur to get the wider campaign moving.

Many presentation or ten minute rule bills, however, are concerned with measures which, in the contemporary climate, would never stand a realistic chance of being passed even if the parliamentary time were available. Such bills are usually best if they are very short and simply drafted, so they can be instantly understood by the layperson. Even so, putting a controversial measure in the form of legislation can often prompt a leap of the political imagination and the printed bills make very effective campaign materials. A bill introduced by Mildred Gordon MP to take account of women's unpaid work is reproduced in its entirety opposite. Tony Benn's Commonwealth of Britain Bill was rather more ambitious in calling for the replacement of the Queen by an elected president, the abolition of the House of Lords and the creation of national Parliaments for England, Scotland and Wales. The bill was introduced in successive Parliaments, achieved national press coverage and was even used as a study text for college courses.

Ballot bills

Ballot bills, often referred to simply as private members' bills, are the only real chance ordinary MPs – and lobbyists – have for getting new legislation on the statute book. As always, parliamentary time is the key factor.

There are only a limited number of days each session, always Fridays, when private members' legislation can be debated. A ballot is therefore held at the start of each parliamentary session to decide which MPs have precedence in introducing bills. Of the 400 or so MPs who enter the ballot, 20 names are drawn, but in fact only the top seven can be fairly sure of getting a full second reading debate.

As the chances of coming in the first seven are slim, few MPs will have decided in advance what their bill might be on. Once the ballot is drawn, the lucky MPs will have nearly three weeks to decide on the subject of their bill, and will be inundated with offers from interest groups, charities, and indeed government, many of whom will have draft bills already prepared. MPs who draw a high place will usually be keen to use the opportunity fully by introducing a measure which has a realistic chance of becoming law. As the success of any bill ultimately requires the support, or at least acquiescence, of government, such private members' bills tend to be focused in scope and, although often controversial, not on issues heavily divided on party-political lines. MPs coming lower down in the ballot will be more ready to champion politically contentious bills, on the theory that if you are going to go down, you might as well go down in a blaze of glory.

What is there in a pressure group's bill that is likely to attract an MP? Obviously it will need to be on a subject in which the MP is interested, and where she feels legislation is necessary. Experienced pressure groups secure assurances from friendly MPs that, should they draw a good place in the ballot, they will introduce a bill on the group's issue. (But MPs have a habit of sliding out of such promises; some swift footwork is still needed from the group when the ballot results are announced.) A bill should be realistic and able to attract support from a wide range of other MPs. Ideally it should also propose something special or of key importance in its field, something to fire the imagination and draw the media glare. The amount

A ten minute rule bill

Counting Women's Unremunerated Work 1

A

BILL

TO

Require government departments and other public A.D. 1989
bodies to include in the production of statistics relating to the gross domestic product and other accounts
a calculation of the unremunerated contribution of
women; and to include this calculation in the Gross
National Product.

W HEREAS women do two-thirds of the world's work
but only receive five per cent. of its income and own
only one per cent. of its assets; and
Whereas the unremunerated contribution of women to all
5 aspects and sectors of development should be recognised; and
Whereas paragraph 120 of Forward Looking Strategies for
the Advancement of Women to the Year 2000 has been agreed by
Governments of the world and ratified by the United Nations
General Assembly on 26 November 1985.
10 Be it therefore enacted by the Queen's most Excellent Majesty, by and with the advice and consent of the Lords Spiritual
and Temporal, and Commons, in this present Parliament assembled, and by the authority of the same, as follows:—

1.—(1) All government departments and other public bodies   Calculation of
15 shall include in the production of statistics relating to the gross   unremunerated
domestic product, a calculation of the contribution of women's   contribution.
unremunerated work to the formal and informal sectors of the
economy.

(2) It shall be the responsibility of these bodies to quantify
the unremunerated contribution of women to agriculture, food
20 production, reproduction and household activities, and the responsibility of the Central Statistical Office to include this quan-
tification in the Gross National Product.

2. This Act may be cited as the Counting Women's Unremu-   Short title.
nerated Work Act 1989.

[Bill 114]   50/2

of research and lobbying back-up a pressure group can guarantee will be crucial. Sponsoring legislation is a major undertaking and if a group can help deliver parliamentary support and offer staff time to work on the bill its pitch will be taken much more seriously. For the MP, choosing a bill is a matter of weighing the attractiveness of a particular measure with its chances of success and it is probably fair to say that as MPs get more experienced, they lean more towards the latter criterion.

Some pressure groups swear by the simple tactic of getting there first, and take part in a mad horse race round Parliament when the ballot results are announced (the second Thursday of the parliamentary session, usually in November) to try and locate and pin down the relevant MPs. While getting in early has its advantages, many MPs won't finally decide until they have to.

An added complication, particularly with government backbenchers, is that the government whips will have a number of 'handout' bills which they offer to MPs to sponsor. From the whips' point of view, this enables them to get through a useful measure for which there is no space in the government's legislative programme and also keeps the MP out of trouble. As far as the MP is concerned, government support will boost considerably his chances of success, getting a new statute to his name, as well as earning him a few brownie points towards political preferment.

The second reading debate on a bill will normally take up most of the day's business on a Friday. Before the end of the day (that is, before the adjournment debate at 2.30pm) the bill's promoters have to 'secure the closure' in order to prevent the debate being adjourned and the bill effectively losing its priority in the timetable. This means calling a division which not only has to be won, but which at least 100 MPs must vote in favour. Getting 100 supporters to stay in Parliament on a Friday when what they really want to do is talk to their constituents, visit factories or just go home, is not easy and requires an extensive lobbying effort by the sponsoring MP, her colleagues and by any supporting pressure groups.

By the time private members' bills return to the floor of the House after their committee stage they will usually take precedence over other bills still waiting for their second reading. The only real hope for bills still in the queue at this juncture is to try and get a second reading without debate, but only one MP has to shout 'Object' in order to foil their chances, and a government whip is usually happy to oblige. (It is this queue which, in theory, presentation bills and unopposed ten minute rule bills have to join, which is why they never stand a chance of progressing.)

For the bills which get as far as Report, things only get tougher. Not only are 100 votes still required to secure the closure on a debate on an amendment, but opponents of the bill are able to deploy a range of delaying tactics. MP after MP makes a time-wasting speech; on occasion they may not even have anything against your bill, but simply want to ensure there is no time for the next bill in the queue! In 1994 the government provoked an uproar when it ensured that a bill on civil rights for disabled people ran out of time by briefing MPs to table a raft of spurious amendments, but the tactic is not uncommon. Once a private member's bill has passed its Commons stages it must progress to the House of Lords and go through exactly the same stages as other bills.

It is important to realise that success in private members' legislation is never just about mustering voting power, as you can always be out-gunned by government. It is more akin to the process of negotiation and pressure described in the section on amending legislation, but writ large. Ivan Lawrence's bill to set up a national lottery for good causes failed to get enough support at second reading but was instrumental in persuading the Conservatives to include the measure as a manifesto commitment at the 1992 election. Roger Berry's bills on disability rights in 1994 and the establishment of a disability rights commission in 1998 also pressured the government to legislate on those issues.

Examples of private members' bills that themselves became legislation include the Public Interest Disclosure Bill to protect whistle blowers in 1998 and a bill to regulate the welfare of dogs kept for breeding in 1999.

Successful private members' bills can be controversial, then, so long as they are also credible. Abortion was first legalised as a result of a private member's bill (David Steel, 1967) and many serious attempts to curtail abortion subsequently have taken a similar form. The pressure group which has perhaps made most consistent use of private members' legislation as a tool of reform is the Freedom of Information Campaign. Amongst several ambitious bills that eventually fell by the wayside but kept up the pressure on government, the Campaign promoted a quartet of private members' bills that did succeed in becoming law, each hacking a chunk out of the edifice of official secrecy: the Access to Personal Files Act 1987, the Environment and Safety Information Act 1988, the Access to Medical Reports Act 1988 and the Access to Health Records Act 1990. The Campaign's efforts eventually led to the Blair government introducing fuller – although flawed – freedom of information legislation.

Select committees

The practice of having a select committee of MPs or peers to examine the work of government or of Parliament in a given field is a long-established one, but the current system of select committees shadowing major government departments dates from 1979. Allegedly regarded by Margaret Thatcher as a device to give MPs something to do and keep them happy, she is supposed to have referred to them as 'occupational therapy for backbenchers'. If the story is true, her comment was a serious misjudgement, as select committees have turned out to be a highly effective means of exposing and thereby influencing government practices.

Departmental select committees usually have 11 members, reflecting party strength in the House, and conduct most of their sessions in public. A committee chooses one of its members to be the chair, who may sometimes come from one of the opposition parties. The committee's task is to examine the expenditure, administration and policy of the department(s) within its brief and associated public bodies. This it does by choosing subjects for investigation, inviting evidence and examining witnesses from both inside government and outside, and publishing reports.

The power of select committees to require witnesses, including government ministers and senior civil servants, to appear before them and answer questions is perhaps their biggest advantage over other forms of parliamentary scrutiny. Select committees have certainly shown themselves ready to use this and their other investigative powers to expose malpractice or incompetence and seriously embarrass the government, for example in 1994 in the foreign affairs committee's inquiry into the linking of arms deals and development aid over the Pergau dam project in Malaysia. The fact that select committees are all-party committees with government backbenchers in the majority means that their reports and published evidence are taken very seriously by the media and can prove especially painful for the executive.

The great drawback of the select committee system is that by the time a committee comes to write its report, it will often be too late to influence the administrative or policy-making process. On some issues, committees have also split on party lines, with opposition members refusing to agree a draft report and even issuing an alternative or dissenting report of their own. But it is undeniable that the very fact that they might have to account for their actions in public before a select committee has had an effect on the work of government officials.

Select committees generally announce in a news release the start of a new inquiry and write to known specialists or major organisations in the field inviting evidence. Anyone can offer to submit evidence; this is best done by contacting the clerk of the relevant committee at the House of Commons, who will give you the terms of reference of the inquiry. Written evidence is best submitted in the form of a concise factual paper with numbered paragraphs, including any recommendations for action. Alternatively, if the evidence is very short it could be put in a letter. You should include a note on your organisation and its authority or expertise in the area under scrutiny. Getting the opportunity to give oral evidence is more difficult, as committees will usually only have time to hear a small number of key witnesses. In any case witnesses are usually expected to give evidence in written form first, so it is easiest to include a request to give oral evidence with your written submission.

Some select committee inquiries go on for many months, while others are much shorter. Committees often have more than one inquiry on the go at a time. There is an increasing trend for committees to choose as subjects for inquiry issues that are already in the news. Having realised that much of their influence comes through the media, they certainly try to pick issues which will catch public interest. A few examples might be of interest: in 2000 the health committee was looking at tobacco and health risks; the foreign affairs committee was considering Kosovo; the agriculture committee was looking at segregation of genetically-modified foods, environmental regulation and farming, and trade liberalisation and the WTO round; and the home affairs committee was considering the double jeopardy rule, controls over firearms, and managing people with severe personality disorders.

Select committees decide on new subjects for inquiry while the current inquiry is still in progress. The committee will usually have a topic or topics in mind, which may be supplanted if something more interesting crops up. This makes it tricky to know when or how to approach a committee to take up your own issue as a suitable subject of inquiry. A letter sent in good time to the clerk, outlining your reasoning with any supporting material, might be useful but almost certainly will not be enough. Ideally you would want to catch the interest of the chair and/or some other members of the committee, but as select committee members cannot really be lobbied as such, this needs to be done tactfully.

In addition to the departmental committees, there are a number of other specialist select committees. Of particular importance are the two committees, one composed of peers and the other of MPs, which consider European legislative proposals (see next chapter), and the mighty public accounts committee, which shines a spotlight on the probity and efficiency with which public money is spent.

The public accounts committee will rarely interview representatives from pressure groups although it does invite relevant written evidence. It regularly spends a couple of hours grilling a permanent secretary as accounting officer for a department. Much of its influence derives from the fact that unlike other select committees, which tend to have a capable but skeleton staff, the PAC is backed up by the information and expertise of the National Audit Office.

15   The European Union and the international scene

Nobody is leaving anybody else alone and isn't ever again going to – Clifford Geertz

In a growing number of areas of policy-making, more decisions are made in Europe than are made at a national level. This includes issues as diverse as free trade and equality between women and men. Arguments about federalism aside, what happens in the UK will be increasingly affected by what happens in the European Union and the wider world. The global village is now a reality not only in terms of communication, but in power relations.

For pressure groups, lobbying the European institutions is guided by one rule over all others: the need to present a *European* case, or one with a wider brief than just the UK. Protectionist lobbies, or those that seek to advance or protect the interests of just one member state of the European Union, find it very hard to make headway. It is important to identify how the issue on which you are working affects people in other member states in order to build arguments and enlist support. On many social issues, this is made easier by the range of European non-profit networks that now exist.

The work of the European Community expanded rapidly in the eighties, but was always focused on achieving and maintaining the internal market, or the free movement of goods, services and people across frontiers. To this primarily inward-looking task, the Maastricht Treaty on European Union added the development of common foreign and defence policies as well as greater cooperation in the fields of justice and home affairs. It also extended the competence of the European institutions to act on social issues (further developed by the Treaty of Amsterdam in 1997). The Union is comprised of the same member states as the European Community, and many commentators have taken to using the term European Union, or EU, when referring to either. In fact, the European Community or EC still exists, and is the legal authority under the European treaties for work in traditional policy areas, including the internal market.

The European power structure

The three main European institutions are the Commission, the Parliament and the Council of Ministers.

▼ The European Commission initiates and drafts legislation, is responsible for ensuring that European law is implemented and manages numerous funds and assistance programmes. Headed by commissioners, including a President, it is based in Brussels and is staffed by some 19,000 officials.

▼ The Council of Ministers is Europe's decision-maker, with the key role of approving legislation. Consisting of ministers from each member state, the Council meets in Brussels and Luxembourg and has a permanent secretariat in Brussels.

▼ The European Parliament comments on and amends draft legislation. Increasingly, it has the power to block certain proposals. Based mainly in Strasbourg, the Parliament is made up of elected MEPs from all the member states.

One of the common problems that arises in understanding how the European institutions work is that it is easy to make the assumption that Parliament, ministers and officials in Europe have broadly similar roles to Parliament, ministers and officials in the UK. As can be seen from the descriptions above, this is not the case. Whereas in the UK it is government ministers who sponsor the majority of legislation, in Europe the responsibility for initiating and directing the legislative programme falls to officials in the Commission. And although the legislative role of the European Parliament has increased in recent years, the principal legislative authority in the EU is the Council of Ministers.

The Commission, Parliament and Council of Ministers are each covered in greater detail below, with a description of how they can be influenced. Influence map 11 illustrates how they interlock, together with other important European institutions.

The authority for decisions made by the European institutions derives from the European treaties, principally the Treaty of Rome, as amended by the Single European Act and the Maastricht and Amsterdam Treaties. In initiating legislative proposals, the Commission is therefore in a very different position to national governments: the Commission's task is limited to carrying forward a programme of work agreed, albeit in very broad terms, in the treaties. Formally, all legislative proposals must start from the Commission, although what passes between it and the Council of Ministers is clearly influential.

The presidency of the Council of Ministers is rotated between member states every six months. At least once every six months, the heads of government of member states meet in a summit known – confusingly – as the European Council. At these meetings the nature

Influence Map 11: The European decision-making process

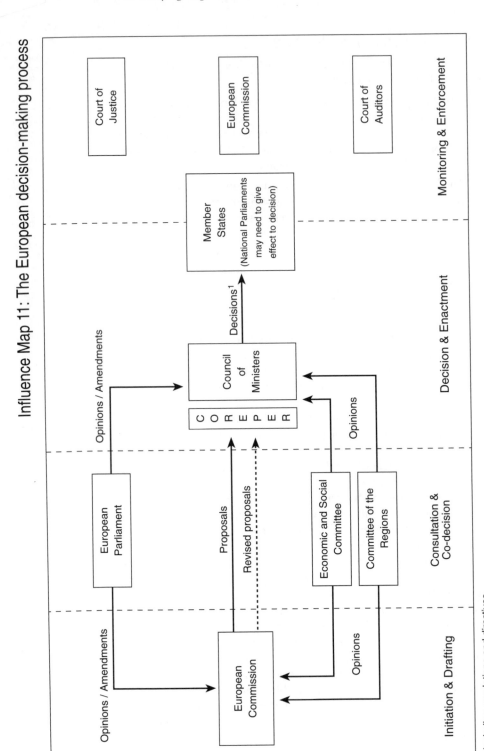

1. Including regulations and directives

of the European Union as a compromise between the varying interests of different member states is most clearly apparent, although it is also visible in the day-to-day work of the European institutions, in particular the Council of Ministers. Negotiations are underway for the current 15 members of the Union to be joined by Cyprus, Hungary, Poland, Estonia, Slovenia and the Czech Republic, followed by others.

The presidency of the Council is theoretically a neutral role, but holding the presidency does give a member state the opportunity to progress debate and decisions on certain issues. When the UK held the presidency in 1998, human rights groups here lobbied the government on the need to strengthen European cooperation on the control of arms exports, leading to an EU code of conduct on arms control.

All the EU's operational programmes are managed by the Commission, which with the Commission's own administrative costs make up all but a few per cent of the EU budget. Over 45% of that budget is still spent on the common agricultural policy, with the next largest budget item being 'structural' policies, or assistance for less developed regions and the reintegration of unemployed people in the job market. More information on obtaining grants from the Commission is given in chapter 3. The Court of Auditors, based in Luxembourg, monitors the EU's financial activities and examines its accounts. As well as an annual report on the EU's finances, it produces reports on specific areas of policy.

Sources of information on the European Union

The European institutions and everyone who works with them often appear to be engaged in an enormous conspiracy to send you voluminous quantities of detailed information, in the process helping to obscure the fact that you are not getting the information you really need. While the institutions conduct their business relatively openly, there is a real problem in acquiring promptly documentation used for decision-making.

Vacher's European Companion is an indispensable reference guide to the people, offices and functions in the European institutions. It includes complete listings of the Directorates-General of the Commission down to unit level, and of MEPs and committees of the Parliament. *Vacher's* is updated four times a year (annual subscription £53, single copies £16.50) and is available from Vacher Dod Publishing Ltd (see appendix B).

The *Official Journal* of the European Commission appears daily: the C-series gives information on programmes and decisions and the L-series is on legislation. The *OJ* is available on subscription from the Stationery Office, but recent issues can be accessed free of charge on the world wide web at *http://europa.eu.int*

The European Union web site at *http://europa.eu.int* provides access to the home pages of all the EU institutions, as well as publications, legislation, calendars, press releases and information on policies. The electronic contact directory for the EU institutions is called IDEA and can be searched either by name or by directorate or office.

Long before anything appears in the *OJ*, the Commission will have issued proposals which generally take the form of 'COM' documents. By the time the final versions are available from the Stationery Office, much water has often passed under the Euro-bridge, so the relevant officials in the Commission should be seen as the main source of such documents. Often, they will supply you with draft 'COM' documents without question; if you encounter problems, try other organisations in your field who may have established relations with the Commission, or the relevant government department in the UK.

General information on the EU

A number of organisations provide useful information on the European Union:

▾ The European Commission supports a network of European Public Information Centres and European Documentation Centres (attached to universities) throughout the UK. These keep up-to-date sets of EU publications; your local library should be able to advise you of the one nearest to you.

▾ The UK office of the European Parliament can provide up-to-date lists of MEPs and other basic information, and has a library which can be consulted by the public. The office is located at 2 Queen Anne's Gate, London SW1, Tel: 020 7227 4300.

▾ The Euro Citizen Action Service (ECAS) publishes a bi-monthly magazine called the *European Citizen* which gives up-to-date information and lobbying hints for associations or non-profit groups. It also runs a wider range of information/consultancy services to help such groups lobby the EU. ECAS is based at rue de la Concorde 53, B-1050 Brussels, Tel: 00 32 2 548 0490, *www.ecas.org*

Finally, of the books that are continually being added to the European information mountain, three may be of particular use to non-profit groups:

A Guide to European Union Funding is published by the Directory of Social Change (DSC) and details over 150 programmes relevant to non-profit groups. Includes examples of work that has been supported and practical tips on making an approach. 1999 edition – £18.95. Available from DSC, see appendix B for address.

Grants from Europe is published by NCVO and contains listings of grant sources and contacts in the Commission, as well as some general advice on exerting influence. 1997 edition – £12.50. Available from Hamilton House Mailings Ltd, see appendix B for address.

Networking in Europe is published by NCVO and also contains some general advice on exerting influence, in addition to listings of European non-profit networks. 1995 edition – £16.95. Available from Hamilton House Mailings Ltd.

The European Commission

The Commission, Europe's civil service, will nearly always provide the first point of contact on any given issue. It is divided into Directorates-General (DGs), each with its specific area of responsibility (see box). As bureaucracies go, it is not large: translators apart, the Commission has fewer than one twentieth of the staff of the UK civil service.

The top level in the Commission is the commissioners themselves, of whom there were 20 in 2000 (this may increase as new member states join the Union). They are essentially political appointments, with the names put forward by individual member states (the larger states put forward two commissioners each, the others only one). Once appointed, however, commissioners are honour-bound to act in the European interest, rather than representing the interests of the countries from which they come. A new Commission is appointed for a five-year term. In contrast to Whitehall, the appointment of a new Commission is accompanied by a major turnover in senior officials.

Each DG is headed by a senior official called the director-general, who is answerable to one of the commissioners. But commissioners also have a *cabinet*, or private office, usually dominated by officials of their own nationality, which is very influential. In practice the extent of the power held by an individual commissioner, both in relation to the Commission itself and to the DG(s) for which she is responsible, will partly depend on the strength of her personality and the political skills of her *chef de cabinet*.

A new proposal will first be drafted by an official in the relevant DG. Consultation with outside interest groups is extensive, but largely informal. The emphasis is on expert or scientific evidence. The point is often made that Commission officials are on the whole more open and accessible than Whitehall civil servants, but they don't advertise the fact and it is important to make your interest known and to do it early. Commission staff come from all the different member states, but English and French are widely spoken. The Commission switchboard is efficient (00 32 2 299 1111), but it is always easier to identify initially the part of the Commission relevant to your issue from the reference books or from outside contacts. Note that the Commission has one main postal address, but that offices are in fact spread around Brussels, so if you arrange a meeting make sure you know where you are going.

Once a draft proposal has been worked over by officials, it will pass to the commissioner's *cabinet*. The time it then takes to go for decision to a meeting of the Commission itself (i.e. of the commissioners) varies greatly, depending on the priority of the issue, but it can be very long. During this time there will be further input from a number of sources including national governments or experts, other DGs with an interest and outside groups. A consultative committee is often set up to advise on the proposal.

Directorates-General and Services of the European Commission

General Services

- ▼ Secretariat General
- ▼ Eurostat (statistics)
- ▼ Press & Communication
- ▼ Publications Office

Policies

- ▼ Agriculture
- ▼ Competition
- ▼ Economic & Financial Affairs
- ▼ Education & Culture
- ▼ Employment & Social Affairs
- ▼ Energy
- ▼ Enterprise
- ▼ Environment
- ▼ Fisheries
- ▼ Health & Consumer Protection
- ▼ Information Society
- ▼ Internal Market
- ▼ Joint Research Centre
- ▼ Justice & Home Affairs
- ▼ Regional Policy
- ▼ Research
- ▼ Taxation & Customs Union
- ▼ Transport

External Relations

- ▼ Common Service for External Relations
- ▼ Development
- ▼ Enlargement
- ▼ External Relations
- ▼ Humanitarian Aid Office (ECHO)
- ▼ Trade

Internal Services

- ▼ Budget
- ▼ European Anti-Fraud Office
- ▼ Financial Control
- ▼ Inspectorate General
- ▼ Joint Interpreting & Conferences
- ▼ Legal Service
- ▼ Personnel & Administration
- ▼ Translation Service

February 2000

The Commission meets once a week to approve proposals and take major decisions, unanimously if possible but, if not, by simple majority. Preparations for Commission meetings are made in a weekly meeting of *chefs de cabinet*. Clusters of commissioners involved on a particular issue may also meet in *ad hoc* groups. Non-controversial or routine proposals tend to be handled through 'written procedure', which means that they can be approved by senior officials, in the absence of objections from commissioners.

Progress on a proposal must be monitored throughout its gestation, however protracted, and representations made on successive drafts and to the different parts of the Commission that are involved. Don't expect your case to be remembered from months back, or that an official will diligently relay your views to the commissioner for you. Try and get an international group together to see the relevant commissioner about a proposal before it is considered by a meeting of the Commission (if you have done your networking, this should be easier than it sounds). At this level, it is not worth taking a delegation from just one member state.

In fact, the sooner you can establish the European credentials of your case, the better. Of all the institutions, the Commission is very much the guardian of the European ideal, tasked with the advancement of European integration. This does not imply that your own arguments have to be pro-European as such, merely that they should be reflected by other member states. If you can back your campaign with arguments and statistics based on the situation around Europe and expressions of support from other member states, your credibility will move onto a different plane.

Once a proposal has been approved by the Commission, it will progress to the Parliament, the Economic and Social Committee and the Council of Ministers (see influence map 11). That is not to say, however, that the Commission lets go. There is a French word *engrenage*, which refers to the 'interpenetration' or constant mixing of officials from different institutions, both national and European. Commission officials talk regularly, for example, with officials from COREPER (see below) and in formulating proposals will take into account what the Council of Ministers, or indeed the European Parliament, is likely to accept. Conversely, when a proposal goes off to be considered by the other institutions, the Commission will continue to play a pivotal role, moderating conflicting opinions, resolving technical issues and ready to prepare a revised proposal for consideration by the Council of Ministers.

The Council of Ministers and COREPER

The Council of Ministers is the perfect example of the general lobbying rule that the more powerful something is, the less accessible it is. The problem, in simplified terms, is this: when you talk to the Commission you are talking to Europe, of which you are a part; when you try and talk to the Council of Ministers, you are confronted with different countries, each with their own national interests.

Member states are represented at Council meetings by the minister responsible for the subject under discussion. Thus the Transport Council will be attended by transport ministers, and so on. Foreign ministers meet frequently in the powerful General Affairs Council. Some of the other Councils, such as those dealing with social affairs, development or health, only meet two or three times a year.

Many Council decisions are in practice made unanimously, although often only because deals have been struck. There is a system of qualified majority voting covering many policy areas, however, and this helps to prevent any one member state from blocking progress. It can only be used if the Commission is in agreement on a proposal, and it enabled much of the legislation needed to complete the single market to be pushed through after 1987. The votes of members are weighted according to population (the UK, France, Germany and Italy get the most) and just over two-thirds are needed to push through a decision. It is understood, however, that if the vital national interests of one member state are at stake, decision will be reached through agreement.

The obvious route for lobbying the Council is thus to lobby the national members, in particular your own country and the country holding the Presidency (see 'The European power structure' above). Bearing in mind how difficult it is to get even your own country to adopt an issue as in the national interest, it is probably a waste of time trying to lobby other member states directly. This must be done through national associations in the countries themselves. The priority will be to build links with associations in those countries due to hold the Presidency of the Council a good year ahead, so they can lobby their ministers well in advance.

When a proposal first arrives from the Commission it will be considered in one of the Council's numerous working parties, composed of the relevant officials from member states together with officials from their permanent representations in Brussels. Departmental contacts in Whitehall should tell you which UK officials are involved. Once the working party has trawled through the proposal, clearing outstanding technical issues and making suggestions, its report and the proposal are considered at a weekly meeting of COREPER, the Committee of Permanent Representatives. It is actually COREPER I, the deputies' committee, which considers matters in the social and environmental fields (COREPER II consists of ambassadors). Apart from determining whether a text is ready for decision by the Council of Ministers, much else will effectively be resolved at COREPER. The Committee, for example, decides whether a matter needs further negotiation by the politicians or whether it is ready for approval without discussion.

The UK's permanent representation in Brussels is known as UKREP (see appendix B for address). UKREP can send you a tiny user's guide which lists contact officials with their telephone numbers, or consult *http://ukrep.fco.gov.uk*

To appreciate the influence of the permanent representations it is only necessary to remember that the national ministers who attend Council meetings are invariably overworked, with European matters only one of their priorities, and often not the most pressing. A ministerial reshuffle back home may even change a national representative at a key stage in the negotiations. Here's what a former minister of trade, Alan Clark, had to say in his *Diaries*, writing with his usual perceptive candour:

'Not, really, that it makes the slightest difference to the conclusions of a meeting what ministers say at it. Everything is decided, horse-traded off, by officials at COREPER, the Committee of Permanent Representatives. The ministers arrive on the scene at the last minute, hot, tired, ill, or drunk (sometimes all of these together), read out their piece, and depart.

'Strange, really. Because the EC constitution is quite well drawn. The Council of Ministers is sovereign, and can/could boss COREPER around. But, as always in politics everywhere, democratic and autocratic, it's the chaps on the spot who call the shot.'

There is little hope of influencing issues of major national or international importance through officials at the permanent representations. This can only be done through national governments. However, many Euro-proposals are very technical in nature, carrying consequences in different member states that are often hard to predict, and in this case concerted briefing of national officials who are members of the relevant working party can pay off.

Council business has become more open following a 1993 decision to give the public a right of access to Council documents. However, getting hold of a working party's report promptly is often difficult (business at the Council of Ministers is generally conducted behind closed doors) but very useful, for it gives information on the position taken by individual member states as well as suggestions for compromise. Some national governments who are habitually more open may make these available to interest groups: try your allies in other member states. At COREPER, some issues can be used almost as bargaining chips, with individual member states making a show of dissent before backing down gracefully. The French call this *proposer monnaie d'échange* – Alan Clark's 'horse-trading'. If your intelligence is sound on the line being taken by the government, you will be in a better position to embarrass them or to press them to hold firm and give your issue a higher priority.

Finally, detailed consideration of Commission proposals is also undertaken by two select committees of the Houses of Parliament, one in the Lords and one in the Commons. The committees prepare reports on the more significant of the proposals and may recommend a debate in Parliament. Of the two, the Lords select committee on the European Communities is probably the more influential, partly on account of its law and institutions subcommittee, which is usually chaired by one of the law lords.

The opportunities for lobbyists are twofold. Firstly, the consideration of proposals by the committees leads to additional information being made available, possibly clarifying the government's position. The appropriate Whitehall department prepares an 'explanatory memorandum' to accompany the draft proposal, which summarises its main effects and includes an assessment of how much it will cost to comply. Secondly, parliamentarians are generally more open to lobbying than officials and can put pressure on the government, whether through the select committees themselves or through other parliamentary techniques. There is an understanding that ministers will not agree to proposals in the Council of Ministers until this parliamentary scrutiny has taken place.

The European Parliament

Direct elections for the European Parliament were only first held as recently as 1979, and for the best part of a decade after that the Parliament was very much an also-ran compared to the Commission and Council of Ministers, its role largely consultative. Its power was significantly boosted by the Single European Act and the Maastricht Treaty, and looks set to increase further, but is still primarily negative in nature: the Parliament can block or veto certain proposals, but has little pro-active power.

In 2000 there were 626 MEPs, divided into seven main political groups plus some independents. The European Socialist Group, is where the British Labour MEPs sit; the British Conservatives are part of the umbrella right-wing European People's Party and European Democrats. Voting tends to follow these political groupings rather than nationality. Although UK MEPs are unusual in each being elected from a particular constituency, representing individual constituents is not really part of their job in the way it is for MPs at Westminster.

The Parliament meets in plenary session for one week every month in Strasbourg. Most of the detailed preparatory work of examining proposals, however, is done in committees of the Parliament (see box), which meet in public in Brussels. Each committee has a *rapporteur* who is responsible for drafting committee reports and who is a key figure for lobbyists. Briefing the *rapporteur* early may save a lot of effort later. A proposal will usually be the subject of a full report by one committee and opinions by others. Committees propose amendments to the draft legislation, which are then voted on in the plenary session.

Committees of the European Parliament

▼ Foreign Affairs, Human Rights, Common Security & Defence Policy (AFET)

▼ Budgets (BUDG)

▼ Budgetary Control (CONT)

▼ Citizens' Freedoms & Rights, Justice & Home Affairs (LIBE)

▼ Economic & Monetary Union (ECON)

▼ Legal Affairs & the Internal Market (JURI)

▼ Industry, External Trade, Research & Energy (INDU)

▼ Employment & Social Affairs (EMPL)

▼ Environment, Public Health & Consumer Policy (ENVI)

▼ Agriculture & Rural Development (AGRI)

▼ Fisheries (PECH)

▼ Regional Policy, Transport & Tourism (REGI)

▼ Culture, Youth, Education, the Media & Sport (CULT)

▼ Development & Cooperation (DEVE)

▼ Constitutional Affairs (AFCO)

▼ Women's Rights & Equal Opportunities (FEMM)

▼ Petitions (PETI)

February 2000

The exact procedure for dealing with Commission proposals varies considerably. The Parliament will receive a proposal when it is first sent to the Council of Ministers and will have an input before the Council comes to a decision. The extent of that input depends on the subject matter of the proposal and what procedure it has been assigned under the European treaties. The main alternatives are as follows:

▼ *Consultation procedure.* Parliament gives its opinion on the proposal, which the Commission then considers in order to put a revised proposal to the Council of Ministers. The Council has to give due regard to Parliament's opinion, but in practice the level of parliamentary influence is not great.

▼ *Cooperation procedure.* Introduced from 1987 under the Single European Act, cooperation procedure gave Parliament an important second reading of the proposal. After the Parliament's original opinion has been considered by the Commission, the Council of Ministers adopts a 'common position'. Parliament than gets a chance to look at the common position and propose further amendments. The Council still has the last word (even if Parliament rejects the common position outright, the Council can adopt it by unanimity) but Parliament's input is very important. Cooperation procedure applied to most proposals under the Single European Act and was extended under the Maastricht Treaty to cover further areas.

▼ *Co-decision procedure.* Introduced under the Maastricht Treaty, this gives Parliament the power of veto in a number of key policy areas. If the Parliament intends to reject the common position, a conciliation committee of the Parliament and the Council of Ministers is convened to try and reach agreement. If the committee does agree a text, it then has to be approved by both institutions. If it fails, the Council can press on with the proposal, but the Parliament may reject it with an absolute majority of its members, in which case the proposal cannot be adopted. A simplified diagram, showing the main stages in the procedure, is given in influence map 12. Its scope having been extended under the Treaty of Amsterdam, co-decision procedure now applies to a very wide range of areas of legislation including the free movement of workers, treatment of foreign nationals, public health, consumer protection, environment programmes and protection, development cooperation, and key areas of social and transport policy.

▼ *Budgetary procedure.* A draft EU budget drawn up by the Commission is given two readings by both the Council of Ministers and the Parliament, following a strict timetable. With a strong majority, the Parliament is able to increase expenditure, within limits, at its second reading in areas such as social policy and cooperation with less developed countries, but is bound by the decisions of the

Influence Map 12: European legislation under the co-decision procedure

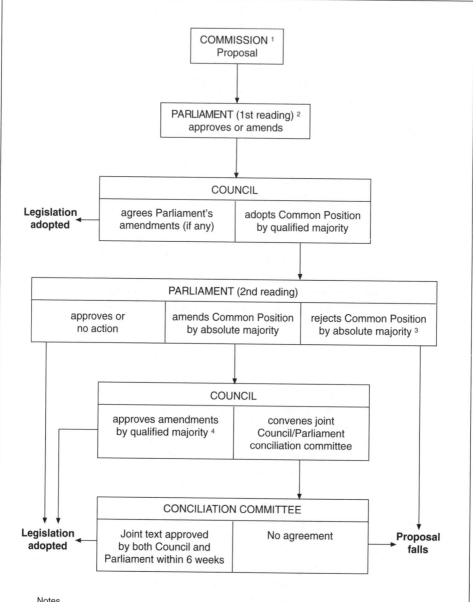

Notes

1 This diagram understates the role of the European Commission, which is involved in facilitating throughout the procedure.

2 The ESC and the Committee of the Regions give their opinion on the proposal at this stage.

3 Under cooperation procedure, the Common Position can still be adopted at this stage by the Council acting unanimously.

4 Or only by unanimity if the amendments are not accepted by the Commission.

Council at second reading in areas of so-called 'compulsory' expenditure, including the massive agricultural subsidies.

An important aspect of much European legislative procedure is that the relative influence of Parliament is dependent on it securing the support of the Commission. If parliamentary amendments are not supported by the Commission, they generally require unanimity in the Council to be adopted, which stacks the odds against them. If the Commission accepts the Parliament's amendments, then the Council can usually adopt the text including those amendments by qualified majority.

The Parliament has by far the most open decision-making procedure of the institutions, so the growth of its legislative role has brought with it greater access for outside groups. The development of the co-decision procedure was also seen by many as reducing the 'democratic deficit' in EU decision-making (although a good part of Parliament's new influence is down to politicking in the conciliation committees).

In addition to influencing legislative proposals, MEPs can be of use to lobbyists in other ways. They can raise issues in Parliament, ask questions, and have an informal role in putting forward new policies to the Commission. Of particular note in this respect is their clout in the process of formulating the EU budget, including the setting of new budget lines. MEPs can also be of help in securing meetings with the Commission.

Under the Parliament's own rules of procedure, 'Every citizen of the European Community has the right, individually or jointly with others to address written requests or complaints (petitions) to the European Parliament'. Petitions should state clearly the name, occupation, address and nationality of every petitioner, and can be sent to your MEP or to the Parliament's London office. Such petitions are often best used as an avenue of complaint rather than just as a show of support on an issue. Briefly state the grounds of your case with any supporting evidence attached. The petition will be forwarded to the Parliament's petitions committee and, if it falls within an area of EU competence, may be investigated, on occasion leading to a formal report.

UK MEPs all have offices in their constituency; the addresses are listed in *Vacher's* or available from the information office of the Parliament. Nearly all of them will also have an assistant in Brussels, contactable through the Parliament switchboard (00 32 2 284 2111). Typically, MEPs will spend a week every month in Strasbourg at the plenary session, and between one and three weeks in Brussels, depending on their committee duties. The rest of the time they are likely to be in their constituencies. (Note that there is little reason for most MEPs to come to London, except perhaps to catch a connecting flight.) Brussels is actually the best place for lobbying MEPs; in Strasbourg they tend to be networking furiously.

Rather like the all-party groups in the UK Parliament, there are a large number of 'intergroups' on specialist issues, consisting of MEPs from across the political groupings. Intergroups play no formal role in the legislative process, but can be a useful focus for briefing and lobbying MEPs. In policy areas which are directly covered by a committee of the Parliament, it makes more sense to concentrate your attention on committee members.

Many intergroups were initiated by outside organisations and rely for their momentum and back-up support on the continued involvement of such organisations. One of the most influential of the intergroups, the eurogroup for animal welfare, was set up largely through the support of the RSPCA.

The Economic and Social Committee and the Committee of the Regions

Where the relevant treaty article so provides, an opinion is required on Commission proposals not just from the Parliament but also from the Economic and Social Committee (ESC or EcoSoc). The ESC is a consultative body representing various economic and social interests in the EU. It is divided into three main groups: employers, employees and 'various interests'. The latter includes agriculture, transport, the professions, consumers, women, and the social economy, including the voluntary sector. The first two are principally industry and commerce, and the unions.

Currently the ESC has 222 members (24 from the UK), nominated by the governments of member states and appointed for a renewable four-year term. Once appointed, members serve in an individual capacity. The ESC has specialised sections covering the main areas of EU competence.

When a proposal is referred to the ESC by the Commission and Council of Ministers, the relevant section appoints a study group to draft an opinion. The role of the study group *rapporteur* is similar to that in committees of the Parliament. The draft opinion will then be considered at section level and at one of the monthly plenaries, where the lobbyist will be looking to influence the three main groups.

Despite being evidence of a strong corporatist streak in the EU, the Economic and Social Committee has little formal influence. Its importance derives from the recognition of its role in bringing professional and technical expertise into the legislative process, and for this reason its opinions will be studied closely by Commission officials (and MEPs). From the lobbyist's point of view, then, the ESC should be seen primarily as a channel of influence to the Commission. The study group and section meetings, incidentally, provide a good opportunity to meet the Commission officials responsible for drafting particular proposals.

Under the Maastricht Treaty, a Committee of the Regions was set up in 1994 to have a parallel role to the ESC, but representing regional and local authorities. Its members are organised by political, rather than professional, groups, and must be consulted on policy areas which have implications for the regions. It has become an important channel of direct influence for the regions in Europe, particularly those whose interests diverge from that of their own member states.

Using European law

EC legislation and other decisions can take a number of different forms which have varying impact. These are glossed in the box opposite, for ease of reference. The most important are regulations and directives, with which member states are obliged to comply.

It is important to note that in signing the European treaties, member states agree to be bound by European law. The member states have definitively transferred sovereign rights to a Community created by them. This leads to what is generally known as the primacy of EC law over national law. If, for example, an EC regulation conflicted with national law in a member state, the regulation would supersede any national provisions.

However, European law is generally designed to work in tandem with the legal orders of member states, or directly through them. Thus much European law takes the form of directives (see box overleaf) which are given legal force in individual member states through national legislation. The rationale behind this is that the prevailing legal, social or economic conditions in individual countries will differ considerably, and that each state is the best authority for deciding how a given measure should be implemented within its own borders. The directive achieves an objective necessary for European policy without giving rise to a host of unforeseen or undesirable consequences in individual member states.

The arbiter of EC law is the European Court of Justice, based in Luxembourg. European institutions may bring actions against a member state, for example for failing to implement legislation properly, or indeed against each other. Organisations or individuals can also appeal against EC rulings (most such actions are dealt with by a Court of First Instance, with a right of appeal to the ECJ). Courts in the UK may also refer a case to the European Court of Justice for a preliminary ruling if it involves aspects of EC law which are not clear, in which case the ECJ's decision is binding. On matters within its jurisdiction, then, it is the European Court of Justice and not the House of Lords which could be described as the highest court in the land.

The Commission has been persuaded to take the UK government to court over issues as diverse as the quality of bathing water in Blackpool and the failure to implement directives relating to collective redundancies and to the transfer of undertakings. Cases considered by the European Court in 1999–2000 included those concerning the protection of public health, the rights of foreign workers, the protection of wild birds, and numerous cases on freedom of movement and on equal treatment for men and women.

The development of European legislative proposals thus has to be monitored both for the threats it may pose to a campaign, but also for its potential in achieving major progress. In many areas, from employment rights to environmental protection, Europe has introduced reforms far beyond what was politically possible to achieve in the UK. The manner in which the UK government implements directives, decisions, or recommendations may call for further campaign action.

The campaign to end cosmetic tests on animals illustrates all of these points. In 1989 the British Union for the Abolition of Vivisection was alerted to the fact that a new Commission proposal could cause a dramatic increase in animal testing for cosmetics. Through direct contact with the Commission, some pressure from MEPs and a lot of

---

A guide to Euro-rules

Regulations
Regulations are directly binding on all member states, laying down the same law throughout the EU. Of all Euro-rules, they are the closest in character to national statute law.

Directives
Directives state an objective which member states are required to achieve within a given period. It is left to each member state to decide how that objective is realised, but it will often require the enactment of national legislation. Directives can be addressed to all member states, or sometimes only to specified ones.

Decisions
Decisions are administrative measures binding on the parties to whom they are addressed, usually individual firms or member states. They are generally used to apply a rule to an individual case (in much the same way as statutory instruments are often used in the UK).

Recommendations and Opinions
These are non-binding measures which are issued by a single European institution. Recommendations urge a particular course of action or form of behaviour on the party to whom they are addressed, while opinions give a view on a particular situation. Effectively, they are a form of political pressure.

Note: The treaty establishing the European Coal and Steel Community (ECSC), which came some six years before the Treaty of Rome, uses different terminology for its legal instruments. The general ECSC decision is directly binding on all member states, whereas ECSC recommendations (like directives) require member states to take such action as is necessary to achieve a stated objective.

noise in the UK media, BUAV managed to get the Commission to agree to produce a new draft text. The strategy was then widened to try and win major reform. BUAV set about establishing a European coalition by trying to find credible animal lobbies in each member state that could campaign in their respective countries. The campaign attracted overwhelming cross-party support in the Parliament which caused the Commission to review its position. Finally, in 1993 the Council of Ministers adopted a cosmetics directive which put in place an animal test ban from 1998, although with numerous qualifications and the possibility of postponement. Animal groups then lobbied to try to ensure that the ban would be given effect.

Notably, European law imposes obligations and confers rights not just on member states but also on their nationals. The European Court of Justice has shown itself prepared to interpret EC law as conferring fundamental rights on individual citizens which can be upheld in national courts. A Dutch national was thus able to take the government to court when she was refused entry to the UK to take up employment with an organisation considered 'socially harmful' by the Home Office. This direct applicability of EC law extends not just to regulations, but also in some cases to directives. Under what is generally known as the 'direct effect doctrine', it is now clear that in certain circumstances Community citizens could bring an action against a public body if they were disadvantaged by government failure to implement a given directive.

Pressure groups in a range of different fields are now turning to European law as a recourse for problems at home. In most cases this need not involve them in litigation: the European Commission, as noted above, is responsible for ensuring that European law is implemented and has powers to clamp down on infringements. When the UK government sought to give the newly privatised water companies an indefinite period in which to bring water standards up to the agreed EC levels of purity, the Commission insisted on a binding commitment to achieve the goal within a set period.

European networks

Few pressure groups will have the resources to maintain a permanent presence in Brussels. Fewer still have the European-wide credibility that makes all the difference in advancing a case to the European institutions. Both these problems, however, can be overcome through networking.

A large number of European networks of non-profits already exist across the social, health, consumer and environmental fields. In many cases, a network will already exist which can provide a channel for your lobbying or a convenient starting point for developing your own contacts with other groups around Europe. Networks vary considerably in size and organisation: some will be formally constituted, perhaps with an office in Brussels, and possibly with a closed membership; others will be more informal. The European Anti-Poverty Network has elected members (many of them community workers) from right across Europe. Most networks will be prepared to send you brief details on their work and their members.

Brian Harvey's *Networking in Europe*, published by NCVO (see appendix C), contains details on literally hundreds of networks and other European-oriented non-profits, with notes on the voluntary sector in other member states and tips on making contact.

Networks often tend to cluster around the programmes and policy areas of the European Commission. In some cases, the appropriate DG has supported setting up a new network if it is relevant to the Commission's work, or at least helped to finance an initial conference or meeting in Brussels (this possibility should not be overlooked if you decide to create a new network, particularly as it may also be the start of an ongoing relationship with the Commission). A handful of networks, such as the NGO Liaison Committee for groups working in less developed countries, have acquired consultative status with the Commission.

Useful pointers are provided by BUAV's approach in bringing together a coalition to lobby on the cosmetics directive (see above). Confining the network to just one organisation in each member state simplifies considerably the problems of organisation and communication, but requires care and effort in finding partners who are both credible and committed. Representation from as many member states as possible is important, although the richer states will probably have to carry most of the costs.

The Euro Citizen Action Service (see 'Sources of information' above) can also provide, for a fee, office facilities in Brussels and help in setting up a European network or public interest group.

International lobbying

There is clearly not enough space in this book to talk about international lobbying in any depth, and the section below is confined to offering signposts to some of the major international institutions with a note on how easily they can be accessed.

The conventional approach to trying to influence other countries in the world is to put pressure on the UK government to lean on them (see chapter 13). This has had some success, particularly when the rights or safety of individual UK subjects are involved, or when the issue in question makes a convenient bargaining tool: the human rights record of the Chinese government in the negotiations on Hong Kong's future, for example. The Foreign and Commonwealth Office, however, is remarkably resistant to pressure and the accountability of the diplomatic service is weak. Peter Hennessy puts his finger on it in his book *Whitehall* when he remarks that diplomats, like the armed forces, think of themselves as serving the Queen, which is subtly different from working for the minister or the government of the day.

On the other hand, more direct approaches to international lobbying have grown in success in recent decades, particularly those based on journalistic techniques of research and exposure. Human rights organisations in the UK and elsewhere offer solidarity to humanitarian or dissident groups in particular countries and provide a vital channel for publicising human rights violations or other grievances to the outside world, drawing support and pressure from the international community.

Notably, working through a national government or working primarily through the international community may not always be compatible. Although they will lobby the UK government and others, groups like Amnesty International are at pains to distance themselves from the views of any national government(s) in order to maintain their reputation for global impartiality. This means at times eschewing the more obvious channels of influence: local Amnesty groups are not, for example, allocated cases of prisoners of conscience held in their own countries, nor do they collect or issue information on their own countries.

The hardest international issues to crack, lobby-wise, are trade and defence, partly because major decisions are invariably taken at the highest level and follow a narrow interpretation of what is in a state's vital national interests. Even large-scale mobilisation of public opinion, as we recently saw across Europe and the US over the WTO, is only effective if it echoes existing sympathies within governments. Policy in these areas is heavily affected by scientific research and commercial or military intelligence, but the secrecy with which they are surrounded makes it difficult to make a realistic contribution. The Western European Union, developed in tandem with the defence component of the European Union under the Maastricht Treaty, does have a parliamentary assembly which includes UK MPs. It can pride itself on being the only parliamentary assembly founded by a treaty with competence in defence matters, but its influence on the WEU's council of foreign affairs and defence ministers is marginal.

The Council of Europe

The Council of Europe, founded in 1949, was the first pan-European association of countries and is now easily the largest, comprising some 41 states from Iceland to Turkey. Not to be confused with the Council of Ministers of the European Union, the Council of Europe has no legislative powers but operates through discussion and agreement. As talking shops go, however, it is very influential, boasting some 160 conventions or agreements that signatory states have agreed to be bound by, ranging in subject from the prevention of torture to crowd safety to medicinal standards. Its work in the human rights field is of particular importance (see below).

The Council of Europe works through two main bodies: the committee of ministers, comprising the foreign ministers of each member country; and the parliamentary assembly, consisting of delegations from each national parliament. The latter is, as you might expect, the more accessible and a list of the UK MPs involved is available from the public information office at the House of Commons. There is also a congress of local and regional authorities of Europe.

The Council's brief is very wide, but it has been most active in intergovernmental work in the fields of human rights, the media, legal cooperation, social and economic issues, health, education, culture, heritage, sport and youth, local and regional government, and the environment. The Council of Europe is based at the Palais de l'Europe (see appendix B for address).

The European Court of Human Rights

The Council of Europe's greatest achievement was also one of its first: the 1950 European Convention on Human Rights. By 2000 this had been ratified by 41 European countries. Taking key provisions from the UN Universal Declaration of Human Rights, the Convention set up for the first time a regional enforcement machinery to protect those rights. In addition to the Council's committee of ministers, this takes the form of the European Court of Human Rights.

A complaint can be made to the European Court of Human Rights by any person or non-governmental organisation (NGO) claiming that one of the states party to the Convention has, to their personal detriment, violated one of the rights or freedoms recognised in the Convention or its protocols. The complainant must first have pursued all appropriate remedies in the state concerned and the application must be made within six months of a final decision by the authorities or courts of that state.

If the complaint is ruled admissible (and the great majority are not), the Court will investigate further and ask the government of the state concerned to respond. Before coming to a judgement on the case, the Court will seek to reach a friendly settlement between the parties. Limited legal aid may be provided.

Notable cases that have come before the Court include those concerning:

▼ use of corporal punishment in schools

▼ detention of mental patients, vagrants, etc.

▼ immigration and deportation measures

▼ parents' access to children in care

▼ prisoners' rights

▼ criminalisation of homosexual activities.

Following the incorporation of the European Convention on Human Rights into UK law in the Human Rights Act 1998 (see chapter 8) the first avenue of recourse for a breach of Convention rights is to a court in the UK. Those who fail to secure a remedy in the UK courts, however, can still go to the European Court of Human Rights.

Pressure groups in the UK, including Liberty, have been particularly active in bringing complaints before the Court. States may also bring complaints against other states. One inter-state case so far referred to the Court concerned methods of interrogating suspects in Northern Ireland. The European Court of Human Rights is based in Strasbourg at Council of Europe (see appendix B for address).

The UN and specialised agencies

The United Nations was set up after the Second World War, according to its charter to 'achieve international cooperation in solving international problems of an economic, social, cultural, or humanitarian character' and to promote respect for human rights. By 2000 it had 188 member states. Each member state has one vote in the General Assembly, the main deliberative organ of the UN. However, peace and security issues are the prime responsibility of the smaller Security Council, which has only 15 members. Five of these are permanent – China, France, the Russian Federation, the UK and the United States – and hold a veto over any Security Council resolution. Half the resolutions since 1945 have been passed in the last decade.

As an assembly, the UN's policy-making role is limited. (It has no equivalent, for example, to the European Commission, with its proactive brief as the motor of European integration.) The UN is very much a melting pot of national interests, dominated by a few countries, most notably the United States. The International Court of Justice in the Hague has jurisdiction to interpret international law and to judge any breaches by states of their international obligations, but only states can be parties in cases brought before the Court.

Pressure group activity in relation to the United Nations takes three main forms:

▼ Using the UN as a forum for publicising particular abuses and embarrassing and pressurising individual member states. There is ultimately the possibility of a Security Council resolution on the issue, if the political will is present.

▼ Building consensus for an international summit (e.g. the conference on women in Beijing in 1995) or a major international agreement or convention (e.g. the Convention on the Rights of the Child). Individual states can then be lobbied to ratify the convention.

▼ Lobbying UN programmes and agencies. These range from humanitarian organisations such as the UN High Commissioner for Refugees, to research bodies, like the UN Institute for Disarmament Research, to the World Bank and the International Monetary Fund, which are classified as UN 'specialised agencies'.

The campaign against the commercial promotion of bottle-feeding is a celebrated early example of successful lobbying through UN agencies and of the fact that pressure groups do not have to be either large or wealthy to be effective at this level. In the late 1970s, non-governmental agencies worked with the UN Children's Fund (UNICEF) and the World Health Organisation (WHO) to act over the tragic consequences of companies' persuading mothers to bottle-feed rather than breastfeed their infants. An International Baby Food Action Network (IBFAN) was set up in 1979, and two years later the World Health Assembly adopted an international code of conduct governing the marketing practices of baby-milk companies. Since then IBFAN has monitored the activities of Nestlé and other baby-milk manufacturers and lobbied to ensure the code is implemented, including putting pressure on WHO to stand by its commitment. Baby Milk Action, the UK representative of IBFAN, only has a handful of staff.

The scope of inter-governmental action, and the number of states invariably involved, mean that to be effective charities or pressure groups will normally have to form international networks or coalitions with like-minded organisations in other countries. The success of the Jubilee 2000 campaign in getting the richer nations to reduce the debt burden of countries in the South is one striking example. The recipe for influence combines accurate research and powerful evidence, strong links between NGOs in the North and those in the South, and the mobilisation of public opinion in individual countries.

Another international network that could lay claim to real success is the Coalition for an International Criminal Court, a broad-based network of human rights organisations and legal experts lobbying for the establishment of an effective, permanent international court to try those accused of war crimes and crimes against humanity. The idea for such court was strengthened by the atrocities in the former Yugoslavia and Rwanda in the 1990s, but the diplomatic obstacles to getting states round the world to accede to the criminal jurisdiction of a new court were immense. During intense negotiations, the coalition circulated up-to-date proposals and working documents to coalition members and also helped to coordinate pressure at the most opportune time in key countries. Following the conclusion of a UN treaty to establish the court in 1998, the coalition was well placed to help its members persuade their national governments to ratify the treaty, sharing best practice and mustering international pressure.

Part 4
Strategy

16   Campaign strategy

It was no abstract question for us. The circumstances of our lives made it a burning luminous mark of interrogation. Where was power and which the road to it? – Nye Bevan

A wide array of campaigning methods are covered in this book. Trying out different techniques, changing tack if things get dull or just in order to see what happens, can often be a productive approach and certainly makes the campaigner's job more interesting. But there must be a way of rationally deciding, in a particular situation, given a specific campaign goal, which method or series of methods should be employed to produce the optimum effect. This is what this chapter is about.

Many of the most successful campaigns of recent decades have been run by single-issue groups and much of what follows draws on the experience of single-issue campaigns. Pressure groups don't of course have to confine themselves to one issue in order to be effective, but what they can benefit from is the precisely focused – in the language of marketing, targeted – approach that is the hallmark of single-issue campaigning.

Modern marketing techniques have revolutionised business in the developed world and they are well on the way to revolutionising politics too. The challenge is to use the power of marketing not to sell products or to raise money, but to advance a cause.

The marketing approach

Campaigners, on the whole, act from conviction. They are moved by a cause, which they then seek to promote as strongly, to as many people, as possible. They are a conduit from a given set of beliefs or values to potential converts. In this, they resemble missionaries.

Company salespeople in the first half of the twentieth century were encouraged to think of themselves in much the same way. They travelled around the country spreading the message, finding as many converts as possible for their product or brand. Quite often, a market for the product simply didn't exist. But by the fifties, even as the culture of 'salesmanship' reached its height, a new approach was already rapidly gaining adherents. Competitive pressures had forced managers to look more carefully at what consumers really needed or wanted and to try to develop products which met those needs. In doing so, they stood the role of the missionary on its head. From now on, the voice of the audience was to come first. This was the marketing concept: innovation driven by the needs of consumers, rather than the convenience of producers. They have been arguing over the distinction in corporate boardrooms ever since.

Managers who embraced marketing did so, incidentally, not for ethical reasons or in reaction at the arrogance of their corporations, but because *it worked*. It was much easier to sell people a product they thought they needed than to push on them something they didn't want.

The implications for campaigners of this marketing revolution are important and difficult. Is it possible on an issue to develop campaigns according to whether they appeal to the priorities and concerns of a specific audience? That would certainly seem to mark a departure from the practice of many pressure groups, where campaigns follow the priorities of the campaigner, and decisions about means as well as ends are often made on ethical grounds. Yet notable successes have been scored, particularly in the environmental movement, by campaigns that have deliberately set out to use the attitudes and worries of their audience as a starting point. Many people would argue that allowing your audience to define a campaign is in fact a more cooperative, or even democratic, approach; but for our purposes here, what is important is that *it works*.

The box overleaf takes two broad causes or movements – antivivisection, and racial justice – and provides examples of a range of campaigns within each. Although each campaign may be seeking to appeal to a number of different audiences, its primary target audience may differ markedly from other campaigns in the same movement. This will affect not just the style and tone of the campaign, but also its declared objectives and the specific issues on which it chooses to work.

Two points of particular importance should be noted:

▼ If any one campaign attempted to expand its work to cover all the approaches illustrated within the movement, it would impair its effectiveness. Impact is gained through clear targeting at a specific audience; messages aimed at very different audiences may be strictly incompatible, or at the least result in confusion and loss of impact.

▼ Each campaign, nevertheless, may derive considerable indirect benefits from the existence of other, perhaps very different, campaigns within the same movement. A moderate group, targeted at the establishment, might find it much more difficult to make headway were it not for the threat of more vociferous groups to which it appears an acceptable alternative. Hard-line groups would make little progress if it were not for the fact that the moderates can continually consolidate the small gains that are won.

'Campaign' here should not necessarily be equated with 'organisation'. Larger organisations with an established profile, particularly if they have a reputation as service-providers, may be able to sustain a number of campaigns aimed at different audiences. For each campaign, however, and all new pressure groups, the priority is to develop a clear message targeted at a specific audience.

The importance of problems

What attracts a particular audience to a proposed change or innovation? Four general factors are notable:

▼ *Compatibility.* The proposed change should fit well with existing values or attitudes held by the audience, and its political or technical understanding.

Different campaigns for different audiences

Anti-Vivisection _____

National Anti-Vivisection Society
Objectives: To convince Parliament and the public that animal experiments are dangerous and to obtain legislation prohibiting all such experiments.
Primary audience: members of the public and their MPs

Humane Research Trust
Objectives: To support research by advanced techniques which replace the use of living animals.
Primary audience: scientists and researchers

Fund for the Replacement of Animals in Medical Experiments
Objectives: To promote alternatives to animal experiments and to work towards reducing the number of animals used and refining procedures to minimise suffering.
Primary audience: universities, industrial companies, government bodies

Beauty without Cruelty
Objectives: To promote cosmetics that have not been tested on animals.
Primary audience: retailers and consumers

Racial Justice _____

A racial equality council
Primary audience: community leaders and local authorities

Runnymede Trust
Primary audience: researchers, government and the media

Project Fullemploy
Primary audience: employers; black workers and business people

Society of Black Lawyers
Primary audience: black lawyers and the legal system

Catholic Association for Racial Justice
Primary audience: the Catholic church

▼ *Superiority*. The change should be identified as an improvement on the existing state of affairs or as conferring some advantage on the audience.

▼ *Simplicity*. The change should be easy to understand and it should be clear how it could be put into practice.

▼ *Leadership*. The change should be promoted or supported by people whom the audience respects or identifies with.

The genesis of any campaign must therefore start from the perceptions, values and environment of the audience. Only when these are understood can the main issues of the campaign be defined, and the means chosen by which it can best be promoted.

In *The Marketing of Ideas and Social Issues* (see appendix C) Seymour Fine constructs the stages in the process by which an issue gains ground and leads to social change (see box below). It is both a model of the growth of awareness and commitment in an individual, and also describes a social process. Acknowledgement that a problem exists leads to suggestions for how it can be dealt with. The more promising or popular ideas gradually firm up to become a set of beliefs. An issue or cause is created; that is to say, a problem backed by social or political pressure for change. People join together to take social action, eventually leading to change. Note the similarities between the stages in this model and the old formula 'Agitate, educate, organise'.

It is important to note that the process begins with the recognition of a problem. Major change is an unsettling prospect for any society and no matter how attractive an innovation appears in theory, there will be an in-built resistance to it unless it is seen to address an existing problem. The first official measure that recognised the special needs experienced by ethnic minority communities in Britain – Section 11 of the Local Government Act 1966 – was in fact a response to the problems faced by local authorities in discharging 'their functions in consequence of the presence within their areas of substantial numbers of immigrants from the Commonwealth whose language or customs differ from those of the rest of the community'. The anti-nuclear movement is at present striving to prove beyond doubt the existence of a causal link between nuclear installations and incidence of leukaemia in the population: if it does so, the uncovering of this 'problem' may well constitute a turning-point in the campaign. Government, too, markets reforms as the solution to social problems: the poll tax was sold to Tory supporters as an ingenious solution to local authority over-spending and to Tory MPs as the policy that

A model of issue adoption

Problems
↓
Reasoning
↓
Ideas
↓
Beliefs
↓
Issue or Cause
↓
Social Action
↓
Social Change

Source: After Seymour Fine

would save them from the political nightmare they faced in the shape of the long-postponed revaluation of properties under the old rating system.

Seymour Fine compares the development of new ideas with business marketing, which is about developing products: 'The marketing view is that products originate out of customers' needs and desires. Ideas are to problems what products are to needs and desires'. In cause marketing, the campaigner specifies the ideas or issues on which the campaign will be conducted so as to resolve some problem facing the target audience.

Decision-makers and channels

So far in this chapter target audiences have been treated as a given, but in fact the choice of audience is one of the key strategic decisions which a campaign must take. In the creation of social change, it is useful to distinguish between two types of agent:

▼ the person or institution who can bring about the desired change, that we can call the power-holder or *decision-maker*;

▼ the person or institution who can influence them, known as the *channel*.

The most common decision-makers, in this sense, are found inside the institutions covered in part three of this book. Classic channels for pressure groups include the media, the professions, and the general public or a section thereof. But the distribution of agency in any particular campaign may be very different. In a public education campaign promoting safer sex, young adults may be the ultimate decision-makers with the Department of Health and gay voluntary groups both constituting key channels.

The significance of the channel is twofold. The more powerful the decision-maker – that is, the greater its control over the issue in question – the more strongly it is likely to favour the *status quo* (on the assumption that the *status quo* will have been largely manufactured or maintained by it). This makes it difficult to access directly. Secondly, channels always exist, even if in some cases the major channels are not that accessible themselves. Some decision-makers enjoy greater discretion over decisions than others, but absolute power is a myth.

Decision-makers and channels are *models* of agency, and most power centres display the characteristics of both, leaning more towards one role on any specific issue rather than the other. The distinction is very important, however, as it enables a campaign to distinguish the key holder(s) of power that the campaign needs to turn in order to succeed, and the people best placed to reach them: in Bevan's terminology, where power is, and the road to it. Some roads may be very well made, but they might be a roundabout way of getting somewhere, or even lead in the wrong direction.

A good illustration is provided by Parliament's role. Parliament is frequently identified as a central target by many pressure groups (and for that reason was included among the other targets covered in part three). But as was made clear in chapters 13 and 14, Parliament ultimately has limited decision-making power and its real significance is more often as a *channel* for pressuring and influencing government. Those campaigns (often naturally drawn to democratic methods) whose main method of operation is to raise support among the public in order to influence Members of Parliament are thus in danger of never getting close to the centre of power.

It should now be clear that the primary audience addressed by a campaign is nearly always a channel. But in choosing an audience for its message, a campaign should not just be swayed by who its friends or its natural constituency are, but by how that audience rates as a channel of influence to key decision-makers.

It is a useful exercise to take a potential campaign objective, and to compile a list in rank order of the people or institutions who hold the power to achieve that objective. For each of the higher-ranking elements on the list, a secondary list should be drawn up of the main influences on that person or institution. The decision-maker ranked first together with the top-ranking channel of influence on that

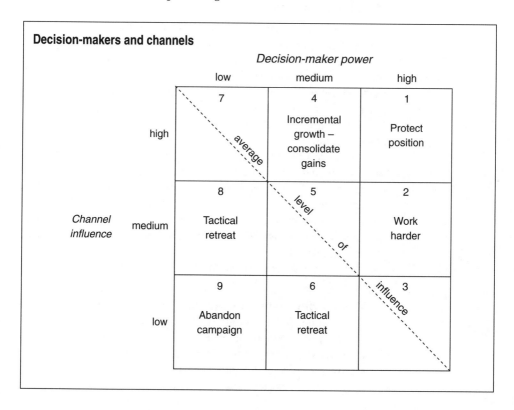

decision-maker represent the most direct route to the achievement of the objective. It will happen only rarely, however, that this route is open to the campaign. Other potential routes will have to be assessed and the calculations involved are made easier by plotting the decision-maker and channel rankings on a 3 x 3 grid (see box on page 353). Clearly, a campaign will have to take into account its own expertise or level of access to a particular channel, but this factor should not be allowed to predominate so as to obscure the campaign's relative distance from the centre of power.

Depending on the issue in question, the campaigns targeting Parliament cited above (channel = public, decision-maker = Parliament) would usually approximate to position 7 on the grid. As key decision-makers are often very difficult to access, many strong campaigns occupy position 4, calling for a strategy of steadily monopolising the decision-makers that are accessible and consolidating gains to prevent them being reversed by other decision-makers. Tact is required. Very occasionally, domination of the channel will limit its own capacity to influence: when CND finally won over the Labour Party to unilateralism in the early eighties, arguably it affected the Party's chances of being elected to government.

Market segmentation

Target audiences differ not only one from another, but also within themselves. That is to say, few audiences are entirely homogenous. A audience of MPs, for example, will range from far right to far left, with all the shades of political allegiance in between. If a target audience does exhibit major variations, a growing pressure group might consider varying its message, or developing separate messages, to cater to each significant section of the audience. This is known as market segmentation.

Developing a range of associated messages or campaigns in this way may well mean that each one will gain less support than a unified campaign would, and there may be problems articulating the different messages. But the justification for segmenting a market is that total market penetration – the total amount of support you win – will be greater than it would be if the audience was treated as one homogenous unit.

A successful strategy of market segmentation will generally depend on three conditions:

▼ That the different sections of the market are large enough, and clearly identifiable enough, to justify developing separate messages for their benefit. If your audience was a collection of MEPs from across Europe, it would probably not be viable to develop separate messages targeted at each nationality. It may work, however, to segment the audience into two or three regional blocks (northern Europeans, Mediterranean countries, etc.) or into major political blocks, depending on the issue.

▼ That sufficiently distinctive messages can be generated to appeal to the differing characteristics of each market segment – it is on this that greater market penetration will depend.

▼ That there nevertheless exists a level of congruity between the different messages, such that they are all seen to contribute to the same basic end and do not undermine each other or create division or suspicion among different groups of supporters.

Market segmentation may be achieved either by modifying an entire campaign, particular messages, or simply the manner or the medium through which the message is communicated to the audience. A pressure group for women's employment rights may lead on equal pay for equal work when targeting workers, for example, and on the glass ceiling when targeting managers. The sub-market of women workers could be further segmented into factory employees and workers in the retail and service industries, with the former reached through union representatives and the latter through leisure media coverage backed up by direct mail.

Most campaigns aimed at the general public, or at raising 'public opinion', are in fact only targeted at certain specific sections of the public. Common criteria for dividing the public for marketing purposes include:

▼ *Socio-demographic criteria*. These include factors such as age, class or socio-economic group, and geographical location.

▼ *Political criteria*. This includes voting behaviour, allegiance to other causes, and membership of societies or other interest groups.

▼ *Lifestyle criteria*. This refers mainly to consumer behaviour – what people spend their money on – and how they spend their time.

The use of lifestyle analysis for the purpose of campaign fundraising is illustrated by the example of Shelter in chapter 3.

The organisation and its credibility

The standard method for assessing the current position of an organisation in relation to its market is SWOT analysis. SWOT stands for Strengths, Weaknesses, Opportunities, Threats, and covers in turn the situation inside an organisation and wider factors in its environment, both of which need to be analysed before an organisational strategy can be formulated. Examples from the range of factors covered in SWOT analysis are given in the box opposite.

The same factor may prove a source of both strength and weakness in an organisation. A large and active membership, for example, will probably be a boon in demonstrating support and coordinating campaign activities, but may be a drag on the policy development of the organisation or its freedom to negotiate. External change, the election of a new government, say, is also likely to hold both opportunities and threats for the organisation. In doing a SWOT it is important to consider the full potential, positive and negative, of each factor.

The distinction between internal and external factors is more than just a convenient way of dividing up the elements impacting on the organisation. Most internal factors will be controllable, or within the power of the organisation to modify, although in a few cases its hands will be tied (for example by its own constitution). Many of the major external factors, on the other hand, are uncontrollable variables: too broad or too complex to realistically admit of modification by the organisation. To the extent that external factors *are* controllable, this will often require a strategic process; rather than being achievable simply at the will of the organisation, it will have to become a campaign objective.

SWOT analysis

INTERNAL

S
T
R
E
N
G
T
H
S

Information
In-house expertise and capacity
Strength and quality of supporters
Contacts and networking
Financial resources
Quality of management

W
E
A
K
N
E
S
S
E
S

O
P
P
O
R
T
U
N
I
T
I
E
S

Movement in target position
Political change
Social/cultural change
Relations with competitors/other bodies
Economic/demographic change
Technological developments

T
H
R
E
A
T
S

EXTERNAL

The results of SWOT analysis should not have the effect of making an organisation concentrate on its weak points. While pressure groups clearly need a range of skills in order to progress, there is little to be gained from becoming the organisational equivalent of Renaissance man. To achieve maximum effect (often to have any effect) a group must focus its efforts on building on its strengths and, specifically, make its strengths play to opportunities in the market or the wider environment. However, if they are in danger of crippling those efforts, certain key weaknesses of the organisation may have to be addressed in order to neutralise their effect. Threats should be carefully monitored with the organisation prepared to adapt as necessary.

Its strengths will also be the main sources of the organisation's credibility. In addition to the broad factors listed in the box, these may include its reputation as a provider of good services, links with its client group, its size and track record, the quality of its research, and the level of 'brand recognition' it commands. Brand recognition is the level of familiarity with the organisation and its outputs possessed by the target audience(s). Together all these factors make up what is known as corporate image, or the overall way in which the organisation is perceived by its audiences.

Credibility is rather like a valve that regulates access to channels of influence and ultimately to decision-makers. Of special importance in this respect is the reference group to which the organisation or its message is perceived to belong. Groups that work on established political issues may quickly find themselves associated in the minds of their audience with one party or side of the political spectrum. This may not be a problem for the immediate audience of supporters, but could prove fatal to gaining access to important other channels. Credentials establishing a campaign's independence are hard won and have to be actively maintained.

The reference group identified in any particular case will depend on the spread of interest groups and the audience in question; it may be positive or negative, sometimes it may be objectively justifiable, sometimes not. A national campaign for smokers' rights would find it difficult to avoid being seen as a front for tobacco producers; a foreign aid agency working with the Philippine government might be hard-pressed to persuade Filipino workers that it was not a GRINGO (Government-Run or -Initiated NGO). If the reference group with which you will be associated by your audience reflects damagingly on the campaign, great care must be taken to distance yourself from it and to modify your corporate image.

Campaign planning

Once the market has been analysed, and the current position of the organisation assessed, the formulation of a strategy can begin. Classically, planning takes place on a number of successive levels, each establishing in more detail the key components of the campaign and moving closer to determining actual operations. These levels are summarised in the box opposite. Note that the process begins from the core aims of the organisation; these are usually defined very broadly and are often written in the organisation's constitution.

There is a temptation with new campaigns to begin by planning activities immediately (i.e. starting from the box in the diagram marked 'operational plan'). The danger with this is that it ignores the particular configuration of power in the area, and the strategic considerations that are a campaign's best chance of making its activities effective.

The informed assessment of potential techniques and the other components of a campaign requires accurate knowledge of the target. If you have not already done so, read the relevant chapters in part three relating to the putative targets of your campaign. Which techniques are appropriate depend not just on the decision-makers you need to reach, but on the issue, the timing and the channels of influence open to the organisation. If you are trying to influence early developments in a new piece of government legislation, lobbying MPs will be next to useless; if you are attempting to question executive action by government, however, MPs will be an important option. There should be enough information in parts two and three of this book to provide initial guidance, for almost any campaign, on which techniques will be appropriate to a given target in a particular situation, but nothing substitutes for individual intelligence on your target.

The definition of specific campaign objectives is what links the broad aims of an organisation to the messy realities of social change. Good objectives display two characteristics:

▼ *They are productive.* If an objective is realised, it should have created a real change which brought the organisation closer to realising its aims. On a big campaign, the objectives can be seen as the building blocks of the campaign strategy.

▼ *They are achievable.* In the event, all objectives may not be achieved, and much progress can be made short of full success, but objectives should always be achievable. These objectives are part of the planning process and are not necessarily those which you will wish to announce publicly. But campaign planning and evaluation depends on being able to specify objectives which you are able to realise. If you continually link campaign activities to objectives which never materialise, you will never be able to find out exactly what works and what does not work (quite apart from demoralising staff).

Typical, achievable campaign objectives might include the passing of amendments to legislation; an agreement to delay implementation of a policy until after further consultation; or recognition of the existence of a problem through ring-fencing a budget or modifying a

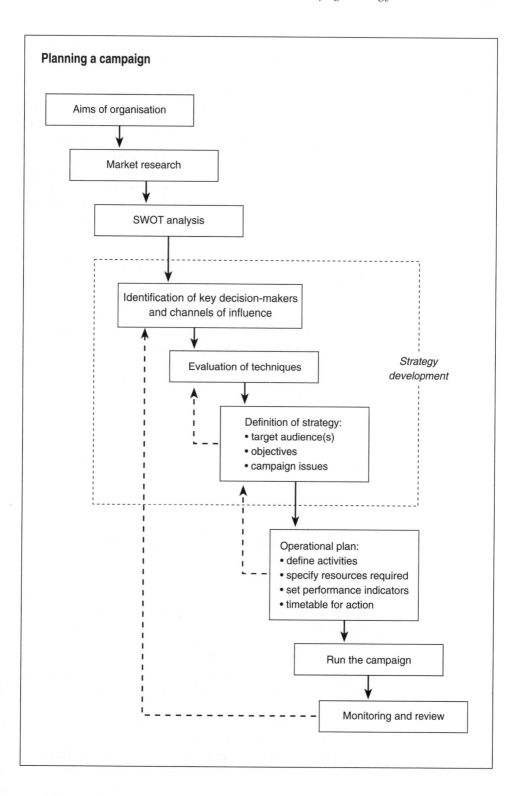

Planning a campaign

Aims of organisation

Market research

SWOT analysis

Identification of key decision-makers
and channels of influence

Evaluation of techniques

Definition of strategy:
• target audience(s)
• objectives
• campaign issues

*Strategy
development*

Operational plan:
• define activities
• specify resources required
• set performance indicators
• timetable for action

Run the campaign

Monitoring and review

procedure. Some objectives might relate to process: the establishment of bilateral negotiations with the target, for example, or the achievement of a certain level of media coverage.

It is also possible to distinguish between primary and secondary objectives, short-term or long-term, etc. If a campaign objective is publicised, choose one that has the capacity to crystallise the energies and emotions generated by the campaign. Ideally it should arouse a similar strength of feeling to the campaign itself, but concentrated on a smaller area. The attempts by gay campaigners to bring the age of gay consent in line with that for heterosexuals is a good example.

Strategy development is not a simple progression from one step to the next. Often the expertise or resource constraints, or other drawbacks, of a particular approach will not become clear until an attempt has been made to turn it into an operational plan, necessitating going back to the level before and trying something different or even starting the process again from the beginning. There is also a major feedback loop which links the outcomes of an ongoing campaign with the formulation of strategy for successive campaigns or a modified version of the current campaign. For feedback to be sufficiently precise, the operational plan should specify performance indicators for measuring progress towards campaign objectives. The monitoring and evaluation of campaigns is discussed in more detail in the next chapter.

Campaign management

Campaign strategy, and in particular social marketing, is often described as if it were a one-stage process; as if the route from 'where we are now' to 'where we want to be' could be completely mapped out from the start. In reality, the environment in which a campaign operates can change rapidly, the campaign itself is subject to a natural dynamic of growth and decline and, most significantly, many social campaigns will encounter opposition every step of the way.

Reaction and counter-reaction

There is a tendency to assume that people in positions of power will argue, act and react in a similar way to the politicians on our television screens and the campaigners who lobby them. This is not the case. Electioneering makes politicians crave publicity. Campaigners, with few other tactics at their disposal, often try and create as loud a noise as possible. But for most people in positions of power, publicity is neither useful nor desirable. Their methods are altogether more subtle and more secure.

Perhaps the greatest problem facing a lobby is that powerful people, whether in government, companies or the professions, very often do not react at all. They don't have to act: inertia is on their side.

In many cases their public accountability is limited so they don't even have to say anything. They can just wait until the campaigner goes blue in the face, starts foaming at the mouth and eventually gives up.

It follows from this that it is necessary to ensure early on that the target *does* react (assuming that more accessible targets are not available). Once the target has, as it were, been flushed out into the open, its reactions, whether positive or negative, can be worked on in the public arena and as often as not turned to the campaign's advantage.

The need to provoke a reaction is one of the main reasons why campaigners resort to direct action. Numerous examples are given in chapter 10. But this approach has its dangers, not least that it can make the campaign appear more extreme, thereby making it all the easier to ignore (particularly if the focus of attention shifts away from the target onto the struggle between the campaigners and the law).

Normally, if a target does not respond to a direct challenge, it will be possible to raise questions through its allies, financial backers, regulatory authorities, or its own members or constituency. Once an issue has been raised, the media can also be relied upon to do much of the actual hounding. The target's initial responses will thus constitute the beginning of a dialogue in which it will have lost one of the privileges of power: not having to justify what it does.

The initial reactions of power-holders, whether in public, private or voluntary institutions, when faced with a pressure group campaign tend to follow a similar pattern:

▼ quietly reassure key colleagues and partners that there is nothing to worry about;

▼ privately discredit the facts and research put forward by the campaign;

▼ marginalise the campaign in any forum by implying that it is extremist or self-interested;

▼ continue to react publicly as little as possible.

Beyond continually trying to drag the target into the public arena there is a limit to what can be done in response to these tactics, bearing in mind that most of them will take place behind closed doors and that a campaign's contacts and access to the establishment will almost certainly be poorer than that of the target. The decisive point is the second one. It is vital for the early success of a campaign that its research is sound and that it can present convincing evidence. If there is a case to answer, the target's peer group will supply the pressure to make sure it is answered.

It is a valuable exercise periodically to do a SWOT analysis on your target (that is, from the target's point of view). Apart from helping you to see things from the other side, it will improve your sense of timing, sensitising you to moments of target vulnerability.

A burst of damaging publicity timed to occur before a shareholders' meeting or a departmental review may be much more effective than one coming just after.

Realistically, most attempts to provoke or damage the target are not aimed at securing instant victory but at dragging it to the bargaining table. Once the campaigning group has established itself as an authority, long-term campaigns settle down to what is in effect, if not in name, a period of stop-start negotiations: compromising, consolidating small gains and resorting to publicity whenever the target shows signs of ignoring or sidelining the campaign. At times it may be politic to congratulate the target publicly, to help paint it with your own colours in order that it may live up to them.

Environmental campaigners' attempt to push the issues of atmospheric pollution and ozone depletion onto the government agenda in the late eighties provides a good illustration of this process. The steady build up of scientific evidence and its presentation in the media led to Margaret Thatcher's watershed speech to the Royal Society in 1988, which explicitly recognised the environmental crisis the world was facing. Applauded by most environmentalists, the speech was welcomed as a demonstration that the government had turned green. With a major advance behind them, environmental groups then encouraged the government to take positive action on pollution and in particular on global warming, later exposing the government's greenness as a sham when little action was forthcoming.

When to sit tight and make progress through quiet consultation or discreet lobbying and when to go on the attack publicly depends on individual circumstances and is one of the hardest decisions faced by the campaigner. The Bedford Box, introduced at the end of this section, provides a strategic tool for helping to get this balance right over different campaign activities. First, however, it would be useful to consider how ideas spread over time.

The diffusion of ideas and the product life cycle

Ideas tend to diffuse through an audience according to a recognisable pattern. Initial take-up of an idea is invariably slow as awareness of the idea spreads. The level of awareness will in fact often rise to near one third of the audience before the idea begins to attract significant support. Once this happens, however, the number of converts or supporters rises exponentially, until saturation point in the audience is approached, when the rate of growth will slow markedly. Plotted on a graph, this pattern takes the form of an S-shaped curve (see box opposite).

It is important to note that this pattern describes a success story. Very many more ideas will be introduced to an audience but will not move beyond a minimal level of support. But looking at the pattern of adoption of successful ideas, numerous scientists, sociologists and other commentators have remarked on the existence of the S-shaped curve. As with all model distributions, there are numerous exceptions to the rule. For example, when an idea nears the end of its period of maximum growth (i.e. below the second point of inflexion of the curve), or before, a number of sub-ideas or variations on a theme can appear which may dislocate support for the original idea but will follow their own dynamic of growth or stagnation.

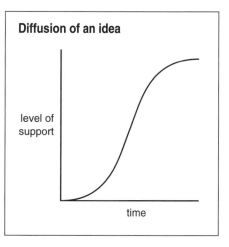

Diffusion of an idea

level of
support

time

The level of support given on the graph is actually the cumulative number of converts over time. Adherence to an idea does not of itself require repeated action (unlike product sales) and therefore the fall-off of support is difficult to gauge but is probably slower and less pronounced than typical declines in product sales. The product life-cycle, while clearly related to the diffusion curve, gives a picture of the volume of sales over time, or the level of *active* support for a cause as expressed in the size of an organisation's membership (see box overleaf). We have moved from a highly informal, difficult-to-monitor process (the spread of an idea) to a more concrete, visible process regulated through exchange (the success of a product).

The product life-cycle (PLC) is probably the most widespread marketing tool in use, even if its applicability to specific situations is hotly debated. The PLC curve has certainly been observed in a wide range of natural phenomena, as well as in social processes other than the sale of products. Seymour Fine notes that mass interest in politics itself, as measured by turnout in US elections, approximates to the standard PLC curve (*The Marketing of Ideas and Social Issues*). The product life-cycle is also very useful for plotting the stages in the growth and decline of a membership-based (single-issue) pressure group.

Four main stages can be identified in the product life-cycle, each calling for a different management emphasis:

▼ *Introduction*. Bearing in mind what was said above, the priority here is to highlight the problem(s) that the campaign is set up to address in order to achieve the level of audience awareness that is necessary to initiate and later sustain solid growth. The staging of a media launch with appropriate pre-launch publicity is designed to maximise public awareness before the new 'product' or campaign formally comes on stream.

▼ *Growth*. The rise in support accelerates as each new supporter reinforces the message with her own peer group, bringing in more

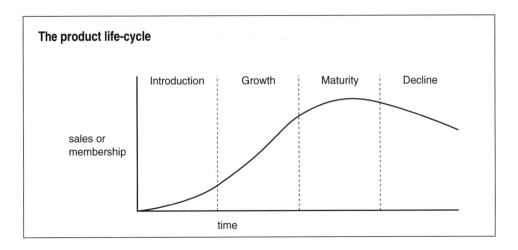

The product life-cycle

Introduction　　Growth　　Maturity　　Decline

sales or
membership

time

converts. Both the introduction and growth stages call for a marketing orientation: developing and presenting issues in order to address directly the concerns of the target audience.

▼ *Maturity.* Growth in new supporters slows, and the need to sustain and deploy the now sizeable body of support calls for an organisational orientation. This is where the benefits of the campaign's expansion can be reaped, but to do so effectively will require considerable managerial capacity and skills.

▼ *Decline.* Support decays, slowly at first and then with increasing pace. The campaign's best chance is to concentrate on audiences where the issue is still strong, squeezing the issue for all it is worth before it dies completely.

There is no typical time-scale for the stages of the product life-cycle, although in busy markets where there are many competing calls on the audience's sympathies the PLC tends to be shorter. Particular stages in the life-cycle may be postponed or compressed, either on account of outside factors, like political change, or through management competence. Assiduous promotion and careful safeguarding of reputation can extend the maturity phase of the cycle for a long time – Coca-Cola has been doing it for decades.

With a small, single-issue pressure group, the phases in the life of the organisation will mirror those of the product life-cycle. At the growth stage the organisation expands rapidly, taking on more staff. A rather flat or haphazard organisational structure will give way to greater division of labour and better definition of roles and responsibilities as the group reaches maturity. At this stage, typically, the founder(s) of the group hand over to a professional manager. Finally a bureaucratic stage is reached where the group ossifies, with the survival of the organisation replacing promotion of the cause as the main priority.

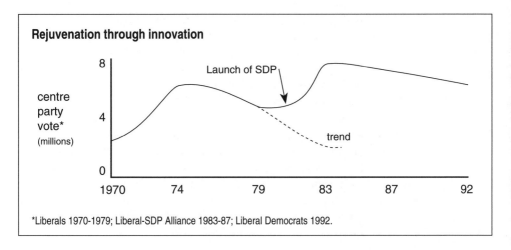

Rejuvenation through innovation

centre party vote* (millions)

Launch of SDP

trend

*Liberals 1970-1979; Liberal-SDP Alliance 1983-87; Liberal Democrats 1992.

Although decline in support for a specific issue can be delayed, it cannot be postponed indefinitely, even with aggressive promotion. In order to continue growing in influence, a pressure group must innovate. Even for a 'single-issue' group, this will involve developing different aspects of the cause and launching new campaigns. A high-profile example of how a cause can be rejuvenated through innovation is provided by the election performance of the centre party in British politics (see box above). Following an exhilarating period of growth in the early seventies, largely on account of public disillusion with the other parties, the Liberal vote showed the onset of a dangerous decline at the end of the decade. The shape of the classic PLC curve was ruptured, however, when in 1981 the launch of the SDP caused centre party support to rise like a phoenix from the ashes of decline.

One of the most important practical applications of the product life-cycle for pressure groups, then, is the benefit of identifying when a campaign is entering maturity. Crucially, once decline has set in, it is very difficult to reverse. It is at the onset of maturity that market research should be used to identify new issues for development. Larger groups or multi-issue campaigns can develop a rolling programme of new issues to highlight, each one postponing the time of full maturity and enabling the group to continue growing in influence.

The campaign portfolio

As a charity or pressure group does grow in size and influence, and perhaps is able to run a number of different campaigns at the same time, considerations arise which will not have been of much concern to the smaller or incipient group. Two will become pressing:

▼ *The need to safeguard the credibility the organisation has acquired.* A pressure group with established influence is a pressure group with something to lose (one reason why successful groups tend to become more conservative over time). Whitehall in particular is very good at granting a group a certain level of access, making it harder for the group to resort to public criticism. Bilateral relations with targets and credibility in the field are highly valuable and need to be protected carefully, but also deployed to maximum effect.

▼ *The rate of change in the wider field.* Any campaign should be aware of environmental opportunities and threats, but the more important a pressure group becomes, the more it will be expected – by supporters, the media and decision-makers – to react to all major developments in its field. This has heavy resource implications. At the same time, policy areas where the rate of change is high are more amenable to outside influence.

Although it may be a factor, the pressure group will rarely be the main influence in dictating the rate of change in its field. This is more likely to be managed by the target itself, or prompted by wider changes in society, the economy or even the natural world. But whether the change is positive or negative, it is important to realise that change itself generates opportunities for influence. The earlier the campaign enters the change process, the greater those opportunities will be.

Managing these different variables – environmental change, campaign resources, and organisational credibility – is a formidable balancing act. On the one hand there is a pull towards conservatism: maintaining a cosy but limited relationship with your audience or with decision-makers, thus under-utilising the credibility that has been built up. On the other, there is a temptation to radicalism: trying to push change too quickly, thereby losing credibility and allowing the organisation to be marginalised.

The Bedford Box has been developed as a management tool to help a group balance its campaigning activities and deploy its credibility and resources to maximum effect (see box opposite). (Marketing professionals will note that it was inspired by the Growth-Share matrix developed by the Boston Consulting Group, but its function is very different.) The Bedford Box plots the rate of change on an issue against the influence of a campaign. It is assumed that this influence will be positive, and that therefore a relatively high level of influence will result in the generation of a social 'good'. Note that this is a measure of the campaign's specific contribution, not the general level of progress on the issue (high influence, and the associated social good, may mean merely slowing down a negative social trend).

Each campaign should be plotted in the space inside the box, according to its relative influence and the general rate of change on the issue with which it is concerned, falling more or less into one of the quadrants:

▼ *Star.* With a high level of influence in a fast-moving area, the campaign is in the driving seat. Heavy resourcing is needed to keep pace with change and maintain influence.

▼ *Steady boat.* Making slow, steady progress out of the public eye, or evolving out of star campaigns when the upheaval has died down, the steady boat is typically steered by established (or establishment) interest groups.

▼ *Question mark.* The pace of events will throw up opportunities, but it is not easy to predict in which direction they will move. Building influence will require the investment of money and credibility.

▼ *Brick wall.* With powerful inertia to be overcome and minimal influence with which to do it, campaigners will feel they are banging away for nothing.

As with any management tool, the value of the Bedford Box for strategic planning will depend on the quality of the information inputted. Assessing the influence of a campaign is a subjective process, difficult for those involved, but the level of bilateral access to

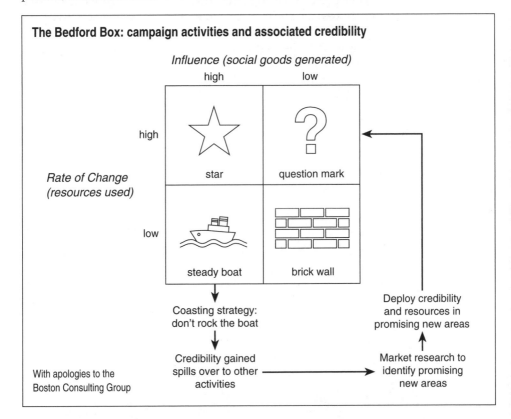

The Bedford Box: campaign activities and associated credibility

Influence (social goods generated)

high   low

Rate of Change
(resources used)

high

star   question mark

low

steady boat   brick wall

Coasting strategy:
don't rock the boat

Credibility gained
spills over to other
activities

Deploy credibility
and resources in
promising new areas

Market research to
identify promising
new areas

With apologies to the
Boston Consulting Group

key decision-makers can often be used as a shorthand for estimating influence. Campaigns run by political parties, where the ultimate target is the electorate, can be positioned precisely in the matrix using opinion poll data. Vote share on an issue is plotted against the rate of change of public opinion.

The catch-22 of campaigning is that credibility is gained through influence but that it is hard to be influential unless you are seen as credible. The Bedford Box provides a framework for managing campaign activities so as to generate credibility which can then be channelled into developing issues in the most promising new areas (bearing in mind that a pressure group needs to develop new issues in order to survive and grow). Steady boat campaigns are important not just because they enable influence to be exercised at little cost, but because they produce an 'excess' of credibility which can be used to back new campaigns in areas identified through audience research as providing opportunities for influencing change. Out of these campaigns will hopefully develop the stars of the future.

The significance ascribed to environmental change in this model is not a suggestion that campaigns should be primarily reactive – quite the opposite. An individual pressure group will necessarily be but one player in a complex process of social change and it will enter that process too late or at the wrong time unless it is sensitive to the patterns of change. Influential campaigns can see their role less as trying to shift the *status quo* than as moulding and manipulating events that are already in flux.

17 Campaign evaluation

We start from our conclusions – Angela Carter

Evaluation is about accessing the benefits of hindsight at the earliest possible opportunity. Through carefully monitoring the implementation of a campaign, and measuring progress towards its objectives, unfruitful approaches can be rectified early and campaign objectives revised or the design strengthened for maximum impact.

Campaigning is a particularly tricky activity to evaluate, however, for two main reasons:

▼ reliable indicators of progress are often hard to find;

▼ social change is typically caused by a complex set of interrelated events and a direct causal link between campaign actions and a change in the policy or practice of the target is often difficult to establish.

As with most strategic processes, campaign evaluation is thus a series of approximations. It will usually combine process evaluation – ensuring that chosen techniques are operating smoothly and are correctly focused – with detailed intelligence on the behaviour of the target(s). Market research may also be a key component of campaign evaluation, particularly with public education campaigns. One point, however, it is best to be unequivocal about. If, having been given time to work, a campaign produces no discernible *effect*, then no matter how impressively staged it may have been, it was not a very good campaign.

The evaluation cycle

In the last chapter, the importance of the feedback loop in the campaign planning process was noted. In fact, planning can be seen not as a straight progression from the definition of aims through to the commencement of operations, but as a cyclical process in which action is periodically reviewed, results assessed against objectives, and the campaign redesigned as necessary. This cycle is shown in the box overleaf.

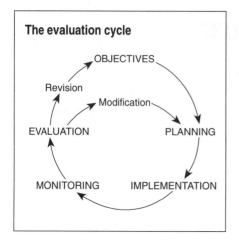

The evaluation cycle

OBJECTIVES

Revision

Modification

EVALUATION

PLANNING

MONITORING   IMPLEMENTATION

For the results to be of much use, evaluation cannot simply be considered when a campaign has finished: it must be built into the planning process. Evaluation is essentially the assessment of a campaign's outcomes in relation to its objectives, so objectives must be carefully defined from the start and indicators found which can measure progress towards those objectives. This is not just to ensure that the evaluation is unbiased, but so that arrangements can be made for collecting the information necessary for monitoring the effects of the campaign during its implementation.

A campaign to promote the use of holistic birthing methods, for example, might identify three main objectives: to win support for its methods among the medical profession, measured by the number of its members who were doctors, nurses, etc.; to acquire respectability among the medical research community, measured by the value of grants obtained from medical research organisations for the establishment and assessment of pilot projects; and finally, to raise awareness of holistic methods in the medical profession and among young women generally, measured by the quantity of coverage received in the medical and women's press and by periodic attitude and awareness surveys. The measure for the first objective requires obtaining information about their profession from new members; for the last objective, an initial pre-campaign awareness survey would be needed against which the later survey results could be compared.

Once objectives have been defined and appropriate measures found, the next step in performing a textbook evaluation is to specify the components of the campaign (i.e. the techniques and resources making up the campaign whose efficacy is being tested) and to identify a control group. This is a group of people or institutions as similar as possible to the target audience, but who are not subject to the campaign and whose behaviour can therefore be used as a yardstick against which the effect of the campaign can be measured. (An alternative is to compare the campaign with other campaigns with similar objectives but with differing components or techniques.) The behaviour of the target audience and that of the control group is monitored and the results analysed to give the detailed evaluation of the efficacy of the campaign.

Control groups are important in public education campaigns which can yield quirky or unexpected results and where success is often measured in shifts in perception rather than direct changes in attitude or behaviour. An objective measure of the precise impact of the campaign is necessary to design future work. Notes on sampling techniques and the use of random procedures are given in chapter 4. For many campaigns, however, control groups will be difficult to identify or simply may not exist; campaigns targeted at central government are a good example. In these situations it may still be possible to establish comparisons with other campaigns using different techniques.

Some objectivity is also achieved by the use of an independent evaluator, who holds no vested interest in the results of the evaluation and who is more distanced from the day-to-day running of the campaign. Ideally, an independent evaluator would also bring with her the experience of having assessed other campaigns or programmes, which could be of great help in designing workable measures or monitoring procedures. For independent evaluation to be a success on a practice as sensitive as campaigning, a relationship of considerable trust has to exist between the pressure group and the evaluator. Conversely, the results of self-evaluation may be less objective but they do have a better record of being implemented. As with planning generally, much of the benefit of self-evaluation lies in the insights gained while carrying out the exercise, and improvements can be made to a campaign on a continuous basis.

Process evaluation

The holistic birth campaign cited above measured one of its objectives, the raising of awareness of holistic methods, by the quantity of relevant media coverage obtained. This is not actually a measure of awareness as such, but of the means by which awareness is created. It is an example of process evaluation.

Process evaluation has a wide application in campaigning because of the difficulties in assessing actual campaign outcomes or effects noted at the start of this chapter. It consists of the assessment of three separate aspects of the campaign process:

▼ *Whether the techniques used are functioning.* What level of coverage is being delivered by the campaign's media relations? What is the response rate from different mailshots, advertisements, insert programmes, etc.? What level of support among MPs and peers has resulted from the campaign's parliamentary work? Where necessary, notes on appropriate monitoring procedures for these techniques and others are given in the relevant chapters. Most are very straightforward but require organised record-keeping on a day-by-day basis.

▼ *Whether the people reached are those at whom the campaign is targeted.* Some techniques appear to be productive without actually reaching the people the campaign needs. Records, reply coupons and monitoring procedures should be designed so that adequate information is received on the level of penetration of the target audience.

▼ *Whether in retrospect the target(s) and channel(s) selected for the campaign are the most appropriate.* The veil of secrecy behind which decision-makers customarily operate will often become more transparent as a campaign progresses, occasionally necessitating a revision in the choice of target. Successive stages in the policy-making process may also be dominated by different people or institutions, with significant new targets or channels of influence appearing over time. Target and channel review is the most neglected of the three aspects of process evaluation considered here, but potentially the most far-reaching.

Although they cannot guarantee success, the three aspects of process evaluation, employed together, will provide a very strong indication of whether or not a particular campaign is on course. Periodically, however, a more fundamental evaluation of the campaign's effect is required.

Impact evaluation

Campaigners will usually know when their objectives have been realised. Moderate success short of the achievement of an objective – such as might justify continuing the campaign – is often much harder to spot. Even if an objective *is* realised, understanding the precise role played by the campaign may not be easy but would prove invaluable to the planning of future campaigns. Both these situations call for process evaluation to be supplemented by an assessment of the impact that process has had on the target.

How impact can be assessed will depend largely on the nature of the target and in particular on the quality of information available about its behaviour. This information will never be complete. In the empirical sciences, causation can be established by creating a controlled environment in which the variables under observation are isolated and subjected to testing. In the social sphere, it is not possible to control for all the variables or possible influences that may exist; as was noted in chapter 4, statistical methods can establish a correlation between variables, but not a cause. These evaluative limitations are not confined to campaigning: all evaluation in the field of social change ultimately depends on the ability of the evaluator to make reasoned inferences on the basis of the evidence available. Admittedly, matters are not helped by the widespread practice in the pressure group world of claiming responsibility for every change in policy and the equally prevalent habit in government of pouring scorn on all such claims.

In a few campaign situations, more than adequate information for the purposes of evaluation will already exist. Legal action is a good example (at least in cases that go to court), where the judgement provides a blow-by-blow account of what worked and what did not. In other instances, interim results, expressions of intent and other indicators, positive or negative, of the behaviour of the target should be matched with the results of process evaluation to build up as complete a picture as possible of the relationship between campaign activities and target reaction.

Often, however, a pressure group will find itself in the position that none of its objectives have been met and conventional indicators of progress are absent. In this situation it may still be possible to measure campaign impact by matching process evaluation results with the information that does exist on the target's behaviour. Examples of what this might involve for different types of campaign are illustrated in the box below. Note that what is being measured is another type of process – this time the impact registered on the target by the campaign.

Public education campaigns can carry out opinion surveys to gauge the shifts in perception that tend to accompany or prefigure changes in public attitudes or behaviour. It might be useful to test awareness of the campaign itself at the same time. With campaigns against companies, impact measures may not just be concerned with target behaviour (as understood through the company's public relations filter) but with external influences on the company triggered by the campaign: drops in sales, the attitudes of suppliers or other partners, even wobbles in the share price.

The sparring that takes place between pressure groups and government results in indications of progress that are often unreliable. The key to monitoring the success of a government lobbying campaign, like so much else in campaigning, is intelligence: up-to-date inside knowledge on who is making decisions, when and on what basis.

Impact measures for evaluating campaign progress

type of campaign	evaluation methods
Public education campaign	Process evaluation plus opinion surveys
Government lobbying	Process evaluation plus intelligence gathering
Legal action	Legal judgement (plus compliance survey where applicable)
Corporate campaign	Process evaluation plus monitoring share price/sales trends/PR outputs
Non-cooperation campaign	Process evaluation plus enforcement cost assessment

Appendix A
Political Activities and Campaigning by Charities

Preface

Charities in England and Wales have a long and distinguished history of contributing to social reform. They continue to make an invaluable contribution to issues central to the well-being of the community today. They do so by their practical work and by their example. They have a proud record of responding to new problems and developing new ways of tackling issues. They also do so by the informed contribution they make to public debate on how issues are best addressed. This can involve participation in issues that engage the political process. Charities cannot under our law be political bodies but this does not mean that they cannot contribute to the political process. The way in which they do so must take account of the constraints which the law places on political activity by charities.

The law is clear that charities must not have political objectives. There is, however, little direct guidance from the courts on the line to be drawn between activities by charities in a political context in pursuance of their objects which are permissible and those which encroach too far into the sphere of politics. Trustees need as clear an understanding of what is permissible as can be given. This leaflet seeks to provide revised and amplified guidance to charity trustees on the extent to which they may properly engage in political activities. It is principally designed to give helpful guidance:

▼ to assist trustees to ensure that any political activities they undertake are within the law;

▼ to indicate how the Commission would respond to allegations or evidence of undue political activities by a charity; and

▼ to afford some reassurance to trustees who follow this guidance that they are acting properly.

In this spirit, Sections 5 and 6 of this leaflet set out specific guidance on the basis of the principles set out on the previous pages on activities which charities may and may not undertake. Given the fact that the guidance is mostly derived from general principles rather than from specific judgements of the courts, it needs to be tested on the basis of practical examples. We will accordingly keep the guidelines under review, to ensure they are developed appropriately in the light of [the] experience of their impact upon the activities of charities.

The guidance was originally published in July 1995. This is the first reprint, clarifying some of the language used in the original publication. We have also responded to questions charities have asked us about their involvement in demonstrations and other forms of direct action by including a new section on that topic.

Our view of the first 18 months has been that the guidance has had a positive reception, and we sense that it is beginning to establish itself as a clear and practicable framework for charities' political and political campaigning activities. We were fortified in that view by the report of the Commission on the Future of the Voluntary Sector (July 1996). That report attached especial importance to our continuing to apply the guidance with flexibility, and we reaffirm our commitment to doing so. Our task in that respect is made easier by charities who discuss with us beforehand any proposed activity over which they have doubts.

We expect to publish further revisions in future and particularly welcome comments on the practical implications of the guidelines as part of our continuing review of their impact. Comments should be sent to our Publications Unit in the Taunton office.

Richard Fries, Chief Charity Commissioner
February 1997

What is this leaflet about?

1. This leaflet gives guidance on the degrees to which charities may engage in political activity. The guidance does not represent a view of what activities are acceptable as of being [of] social or moral worth, but seeks to describe what activities we consider charities can properly undertake under the existing law.

Meanings of expressions used in this leaflet

2. In this leaflet:

Governing document means any document which sets out the charity's purposes and, usually, how it is to be administered. It may be a trust deed, constitution, memorandum and articles of association, will, conveyance, Royal Charter, or Scheme of the Commissioners.

Political activity means any activity which is directed at securing, or opposing, any change in the law or in the policy or decisions of central government or local authorities, whether in this country or abroad.

Political purpose means in essence any purpose directed at:

▼ furthering the interests of any political party; or

▼ securing, or opposing, any change in the law or in the policy or decisions of central government or local authorities, whether in this country or abroad.

Trustees means charity trustee. Charity trustees are the people who are responsible for the general control and management of the administration of the charity. In the charity's governing document they may be called trustees, managing trustees, committee members, directors or governors, or they may be referred to by some other title.

Charitable purposes mean those which the law regards as charitable. These have been extended and developed by decisions of the Court and ourselves over the years by comparison with purposes originally held to be charitable. This development of law reflects changes in social conditions, and the process continues today. Charitable purposes are characterised by a desire to benefit others for the public good; this is known as public benefit. To be a charity, all purposes of an organisation must be exclusively charitable; a charity cannot have some purposes which are charitable as well as others which are not. A charity's charitable purposes are usually expressed as its objects.

Section 1: Introduction

3. Charities operate for the public benefit and their contribution to public life is immense. It includes tackling new issues and developing new ways of dealing with problems. Charities have a wealth of knowledge and experience which they can contribute to the solution, as well as the treatment, of problems relating to their area of work. The nation would be impoverished if charities were cut off entirely from public debate and the opportunity to inform decision-makers.

4. Charities must not be political organisations. But they are not precluded from all political activity. A distinction must be made between political **purposes** and political **activities**. The Courts have made it clear that a body whose stated purposes included the attainment of a political purpose cannot be charitable (Section 2 of this leaflet amplifies this). A body whose purposes **are** charitable (and therefore do not include a political purpose) **may** nevertheless engage in activities which are directed at securing, or opposing, changes in the law or in government policy or decisions, whether in this country or abroad (in this leaflet the expression "political activities" is used in this sense). But charities cannot engage in such political activities without restraint. In this there is a crucial difference between them and non-charitable voluntary bodies. Other voluntary bodies, unlike charities, having complete freedom within the law to support any cause they like. Charities on the other hand are restricted in the extent to which they can engage in political activities by the legal rules applying to them by virtue of their charitable status.

5. The degree to which charities may engage in political activity is the subject of this leaflet. The Guidance does not represent a view of what activities are acceptable as being of social or moral worth but seeks to describe what activities we consider charities can properly undertake under the existing law.

6. In any case where trustees remain uncertain as to the legality of proposed activities they should not hesitate to consult their legal advisers or to seek advice from us.

Section 2: Charitable status: definition of a political purpose

7. What charities are allowed to do is determined by their 'purposes', the objects for which they are established, as set out in their governing document. An institution whose stated purposes include the attainment of a political purpose cannot be a charity. This is clear from a number of cases decided by the Courts. The reason for this is that charities must be constituted for the public benefit. The Courts have made it clear that they will not determine whether a political purpose is or is not for the public benefit. Such questions are for political debate and Parliamentary determination.

8. Briefly, the Courts have held that purposes designed to promote the interests of a political party (an expression which is used in this leaflet to mean any local, national or European political grouping) or to seek or oppose changes in the law or government policy or decisions, whether in this country or abroad, are political purposes and not, therefore, charitable. It is possible to derive from the decisions of the Courts certain basic principles about political purposes and these are set out in the Annex to this leaflet.

Section 3: Extent to which charities may engage in political activities

9. Although an organisation established for political purposes can never be a charity, the trustees of a charity may do some things of a political nature as a means of achieving the purposes of the charity.

10. This principle, although easy to state, is not always easy to apply in practice. In applying it charity trustees must take particular care, since the dividing line between proper debate in the public arena and improper political activity is a difficult one to judge. The guidance given in this leaflet, which is drawn from the principles established by the Courts, is designed to help trustees to determine that line in relation to a range of activities. Any political activity undertaken by trustees must be in furtherance of, and ancillary to, the charity's stated objects and within its powers.

11. To be ancillary, activities must serve and be subordinate to the charity's purposes. They cannot, therefore, be undertaken as an end in themselves and must not be allowed to dominate the activities which the charity undertakes to carry out its charitable purposes directly. The

trustees must be able to show that there is a reasonable expectation that the activities will further the purposes of the charity, and so benefit its beneficiaries, to an extent justified by the resources devoted to those activities.

12. Where these requirements are met, trustees of charities may properly enter into dialogue with government on matters relating to their purposes or the way in which the trustees carry out their work. They may publish the advice or views they express to Ministers. They may also seek to inform and educate the public on particular issues which are relevant to the charity and its purposes, including information about their experience of the needs met in their field of activities and the solutions they advocate. But they must do so on the basis of a reasoned case and their views must be expressed with a proper sense of proportion.

13. Trustees must not advocate policies, nor seek to inform and educate, on subjects and issues which do not bear on the purposes of their charity. Moreover, the manner and content of any support of, or opposition to, legislative or policy change must be consistent with these guidelines.

14. In summary, therefore, a charity can engage in political activity if:

▼ there is a reasonable expectation that the activity concerned will further the stated purposes of the charity, and so benefit its beneficiaries, to an extent justified by the resources devoted to the activity;

▼ the activity is within the powers which the trustees have to achieve those purposes;

▼ the activity is consistent with these guidelines; and

▼ the views expressed are based on a well-founded and reasoned case and are expressed in a responsible way.

Section 5 of this leaflet gives more detailed guidance on the acceptability of particular kinds of political activity.

15. Because of the need to meet these requirements it is important that any charity undertaking political activities has adequate arrangements in place for the commissioning, control and evaluation of such activities by its trustees (who are, of course, ultimately responsible for ensuring that they are properly conducted).

Section 4: Campaigning

16. Campaigning by charities to mobilise public opinion to influence government policy can arouse strong feelings. On the one hand, many people think that charities should be allowed, and indeed have a duty, to campaign freely to change public policy on any issue if it is relevant to their work and if they have direct experience to offer. On the other hand, some argue that such campaigning is a misuse of charity funds, a misdirection of effort by charities and a misuse of the fiscal concessions

from which charities benefit. This is particularly so if the charity appears to favour a particular political party or a policy of a political party.

17. By the very nature of their knowledge and social concern, however, some charities are well placed to play a part in public debate on important issues of the day and to make an important contribution to the development of public policy. Others will invariably be drawn into such debate. It would be wrong to think that this cannot and should not happen: it is open to charities to engage in campaigning activities, provided the requirements set out in Section 3 of this leaflet are satisfied.

18. Whether a charity can properly engage in campaigning will, therefore, depend upon the nature of its purposes, its powers and the way in which it contributes to public debate. Where charities wish to raise issues in a way which will inform public debate and influence decisions of public bodies, great care must be taken to ensure that the issues concerned are relevant to their purposes and that the means by which they raise them are within their powers and consistent with these guidelines.

19. A charity should not seek to organise public opinion to support or oppose a political party which advocates a particular policy favoured or opposed by the charity. It is inevitable that sometimes a policy put forward by a charity coincides with that of a particular political party, or a political party decides to adopt such a policy. It does not follow that the charity is prevented from promoting its policy on the issue. However, it may influence how it does so. In such case the charity should take particular care – especially to ensure that the independence of its view is explained and understood.

20. Where a charity can properly campaign, the information provided to the public in support of the campaign as a whole must be accurate and sufficiently full to support its position. In arguing its case a charity is not restricted to using print media alone. If it uses a communications medium the nature of which makes it impracticable to set out the full basis of the charity's position, without the need to set out the full factual basis and argument lying behind that position. It must be able to set out its full position, however, if called upon to do so.

21. Provided all other requirements are met, material produced in support of a campaign may have emotional content. Indeed, we accept that in the areas in which many charities work it is difficult to avoid engaging the emotions of the public. But it would be unacceptable (except where the nature of the medium makes it impracticable to set out the basis of the charity's position) for a charity to seek to persuade government or the public on the basis of material which was **merely** emotive.

Section 5: What political activities are allowed?

22. A charity may undertake only those activities which further its purposes and which are authorised by its governing document. If the activity involves campaigning, then in all cases the manner in which it is conducted must be in accordance with the principles set out in Section 4 of this leaflet.

23. Where this is the case, a charity may engage in activities of the kinds shown below. Examples of activities in which a charity must **not** engage are shown in *italics*.

Influencing government or public opinion

24. A charity may seek to influence government or public opinion through well-founded, reasoned argument based on research or direct experience on issues either relating directly to the achievement of the charity's own stated purposes or relevant to the well-being of the charitable sector.

25. A charity may provide information to its supporters or the public on how individual Members of Parliament or parties have voted on an issue, provided they do so in a way which will enable its supporters or the public to seek to persuade those Members or parties to change their position through well-founded, reasoned argument rather than **merely** through public pressure.

26. A charity may provide its supporters, or members of the public, with material to send to Members of Parliament or the government, provided that the material amounts to well-founded, reasoned argument.

27. A charity may organise and present a petition to either House of Parliament or to national or local government. It is advisable to ensure that the purpose of the petition is stated on each page.

28. *A charity must not base any attempt to influence public opinion or to put pressure on the government, whether directly or indirectly through supporters or members of the public, to legislate or adopt a particular policy on data which it knows (or ought to know) is inaccurate or on a distorted selection of data in support of a preconceived position.*

29. *A charity must not participate in party political demonstrations.*

30. *A charity must not claim evidence of public support for its position on a political issue without adequate justification.*

31. *Except where the nature of the medium being employed makes it impracticable to set out the basis of the charity's position, a charity must not seek to influence government or public opinion on the basis of material which is merely emotive.*

32. A charity must not invite its supporters, or the public, to take action in support of its position without providing them with sufficient information to enable them to decide whether to give their support and to take the action requested. In particular, a charity must not invite its supporters or the public to write to their Members of Parliament or the government without providing them with sufficient information to enable them to advance a reasoned argument in favour of the charity's position.

33. A charity whose stated purposes include the advancement of education must not overstep the boundary between education and propaganda in promoting that purpose. The distinction is between providing balanced information designed to enable people to make up their own mind and providing one-sided information designed to promote a particular point of view.

Responding to proposed legislation

34. A charity may provide, and publish comments on possible or proposed changes in the law or government policy, whether contained in a Green or White Paper or otherwise.

35. A charity may, in response to a Parliamentary Bill, supply to Members of either House for use in debate such relevant information and reasoned arguments as can be reasonably be expected to assist the achievement of its charitable purposes.

Advocating and opposing changes in the law and public policy

36. A charity may advocate a change in the law or public policy which can reasonably be expected to help it to achieve its charitable purposes and may oppose a change in the law or public policy which can reasonably be expected to hinder its ability to do so. In either case the charity can present government with a reasoned written argument in support of its position. It may well publish its views and may seek to influence public opinion in favour of its position by well-founded reasoned argument.

Supporting, opposing and promoting legislation

37. A charity may support the passage of a Bill which can reasonably be expected to help it to achieve its charitable purposes and may oppose the passage of a Bill which can reasonably be expected to hinder its ability to do so.

38. A charity may spend its funds on the promotion of public general legislation provided it has the power to do so and the legislation can reasonably be expected to further its charitable purposes.

Commenting on public issues

39. A charity may comment publicly on social, economic and political issues if these relate to its purpose or the way in which the charity is able to carry out its work.

Supporting political parties

40. A charity may advocate a particular solution if it can reasonably be expected to further the purposes of the charity, even though that solution is advocated by a political party. If it does so it must make plain that its views are independent of the political party.

41. *A charity must not support a political party.*

Acting with other bodies

42. A charity may affiliate to a campaigning alliance, even if the alliance includes non-charitable organisations, provided certain conditions are met. First, the charity must carefully consider the alliance's activities, and the implications of the charity's being associated with them, and should only affiliate if affiliation can reasonably be expected to further the charity's own charitable purposes. Second, since a charity may not undertake through an alliance, activities which it would be improper for it to undertake directly. If the alliance engages in such activities the charity must dissociate itself from them and take reasonable steps to ensure that its name, and any funds its has contributed, are not used to support them.

Providing information

43. A charity may provide factual information to its members and those interested in its work in seeking to inform their Members of Parliament and others on matters related to the purposes of the charity.

44. A charity may employ Parliamentary staff to inform Members of Parliament on matters relevant to its purposes.

45. *A charity must not provide information which it knows, or ought to know, to be inaccurate, or which has been distorted by selection to support a preconceived position.*

46. *A charity must not provide supporters or members of the public with material specifically designed to underpin a party political campaign or for or against a government or particular MPs.*

47. *A charity must not issue material which supports or opposes a particular political party or the government.*

Forthcoming elections

48. A charity may respond to forthcoming elections, whether local, national or to the European Parliament, by analysis and commenting on the proposals of political parties which relate to its purposes or the way in which it is able to carry out its work, provided that it comments in a way which is consistent with these guidelines and complies with all the relevant provisions of electoral law.

49. A charity may also bring to the attention of prospective candidates issues relating to its purposes or the way in which it is able to carry out its work, and raise public awareness about them generally, provided that the promotional material is educational, informative, reasoned and well-founded.

50. *A charity must not seek to persuade members of the public to vote for or against a candidate or for or against a political party.*

Conducting and publishing research

51. A charity which conducts research must ensure that it is properly conducted using a methodology appropriate to the subject. If the research is undertaken to test a hypothesis arising from a charity's own experience or earlier research, it must be undertaken objectively to test that hypothesis rather than merely to support a preconceived position or objective. The aim in publishing the results of the research must be to inform and educate the public.

52. *A charity must not distort research, or the results of research, to support a preconceived position or objective.*

53. *A charity must not promote the results of research conducted by itself or others which it knows, or ought to know, to be flawed.*

54. *A charity must not undertake research for another body where it is clear that body intends to use the research for party political or propagandist purposes.*

55. We will be producing a further leaflet on charities and research, which will give more guidance in this area.

Seeking support for government grants

56. A charity may seek the support of Members of Parliament where a question arises as to whether a government grant to the charity is to be made or continued.

Section 6: Charities involvement in demonstrations and direct action

57. Charities may wish, as part of a campaign, to organise, promote or participate in some kind of demonstration or direct action. If this involves nothing more than the provision of reasoned argument or information (such as the handing out of leaflets in a public place) the principles stated earlier in the leaflet will apply to it and no particular difficulties should normally arise, whether from the point of view of organising the event or of deciding whether it is one in which the charity can properly be involved.

58. Different considerations apply if an event moves beyond the mere provision of reasoned argument or information (as may be the case, for

example, with marches, rallies, or peaceful picketing). This will be so even if elements of the event, such as the speeches made before a march, involve the provision of reasoned argument or information.

59. As in the case of other types of political activity, a charity can only organise, promote or take part in activity of this kind if it forms part of a well-founded and properly argued campaign which, seen as a whole, satisfies the requirements set out in Section 3. We will respond to any failure to meet this basic requirement in the same way as any other breach of these guidelines (see Section 7).

60. There are other matters which must also be considered by charities proposing to engage in demonstrations or direct action.

61. Whilst events of this nature may be thought to offer significant opportunities in terms of publicising a charity's position or showing the extent of public support for it on the matter in question, they can also involve significant risks.

62. Precisely because they go beyond the merely educative or informative, some people will regard any involvement by a charity in activities of this kind as inappropriate. As a result, the participation of a charity in a demonstration or direct action may damage public support for it, or even for charities generally. The further the activity moves away from reasoned argument and debate, and the more it affects the rights of others, the more likely it is that this will happen.

63. Additionally, events such as demonstrations and rallies can of course present real problems of control. Since the law relating to public order is complex and in parts unclear, there is considerable potential for the commission of an offence by the charity, its officers or those taking part.

64. The risks of incurring civil or criminal liability, and of adverse publicity, are of course increased significantly if an event is badly organised or if other groups who do not share the aims of the organisers become involved.

65. In our view, therefore, any charity considering taking part in demonstrations or direct action must consider the implications of doing so very carefully, from the point of view of both the possible impact on public support and potential civil or criminal liability.

66. A charity should assess whether or not it needs to seek its own legal advice on the lawfulness of what it has in mind, with a view to satisfying itself that there is no significant risk of any civil or criminal proceedings being brought against it, its trustees or members or those taking part. The greater the risk of interference with the rights of others, the more important it is that such advice should be taken, and the less likely that the activity can be justified in terms of the charity trustees' duties not to expose the property of the charity to risk.

67. Should the charity decide to proceed, the duty imposed on all charity trustees to act prudently will require its charity trustees to take reasonable steps to ensure that the event in question:

▼ receives thorough and appropriate advance preparation (including, where necessary, liaison with the police and other authorities);

▼ is at all times fully under the control of the charity (or of the organisers of the event, where the charity is not solely responsible for organising it);

▼ is peaceful;

▼ does not take such form, and is not conducted in such a way, as to give rise to a significant risk of civil or criminal proceedings being brought against the charity, its trustees or members or those participating in the event; and

▼ does not take such form, and is not conducted in such a way, as to bring the charity, or charities generally, into disrepute (as a result, for example, of being intimidatory, provocative or excessively disruptive of the life of the community).

68. Should charity trustees fail to take such reasonable steps, and their charity incur financial loss as a result (e.g. by incurring a liability to a third party following a demonstration which gets out of control) the trustees may be exposed to a claim for want of prudence in their administration of the charity, which could result in financial claims against them personally.

69. A charity should consider carefully before requiring its staff to take part in a demonstration or other form of direct action. One important consideration is that it is an implied term of employment contracts that the employer must not require the employee to do an unlawful act. While no charity will deliberately require its staff to do something that the charity knows is unlawful, equally it must take care that any instructions it gives to its staff are capable of being fully carried out in a way which will not involve, or be likely to involve, the staff in any unlawful act.

70. Finally, there can generally be no objection to members or officers of a charity participating in an individual capacity in demonstrations or direct action organised by others. Charities need to take reasonable steps, however, to ensure that if members or officers do take part **in an individual capacity**, there is no misunderstanding as to the basis of their participation. In particular, a charity should not do anything (such as supplying placards or badges for the purpose) which might suggest that participants are taking part as official representatives of the charity.

Section 7: What penalties are there for carrying out unacceptable political activities?

71. The pursuit of improper political activities by charities is a misuse of charity funds and can lead to the loss of tax relief on funds applied for that

purpose. It may also be regarded as amounting to the use of a charity as a vehicle for the personal views of its trustees. It can therefore bring about a loss of support for the charity and damage the good name of charities generally.

72. We therefore expect trustees to comply with these guidelines. Where it appears that they have failed to do so we will take the matter up with them to seek an explanation.

73. In the absence of a satisfactory explanation a range of possibilities arise, including simply giving advice to the trustees, taking proceedings against them for repayment of the funds applied on the activities in question (including any additional tax liability incurred as a result) and restricting future political activity.

74. The action taken by us will depend upon all the circumstances of the case, including:

▼ the scale and nature of the activity in question;

▼ whether the charity has engaged in improper political activities before; and

▼ the attitude of the charity trustees.

75. Political activity by the trustees of a charity would not normally affect its charitable status and be reason for removing it from the Register of Charities, as the issue would concern the propriety of the trustees' management of the charity rather than the nature of the charity's purposes. If, however, the trustees could argue successfully that the express purposes of the institution were wide enough to cover impermissible political activities, then the question of whether the organisation was established for exclusively charitable purposes would arise, and could lead to its removal from the Register of Charities.

Section 8: Conclusion

76. The extent to which charities are allowed to promote, support or take part in political activities has to be considered in each case in the light of all the relevant circumstances. It is not sufficient for the trustees simply to **believe** that their activities will effectively further the purposes of the charity; there must be a **reasonable expectation** that this is so. Trustees should not hesitate to consult their legal advisers, or to seek advice from us, before undertaking any activity which might be beyond the proper scope of the charity.

77. We are always willing to give advice on any specific problem a charity may have in this connection (on the distinction between education and propaganda, for example, or between an ancillary purpose and a main purpose) and to consider the draft of any publications such as advertisements, appeals, newsletters, etc. on which trustees have doubts.

Annex – Summary of Principal Court Decisions Relating to Political Purposes

1.   A trust for the attainment of a political purpose is not charitable since the Court has no way of judging whether a proposed change in the law will or will not be for the public benefit – **Bowman v Secular Society Ltd [1917] AC 406**, at page 442; **National Anti-Vivisection Society v Inland Revenue Commissioners [1948] AC31**, at page 49 and 62.

2.   The expression "political purpose" is not confined to party politics but includes the promotion of any change in the law – **Inland Revenue Commissioners v Temperance Council of Christian Churches of England and Wales [1926] 10 Tax Case 748; National Anti-Vivisection Society v Inland Revenue Commissioners [1948] AC 31**, at pages 51 and 61.

3.   To promote the maintenance of the existing law, or a particular line of political administration and policy, is also a political purpose – **Re Hopkinson [1949] 1 All ER 346**, at page 350; **Re Koeppler's Will Trusts [1948] Ch 243**, at pages 260 and 261. But a trust to promote the enforcement of an existing law may be charitable if its effect is to promote a charitable purpose – **Re Vallance (1876) 2 Seton's Judgements (7th ed) 1304; Re Herrick (1918) 52 ILT 213**.

4.   Political propaganda in the guise of education is not charitable – **Re Hopkinson [1949] 1 All ER 346**.

5.   A trust for the education of the public in or in accordance with one particular set of political principles is not charitable – **Re Hopkinson [1949] 1 All ER 346; Re Bushnell [1975] 1 All ER 721**. But a trust for the education of the public in forms of government and in political matters generally can be charitable – **Re The Trustees of the Arthur McDougall Fund [1956] 3 All ER 867**.

6.   Although an association for promoting some change in law cannot itself be a charity (see 1 and 2 above), an organisation would not necessarily lose its rights to be considered a charity if, as a matter of construction, the promotion of legislation were one among other lawful purposes ancillary to good charitable purposes; it is a question of degree – **National Anti-Vivisection Society v Inland Revenue Commissioners [1948] AC 31**, at pages 49 and 62.

7.   Research, to be charitable, must be directed to increasing the store of communicable knowledge in a public, as opposed to a private, way – **Re Hopkin's Will Trusts [1956] Ch 669**.

8.   In **McGovern v Attorney General [1982] Ch 321** (the Amnesty International Trust case), Mr Justice Slade concluded that a trust for political purposes can never be regarded as being for the public benefit in the manner which the law regards as charitable. Such trusts include those of which a direct and principle purpose is either:

(i)   to further the interests of a particular political party; or

(ii)   to procure changes in the laws of this country; or

(iii) to bring about changes in the laws of a foreign country; or

(iv) to bring about a reversal of Government policy or of particular decisions of governmental authorities in this country; or

(v) to bring about a reversal of Government policy or of particular decisions of governmental authorities in a foreign country.

The judge made it clear, however, that if all the main objects of the trust are exclusively charitable, the fact that trustees may have incidental powers to employ political means for their furtherance would not deprive the trust of its charitable status.

Mr Justice Slade's list is not exhaustive and in **Re Koeppler's Will Trusts [1948] Ch 243**, at page 260 Mr Justice Peter Gibson added to it "trusts to oppose a particular change in the law or a change in a particular law", following Mr Justice Vaisey in **Re Hopkinson**, (see paragraph 3 of this annex).

9. Charities cannot engage in public campaigning to influence public opinion on political issues unrelated to their own charitable objects. In **Baldry v Feintuck [1972] 2 All ER 81**, support by a student union for a campaign of protest against the Government's policy of ending free milk to school children was held to be a non charitable application of funds. In **Webb v O'Doherty and Others (Times Law Report, 11 February 1991),** support by a student union for a campaign against the Gulf War was held to be a non charitable application of funds. Similarly it is improper for a charity to join or otherwise provide support to a non charitable organisation as a means of furthering a political purpose unrelated to its charitable objects. In **Webb v O'Doherty** affiliation to bodies carrying out a campaign against the Gulf War was held to be unlawful for a charity.

Appendix B
Useful organisations and addresses

Advertising Agency Register (AAR)
26 Market Place
London W1
Tel: 020 7612 1200

BBC Appeals Advisory Committee
Broadcasting House
London W1A 1AA
Tel: 020 7580 4468

British Library
96 Euston Road
London NW1 2DB
Tel: 020 7412 7677

British Library Lloyds TSB
Business Line, Tel: 020 7412 7454
British Library's charged research
service, Tel: 020 7412 7457
Simple queries answered free of charge
on the Business Line; if more in-depth
research is required, a charge will be
made through the research service, for
which an initial quotation can be
provided.

British Library's newspaper library,
Colindale Avenue, London
NW9 5HE, Tel: 020 7412 7353

Butterworth Ltd
Legal Publishers
35 Chancery Lane
London WC2A 1EL
Customer Service line:
020 8662 2000

Barrow Cadbury Fund and **Barrow**
Cadbury Trust
Eric Adams (Director) or Dipali
Chandra (Deputy Director)
2 College Walk
Selly Oak
Birmingham B29 6LQ
Tel: 0121 472 0417

Certification Office for Trades
Unions and Employers
Associations
Brandon House
180 Borough High Street
London SE1 1LW
Tel: 020 7210 3734

Charity Commission for
England and Wales
Central enquiry line, Tel: 0870 333
0123; Minicom: 0870 333 0125
Website: www.charity-commission.
gov.uk

Harmsworth House
13–15 Bouverie Street
London EC4Y 8DP
Fax: 020 7674 2300

2nd Floor, 20 Kings Parade
Queens Dock, Liverpool L3 4DQ
Fax 0151 703 1555

Woodfield House
Tangier, Taunton
Somerset TA1 4BL
Fax 01823 345 003

Committee of Advertising Practice (CAP)
Tel: 020 7580 4100
Fax: 020 7580 4072
E-mail: advice@cap.org.uk
Website: www.cap.org.uk

CAP offers a free copy advice service to intending advertisers to help them avoid provoking complaints (or at least reduce the chances of a complaint being upheld).

Community Matters (National Federation of Community Organisations)
8–9 Upper Street
London N1 0PQ
Tel: 020 7226 0189

Companies House
Website: www.companies-house.gov.uk

21 Bloomsbury Street
London WC1B 3XD
Tel 029 2038 0801

Crown Way
Cardiff CF14 3UZ
Tel: 029 2038 8588

37 Castle Terrace
Edinburgh EH1 2EB
Tel: 0131 535 5800

IDB House
Chichester Street
Belfast BT1 4JX

Consumers Association
2 Marylebone Road
London NW1 4DF
Tel: 020 7770 7000
Fax: 020 7770 7600

The Council of Europe
Palais de l'Europe
F-67075 Strasbourg Cedex
France
Tel: 00 33 3 88 41 2000
Website: www.coe.int

CSV Media
237 Pentonville Road
London N1 9NJ
Tel: 020 7278 6601

Direct Marketing Association
Haymarket House
1 Oxenden Street
London SW1Y 4EE
Tel: 020 7321 2325

Directory of Social Change (DSC)
24 Stephenson Way
London NW1 2DP
E-mail: info@dsc.org.uk
Website: www.dsc.org.uk
Publications
Tel: 020 7209 5151; Fax: 020 7209 5049
Courses and Conferences
Tel: 020 7209 4949; Fax 020 7209 4130
Marketing and Research
Tel: 020 7209 4422; Fax 020 7209 4130
Charityfair and Charity Centre
Tel: 020 7209 1015; Fax 020 7209 4130

Disclosure Information Centre
Primark
1 Mark Square, Leonard Street
London EC2A 4EG
Tel: 020 7566 1910
Website: www.disclosure.co.uk

The Ethical Investment Research Service (EIRIS)
80–84 Bondway
London SW8 1SF
Tel: 020 7928 3649

Euro Citizen Action Service (ECAS)
rue de la Concorde 53
B-1050 Brussels
Belgium
Tel: 00 32 2 548 0490
Website: www.ecas.org

Europa Publications
11 New Fetter Lane
London EC4P 4EE

Tel: 020 7822 4300
Fax: 020 7822 4319
Website: www.europapublications.
co.uk

European Commission
Switchboard: 00 32 2 299 1111

**The European Court of
Human Rights**
Council of Europe
F-67075 Strasbourg Cedex
France
Tel: 00 33 3 88 41 2018
Website: http://echr.coe.int

European Parliament
Switchboard: 00 32 2 284 2111

**The UK office of the European
Parliament**
2 Queen Anne's Gate
London SW1
Tel: 020 7227 4300

European Union
Website: http://europa.eu.int
*Provides access to the home pages of all
the EU institutions, as well as publications, legislation, calendars, press
releases and information on policies.*

Foundation Center
79 Fifth Avenue
New York
New York 10003
USA
Tel: 00 1 212 620 4230
Website: www.fdncenter.org

Free Representation Unit
Peer House
8 Verulam Street
London WC1X 8LZ
Tel: 020 7831 0692

Hamilton House Mailings Ltd
(for NCVO publications)
Earlstrees Court

Earlstrees Road
Corby NN17 4AX
Tel: 01536 399016
Fax: 01536 399012

House of Commons
London SW1A 0AA

House of Commons main line:
020 7219 3000
Website: www.open.gov.uk
*Extensive information on both
government departments and public
bodies*

House of Commons Public
Information Office: 020 7219 4272

House of Lords

House of Lords Journal and
Information Office: 020 7219 3107

**Industrial Common Ownership
Movement (ICOM)**
74 Kirkgate
Leeds LS2 7DJ
Tel: 0113 246 1737
Fax: 0113 244 0002

**Institute of Charity Fundraising
Managers (ICFM)**
Market Towers
1 Nine Elms Lane
London SW8 5NQ
Tel: 020 7627 3436

Jane's Information Group
Sentinel House
163 Brighton Road
Coulsdon, Surrey CR5 2YH
Tel: 020 8700 3700
Website: www.janes.com

Labour Research
78 Blackfriars Road
London SE1 8HF
Tel: 020 7928 3649

Law Centres Federation
Duchess House
18–19 Warren Street
London W1P 5DB
Tel: 020 7387 8570
E-mail: info@lawcentres.org.uk
Website: www.lawcentres.org.uk

Legal Action Group
242 Pentonville Road
London N1 9UN
Tel: 020 7833 2931
Fax: 020 7837 6094
E-mail: lag@lag.org.uk

Liberty (National Council for Civil Liberties)
21 Tabard Street, London SE1 4LA
Tel: 020 7403 3888
Fax: 020 7407 5354
Legal advice service,
Tel: 020 7378 8659

The Market Research Society
15 Northburgh Street
London EC1V 0JR
Tel: 020 7490 4911

Media Trust
3–7 Euston Centre
Regent's Place
London NW1 3JG
Tel: 020 7874 7600
Website: www.mediatrust.org.uk

National Association of Citizens Advice Bureaux
115–123 Pentonville Road
London N1 9LZ
Tel: 020 7833 2181
Fax: 020 7833 4371

National Association of Councils for Voluntary Service (NACVS)
3rd Floor, Arundel Court
177 Arundel Street
Sheffield S1 2NU

Tel: 0114 278 6636
Fax: 0114 278 7004
E-mail nacvs@nacvs.org.uk
Website: www.nacvs.org.uk

The National Consumer Council
20 Grosvenor Gardens
London SW1W 0DH
Tel: 020 7730 3469

National Council for Voluntary Organisations (NCVO)
Regent's Wharf
8 All Saints Street
London N1 9RL
Tel: 020 7713 6161
Fax: 020 7713 6300
(for NCVO publications, contact Hamilton House Mailings)

National Lottery Charities Board
St Vincent House
16 Suffolk Street
London SW1Y 4NL
Tel: 020 7747 5299
Application packs can be obtained by calling 0845 791 9191 or on the web at www.nlcb.org.uk

Network for Social Change Ltd
BM Box 2063
London WC1 3XX

Northern Ireland Assembly Ombudsman/Commissioner for Complaints
Freepost
Belfast BT1 6BR
Tel: 0800 343 424

Northern Ireland Council for Voluntary Action (NICVA)
127 Ormeau Road
Belfast BT7 1SH
Tel: 028 9032 1224
Fax: 028 9043 8350

**Parliamentary
Communications Ltd**
10 Little College Street
London SW1P 3SH
Tel: 020 7858 1555

Parliamentary Profile Services Ltd
34 Somali Road
London NW2 3RL
Tel: 020 7222 5884

Parliamentary website
www.parliament.uk
*Detailed information on parliamentary
activity.*

**Pensions and Investment
Research Consultants (PIRC)**
4th Floor, Cityside
40 Adler Street
London E1 1EE
Tel: 020 7247 2323

Police Complaints Authority
10 Great George Street
London SW1P 3AE

**Police Operations at the Palace of
Westminster**
Tel: 020 7219 6882

**Special events office,
Charing Cross police station**
Tel: 020 7321 7524

The Public Law Project
Birkbeck College
Malet Street
London WC1
Tel: 020 7467 9800

The Public Records Office
Ruskin Avenue
Kew
Surrey TW9 4DU
Tel: 020 8876 3444

Release
388 Old Street
London EC1V 9LT
Tel: 020 7729 5255

Release's helplines providing
emergency help and advice in
case of arrest:
Tel: 020 7603 8654 (24-hours)
020 7729 9904 (office hours)

Registry of Friendly Societies
Victory House
30–34 Kingsway
London WC2B 6ES
Tel: 020 7663 5025

**The Joseph Rowntree
Reform Trust**
Lois Jefferson (Trust Secretary)
The Garden House
Water End
York YO30 6WQ
Tel: 01904 625 744

**Scottish Council for Voluntary
Organisations (SCVO)**
18–19 Claremont Crescent
Edinburgh EH7 4QD
Tel: 0131 556 3882
Fax: 0131 556 0279

**Scottish Human Rights Centre
(formerly the Scottish Council for
Civil Liberties)**
146 Holland Street
Glasgow G2 4NG
Tel: 0141 332 5960
Fax 0141 332 5309
E-mail: shrc@dial.pipex.com
Website: www.shrc.dial.pipex.com

**Stationery Office Publications
Centre**
PO Box 276
London SW8 5DT
Tel: orders on 020 7873 9090 and
enquiries on 020 7873 0011

Trades Union Congress
Congress House
Great Russell Street
London WC1B 3LS
Tel: 020 7636 4030
Fax 020 7636 0632

UKREP
10 Avenue d'Auderglem
1040 Brussels
Belgium
Tel: 00 32 2 287 8211
Website: http://ukrep.fco.gov.uk
UK's permanent representation in Brussels

Vacher Dod Publishing Ltd
PO Box 3700
Westminster
London SW1E 5NP
Tel: 020 7828 7256

Wales Council for Voluntary Action (WCVA)
Baltic House
Mount Square
Cardiff CF10 5FH
Tel: 029 2043 1700
Fax: 029 2043 7701

Appendix C
Useful publications

Titles published by the Directory of Social Change (DSC) and Charities Aid Foundation (CAF) are available from the Directory of Social Change, Publications department, 24 Stephenson Way, London NW1 2DP. Call 020 7209 5151 or e-mail info@dsc.org.uk for more details and for a free publications list, which can also be viewed at the DSC website: www.dsc.org.uk
Prices were correct at the time of going to press but may be subject to change.

Aslib Directory of Information Sources
edited by Keith W Reynard and Jeremy M E Reynard
Aslib Publications
10th edition 1999

Hard copy alone
£295.00   ISBN 0 85142 409 0

Combined hard copy and CD-ROM
£360.00   ISBN 0 85142 418 X

Additional copies of CD-ROM
£30.00 each   ISBN 0 85142 425 2

Benn's Media
Miller Freeman Information Services
2000

UK volume   ISBN 86382 429 3

Europe volume   ISBN 0 86382 430 7

World volume   ISBN 0 86382 431 5

£152.00 each or £325 for set of three volumes (reduced price available for subscriptions)
Miller Freeman Informations Services, Miller Freeman UK Ltd, Riverbank House, Angel Lane, Tonbridge, Kent TN9 1SE, Tel: 01732 377591; Website: www.mfinfo.com

British Archives: A Guide to Resources in the United Kingdom
edited by Janet Foster and Julia Sheppard
Macmillan
3rd edition September 1995
£85.00   ISBN 0 333 53255 4

Civil Service Yearbook
produced by the Cabinet Office
33rd (2000) edition December 1999
£40.00   ISBN 0114301573
available from the Stationery Office Publications Centre (see appendix B)

Complete Fundraising Handbook
Sam Clarke & Michael Norton
DSC
3rd edition 1997
£14.95   ISBN 1 900360 09 8

Corporate Events Services
published annually by Showcase Publications
9th edition 1999/2000
£30.00
Showcase Publications, 38c The Broadway, London N8 9SU, Tel: 020
8348 2332; Fax: 020 8340 3750: E-mail: info@cesbook.co.uk Website:
www.cesbook.co.uk

Current British Directories
CBD Research Ltd
13th edition 1999
£165.00
ISBN 0 900246 75 8
ISSN 0070 1858
CBD Research Ltd, Chancery House, 15 Wickham Road, Beckenham,
Kent BR3 5JS, Tel: 020 8650 7745; Fax: 020 8650 0768;
E-mail: cbdresearch@compuserve.com Website: www.glen.co.uk/cbd

Dod's Parliamentary Companion
Vacher Dod Publishing Ltd (see appendix B)
181st edition 2000
ISBN 090570228X

Directory of Grant Making Trusts
CAF
1999/2000 edition
£89.95   ISBN 1 85934 078 4

Ecodefense: A Field Guide to Monkey-wrenching
edited by Dave Foreman and Bill Haywood
Abbzug Press, Chico, California
3rd edition 1993
$20.00   ISBN 0963775103

Freedom of Information Handbook
David Northmore
Bloomsbury
1990   ISBN 0747508771
Out of print

Grants from Europe
Ann Davison
NCVO
8th edition 1997
£12.50   ISBN 0 7199 1502 3
available from Hamilton House Mailings Ltd (see appendix B)

Guide to European Union Funding
Peter Sluiter & Laurence Wattier
DSC
1st edition 1999
£18.95   ISBN 1 900360 50 0

Guide to Funding from Government Departments and Agencies
Susan Forrester & Ruth Pilch
DSC
1st edition 1998
£18.95   ISBN 1 900360 42 X

Guide to the Major Trusts
DSC
Volume 1 (Top 300 trusts)
Luke FitzHerbert, Dominic Addison & Faisel Rahman
7th edition 1999/2000 *(new edition January 2001)*
£19.95   ISBN 1 900360 38 1

Volume 2 (Next 700 trusts)
Sarah Harland, Louise Walker & Dave Casson
4th edition 1999/2000 *(new edition January 2001)*
£19.95   ISBN 1 900360 52 7

Volume 3 (Further 400 UK-wide trusts, plus trusts in Northern Ireland, Scotland and Wales)
Sarah Harland & Louise Walker
1st edition 2000/20001
£17.95   ISBN 1 900360 69 1

CD-ROM Trusts Guide
DSC
2nd edition 1999/2000
£129.25 (£110.00+VAT)   ISBN 1 900360 64 0
This will be replaced early in 2001 by a CD-ROM which contains the DSC and CAF databases of trusts.

Trust Monitor
published 3 times a year by DSC
2000 annual subscription price £30.00
ISSN 1369 4405

Guide to UK Company Giving
John Smyth
DSC
3rd edition 2000
£25.00   ISBN 1 900360 68 3

CD-ROM Company Giving Guide
DSC
2nd edition 2000
£99.88 (£85.00+VAT)   ISBN 1 900360 74 8

Corporate Citizen
published 3 times a year by DSC
2000 annual subscription price £30 for voluntary groups, £55 for others
ISSN 1353 0100
Website: www.dsc.org.uk/corporatecitizen

List of Ministerial Responsibilities
produced by the Cabinet Office
November 1999 edition
£5.00
available from Central Secretariat, Cabinet Office, Room 132E/1, Horse Guards Road, London SW1P 3AL, Tel: 020 7270 1865.
Please make cheques payable to 'Cabinet Office Votes Cash Account'
The List can also be viewed at: www.cabinet-office.gov.uk

The Marketing of Ideas and Social Issues
Seymour Fine
New York, Praeger
(1981 quoted), 1997 latest
ISBN 0 03 059277 1

Media Law
Geoffrey Robertson QC and Andrew Nicol
Penguin
1992
ISBN 0140138668

Municipal Yearbook
edited by Katie Brown
Newman Books
2000
Two volumes (not sold separately) £173 plus £5.00 p&p per copy
in the UK
ISBN 02076298171
Also available on CD-ROM
Newman Books, 32 Vauxhall Bridge Road, London SW1V 2SS,
Tel: 020 7973 6624; Fax: 020 7233 5057; Website:
www.newmanbooks.co.uk

Networking in Europe
Brian Harvey
NCVO
2nd edition 1995
£16.95   ISBN 0 7199 1460 4
available from Hamilton House Mailings Ltd (see appendix B)

Official Journal of the European Union.
appears daily – C-series gives information on programmes and
decisions, L-series is on legislation.
Available on subscription from the Stationery Office; recent issues can
be accessed free of charge on the world wide web at http://
europa.eu.int

Public Bodies
published for the Cabinet Office by the Stationery Office
(December) 1999
£24.95   ISBN 0 11 430159 x
available from the Stationery Office (see appendix B)

Regional Trends
edited by Jill Matheson and Alison Holding
produced by Office for National Statistics
(September) 1999
£39.50   ISBN 011621158x
available from the Stationery Office (see appendix B)

Shareholder Action Handbook
Craig Mackenzie
New Consumer Ltd
1993
ISBN 1 897806 00 0

Social Trends
edited by Jill Matheson and C Summerfield
produced by Office for National Statistics (January) 2000
£39.50   ISBN 011621242x
available from the Stationery Office (see appendix B)

Vacher's European Companion
published quarterly by Vacher Dod Publishing Ltd (see appendix B)
annual subscription £53.00
single copies £16.50
ISBN x100000542

Vacher's Parliamentary Companion
published quarterly by Vacher Dod Publishing Ltd (see appendix B)
A5 format (ISBN x100000858)
A6 format (ISBN x100000541)
single copies £11.50 each

Whitehall Companion
(December) 1999
£165.00   ISBN 0117022632
available from the Stationery Office (see appendix B)

Who's Who
published annually by A&C Black Publishers Ltd
2000
£115   ISBN 07136 5158 x
A&C Black Publishers Ltd, 35 Bedford Row, London, WC1R 4JH, Tel:
orders on 01480 212 666; enquiries on: 020 7242 0946; Fax: 020 7831
8478; E-mail: enquiries@acblack.co.uk

Who's Who in the City
Waterlow Professional Publishing
2000
£139.00   ISBN 185783853x

Willings Press Guide
Nesta Williams
Hollis Directories
2000
£225.00   ISBN 0900967145

Writer's Handbook
edited by Barry Turner
published annually by Macmillan
2000
ISBN 0333725751

List of Information Boxes

Sources of information on grant-making trusts and foundations 51

Sources of information on international grants 64

Information on companies and independent organisations 71

Census data from the Office for National Statistics 74

The think-tanks at a glance 78

Useful web sites 121

The investigators... 178

Business Directories 230

Sources of information on politicians and Parliament 293–4

General information on the EU 328

List of Influence Maps

1 Environment of the modern company 224

2 Secondary targets 241

3 Structure of a local authority 247

4 Lobbying for a grant 253

5 Influencing contracted-out services 262

6 Central government 265

7 Organisation of a government department 271

8 The creation of legislation 278

9 The House of Commons 302

10 Passage of a government bill through Parliament 314

11 The European decision-making process 326

12 European legislation under the co-decision procedure 336

Index

Access to Health Records Act 1990, 321
Access to Medical Reports Act 1988, 321
Access to Personal Files Act 1987, 321
Action for Victims of Medical Accidents, 59
Action on Smoking and Health (ASH), 59
Acts of Parliament, *see Legislation*
Adam Smith Institute, 57, 78
Adjournment debates, 309-10
Advertising, 36, 38, 43, 92-117
    agencies, 100-1, 111
Advertising Agency Register, 101
Advertising Standards Authority, 112, 166, 239-40
Agencies (government), *see Quangos*
Aims of Industry, 57
Alinsky, Saul, 197, 217
All-party groups, 292, 294
Amnesty International, 27-8, 31, 47, 54, 58, 59, 96, 123,
    126, 150-1, 282, 343
Animal Aid, 214
Annual general meeting (AGM), 36, 116, 231-4, 240
Anti-Apartheid Movement, 47, 197, 238-9
Anti-Slavery International, 59
Arrest, 19, 191-4, 211-13, 218
Association of London Authorities, 108
Audience, 92-3, 95, 105-7, 349-57, 362-65
Audit, 257-60, 289, 327
Audit Commission, 258-9, 261, 289
Audit Commission Act 1998, 259

Baby Milk Action, 346
Barrow Cadbury Fund Ltd, 54-5
BBC Children in Need Trust, 51
Beauty Without Cruelty, 238, 350
Bedford Box, 347-9, 362, 366-8
Benefits (events), *see Events*
Benn, Tony, 318
Bills, *see Legislation*
Blair, Tony, 9, 10, 304
Borman, William, 200
Boycotts, 200, 218, 237-9
Bradman, Godfrey, 50, 180
Brando, Marlon, 197
Brent Housing Action Campaign, 197
British Atlantic Committee, 59
British Medical Association, 237
British Union for the Abolition of Vivisection (BUAV), 340-2
Broadcasting Complaints Commission, 152
Budget, The, 282-3
Bush, George, 197
Butler-Sloss, Lord Justice, 156

Cabinet, 264-70, 277-80, 282-3
Campaign Against the Arms Trade, 230
Campaign for Nuclear Disarmament (CND), 114, 185,
    188, 354
Campbell, Alastair, 9
Catholic Association for Racial Justice, 350
Centre for Policy Studies, 78
Channels (of influence), 352-4

Charitable purposes, 24-8, 46, 51-2
Charitable status, 15, 24-34, 35, 46
Charitable Uses Act 1601, 24-5
Charities Act 1992, 44, 49
Charities Act 1993, 28
Charities Aid Foundation, 51
Charity Commission, 25, 27-8, 31-4, 45, 51, 52, 71, 79, 288-9
Charter 88, 54, 99-100
Child Poverty Action Group, 54, 170, 281
Christian Aid, 96
Cinema, 100, 110-11
Citizens Advice Bureaux, 213
Civil disobedience, 202-19
Civil Liberties Trust, 34
Civil proceedings, *see Legal action*
Civil servants, 73, 75, 216, 263-90
Clark, Alan, 269, 332-3
CLEAR (Campaign for Lead-Free Air), 50
Coalition for an International Court, 346
Comic Relief, 51
Commercial participators, 49
Commission for Local Administration, 178, 257
Commission of the European Communities, *see
    European Commission*
Committee of 100, 197
Committee of Permanent Representatives (COREPER),
    331-4
Committee of the Regions (EU), 338-9
Community charge, *see Poll tax*
Community Legal Service, 148, 180
Community Matters, 23, 29
Companies (for-profit), 11, 34, 35, 47, 57-8, 71, 116,
    222-42, 373
Companies Act 1985, 18, 228, 229, 231, 233
Companies House, 71, 226, 228-9, 234
Company limited by guarantee, 15, 17-20, 23, 25, 46
    charitable, 29
Conservative Party, 16, 36, 77, 230, 285, 301, 304
Constitution, 15-21, 28-9, 32-33, 36
Consumer action, 159, 196, 218, 223, 237-42
Contracting out, 245, 261-2
Contracts, 14-18
Copyright, 67, 113-14
Copywriting, 95-8
Corporate identity, 96
Council of Europe, 72, 343-5
Council of Ministers (EU), 324-7, 331-8, 341
Councils, *see Local authorities*
Councillors, 245-57
Court of Auditors (EU), 327
Courts, 154-8, 160, 162-3, 164-5, 179-80, 194-6,
    339-41, 344-5
Credibility, 67-8, 355-7, 365-6
Criminal Justice and Public Order Act 1994, 172, 183, 204-5
Criminal Law Act 1977, 203-4
Crown Prosecution Service, 156-9

Defamation, 113, 114-17, 240
Defamation Act 1952, 115
Defamation Act 1996, 116-17, 128

Demonstrations, 8, 19, 182-94, 240
Demos, 57, 78
Departments, *see Government*
Design, 98-100
Devolution, 284-7
Diplock, Lord, 167
Direct action, 11, 199-219, 240, 242, 361
Direct mail, 23, 35, 37, 40-4, 92-3, 100-1, 111
Direct Marketing Association, 43
Directory of Social Change, 51, 58, 59, 134, 140, 230
District auditor, 258-60
Donations, 29-30, 37-46, 50, 57-8, 97, 107, 109-10
Donor profiling, 37-8, 40-3, 93

Early day motions, 307-9
Earth First!, 208
Economic and Social Committee (EU), 338-9
Electronic picketing, *see Picketing, electronic*
El Salvador Committee for Human Rights, 48
Embargoes, 138-40
Employee action, 235-7
Employment Acts, 235
Employment Policy Institute, 78
Encryption, 129-30
Entryism, 215-16
Environment, 7, 11, 26, 63, 81, 95, 124, 159, 202-3, 214-15, 238, 362
Environment and Safety Information Act 1988, 321
Environmental Defense Fund, 124
Equal Opportunities Commission, 59
Ethical Investment Research Service, 230
Euro Citizen Action Service, 328, 342
European Anti-Poverty Network, 342
European Commission, 63, 324-31, 335-42
European Council, 325, 327
European Court of Human Rights, 171-7, 344-5
European Court of Justice, 158, 339-40
European Parliament, 324-8, 331, 334-8
European Social Fund, 63
European Union, 10, 63, 72, 258, 324-3
Evaluation, 110-111, 369-73
Events, 47-9
Excalibur database, 150
Exclusives, 143-4

Fabian Society, 77-8
Fine, Seymour, 351-2, 363
Ford Foundation, 64
Foreign and Commonwealth Office, 59
Foreign Policy Centre, 78
Foreman, Dave, 208
Foundation Center, 64
Foundations, 29, 35, 50-5
    non-charitable, 53-5
Freedom of information, 73-5, 321
Freedom of Information Bill, 73-5
Freedom of Information Campaign, 321
Free Representation Unit, 180
Friends of the Earth, 50, 95, 143, 197, 238
Fund for the Replacement of Animals in Medical
    Experiments (FRAME), 350
Fundraising, 19, 21, 30, 35-64, 191

Gandhi, MK, 200-202, 211, 216, 237
Gatsby Charitable Foundation, 50

Gay rights, 62, 189, 209-10, 360
Genetically-modified (GM) food, 11, 208-9, 239
Gordon, Mildred, 318
Government (lobbying), 27-8, 32, 35, 42, 59, 68, 72-6,
    112-14, 151, 155-6, 165, 215, 216, 228, 263-90, 291,
    300-23, 373
    agencies, *see Quangos*
    departments, 59, 73, 75, 103, 166, 177, 178, 226, 263-90
    local, *see Local authorities*
Government of Wales Act 1998, 287
Grants, 20, 29, 50-64, 253
Greater London Council, 60
GreenNet, 64
Greenpeace, 42, 95, 171, 198, 216, 232

Haldane, RB, 281
Hand bills, *see leaflets*
Harvey, Brian, 342
Haywood, Bill, 208
Health authorities, 63, 159-60
Health Education Authority, 97
Health Services and Public Health Act 1968, 60
Healthcare Foundation, 52
Hennessy, Peter, 342
Heseltine, Michael, 168
Homelessness, 24, 165, 168, 203
House of Commons, Lords, *see Parliament*
Housing Act 1985, 60
Howard, Michael, 165, 289
Human Rights Act 1998, 7, 10, 171-7, 194, 345
Humane Research Trust, 350

Income and Corporation Taxes Act 1988, 46
Index on Censorship, 64
Industrial and provident society, 14, 19
Industrial Common Ownership Movement, 23
Industry and Parliament Trust, 57
Ingham, Sir Bernard, 151
Inserts, 36-8, 43, 100, 104
Institute for Public Policy Research, 78
Institute of Charity Fund-raising Managers, 49
Institute of Economic Affairs, 24, 77-8
Institute of Fiscal Studies, 77-8
International Baby Food Action Network (IBFAN), 346
International campaigning, 27-8, 342-6
International Centre for the Legal Protection of Human
    Rights, 64
International Court of Justice, 345
International Criminal Court, 346
International Freedom Foundation, 33
International Monetary Fund, 346
Internet, 10-11, 69, 118-30, 189, 194, 217, 241
Interviews, 86-9, 145-9
IranAid, 45

Jane's Information Group, 229
Jones, W Alton, Foundation, 64
Judges, 154, 158, 163
Judicial review, 8, 153, 164-71, 256, 290

Labour Party, 36, 44, 58, 60, 215, 285, 301, 304, 354
Labour Research, 230
Law Centres Federation, 161
Lawrence, Ivan, 321

Lawrence, Stephen, 150,156
Leaflets, 36, 38-9, 92, 101, 189
Legal action, 8, 14-15, 18, 112-17, 153-81, 237, 240, 256, 290, 339-41, 372-3
Legal Aid, 180
Legal structure, 154-8
   of pressure groups, 14-19
Legislation, 20, 33, 72, 154, 176-7, 277-80, 312-21
   European, 325-6, 334-8, 339-41
   see also individual Acts of Parliament
Letters
   to MPs, 297-300
   to the press, 144-5
Leverhulme Trust, 50
Libel, *see defamation*
Liberal Democrats, 36, 285, 304, 365
Liberty, 34, 58, 211, 213, 345
Lincolnshire and Nottinghamshire Against Nuclear Dumping, 214
Livingstone, Ken, 60
Local authorities, 44, 102-3, 206, 243-62
   finance, 257-8
   grants from, 60-3
London Boroughs Grants Scheme, 63
Local Government (Access to Information) Act 1985, 250
Local Government Act 1966, 351
Local Government Acts 1972, 1985, 1986 and 1988, 60-2
Local groups, 21-3
Low Pay Unit, 59, 152
Lynx, 47, 116

Maastricht Treaty on European Union, 10, 324-5, 334-5, 339, 343
MacArthur Foundation, 64
MacKenzie, Craig, 231
Macnaghten, Lord, 25
Magistrates, 156-8
Mail-bombing, 126-7, 217, 241
Major, John, 10, 206, 269
Mailing lists, 37-8, 40-4
Management committee, 17-18, 20-2, 25, 30, 34
Marches, see *Demonstrations*
Market research, 41, 79, 359
Market Research Society, 88
Market squeeze, 237-9
Marketing, 7, 43
   of causes, 348-55
Mass lobbies, 311-12
Media, 7-9, 33, 36, 89-90, 131-52, 188, 196-8, 202, 275-7, 290, 370-1
   see also *Press*
Members of Parliament, 32, 92, 178, 256, 260-1, 274-5, 291-323, 343-4, 353, 358
Members, membership, 15-18, 20-3, 35-40, 49
MIND (National Association for Mental Health), 161
Ministers, 75, 131, 167, 263-90, 313, 322, 331-4
Mitchell, Austin, 300
Monitoring, 110-11, 369-73
Monkey-wrenching, 207-9, 219
MPs, *see Members of Parliament*

Nader, Ralph, 66
Nairne, Sir Patrick, 288
National Anti-Vivisection Society, 350
National Assembly for Wales, 284-5, 287
National Association for the Care and Resettlement of Offenders (NACRO), 294

National Audit Office, 289
National Childcare Campaign, 59
National Consumer Council, 240
National Council for Civil Liberties, *see Liberty*
National Council for Voluntary Organisations, 23, 29, 59, 64, 294
National Front, 62
National Health Service, 68, 284
National Lottery Charities Board, 55-7
Network for Social Change, 50, 55
Network Foundation, 55
Networks, 17, 341-2
News, *see media*
Newsletter, 37-8, 189
News releases, 137-8
Nicaragua Solidarity Campaign, 47
Nicol, Andrew, 114
Non-cooperation, 205-7, 373
Northern Ireland Assembly, 244
Northern Ireland Council for Voluntary Action, 23
Northmore, David, 75
Nuffield Foundation, 50

Objects, 17-21, 24-34, 51-2
Obstructions, 202-3
Occupations, 203-5, 218
Office for National Statistics, 72
Officers (local authority), 243, 246-55
Official Secrets Acts, 203
Officials, *see civil servants*
Ombudsman, *see Parliamentary Commissioner*
Opinion polls, 8, 88-9
Oxfam, 32-3, 46, 108
Oxleas Wood, 202

Pankhurst, Emmeline, 76
Parents Against Tobacco, 52
Parliament, 62, 72-5, 153-5, 165-7, 184, 189, 202, 209, 275, 277, 291-323, 353-4
Parliamentary Commissioner for Administration, 73, 177-9
Parliamentary questions, 75, 151, 288, 305-7, 310-11
Parties (political), 27-8, 35-6, 112, 300-4
Passing off, 113-14
Peace through NATO, 59
Peers, 297-8, 303-4, 316
Pensions and Investment Research Consultants, 234-5
Petitions, 7, 254, 311, 337
Picketing, 155, 181, 183, 194-6, 210, 218, 228
   electronic, 11, 126, 242
Picture stories, 142-3
Pinochet, Augusto, 7, 150-1
Planning, 357-60
Police, 155, 164, 181, 182-7, 189-95, 202, 204, 211-13, 219, 240, 312
Police and Criminal Evidence Act 1984, 211-12
Police Complaints Authority, 212
Policy Studies Institute, 78
Political activities by charities, 24, 31-4, 61-2
Political purposes, 27-8, 31-2
Poll tax, 7, 11, 193, 197, 199, 205-7, 216, 351-2
Positioning, 93-5, 97
Posters, 92, 100, 102, 107-8, 111, 189
   fly-posting, 102-4
Press, 11, 69-70, 131-45, 149-52, 155, 229
   advertising, 92, 94-5, 99-100, 105-7, 111
   see also *Media*

Press releases, *see News releases*
Press conferences, 141-2
Prime Minister, 263-7, 279, 306-7
Private members' bills, 52, 316-21
Product life-cycle, 362-5
Professional fundraisers, 44, 49
Project Fullemploy, 350
Protection from Harassment Act 1997, 210-11
Proxy votes, 234-5
Public collections, 44-5
Public education campaigns, 20, 92-3, 352, 355, 370-1, 373
Public expenditure, 282-4
Public Health Acts, 156, 168
Public Law Project, 171
Public Order Act 1936, 187
Public Order Act 1986, 182-4, 187, 192-3
Public Records Office, 76
Public Service Agreements, 273
Publications, 37, 46-7, 89-91, 112-15

Questionnaires, 81, 86-9
Quangos, 8, 9-10, 59, 287-90
Quotes, 145-49

Racial justice, 55, 62, 79-80, 159, 160, 349-50
Radio, 92, 108-10, 131, 136, 140, 145-9
Registration, 15-16
    as a charity, 15, 28-9, 32
    as a company, 16, 18
Registry of Friendly Societies, 19, 71
Release, 192, 213
Reply forms, 39, 101, 111
Representation of the People Act 1983, 256
Research, 8, 37-8, 42-3, 52, 66-91, 240, 361
    see also *Market research*
Revolution, 200, 219
Robertson, Geoffrey, QC, 114
Rocques, Richard, 181
Rose Theatre Trust, 170
Rowland, Tiny, 226
Rowntree, Joseph, Foundation, 89
Rowntree, Joseph, Reform Trust, 54
Royal Institute of International Affairs, 77-8
RSPCA, 338
Ruddock, Joan, 292
Runnymede Trust, 350

Sabotage, 207-9, 219
Satyagraha, 200-2
Scotland Act 1998, 285
Scott, Lord Justice, 156
Scottish Council for Voluntary Organisations, 23
Scottish Executive, 284-7
Scottish Human Rights Centre, 182
Scottish Parliament, 284-7
Select committees, 321-3
Shareholder action, 222, 231-5
Sharp, Gene, 219
Shelter, 24, 40-2, 48
Single European Act, 10, 325, 334-5
Sit-downs, 202-3, 218
Slander, *see Defamation*
Social Market Foundation, 78

Socialist Workers Party, 99
Society of Black Lawyers, 350
Soros, George, 50
Special Advisers, 9, 275-7
Spies for Peace, 66
Spin doctors, *see Special advisers*
Sponsorship, 57-8
Standing committee, 313-15
Statutory Instruments, 113, 280, 314, 316
Statistics, 72-89, 372
Steel, David, 321
Stewards, 189-91
Stone, Dr Richard, 260
Strategy, 347-73
Straw, Jack, 165
Strikes, 219, 228, 235-7
Stunts, 108, 196-8
Subscriptions, 29, 37-40
Supply-side campaigning, 8, 11, 237-42
SWOT analysis, 355-7, 359, 361

Target audience, *see Audience*
Tax, 28, 30, 46
    reliefs, 29, 32-4
Telephone fundraising, 35, 44
Telemarketing, *see Telephone fundraising*
Television, 108-10, 134, 136-7, 140, 142-3, 145-9
    advertising, 92, 105, 108-10
Templeman, Lord, 155
Ten minute rule bills, 316-19
Terrorism Bill, 209
Thatcher, Margaret, 10, 75, 151, 155, 269, 281, 307, 321-2, 362
Think-tanks, 76-8
Trade Union and Labour Relations (Consolidation) Act 1992, 58, 195-6, 210
Trade unions 35-7, 58-9, 71, 112, 161, 165, 168, 195, 210, 214, 223, 230, 235-7, 242
Trading, 30, 45-8
Treasury, 178, 282-4, 285, 287
Treaty of Amsterdam, 324-5, 335
Treaty of Rome, 325, 340
Trespass, 183, 203-5, 218
Trusts, 16, 19, 25-8, 30, 31-4
    grant-making, *see Foundations*
Twyford Down, 202-3

UKREP, *see Committee of Permanent Representatives*
Ultra vires, 20, 167-70, 256
UNICEF, 346
Unincorporated associations, 15-17, 19-20, 23, 25, 29, 46, 116, 237
Union of Communication Workers, 326-7
Unions, *see Trade unions*
United Nations, 72, 123, 344-6
United Nations Association, 59
Urban Trust, 79-80, 83, 87

Wales Council for Voluntary Action, 23
War on Want, 34
Welsh Assembly, *see National Assembly for Wales*
Western European Union, 343
Whitehall, 76, 131, 207, 263-90
Widdecombe, Ann, 282
Wilson, Des, 144

Women's rights, 196-7, 199, 267, 355
Women's Action Coalition, 198
Women's Social and Political Union, 196
Woolf, Lord, 178
Workers Against Racism, 45
World Bank, 346
World Development Movement, 165
World Health Organisation, 346
World Trade Organisation, 323, 343
World Wide Web, *see under Internet*

Yellowlees, Sir Henry, 144

MARK LATTIMER is the Communications Director at Amnesty International UK, where his experience includes ground-breaking campaigns such as the Pinochet case and the campaign for a Human Rights Act. Previously, he was the first Head of Policy at the National Lottery Charities Board and the Head of the Public Affairs Unit at the Directory of Social Change. He is also a Director of the London Housing Foundation.

In addition to human rights, his campaigning experience covers fields as diverse as the National Health Service, the funding of voluntary organisations, and ethical investment. He is the author of a number of books including *The Gift of Health: the NHS and the Mixed Economy of Healthcare*.